COMPUTER APPLICATIONS AND HARDWARE

COMPUTER APPLICATIONS AND HARDWARE

By

Ramesh Bangia
B.Sc. Dip. Comp. Sc. (IIT D)
Formerly: Incharge Computer Centre,
Hindustan Copper Limited, New Delhi
Ex. Managing Editor: Software Today

FIREWALL MEDIA
(An Imprint of Laxmi Publications Pvt. Ltd.)
BANGALORE • CHENNAI • COCHIN • GUWAHATI • HYDERABAD
JALANDHAR • KOLKATA • LUCKNOW • MUMBAI • RANCHI
NEW DELHI • BOSTON, USA

Published by :
FIREWALL MEDIA
(*An Imprint of Laxmi Publications Pvt. Ltd.*)
113, Golden House, Daryaganj,
New Delhi-110002

Phone : 011-43 53 25 00
Fax : 011-43 53 25 28

www.laxmipublications.com
info@laxmipublications.com

Price : **Rs. 290.00** *Only.* *First Edition* : 2008

OFFICES

India

© **Bangalore**	080-26 61 15 61
© **Chennai**	044-24 34 47 26
© **Cochin**	0484-239 70 04
© **Guwahati**	0361-254 36 69, 251 38 81
© **Hyderabad**	040-24 65 23 33
© **Jalandhar**	0181-222 12 72
© **Kolkata**	033-22 27 37 73, 22 27 52 47
© **Lucknow**	0522-220 95 78
© **Mumbai**	022-24 91 54 15, 24 92 78 69
© **Ranchi**	0651-230 77 64

USA

Boston
11, Leavitt Street, Hingham,
MA 02043, USA

FCO-2985-290-COMP APPLICATION & HARDWARE **C—15320/08/02**
Typeset at : Kalyani Computer Services, New Delhi. ***Printed at :*** **Ajit Printers**

Contents

1 Introduction to Computers

Definition of Personal Computer

There is a story that 5 blind men came across an elephant. Each one of them touched the different parts of its body. The one who touched the trunk said that the elephant was like a snake; the one who held the tail, said that it was like a rope. The ones holding other parts of its body said different things.

Like elephant, a computer is made of different parts which when looked at from any user angle will give a different definition. We should just remember that a computer:

1. Cannot think
2. It has vast capabilities of calculations like addition, substraction, etc. and
3. It is totally under the control of the user.

So, we can say that a computer is a machine, totally at the command of the user, which can perform operations at a much higher speed than a human being.

So may times you have seen or heard that a telephone bill or an electricity bill has been wrongly prepared and the amount charged is enormous. It is not because of computer's mistake but it is so since the meter reading given to the computer was wrong, possibly the reading was wrongly taken by the meter reader who had gone to the house to read and record the meter reading.

Therefore, we understand that there is nothing magical about a computer. It is actually a friendly machine which is totally at your command. Do you remember the story Aladdin and the Magic Lamp? Just like the Genie of the magic lamp, a computer will obey your command. If you make a mistake in giving commands to the computer, it will carry out these commands giving wrong results.

Thus, the Computer is a machine which works on the raw Data given to it and gives out meaningful results in the form of Information.

Computer Age

Though the first fully operational electronic computer was introduced to the world in 1946, but the historian assumes the starting of a computer age from 1951, when first commercial computer UNIVAC was introduced. The remarkable thing about the computer age is that so much has happened in so much short time. We have leapfrogged four generations of technology in about 50 years - a span of time whose events are within the memories of many people today. The first three computer generations are pinned to three technological developments:

1. vacuum tube

2. transistor and
3. integrated circuit

Each has drastically changed the nature and size of computers. We define the timing of each generation according to the beginning of commercial delivery of the hardware technology. Defining subsequent generations has become more complicated because the entire industry has become more complicated.

Uses of Computers

There are lots of uses of computers. In fact, in our everyday life it is used in almost every step. Some of the places where it is used is listed below. I have listed them alphabetically.

Airlines booking	Now you can book your ticket for a flight leaving New York while sitting in Melbourne. All the airlines are interconnected through computers. The same goes for Railways but it is restricted to individual countries only.
Banks	Computers in Banks have made it possible that you can get your account information while sitting at home only. For this your bank must be an e-bank, which most of them are. ATMs are another computer applications of banks.
Business	For most of the companies, all the work relating to accounts is now done on computers, for accuracy and speediness. You can even have your correspondence on it.
Cartoons	There are various programs available in computers which allow you to create animations. By learning them you can become an expert animator. You may even make a movie of your own.
Cinema	Now a days most of the film editing is done by computers. You can add and delete film clips at a snap using computers. In fact, some movies are totally made using computers. Films like Toy Story are made using computers.
Defence	America has used the computers in defence for the fullest with pin pointing the position of enemy targets. Most of the missiles these days are computer controlled.
DTP	It has revolutionized how composing for printing used to done. Now every book for printing is composed on computer since it is very easy to edit and read on screen.
Education	Computers can help in teaching too. In fact this books on computers was created using computers. Most of the schools now use computers for accounting, students record management, papers preparation and even results compilation.
Home	At home it has become an additional entertainment media. You can use it for playing games, watching movies, listening to songs,

	writing letters, creating your own database of friends, etc., the options are unlimited.
Library	Maintaining the records in library manually used to be a very cumbersome method. Computers have dramatically changed the way the cataloging is done in libraries.
Medicine	Lots of research in medicine is done using computers. Doctors now a days can see the complete inside of the human beings using the computers.
Space Technology	All the movements of the satellites are controlled using computers.
Weather	Using computers and satellites you can predict the weather for the next few days. In fact, the biggest computer in India is with the Meteorological Department of India, at New Delhi.

Personal Computer and its Parts

If you see, the computer is physically divided into 3 main parts:

Monitor

It is like the TV and all the information is displayed here.

Central Processing Unit

It is the main processing unit where all the processing takes place.

Keyboard

It is like the typewriter and is used to give information to the computer.

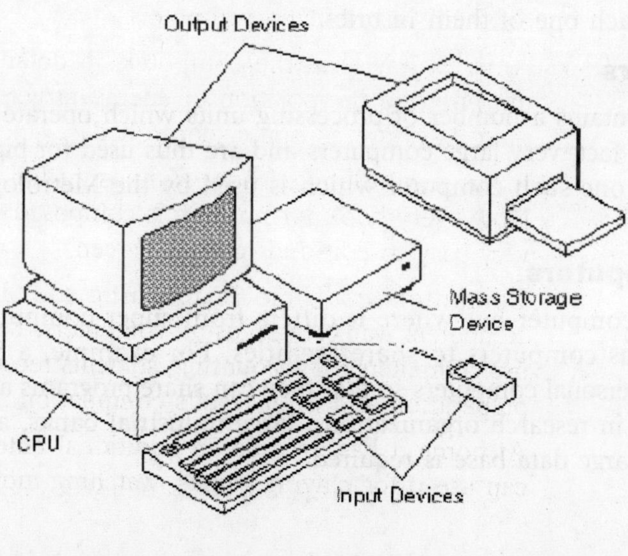

Generation of Computers

Development of computer over the ages can be divided into 5 generations. These are listed below with the year when they have been around and what was the main storing method:

First Generation	This was based on Thermionic Valve or so called Vacuum Tube	1949
Second Generation	This was based on Transistors	1956
Third Generation	Integrated Circuits or ICs	1966
Fourth Generation	Microprocessors Chips	1975
Fifth Generation	Large Scale Integration Systems	1980

Personal Computers

In 1981, IBM introduced the first Personal Computer. Since then, IBM has brought out different versions/models with variations of floppy disks, hard disks, chips, etc., making them faster and faster.

The various versions of IBM PC compatible computers. The latest being Pentium V computer based on Pentium V chip.

Classification of Computers

If we classify the computers by their sizes, we would have the following classification:

- Super Computers
- Mainframe Computers
- Super Mini Computers
- Mini Computers
- Micro Computers or Personal Computers

Let us read about each one of them in brief.

Super Computers

A supercomputer contains a number of processing units which operate in parallel to make it faster. They are in fact, very large computers and are thus used for bigger applications. In India, there is only one such computer which is used by the Metrological department in weather forecasting.

Mainframe Computers

It is again a large computer but where it differs from super computer is that it can be connected to various computers to share facilities. For example, a System/370 can be attached to several personal computers so that they can share programs and data. Mainframe computers are used in research organizations, large industrial banks, airlines, and railway reservations where large data base is required.

Super Mini Computers

These are cross between minicomputers and super computers. They are commonly used as dedicated computers, for one processing function at a time.

Mini Computers

They are inferior to mainframe computers both in speed and storage. They can also support various terminals. In fact, they can support upto 100 terminals. Minicomputers have operating systems with multitasking and network capabilities enabling them to serve more than one user.

Laptops

In recent years design changes have reduced the size of some microcomputers, making computer technology portable and affordable. Laptop computers are roughly the size of a large notebook. Their power source, a battery is completely self-contained yet can be recharged from an electrical outlet. Laptops sometimes called notebook computers, can contain more than 20 GB of hard disk memory, 64 MB of RAM, CD Drive, mouse, keyboard and a colour display.

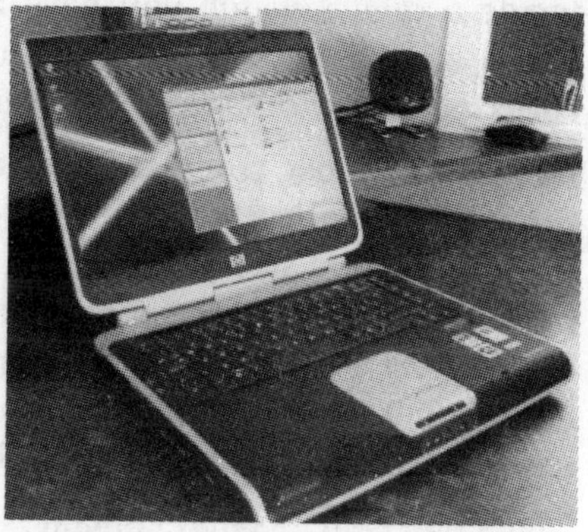

Power adapters can be used to plug into any electrical outlet throughout the world. It can be connected with an additional battery or serial port, a network or fax equipment. Laptops are not as inexpensive as their size may suggest, many carry a prize tag equivalent to full-size personal computer for business.

Inside the PC

Central Processing Unit is actually the main brain of the computer system. It is here that the whole processing takes place. It consists of 4 main units:

Primary Storage
Arithmetic Logic Unit
Control Unit
Output Unit

Let us read about them one by one.

Primary Storage Unit

This is main storage area, which is also called the main memory area. Its main functions are listed below:

1. Holding the data in its memory till it is required to be processed.
2. Holding the result of the processed data.
3. Holding program instructions which are required for processing.

Arithmetic Logic Unit

This is used for the most of the logical processing, for example, for calculations or comparisons. The arithmetic operations like, +, –, *, and / are performed here. The logical operations like, <, >, =, <=, >=, and <> are also performed here. In most of the arithmetical operations the result is in numerical form while in the case of logical operations the result can be YES/NO or TRUE/FALSE.

The arithmetic logic unit (ALU) is a digital circuit that calculates an arithmetic operation (like an addition, subtraction, etc.) and logic operations (like an Exclusive Or) between two numbers. The ALU is a fundamental building block of the central processing unit of a computer. Many types of electronic circuits need to perform some type of arithmetic operation, so even the circuit inside a digital watch will have a tiny ALU that keeps adding 1 to the current time, and keeps checking if it should beep the timer, etc...

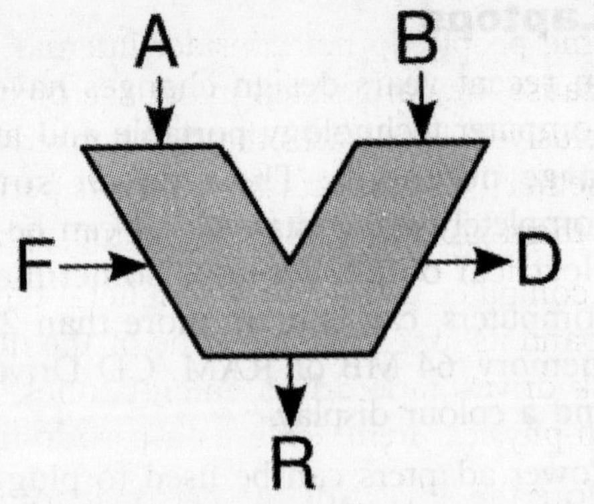

A typical schematic symbol for an ALU: A & B are operands; R is the output; F is the input from the Control Unit; D is an output status

By far, the most complex electronic circuits are those that are built inside the chip of modern microprocessors like the Pentium. Therefore, these processors have inside them a powerful and very complex ALU. In fact, a modern microprocessor (or mainframe) may have multiple cores, each core with multiple execution units, each with multiple ALUs.

Many other circuits may contain ALUs inside: GPUs like the ones in NVidia and ATI graphic cards, FPUs like the old 80387 co-processor, and digital signal processor like the ones found in Sound Blaster sound cards, CD players and High-Definition TVs. All of these have several powerful and complex ALUs inside.

Control Unit

This unit controls the flow and manipulation of data and information. It also controls the flow of data from input devices to memory and from memory to output devices.

Output Unit

The output unit consists of the output devices attached to the computer. These devices take machine-coded output results from the processor and convert them into a form that can be understood by the user.

Overview of Computer Hardware

Hardware is a term used to describe the physical components of the computer, any computer part which you can see and touch, such as Computer Monitor, Keyboard, Mouse, etc., is hardware. Any accessory or device connected to the computer, such as the printer is also hardware.

Computer Peripherals

A peripheral is a piece of computer hardware that is added to a host computer in order to expand its abilities. More specifically, the term is used to describe those devices that are optional in nature, as opposed to hardware that is either demanded or always required in principle.

The term also tends to be applied to devices that are hooked up externally, typically through some form of computer bus like USB. Typical examples include joysticks, printers and scanners. Devices such as monitors and disk drives are not considered peripherals when they are not truly optional.

Some people do not consider internal devices such as video capture cards to be peripherals because they are added inside the computer case; for them, the term peripherals is reserved exclusively for devices that are hooked up externally to the computer. It is debatable however whether PCMCIA cards qualify as peripherals under this restrictive definition, because some of them go fully inside the laptop, while some, like WiFi cards, have external appendages

In computer hardware, a peripheral device is any device attached to a computer in order to expand its functionality. Some of the more common peripheral devices are printers, scanners, disk drives, tape drives, microphones, speakers, and cameras. A device can also refer to a non-physical item, such as a pseudo-tty, a RAM drive, or a network adapter.

Before the advent of the personal computer, any connected device added to the three base components—the motherboard, CPU and working memory (RAM, ROM, or core)—was considered to be a peripheral device.

The personal computer has expanded the sense of what devices are needed on a base system, and keyboards, monitors, and mice are no longer generally considered to be peripheral devices.

Overview of Operating System

An operating system (OS) is a set of computer programs that manage the hardware and software resources of a computer. It processes raw data which is given to the computer as input. It then allocates and manages the tasks of the internal system resources of the computer. It is the operating system which performs basic tasks such as controlling and allocating memory, prioritizing system requests, controlling input and output devices, facilitating networking and managing file systems.

Most operating systems come with an application that provides an interface to the operating system managed resources. These applications have had command line interpreters as a basic user interface, but more recently have been implemented as a Graphical User Interface (GUI) for ease of operation.

Operating Systems themselves have no user interfaces; the user of an operating system is an application, not a person.

The operating system forms a platform for other system software and for application software. Windows, Linux, and Mac operating system are some of the most popular Operating System's.

Types of Operating Systems

Operating system can be classified into various categories, with respect to the type of processing, it supports. Following are the main types of Operating System:

Batch Operating System

Batch processing requires that a program, its related data and relevant control commands sould be submitted together, in the form of a Job. Batch operating system allows no interaction between the users and the executing programs. Thus the programs that have long execution times (like payrolls, forecasting, statistical analysis and large scientific number-crunching programs) and require little operator interaction during execution, were well served by Batch Processing. However, due to long turn-around delays and infeasibility of online debugging, the Batch Processing was not at all suitable for software developement.

Batch operating system allows no interaction between the users and the executing programs.

The typical features of a batch operating system were:

1. **Scheduling**. The scheduling of jobs was normally in the order of their arrival, i.e., First Come First Served (FCFS). This criteria provides a fair deal to the jobs, but suffers from long average turn-around time and average waiting time, since some short jobs may have to wait for unduly long periods to get executed, if some long jobs are laready queued ahead of the short jobs. To overcome this limitation, another criteria known as Shortest Job Next, was evelved, which offered preference to pending shorter jobs over the long jobs. This offered much better his averave turn around time and average waiting time of the pending jobs.
2. **Memory Management**. Memory used to be divided into two permanent partitions—one permanently occupied by the resident portion of the operating system and the other dynamically used to load the transient programs for execution. When a transient program terminates, it vacates the memory partition occupied by it and the same is assigned to other waiting transient program.
3. **I/O Management**. Since, only one program used to be under execution at a time, there was no contention for the allocation of I/O Devices. So, a simple program-controlled I/O approach was good enough to access the I/O Devices.
4. **File Management**. Since, ther used to only one program accessing the files at a time, there was no need of providing concurrency control.

   Thus, in a nutshell the Batch operating system was limited to a Loader and some simple Device Drivers.

Multi-programming Operating System

A multi-programming system permits multiple programs to be loaded into the memory and execute the programs concurrently. A program in execution is called a "Process" or a "Task".

The concurrent execution of programs has a significant potential for improving the utilization of system resources and thus enhanceing the system thourghput, as compared to batch and serial processing.

This potential is exploited by multi-programming operating system, which multiplexes the computer resources amongest a multitude of concurrent programs. A program in execution is called a Process. When a running process requests ome I/O, it goes to "Wait" state. Then another Ready process (i.e., one of the processes from the "Ready" queue) is scheduled to "Run". So, when a process goes for I/O, the CPU is not left idling. When the I/O requested by a Waiting process is completed, it is transferred from "Waiting" to "Ready" state and wait to be scheduled, as per the predecided scheduled criteria.

Time-sharing Interactive Operating System

The time-sharing interactive systems belong to the era of a large mainframe systems, that were made available to a large number of users for accessing concurrently in an interactive mode. Each user used to interact with the system through a separate Video Terminal. A programmer could enter its source code using sophisticated editors, compile the source code, link the object code and run the executable code interactively.

At any stage, the user could interact with the execution of its program. Debugging could be performed online. This reduced the time needed for pgrogam development, drastically. The operating system served the interactive users, in a round-robin fashion, allowing a fixed time-slice for each user to have control of the CPU. Since, the operators were interacting through slow I/O devices, each user had a feel as if the CPU was available solely to itself. So, the computation capacity of the CPU is multiplexed evenly, amongst the interactive users.

At any stage, the user could interact with the execution of its program. Debugging could be performed online.

So, time-sharing systems were large multi-programmed multi-user systems, designed for program development. One of the major requirements of such a system is good terminal response. It should give an illusion to each user as if the entire computer resoures are available to itself, solely. It should provide an equitable share of common resources to each user. For example, when the system is overloaded, the program with higher processing requirements is made to wait longer.

Most time-sharing systems use time-sliced, non pre-emptive scheduling. It has FCFS Queue; and a program requiring service is put at the end of the queue. When the process reaqches the front of the queue, service is put at the end of the queue. When the process reaches the front of the queue, it is despatched.

If it is not completed withing the time slice, it is pre-empted at the end of the time-slice and put at the end of the queue. Now, it has to wait for the next time-slice, to resume its execution from the point where it left at the end of previous time-slice. A process continues to run in bursts like this, till it terminates.

The main features of a time-sharing interactive operating system are:

1. **Memory Management**. The memory management in time-sharing systems provides for isolation and protection of co-resident programs. Since, the programs are being executed on behalf of different users, they do not involve much of inter-process communication.
2. **I/O Devices Management**. I/O Management must be sophisticated enough to cope with the requirements of multiple users, contending for multiple devices. However, due to realtively slow speed of terminals and users, processing of terminal-interrupts would not be so critical. As in most multi-user environments, allocation and de-allocation of devices must be handled in a manner so as to provide the system integrity, while attempting to optimize the system perfomance.
3. **File Management**. Since multiple users will be sharing access to multiple files, the file management must provide protection and access control.

Real Time Operating System

If refers to the environment of embedded systems, with a very rigid rquirement ot complete ther processing of input data, in a pre-specified time. The input data, in such systems, is invariable received from real-world sensors. The outputs may be used to control some real-world processes.

For example, an Adir Defense system, receiving information about aircraft movements from radars and control waspons for the elimination of hostile aircraft. For such an application, it can be well appreciated that the processing of data inputs, within specified time limits, is absolutely critical.

So, the real time systems are used in environments, where a large number of events, mostly external to the computer system, must be accepted and processed to a highly time-bound manner (with specified dealiners).

Such applications include process control in indusry (like stell, petro-chemical plants, thermal plants and nuclear plants, etc.), military systems for processing of sensor information and weapon control, telephone switching equipment, flight control, real-time simulations, etc.

1. **Scheduling**. A primary objective fo a real-time system is to provide quick response to external events, so as to meet the specified deadlines of processing. Such systems have to be multi-tasking (may not be multi-user). The scheduling is normally priority-based pre-emptive, in which the processes handling he priority process becomes ready to run, it preempts a lower priority running process. User convenience and resource optimization are of secondary concern. Such systems may be expected to handle thousands of interrupts per second, with a stringent requirement of not missing even a single event.
2. **Memory Management**. The memory management is relatively less demanding, since the process population is more or less static and memory is so designed that

most of the processes will always be memory resident, in order to provide a quick response. In fact, the programs are normally ROM resident. But, the processes have closer interaction. This requires features that enable sharing of memory, amongst processes and at the same time provide protection from each other.

3. **I/O Devices Management**. Time critical device management is one of the major requirements of real time systems. The external events and data have to be accepted and processed, in a highly time-bound manner. This is implemented using interrupt mechanism. The system calls allow the users to connect the devices and access Interrupt Service Routines (ISRs) directly, so as to achieve a good response time.
4. **File Management**. The file management is not very critical, since most of the real-time databases will be memory-resident. Some embedded systems may have program and static data on ROM and may not need any online secondary devices at run-time. The dynamic databases are maintained in ROM. If at all any files are to accessed, as in the case of large real-time systems, the primary objective is fast access.

Category of Real Time Operating Systems

1. **Hard Real Time Operating System**. In Hard Real Time Systems, all critical tasks have to be completed stricly within the specified time limits. Not meeting the dealines can be catastrophic; like an embedded system controlling the operation of a refinery. In such systems, all code and data must be in RAM/ROM. All kernel delays must be bounded. So, the Operating System should not have any unncessary frills. Interrupt mechanism must be optimized, so as to respond to the real world inputs, with minimal delays.
2. **Soft Real Time Operating System**. This is less restrictive type of real time system. If the input data is not processed within specifed time intervals, the results may not be catastrophic, but the output may lose its utility. For example, in a system monitoring flight path of an aircraft, the delayed information will have no utility. In such systems, tasks are divided into two categories—Real Time Tasks and Non-Real Time Tasks. The Real-Time Tasks are accorded priority over the other tasks. Any output from such systems would be useful, only if it is produced within a specified time after reeiving the corresponding inputs. So, the kernel delays must be bounded. The soft real time systems are not suitable for industrial and defense use, since the delays are not uncertain.

Combination Operating System

Different types of operating systems are optimized or geared up to serve the needs of specific environments. However, sometimes an environment may be a hybrid of such environments, for example the same computer may be used as software development platform and as a target machine in a real-time environment. For this reason, the commercial operating systems like UNIX, VMS, etc., are designed to provide a large set of services, catering to the need of various environments. If batch and interactive jobs are being run simultaneously, lower priority is assigned to batch jobs. In fact, the batch jobs may be used as filter, executed only when system reaources are idling. The processes, hndling real-time interrupts to receive real-world events and inputs, will be assigned higher priority. Such systems would normally employ time-sliced, priority-based preemptive scheduling. A combination operating system will be one which caters for the needs a wide spectrum of target environments. For obvious reasons, such operating systems will not be optimized for a specific environment.

If batch and interactive jobs are being run simultaneously, lower priority is assigned to batch jobs.

Distributed Operating System

A Distributed operating system caters for a distributed environment, wherein a collection of anutonomous computer systems, capable of communicating and cooperating with each other through network, are connected to each other through a LAN/WAN. A Distributed operating system governs the operation of such a distributed system and provides a virtual machine abstraction to its users. Key objective of Distributed operating system is tranparency, i.e., the resource distribution must be hidden from the users and the application programs, unless they need to determine this information, in which case the information is provided through system services, provided the user has authorization for the same. The Distributed operating system provides means for system-side sharing of resources like computational capacity, I/O and files, etc.

A Distributed operating system governs the operation of such a distributed system and provides a virtual machine abstraction to its users.

Thus, it should also cater for the following services:

- Global Naming of resources
- Distribution of computations
- Enabling processes to access remote resources
- Enabling processes to communicate with remote processes.

Importance of Operating Systems

As we know the importance of operating system in a computer system. It is there to run the computer and that too without any fault. For this we look at the various needs, goals, services and characteristics of the operating system.

Needs of Operating Systems

Initially the computers were introduced as bare machines. The programs in them were developed by manually translating squeezes of instructions into binary or some other code where base is usually an integer power of 2. Then the instructions and data were entered into computer by means of consolde switches or throguh a hexadecimal keyboard. Then address of first instruction was loaded into program counter to start execution of the program.

Results were obtained by examining the contents of the relevant registers and memory locations. Input/output devices were controlled by the executing program itself. There was no concept of any supporting system software at all.

User had to do mostly all of sub-controlling jobs manually or through program. The need was of a user who knew each and everything about machine. A general/naive user was not at all able to work on ocmputer.

At that time the following needs gave birth to the system software and development of operating system.

1. For fast and automatic working. As the maual entry and working in absence of system software result into the slow speed of processing so a need of such a software was felt which could do most of the intermediate job automatically so that user has to least bother about machines working, resutling into fast and automatic working of the machine. The operating system automates the sequencing of operations involved in program execution.
2. For better utilization of system Resources: The bare machine approach was not very efficient. With this approach, running of computer system may require frequent manual loading of programs and data. This results in low utilization of system resources. To overcome this problem operating systems with multiuser environment were developed. In absence of operating system even with the help of editors, debuggers and loaders the program development process was very slow.
3. To realize the resource utilization potential of batch processing, a mounted batch of jobs must be executed automatically, without slow human intervention and their results into the development of operating system.
4. To proived a human interface which could present a communication mode for both of them, the operating system was developed.
5. To match the speed of fast processors and comparatively slow I/O devices the need of operating system was felt.

Goals of Operating Systems

Any operating system should meet the following major goals:

1. Optimizethe use of computer resources so as to maximize its throughput.
2. Create a user-friendly computing environment for accessing the computer resources.

To fulfill these two goals operating system started from command mode and travelled upto graphical user interfaces, i.e., the operating system progressed and became more and more friendly. To facilitate the use of hardware resources researches developed different types of operating systems which also consider the user and time requirements. Various types of operating systems are developed over 45 years and they are discussed earlier.

Services of Operating System

An operating system provides an environment for the execution of user programs. Operating System provides certain services to the prorams and to the users of those programs for the accessing of system resources.

Some of the common services are:

Program Execution: The main purpose of operating system is to provide an efficient and convenient environment for the execution of programs. So, an operating system must provide various functions for loading of a program into RAM and execute it. Each executing program must terminate, either normally or abnormally.

I/O Operations: A running program would need I/O operations for reading-in of input data and for outputting of results. This I/O may be from/to a file or from/to an I/O device. For each device, some special functions may be necessary (such as rewind a tape, clear screen, etc). All these operations are manged by an operating system.

File Manipulations: Each executing program would need to create, delete and manipulate files, which is managed by the operating system.

Communications: Operating system manages inter-process communication between the processes, executing on the same computer or running on different computers in a distributed/multi-processor environment. An operating system would provide mechanisms for this inter-process communications like mailboxes, shared memory, etc.

Error Detection and Recovery: Errors may occur during execution of a program; like divide by zero, memory access violation, etc. The operating system should provide for detection such errors (or exceptions) and handle recovery (called Exception Handling).

Resource Allocation: When multiple users are logged onto the system or multiple jobs are runing concurrently, resources would need to be shared amongst them. The operating system would decide on the allocation of resources; like the CPU scheduling algorithm wili determine the control of CPU amongst the concurrent processes. Similarly, there will be routines for the allocation and de-allocation of other resources like memory, I/O devices, files, etc.

Accounting: It relates to the accounting of resources used by each user in a multi-user environment. Resource usage statistics may be useful in planning the futuristic requirements of an enterprise.

System Protection: This is also a service provided to ensure that the users and user processes are protected from each other. For example, when a process is having an exclusive access to a device allocated to it, no other process would be granted access to that device during that period. Also, no process would be permitted to access a memory location in a segment not assigned to that process. This service ensures that a process can execute safety.

Introduction to DOS

DOS translates the commands that we enter through the keyboard into signals that can be interpreted by the computer. The CPU (Central Processing Unit) processes the raw data as per the commands we feed (Input) into the computer and returns the results (gives the Output).

The results are displayed on the Monitor in our language. The results can also be printed on a printer. Directed by the instruction that we type, the DOS operates and controls the operating system. With DOS we can do the following:

- Create new files
- Delete old files
- Rename existing files
- List all the files in the hard disk or floppy
- Enhance the storage capacity of the disk
- Format new floppy or hard disk for usuage
- Reorganize the storage files on the disk
- Make back up files on the hard disk or to the floppy diks
- Scan for viruses

Type of DOS Commands

There are 2 types of DOS commands, mainly, Internal and External commands.

Internal Commands

These commands can be given from the DOS prompt, irrespective of the fact the command is there in the DOS directory or not. These can be said to be the in-built commands of DOS.

For example, the following commands are internal commands:

Chdir It changes the current directory, shortname is CD.

Cls It clears the screen.

Copy It is used for copying files, read more about it later in the chapter.

Copy cont It is used to create a quick batch file.

Ctty This command is used to redirect the keyboard and screen to the serial port.

External Commands

These commands are such they have to be present in the hard disk to be used.

Some of external commands are given below:

Append It lets programs open data files as if they were in the current directory.

Assign It is used to reassign drives when programs work only with specific drives.

Attrib It changes file attributes, which are settings in every DOS file.

Backup/Restore It lets you backup your hard disk onto as many floppies as required. Restore command can be used to use backedup files.

Chkdsk It checks disk status, memory status, files and flags unidentifiable files.

Comp It compares two files for identical content and reports up to 10 mismatches.

File Structure in DOS

All the data in the computer is stored in terms of Files. Each file is unique and is identified by name, date and time of creation, number of bytes, etc. The name of the file usually in the form of 8 + 3 digits (also called 8.3 rule) which is recognised by DOS. The 8 digits are reserved for the first name and the next 3 for the extension, which signifies the type of the file.

A typical filename in DOS can be represented as:

MSM.COM

where

MSM is the first name

. is always there

COM represents the last name or popularly called extension

Storage of Files

Files are stored in the hard disk just as we store packets in godown. A hard disk is divided into various subdirectories like rooms in a house. When you start your PC, the first directory that you see is the root directory. The root directory can be compared to a house. Within a subdirectory, you can have another subdirectory and files. You can create and delete these directories yourself. Related files are kept in the same directory.

Seeing the File

If you want to see the files or subdirectories available in a particular directory, you use the DIR command. Simple DIR command produces the display shown on the next page.

All the files in this directory will be listed along with the information like name, extension, number of bytes, data and time of creation. At the end, the total number of files in the directory is given along with the total number of bytes used. The total number of bytes remaining free in the hard disk is also given.

```
PR_ADDC  DBF            872  12-13-02  7:23p pr_addc.DBF
PR_ADDC  CDX          9,216  12-13-02  7:23p pr_addc.CDX
MTNL_G~1 DBF            360  12-13-02  7:23p mtnl_groupc.DBF
OUT      TXT            132  12-18-02  3:59p out.txt
C&CGOLD       <DIR>          01-26-03 12:52a c&cgold
        26 file(s)        281,630 bytes
        13 dir(s)          189.29 MB free

C:\>
```

Another way of using the DIR command is DIR/P.

The /P added to DIR, stands for pagewise. Suppose there are a large number of files and subdirectories within a directory. Now when you use DIR command, you will find that most of the file names scroll past the screen and only the last few entries are displayed. This may result in your not seeing the required file which may appear in the first lot. For this you should be able to stop and continue at will, the scrolling of the listing to look for a particular file. The following command gives you that option:

Once the screen has been filled up, the listing on the screen will stop with this message at the bottom:

```
Press any key to continue . . .
```

When you do press any key, the monitor will again display the next screen and stop. You can repeat this till all the files in the directory have been displayed.

```
 Directory of C:\

USERS    TXT            90  01-05-02  5:46p USERS.TXT
FRUNLOG  TXT         1,012  04-20-99  9:59a FRUNLOG.TXT
AUTOEXEC BAT            35  12-11-02  1:23p AUTOEXEC.BAT
CONFIG   SYS            10  11-14-02  9:05a CONFIG.SYS
WINDOWS        <DIR>        04-20-99  9:46a WINDOWS
PROGRA~1       <DIR>        11-13-01 11:31a Program Files
SETUPXLG TXT         1,104  06-01-02  2:31p SETUPXLG.TXT
INFERNO  LOG            67  08-17-01  8:20p inferno.log
PM65           <DIR>        08-18-01 10:53a PM65
KPCMS          <DIR>        08-18-01 10:54a KPCMS
ACROBAT3       <DIR>        08-18-01 10:54a Acrobat3
PSFONTS        <DIR>        08-18-01 10:54a psfonts
SCANDISK LOG         2,393  02-21-03 10:50a SCANDISK.LOG
ADOBEAPP       <DIR>        08-18-01  8:58p ADOBEAPP
WINZIP         <DIR>        08-18-01 11:34a WinZip
WINDOW~1 BMK            63  08-21-01  6:30p WINDOWSWinHlp32.BMK
NCDTREE        <DIR>        09-12-01  7:58p NCDTREE
LOGFILE  TXT           108  09-30-01 12:36a LOGFILE.TXT
TRACE    LOG             0  11-06-01  2:07p TRACE.LOG
Press any key to continue . . .
```

Another option is DIR/W.

The /W stands for widthwise display. This command is used when you want to see only the names of the files and are not interested in any detail. This results in the appearance of file names on the screen in groups of 3-4. Usually, all the files are listed together on the screen. If however, the files still don't fit together on the screen, you can give the command DIR/W/P. Then the following will be displayed:

Creating and Changing Directory

To create a new directory, you have to assign a name to it. This should, as far as possible, signify the type of data or programs you are going to store into it. The command is given as following:

```
MD SACHIN
```

This will create a new directory by the name of SACHIN. In the beginning, it is blank. Your cursor will remain at the position of its start.

Supposing you want to enter this or any other directory, then the command will be:

```
C:\>dir/w/p

 Volume in drive C has no label
 Volume Serial Number is 2919-10EC
 Directory of C:\

USERS.TXT       FRUNLOG.TXT     AUTOEXEC.BAT    CONFIG.SYS      [WINDOWS]
[PROGRA~1]      SETUPXLG.TXT    INFERNO.LOG     [PM65]          [KPCMS]
[ACROBAT3]      [PSFONTS]       SCANDISK.LOG    [ADOBEAPP]      [WINZIP]
WINDOW~1.BMK    [NCDTREE]       LOGFILE.TXT     TRACE.LOG       WINZIP.LOG
STUB.LOG        [MYDOCU~1]      ADOBEWEB.LOG    NETLOG.TXT      COMMAND.COM
FRONTPG.LOG     [SCANJET]       AILOG.TXT       [SIERRA]        TMP.INI
CONFIG.000      AUTOEXEC.000    USER.DEF        AUTOEXEC.001    PR_ADDC.DBF
PR_ADDC.CDX     MTNL_G~1.DBF    OUT.TXT         [C&CGOLD]
        26 file(s)        281,630 bytes
        13 dir(s)          189.27 MB free
```

Change Directory

This command can be given as following:

```
C:\>CD  SACHIN
C:\>SACHIN>
```

This means that you have entered the directory called SACHIN. However, if you are in any other directory and want to enter the SACHIN directory from there, the command becomes:

```
C:>CD\
```

The backslash (\) means that you are entering a different directory. Actually (\) means more than that. If you type CD\ at the DOS prompt of any subdirectory, your cursor reaches the root directory. This is a quick way to go to the root directory, skipping several levels of subdirectories. If you write only CD then it will show the current directory.

```
C:\>cd windows

C:\WINDOWS>
```

Remove Directory

Sometimes, it is possible that you have finished using a software and do not want to keep it or have finished with a project and taken the backup too and don't want to burden your hard disk by keeping it. In this case you would like to remove the directory all together. This would help in having more space for working. This command has to be given from outside the directory which you want to remove. So, if you are in the directory, go out from it and then give the remove directory command. You can use either RD or RMDIR. The command is given as:

```
RD  SACHIN
```

Before, you do this, however, you must make sure that you have removed all the files in the directory by using the DEL command. If you have not done so, this command will give you the message that the directory is not empty and cannot be deleted.

DOS commands

Now you will be introduced to various DOS commands, mainly copy, delete, rename, etc.

Copying a File

It is used to copy file or files from one directory to another or to shift to another drive. The command given is:

```
Copy  sachin.doc  a:sachin.doc
```

Here the file sachin.doc would be copied to drive A with the same name, i.e., sachin.doc. If you want to change the name, that is also possible. Then after the a: type the new name.

Another way of using the copy command is by using the wild card option, i.e., *. This is how it is used:

```
Copy  *.doc  a:
```

The above command will copy all files ending with doc to the floppy drive a. Let us use * at both the places, for example:

```
Copy  *.*  a:
```

This will copy all files irrespective their names or extensions to drive a.

You can, if you want, copy files starting with an alphabet. For example:

```
Copy  l*.doc  a:
```

will copy all doc files starting with l.

Xcopy

This command is an extended command of copy. Here you can copy any number of files from any place in the hard disk to another place. The command is written as:

```
Xcopy  source:path   target:path  switches
```

where you have to define the path of the source files and similarly define the path of the target. Various switches used here are listed below:

Switch	*Action*
/A	Copies only those files matching the source specification that also have their archieve bit set.
/D:date	Copies file sthat were modified on or after the specified data.
/E	Creates subdirectories on the target location, even if there are no files in them.
/M	Resets the archive bit in a file after making the copy.
/P	Issues a prompt asking you to confirm the copy of each source file.
/S	Copies files matching the source specification that are found in sub directories

	nested below the source subdirectory.
/V	Performs a verification check against the image of the file in memory.
/W	Causes XCOPY to pause before making copies allowing you an opportunity to change disks in the source drive if necessary.

For example,

```
Xcopy c:\sachin\*.doc a:
```

This command will copy all the doc files from the sachin subdirectory to the drive a.

Backup

There are times when you need to backup files to another drive to save the disk space area. The command is used as:

```
MSBACKUP file(s) /switches
```

where file(s) are the files which have to be backedup. Following switch options are available:

Switch	*Action*
/BW	Starts MSBACKUP in black-and-white for monitors that have trouble displaying the screen colours.
/TD	Backups up all files named in the specification file that have changed since the last full backup.
/TF	Backs up all files named in the specification.
/TI	Backs up all files named in the specification file that have changed since the last full backup.

Deleting a File

By deleting the name of a file, you remove it completely, including its contents. So be very sure that you are not going to need the file again before giving the delete command. You can delete a file by giving its full name. For example, when you give the following command:

```
DEL SACHIN.DOC
```

This would delete the file called sachin.doc.

Date and Time

These commands are used to display system time and date. By simply typing Date and Time, you can see the system date and time. What's more you can change them too, by retyping the Date and Time in the same format as displayed. Date is usually displayed in the format of Day and mm-dd-yyyy, where dd, mm and yy have the usual notations. Time is shown in terms of hours, minutes, seconds, etc. You can opt to display the time in 12-hour or 24-hour format.

```
C:\>time
Current time is  1:44:33.97p
Enter new time: _
```

```
C:\>date
Current date is Mon 04-21-2003
Enter new date (mm-dd-yy):
```

Prompt

If you do not like the usual C:\ format, you can change it various other options available under DOS. The various switch options are:

Switch	*Action*
PROMPT	This option is used to get the default setting.
String	Specifies the text that you want to display as your system prompt.
$$	$(dollar sign)
$_	Carriage return/linefeed.
$B	| (bar or pipe symbol)
$D	Current date
$e	Escape code (you cannot use E instead)
$G	> (greater than symbol)
$H	Backspace (erases the preceding character)
$L	< (less than symbol)
$N	Current drive
$P	Current drive name and path name
$Q	= (equal sign)
$T	Current time
$V	System DOS version number

```
D:\>prompt $D

Mon 04-21-2003
```

Renaming a File

Sometimes, you may not like the name that you gave to a file. You may want to give it a new name without distributing the contents of the file. For this, you use the Rename command as following:

```
REN SACHIN.DOC GOLDEN.DOC
```

This will result in changing the name of the file from sachin.doc to golden.doc. Remember to put a space in between the two file names.

Restore

Once you backup the file, you must restore them too. The command for this is:

```
Restore source drive: target drive: /switches
```

where source drive has the files which have been backed up. Various switch options are:

Switch	*Action*
/A:mm-dd-yy	Restores only those files that were modified on or after the specified date, where mm is the month, dd is the day and yy is the year.
/B:mm-dd-yy	Restores only those files that were modified on or before the specified date, namely mm-dd-yy.
/D	Displays file name(s) on the backup disk but does not restore them.
/E:hh-mm-ss	Restores those files modified at or earlier than the specified time, where hh is the hour (in 24 hour format), mm is the minutes after the hour, and ss is the seconds.
/L:hh: mm: ss:	Restores only those files that were modified at or after the specified time.
/M	Restores files that were modified since the last backup was made.
/N	Restores files that were deleted since the last backup.
/P	Prompts to confirm the restoration of files that were changed since the last backup or marked as read-only files.
/S	Restores files in sub directories nested below the specified target subdirectory.

Changing the Attrib

Each file in DOS has various attributes attached to it. These attributes decide the fate of the file. Among them are read-only, hide, etc. So you can change the attribute of a file using the command called Attib, and the options attached to it. The command is:

```
Attrib modes path /switches
```

where path is the path of the file whose attributes you want to change. Various switches in use are:

Switch	*Action*
+A	Changes file setting to archived.
–A	Changes file settings to not archived.

+H	Changes specified file(s) to hidden, which means the file(s) will not be visible to most DOS operations.
–H	Makes hidden files visible again.
+R	Changes specified file(s) to read-only which means the file(s) cannot be overwritten or erased.
–R	Changes specified file(s) to read write which means, the file may be overwritten or erased.
+S	Marks specified file(s) as DOS system file(s).
–S	Removes DOS system-file setting.
/S	Used with the file names that contain wildcard character or subdirectory names without file names. This option will include matching files in sub directories nested below the current subdirectory.

Type

This command is used to see the contents of a text file. The command is:

```
Type filename
```

where filename is the name of the file whose contents you have to see. Since this shows the plain listing of the files, it is adviced that you use this command mainly for plain text files and not for formatted document files.

```
C:\>type out.txt
Num cars in race = 4
Num cars in race = 4
Num cars in race = 4
Num cars in race = 4
Num cars in race = 4
Num cars in race = 4
```

You can use | More to see all the contents of the file.

This is not the end of the DOS commands, there are more. The commands given here are just to give you an idea of the type of commands available under DOS. You can get the complete list of commands of DOS by typing

?

at the DOS prompt.

DOS Commands

Since DOS is a command based operating system, I give a complete list of DOS commands which can be used as per its syntax.

Append

SET SEARCH PATH FOR DATA FILES

Syntax: APPEND [[d:] path [d:] path [...]] [/x[;ON /off]] [/[path[:ON/OFF]] [/E]

Description With APPEND installed, DOS will automatically search APPENed directories for data files. The /X:ON switch allows APPEND to work with a wide range of applications. /E allows the APPEND path as an environment variable so that the path string can be edited using the SET command. If a /E switch is used, APPEND ignores path parameters on the same lines.

Assign

REDIRECT DRIVE ACCESSES

Syntax: ASSIGN [x[:] = y [:] [...]]]/STATUS]

Description ASSIGN allows you to accesses from one floppy drive to another floppy drive or a hard disk. Once accesses are redirected, all further reads and writes to drive x are automatically redirected to drive y.

attrib

CHANGE FILE ATTRIBUTES

Syntax: ATRIB [+A-A] [+H-H] [+R-R] [+S-S] [[d:] [path] file name] [/S]

Description ATTRIB allows you to display, or alter the attributes of a file. Running without a + or - switch displays the attributes of the specified file or files. With a + or - switch, it sets or clear the specified attribute. If file name is omitted, ATTRIB sets or displays the attributes of all the files in the current directory. The /S switch causes ATTRIB to process files in the specified directory.

backup

BACK UP FILES

Syntax: BACKUP source destination [/A] [/F[:size]] [/1 [:log]] [/M] [/S] [/D:date [/T:time]

Description BACKUP lets you back up hard disk files to floppies. If you omit the /F switch or use it but do not specify size, BACKUP formats destination disks to the highest capacity the drive supports.

buffers

SET DISK BUFFER COUNT

Syntax: Buffers = n [,m]

Description To speed disk accesses, DOS maintains an array of internal disk buffers where data going to and from disk is cached in case it is requested again. BUFFERS specifies the number of disk buffers and the size of the secondary cache. Normally, BUFFERS is optimized for programs that perform random reads and writes. However, increasing the size of the secondary cache benefits programs that perform sequential disk accesses. The default values for a depend on the amount of RAM in your system and the size of your hard disk.

call

CALL BATCH PROGRAM

Syntax: CALL [d:] [path] filename [parameters]

Description CALL gets a batch program from another batch file. When the CALLed batch program terminates. Control returns to the program that executed the CALL.

chcp

CHANGE CODE PAGE

Syntax: CHCP [nnn]

Description CHCP changes the active code page. Before switching to a code page, you must execute an NLSFUNC command to install DOS's national language support functions and prepare the code page with the MODE command. If CHCP is run without a code page number, it displays the number of the active page.

chdir (cd)

CHANGE DIRECTORY

Syntax: CD [d:] [path]

Description CD changes the current directory. Run with no parameters, it displays the name of the current directory on the current drive. Run with a d: parameter but without a path parameter, it displays the name of the current directory, on the specified drive.

chkdsk

CHECK DISK

Syntax: CHKDSK [[d:] [path] filename] [/F] [/V]

Description CHKDSK checks a disk's file allocation table, directory entries for errors. If the /F switch is specified, CHKDSK corrects the errors it finds. If /V is included, it also displays the names of the files as it encounters them. If you specify a filename, CHKDSK tells you whether the file is fragmented and, if it is, how many noncontiguous blocks it is stored in.

choice

ALLOWS TO ENTER TEXT FOR DISPLAY

Syntax: CHOICE [/C[:]keys] [/N] [/S] [/T[:]c, nn] [text]

Description Displays a prompt and waits for you to type a character. You can supply the prompt and the list of allowed characters. You will mainly want to use this command in batch files to add simple menus to your batch files.

command

START COMMAND PROCESSOR

Syntax: Command [comspec] [device] [/C command] [/E:size] [/MSG] [/P]

Description COMMAND.COM is the command processor DOS loads by default. If you want to instal it and specify any of the parameters shown above, you must install it with a SHELL = directive in CONFIG.SYS. The comspec parameters tell COMMAND.COM where to find its own image on disk so that it can load itself when needed.

copy

COPY ONE OR MORE FILES

Syntax: To copy a file or files

COPY source [/A/B][destination][/A/B][/V] [d:]. [path] filename2 [/A/B][+...][destination] [/A/B] [/V]

Description The COPY command has two distinct uses: copying files and concatenating files. A /A or /B switch applies to the file proceeding the switch and to all subsequent files until another switch is encountered. You can create a duplicate with a different name by specifying a file name for destinations. You must specify a destination file name if the file is being copied to the same directory.

country

SPECIFIES ACTIVE COUNTRY

Description The command specifies the country of working and its information. The command is usually used in the CONFIG.SYS file.

ctty

CAUSES THE TERMINAL DEVICE TO CONTROL MONITOR

Syntax: CTTY device

Description This command allows you to change the console device from the normal keyboard and display to an external device, such as a computer terminal.

date

SET SYSTEM DATE

Description DATE sets the system date. Normally, dates are entered in mm-dd-yy format. However, the format for date may change if you use the COUNTRY directive to adopt the conventions of another country. If DATE is run without a date parameter, it displays the current date and prompts you to enter a new one.

dblspace

ACCESS DOUBLESPACE

Syntax: DBLSPACE

or

DBLSPACE /command

Description This program allows you to compress existing disks and to create new compressed volumes. Once you have compressed volumes, DBLSPACE allows you to manage these compressed volumes and to create new compressed volumes.

debug

STARTS PROGRAM DEBUGGER

Syntax: DEBUG [[d:] [path] filename [parameters]

Description DEBUG is DOS's built in program debugger, which is useful for testing, creating and modifying short COM files, entering and testing short assembly language programs, and inspecting the contents of memory. Once it is started, you can type the following commands at its command prompt.

?	Displays a list of commands
A	Assemble instruction mnemonics
C	Compare two blocks of memory
D	Display the contents of a block of memory
E	Enter data into memory
F	Fill a block of memory
G	Run the current program
H	Perform hexadecimal arithmetic
I	Input a value from a I/O port
L	Load data from disk
M	Move a block of memory
N	Name the current program
O	Output a value to an I/O port
P	Execute the next program instruction, proceeding through loops and subroutines

Q	Quit
R	Display and modify register values
S	Search a block of memory
T	Execute the next program instruction
U	Unassemble machine code instructions
W	Write data to disk
XA	Allocate expanded memory
XD	Deallocate expanded memory
XM	Map expanded memory page
XS	Display expanded memory status information

defrag

CHECK FOR FRAGMENTATION OF FILES

Syntax: defrag [/lcd] [/bw] [/g0]

defrag [drive:] /u [/b] [/skiphigh] [/lcd] /bw] [.g0] [/h][/q]

defrag [drive:] /f[/s[:] order] [/b] [/skiphigh] [/lcd] /bw] [/g0] [h]

defrag [drive:] q [/b] [/skiphigh] [/lcd] /bw] [g0] [/h]

Description DEFRAG mainly separates out the free space and file space in the disk. It helps in speeding up the read-write of the disk.

del

DELETE FILE

Syntax: DEL [d:] [pat] filename [/p]

Description The DEL command deletes a file or set of files from disk. If you use the /p switch DOS prompts you with the name of each file before it is deleted. Filename may include wildcards.

deltree

DELETE A DIRECTORY

Syntax: DELTREE [/y] [drive:] path

Description DELTREE provides a single command for deleting all the files of the directory and its bus-directories.

device

LOAD DEVICE DRIVER

Syntax: DEVICE=[d:] [path] filename [parameters]

Description DEVICE loads a special type of program called an installable device driver into memory at start-up. DOS comes with ten installable device drivers. Other device drivers are frequently shipped with add-on peripherals such as disk drives and tape drives. If you omit path, DOS assumes the drivers installed and see where they were loaded with the MEM/P command.

devicehigh

LOAD DEVICE DRIVER HIGH

Syntax: DEVICEHIGH [SIZE=size] [d:] [path] filename [parameters]

Description DEVICEHIGH works just like DEVICE except that it loads installable device drivers in upper rather than conventional memory. The size parameter specifies the minimum amount of upper memory required to install the driver. Before DEVICEHIGH may be used, both HIMEM.SYS and EMM386.EXE must be installed, and DOS must be started with the statement DOS=UMB in CONFIG.SYS. If there is not enough room in upper memory to loaded the driver, or if the size of the largest remaining UMB is less than size DEVICEHIGH loads the driver in conventional memory instead.

dir

DISPLAY DIRECTORY LISTING

Syntax: DIR [d} [path] filename] [/A:attr]]/B] [/L][/O:order] [/P][/S][/W][/C][/CH]

Description The DIR command lists the contents of the current/specified directory(s). Numerous switches, most of which were added in ver. 6.0 give you a great deal of flexibility in formatting output.

diskcomp

COMPARE DISKS

Syntax: DISKCOMP [d1: [d2]] [/1] [/8]

Description DISKCOMP compares the contents of two disks and reports discrepancies. If you omit d:.DISKCOMP uses d1.: for both disks, prompting you to insert and remove disks as needed. If you omit both drive parameters, DISKCOMP uses the current drive for both. In general, DISKCOMP cannot compare unlike disk types.

diskcopy

COPY DISK

Syntax: DISKCOPY [d1: [d2:]] [/l] [/v]

Description DISKCOPY performs a sector-by-sector disk copy, duplicating the source disks, prompting you to swap disks as needed. If you omit both drive parameters, DISKCOPY defaults to the current drive. If the destination disk DISKCOPY cannot be used on hard disk, and in general, will not work with unlike disk types.

dos

CONFIGURE DOS

Syntax: DOS = [HIGHLOW] [UMB/NOUMB]

Description The DOS directive specifies where DOS should be loaded and whether it is to establish a link to upper memory. DOS = HIGH loads most of DOS itself into the 64K region of extended memory known as the HIGHMEMORY AREA (or HMA for short). LOW loads DOS the normal way, in conventional memory so that TSRs and device drivers can be loaded high with the LOADHIGH and DEVICEHIGH commands. When DOS = UMB is specified, DOS USES HIMEM.SYS to claim all the UMBs created by EMM386.EXE for itself so that no one else may use them. The default is DOS=NOUMB.

doskey

INSTALL COMMAND-LINE ENHANCER AND MACRO RECORDER

Syntax: DOSKEY [REINSTALL] [/BUFSIZE = size] [/MACROS] [/HISTORY] [/INSERT /OVERSTRIKE] [macro = [text]]

Description DOSKEY is a memory-resident utility that adds four new features to the command line.

With it installed you can:

— Edit text on the command line using the Left and Right, Ctrl+Left and Ctrl+Right, Home, End, Ctrl+End, and Esc keys

— Recall past commands using the Up and Down Arrow. PgUp. PgDn, F8, and F9 keys. Pressing F7 displays numbered command history. You can execute specific command by pressing F9 and entering the number of the command or recall a particular command by typing the first few characters and pressing F8. Alt+F7 clears all the commands Enter multiple commands on a single command line by separating them with Ctrl+T, which shows up on the screen as the symbol for a paragraph marker.

— Create command macros that act like internal DOS commands. DOSKEY understands the following special metacharacters in macro definitions

$B	Piping operator (|)
$G	Output redirection operator (>)
$L	Input redirection operator (<)
$T	Command separator, Ctrl+T (#)
$$	Dollar sign
$1 to $9	Replaceable parameters 1 through 9

$* All command line parameters

dosshell

START THE DOS SHELL

Syntax: DOSSHELL [G[:res[n]^T[:res[n]/B

Description DOSSHELL starts the DOS Shell, a mouse driven graphics user interface that serves as an alternative to the command line. Through the Shell you can change drives and directories, perform file operation launch programs and load several programs at once and switch among them a process known as task-switching.

DRIVPARM

DEFINE DRIVES PARAMETERS

Syntax DRIVPARM=/D:drive[/F:from][/H:hands)[/S :sectors) [/T:tracks] [/N] [/C] [/I)

Description: DRIVPPARM modifies the internal drive parameter tables that DOS sets up to characterize block all devices attached to your PC. You can characterize a device by the form factor or by the number of heads, sector and tracks it contains.

ECHO

ENABLE OR DISABLE OR DISPLAY A MESSAGE

Syntax ECHO [ON/OFF] [message]

Description The ECHO command enables or disable command echoing in batch files or outputs a message from a batch file. If ECHO is enabled batch file commands are echoed to the screen (displayed on the screen as they are executed); if ECHO is disabled, batch file commands are not echoed to the screen.

EDIT

START DOS EDITOR

Syntax EDIT [[d:] [path]filename] [/B] [/G] [/H] [/NOHI]

Description The DOS Editor is a mouse-driven full-screen text editor that serves as a functional replacement for EDLIN. Use it any time you need to edit a text file, whether it's a short AUTOEXEC.BAT file or a larger text file created by an other program.

EMM 386

CONTROL EMM386.EXE DRIVER

Syntax EMM386 [ON/OFF/AUTO] [W=On/OFF]

Description The EMM386 command controls DOS's EMM386 EXE driver. The command is only valid if the driver is installed through CONFIG.SYS.

Run without command-line parameters, EMM386 ON enables the driver, and EMM386 OFF temporarily disables it. EMM386 AUTO places the driver in AUTO mode, which is similar to On except that expanded memory services are provided only when a program calls for them, not before (provided EMM386.EXE was not installed with a NOEMS switch, which would prevent it from providing expanded memory services). The W=ON and W=OFF switches enable and disable support for math coprocessors.

ERASE

DELETES THE SPECIFIED FILE

Syntax	ERASE [drive:] [path]filename [/P]
Description	See DEL for more details.

exit

TERMINATE COMMAND PROCESSOR

Syntax	EXIT
Description	If you are running inside a secondary command processor (for example, you have shelled to DOS from WordPerfect), EXIT is the command you type to terminate the command processor and return to the program that launched it. EXIT is ignored by the primary command processor.

expand

EXPAND FILE

Syntax	EXPAND [d:] [path] filename 1 [...] destination
Description	EXPAND expands compressed files on the disks that came in your DOS package. Wildcards are not accepted for filename, but you can specify multiple filenames. Destination specifies where the expanded files will be placed and may consist of a drive name, a path name, a file name in destination if only one file is being expanded.

fasthelp

DISPLAYS INFORMATION ABOUT ALL DOS COMMANDS

Syntax	FASTHELP [command] [command] ?
Description	This command is a fast way to get simple help on DOS commands. When you enter FASTHELP by itself, it displays a listing of all the DOS commands in alphabetical order with a brief one-line description for each command.

fastopen

INSTALL FASTOPEN

Syntax FASTOPEN [d:] [n] [...] [/x]

Description FASTOPEN speeds up hard-disk operations by caching information about the physical locations of files on the disk so that once they are opened more quickly the second time. The n parameter specifies how many files FASTOPEN can retain information about at one time on a per-drive basis. Each file increase FASTOPEN's size in memory by about 48 bytes. You can conserve memory by using the /X switch (which allocates space for the cache in expanded memory rather than conventional memory) or by loading FASTOPEN into upper memory with the LOADHIGH command on compatible systems.

fc

COMPARE FILES

Syntax FC [d:] [path] filename 1 [d:] [path] filename 2 [/A] [/B] [/C] [/L] [/LBn] [/lines] [/N] [/T] [/W]

Description The PC commands in COMP's more sophisticated cousin, and is a powerful tool for comparing files of any type. By default comparisons are performed in ASCII mode unless one more of the files being compared has extensions .EXE, .COM, .SYS, .OBJ, .LIB, or .BIN.

fcbS

SET LIMIT ON FILE CONTROL BLOCKS

Syntax FCBS = X

Maximum number of file control blocks that can be opened at one time (default = 4, range = 1 to 255)

Description FCBS lets you specify the maximum number of file control of file control blocks that can be open in the system concurrently. DOS limits the number of file control blocks that can be opened in the system at one time, because having too many of them open can adversely affect network performance. Once the limit is reached, DOS closes old file control blocks when new ones are opened.

fdisk

CONFIGURE HARD DISK

Syntax FDISK

Description FDISK is the tool DOS provides for setting up and managing hard-disk partitions. With it, you can

* Create and remove DOS partitions, primary and extended.
* Assign drive letters to and remove them from extended DOS partitions.
* Specify what partition is the active partition.

* Display partition data

DOS supports partitions upto 2GB. Note that when you delete a partition using FDISK all the data stored in the partition is lost.

files

SET LIMIT ON OPEN FILES

Syntax FILES = x

Description FILES determines how much space DOS reserves in low memory to hold information about files opened with DOS's handle-based file functions and thus sets the limit on the number of files that can be opened at once. Five file handles are reserved for DOS's own internal device drivers, so the number of files handles available to application programs is actually five less than the setting of FILES.

find

FIND CHARACTER STRING

Syntax FIND [/C] [/l] [/N] [/V] string [[d:] [path] filename]

Description FIND searches a file for a stream of characters input to it for a specified text string and either displays the lines that contain the string or, if it was starting with a /V switch, displays a count of lines that contains or do not contain the text string rather than the lines themselves. The /l switch performs searches without regard to case. If no file name is specified, FIND acts as a filter command and expects input to be provided to it via an input redirection or piping operator. By default, searches are case sensitive.

for

EXECUTE COMMAND FOR EACH ELEMENT OF A SET

Syntax FOR %% variable IN (set) DO command

Description The FOR command executes command once for each member of set. Each time through the loop he next member of set is substituted for %% variable. If set includes wildcards, the wildcards are expanded as if they were file names.

format

FORMAT DISK

Syntax FORMAT d:[/l] [/4] [/8] [/B] [P:size] [/N:Sectors] [/T:tracks] [/Q] [/S] [/U] [/V: [label]]

Description The FORMAT command is sued to format hard-disk partitions and floppy disks. FORMAT creates a boot sector, two copies of the file allocation table and the root directory on the disk or partition so that DOS can store files there. DOS supports 3 types of formats:

The Safe Format (default): Safe formats disks can be unformatted with the UNFORMAT command. The Quick Format. Quick formatting is much faster than safe formatting but can only be performed on disks that have been formatted before. Quick formatted disks, like safe formatting disks may be unformatted.

The Unconditional Format: Unconditional formatting destroys everything on the disk so that the UNFORMAT command cannot recover it. You can combine the /Q and /U switches to perform a very fast format. However, you may not be able to unformat a disk formatted this way.

goto

SPECIFIES THE LINE TO GO TO

Syntax	GOTO label
Description	This command allows you to control the order in which DOS executes lines in a batch file.

graphics

SET THE GRAPHIC MODE OF PRINTER

Syntax	GRAPHICS [type] [drive] [path] filename] [/R] [/B] [/LCD] [/PRINTBOX | STD | /PRINTBOX | LCD]
Description	This command allows you to use the Print Screen key on your keyboard to print graphics screens.

help

DISPLAY HELP FOR DOS COMMAND

Syntax	HELP [command]
Description	HELP invokes on-line help for a DOS command the same help that is invoked when the command is run with a /? switch. Running HELP with no command name following it displays a list of all of DOS commands.

if

EXECUTE COMMAND CONDITIONALLY

Syntax	To test an exit code returned by a program
	IF [NOT] ERRORLEVEL exitcode command
	To compare two strings:
	IF [NOT] stirng1 = sting2 command
	To see if a file exists in a specified location on disk
	IF [NOT] EXIST [d:] [path] filename command

Description The IF command allows a batch file to perform a test and act based on the results of the test.

The IF ERRORLEVEL form of the command returns true if the exit code from form the program most recently executed is equal to or higher than exitcode. The string comparison form of the command returns true if the two string are equal.

The IF EXIST form of the command returns true, if the file exist in the specified location.

include

INCLUDES THE CONTENTS OF ONE CONFIGURATION BLOCK WITHIN ANOTHER

Syntax INCLUDE = blockname

Description This command allows you to include the CONFIG.SYS lines from one menu block in another.

install

INSTALL MEMORY-RESIDENT PROGRAM

Syntax INSTALL = [d:] [path] filename [parameters]

Description INSTALL lets you load TSRs from CONFIG.SYS rather than from the command line. If you do not include a path to the file, INSTALL looks for it in the root directory of the drive DOS was started. You must include the file name extension.

interlnk

CONNECTS TWO COMPUTERS

Syntax INTERLNK [client[;]=[server][:]

Description Interlnk is a DOS 6.0 feature that allows you to connect two computers together using a special serial or parallel cable. Using this command and INTERSVR, you can have the disk drives and/or printers on once computer appear on the other computer.

intersvr

STARTS THE INTERLNK SERVER

Syntax INTERSVR [drive[...] [/X=drive:[...] [/LPT:[n|address] [/BAUD|rate] [B] [/V]

For copy use

INTERSVR /RCOPY

Description This command is half the Interlnk system, which allows you to connect two computers together with a serial or parallel cable in order to share disks and/or printers.

join

JOIN DISK TO DIRECTORY

Syntax JOIN [d1: [d2:] path] [/D]

Description JOIN establishes a logical link between a disk and a remote directory, making it appear that an entire disk is actually a subdirectory on another drive. For example, after typing

JOIN A: C:\A DRIVE

typing

DIR C:\A DRIVE

will display a list of the files on the disk in drive A. You can only JOIN drives to empty directories running JOIN without command line parameters list the drives currently JOINED running it with a / D switch cancels JOIN for the specified drive. While a drive is JOINed, it cannot be accessed by drive letter.

keyb

ALTER KEYBOARD LAYOUT

Syntax KEYB [xx[, [yyy] [,[d:] [path] filename]]] [/E] [/D:nnn]

Description KEYB is a TSR that remaps your keyboard to one of the alternate layouts diagrammed in your DOS manual. With KEYB installed, you can revert to the default configuration by pressing Ctrl+Alt+F1 and return to the new configuration by pressing Ctrl+Alt+F7.

label

SET VOLUME LABEL

Syntax LABEL [d:] [label]

Description The LABEL command lets you create, modify and delete the volume label assigned to a disk. If you run it without a label parameter LABEL displays he current label (if one exists) and prompts you to enter a enter a new one. If you press Enter without entering a new label, LABEL asks you whether you want to delete the current label.

lastdrive

SPECIFY HIGHLIGHT DRIVE LETTER DOS WILL SUPPORT

Syntax LASTDRIVE = x

Description When DOS starts up, it reserves room for information about five logical drives (the current directory for the drive, the address of the device drive that services the drive, and so on) in low memory. If you plan to use a drive letter higher than E, you must use LASTDRIVE to reserve room for it.

loadfix

LOAD PROGRAM ABOVE 64K MARK

Syntax LOADFIX [d:] [path] filename [parameters]

Description When DOS is loaded in the HMA, there is a very good chance that programs will be loaded and run in the first 64K of memory. However, some programs do not run properly in this region. The LOADFIX searches the PATH for executable files. The filename parameter does not have to include the filename extension.

loadhigh (lh)

LOAD MEMORY-RESIDENT PROGRAM IN UPPER MEMORY

Syntax LOADHIGH [d:] [path] filename [parameters]

Description The LOADHIGH command loads a program into upper memory blocks (UMBs) established between 640K and 1Mb on 386 and 486PCs by the EMM386.EXE driver. Before LOADHIGH may be used both HIMEM.SYS and EMM386.EXE must be installed, and DOS must be started with the statement DOS=UMB in CONFIG.SYS. If there is not enough room to load the specified program in uppermemory, LOADHIGH loads it in conventional memory, LOADHIGH automatically searches the PATH for executables to load. The filename parameter need not contain an extension.

mem

DISPLAY MEMORY USAGE

Syntax MEM [/CLASSIFY /DEBUG PROGRAM]

Description The MEM command profiles memory usage. Run without a command line switch it displays vital statistics on memory usage such as the largest executable program size and the total amount of memory installed. The command line switches provide information about what is loaded in memory and where they may be abbreviated /C /D and /P..

memmaker

OPTIMIZES COMPUTER MEMORY USUAGE

Syntax MEMMAKER [/B] [/BATCH] [/SESSION] [/SWAP:drive] [/T] [UNDO] [/W | n,m]

Description MemMaker is memory optimizer. It configures the statements in your CONFIG.SYS and AUTOEXEC.BAT to maximize the amount of available conventional memory.

menucolor

SET STARTUP MENU COLOURS

Syntax MENUCOLOR = x[,y]

Description This command sets the colours for a CONFIG.SYS startup menu.

menudefault

SETUP DEFAULT MENU ITEM

Syntax MENUDEFAULT = blockname [,timeout]

Description This command allows you to select which item from your startup menu will be highlighted initially. You can also tell DOS to select this item automatically.

menuitem

DEFINE AN ITEM ON THE STARTUP MENU

Syntax MENUITEM = blockname [,menu-text]

Description This command inside your CONFIG.SYS file defines a single menu item and must be part of a larger menu block. This also allows you to choose between multiple configurations.

mirror

SAVE DISK INFORMATION

Syntax To create a back copy of a hard disk's partition tables

MIRROR / PARTN

To create a mirror file on a disk for use by the UNFORMAT command MIRROR D:[/l]

To make MIRROR memory resident and have it perform delete tracking for the UNDELETE command

MIRROR / I drive [...entries] [...]

To remove MIRROR from memory

Description The MIRROR command performs three distinctly different functions. One, it creates backup copy of a hard disk's partition tables so they can be restored if they become corrupted. Two, it creates mirror file that the UNFORMAT command can use to restore the disk if it becomes damaged or is inadvertently formatted. Three, it performs a function known as delete tracking which enables the UNDELETE command to restore some files that could not be restored using conventional methods. The default value for entries depend on size of the disk that delete tracking is being performed on.

mkdir (md)

MAKE DIRECTORY

Syntax MD [d:] path

Description The MD command creates a new subdirectory.

mode

CONFIGURE DEVICE

Syntax: To configure a printer attached to a parallel port

MODE LPTn [:][COLS=columns][LINES=lines] [RETRY=r]

MODE device CODEPAGE SELECT = yyy

MODE device CODEPAGE RESEARCH

MODE device CODEPAGE / STATUS

Description: The MODE command is actually many command in one. You can use it to:

* Set the number of characters per inch and lines per inch for IBM compatible printers
* Initialize a serial port to the desired baud rate parity setting number of data bits, and number of stop bits
* Display the status of one or more devices
* Redirect printer output from an LPT port to a COM port
* Prepare select refresh and display the status of code pages
* Set the number of rows and columns of text displayed on an EGA or VGA video adapter
* Set the typematic rate and delay interval on selected keyboard.

more

DISPLAY SCREENFUL OF INFORMATION

Syntax: MORE <source>

or

a command / MORE

Description: MORE accepts a stream of input data and outputs it one screenful at a time pausing for a keystroke at the end of each screen. Input must be supplied to the command by an input redirection or piping operator.

move

MOVES ONE OR MORE FILES

Syntax: MOVE [drive:] [path] filename [,[drive:] [path] filename[...]] destination

Description: This command has two uses. First, as its name suggests, it can move a file or group of files from one directory to another.

msav

SCAN COMPUTER FOR KNOWN VIRUSES

Syntax MSAV [drive:] [/S /C] [/R] [/A /L] [/N] [/P] [/F] [/VIDEO]

Description This is a DOS program that will scan your memory and disks for viruses. It can also remove viruses that it finds.

msbackup

BACKUP ONE OR MORE FILES

Syntax MSBACKUP [Setup file] [BW | /LCD | /MDA]

Description This command allows you to back up an entire hard disk to a set of floppy disks, even when you have some files that are too large to fit on a single floppy disk

msd

PROVIDES DETAILED SYSTEM TECHNICAL INFORMATION

Syntax To create a report

MSD [/I] [/F[drive:] [path] filename [/P[drive:] [path] filename] [/S[drive:] [path] [filename]

To check only the Technical Information

MSD [/B] [/I]

Description Records the configuration of your system for use in tracking down and troubleshooting problems.

numlock

SET NUMERIC LOCK ON OR OFF

Syntax NUMLOCK = [ON:OFF]

Description This command controls whether the Num Lock state is turned on or off (normally you have to press the Num Lock key to change this state).

path

SET SEARCH PATH FOR EXECUTABLE FILES

Syntax PATH [[d:]path[:d]path] [;...]

Description The PATH command creates a list of directories that DOS searches for executable files whenever you type a command that is not an internal DOS command. Running PATH with no command line parameters display the current PATH running it with nothing but a semicolon cancels the current PATH, PATH strings are stored as environment variables so you can also create and modify them with the SET command.

pause

PAUSE BATCH FILE EXECUTION

Syntax PAUSE

Description PAUSE pauses a batch file and displays a message "Press any key to continue".

power

TURNS POWER MANAGEMENT ON OR OFF

Syntax POWER [ADV[:MAX | REG | MIN | STD | OFF]

To display current power setting type

POWER

Description To be used alongwith POWER.EXE device driver. The power command allows you to change the power management settings on a laptop computer from the command line.

print

INSTALLS PRINT SPOOLER

Syntax PRINT [/D:device] [/B:size] [/U:ticks1] [/M:ticks2] [/S:ticks3] [/Q:qsize] [/T] [d:] [path]filename [...] [/C] [/P]

Description PRINT is a TSR that allows text files to be printed in the background while you work in the foreground. The /U, /M and /S switches allow you to finetune PRINT so that files print quickly but don't steal too much time away from foreground tasks. The /B and /Q switches let you specify the sizes of the internal buffers PRINT set up. The /C, /P and /T switches let you control what goes into and out of the print queue. A /P or /C switch affects the file whose name precedes the switch and all subsequent files until another /P or /C switch is encountered. PRINT should be used to print text files only, printing binary files can produce strange results. To list the files currently in the print queue, run PRINT by itself on the command line.

prompt

CONFIGURE COMMAND PROMPT

Syntax PROMPT [prompt string]

Description The PROMPT command defines the appearance of the DOS prompt. You can include the following metacharacters in a prompt string:

$b	Piping operator (|)
$d	Current date
$e	Escape character
$g	Output redirection operator (>)
$h	Backspace (delete previous character)
$I	Input redirection operator (<)

$n	Current drive
$p	Current Drive and Directory
$q	Equal sign)=)
$t	Current time
$v	DOS version number
$_	Carriage return

Run without a prompt string parameter PROMPT restores the default DOS prompt which is equivalent to typing the command PROMPT $$n$g.

qbasic

START QUICK BASIC INTERPRINTER

Syntax QBASIC [/B] [/EDITOR] [/G] [/H]; /MBF| [/NOHI] [/RUN] [d:] [path] [filename]

Description The QBASIC command starts the QBASIC Interpreter, and interpreted BASIC programming environment based on Microsoft Quick BASIC. The /MBF switch is useful for running QBASIC programs that read and write data files created by GW-BASIC or BASICA.

rem

DEFINE COMMENT LINE

Syntax REM [comment]

Description REM can be used in batch files and in CONFIG.SYS file to declare comment lines.

rename (ren)

RENAME FILE

Syntax REN [d:] [path] filename filename2

Description The REN command renames a file. You cannot specify a drive or path with filename2 because the file cannot be renamed to another drive or directory. You can use wild cards too.

replace

REPLACE FILES

Syntax REPLACE [d:] [path] filename destination [/A] [/P] [/R] [/S] [/U] [/W]

Description REPLACE can be used in two distinctly different ways to replace files of certain name at the destination or add files that don't already exist at the destination. It will not replace read-only files unless the /R switch is used.

restore

RESTORE BACKED UP FILES

Syntax RESTORE source destination [/A:date] [/B:date] [/D] [/E:time] [/L:time] [/M] [/N] [/P] [/S]

Description RESTORE restores files backed up with the BACKUP command. You can list the name of files on the backup disk with the /D switch which list all files that match filename without actually restoring them. When RESTORE is started it prompts you to insert the backup disks in the same order that they were inserted during the backup operation, so it is a good idea to have them labeled.

rmdir (rd)

REMOVE DIRECTORY

Syntax RD [d:] path

Description RD removes a subdirectory. It is the counterpart to MD which creates a subdirectory. A subdirectory cannot be removed unless it is devoid of files and other subdirectories.

set

SET ENVIRONMENT VARIABLE

Syntax SET [variable=[string]]

Description SET creates, deletes, modifies, typing SET by itself lists all the environment variables currently defined. Specifying a variable name and a text string creates that environment variables currently defined. Specifying a variable name and a text string creates that environment variable and sets it equal to the string. If you include the variable parameter but omit string the environment variable is deleted.

setver

SET DOS VERSION

Syntax SETVER [d:path] [filename] [n,nn] [/DELETE] [/QUIET]

Description Some program check the version of DOS that is being used and refuse to run under version 6.0. SETVER lets you set the version number that DOS will report to application programs on a program-to-program basis. To remove an entry from the table that DOS maintains internally, use the /DELETE switch. Run without switches SETVER lists the file names in the table along with the DOS versions that are reported to them. SETVER is only effective if SETVER.EXE is loaded with a DEVICE or DEVICEHIGH directive in CONFIG.SYS.

share

INSTALL FILE SHARING SUPPORT

Syntax SHARE [/F:size] [/L:locks]

Description SHARE installs the component of DOS that supports file sharing and file locking on networks. With SHARE installed, programs written for networked environments can access files cooperatively ensuring that one program does not destroy what another has done.

shell

SPECIFY COMMAND PROCESSOR

Syntax SHELL = [[d:] path] filename [parameters]

Description The SHELL directive specifies what command processor is used to read and process your commands. The default command processor is COMMAND.COM.

sort

SORT TEXT

Syntax SORT [/R][/+nn] <source [>destination]

or

command /SORT [/R][/+nn] [>destination]

Description SORT accepts a stream of input data and sorts it. If destination is not specified. SORT sends its output to the screen. Input must be supplied to the command by an input redirection/piping operator.

stacks

CONFIGURE SYSTEM STACKS

Syntax STACKS = n/s

Description To prevent system from crashing when hardware interrupts occur too quickly in succession DOS intercepts selected hardware interrupts and assigns them each a stack from an array of stacks it maintains internally. STACKS specifies the number of stacks created at start-up the number of bytes allocated to each stack. On an 8086- or 8086-based PC, the default is STACKS=0. On all others, the default is STACKS=9, 128.

subst

SUBSTITUTE DRIVE FOR DIRECTORY

Syntax SUBST [d1:d2] path [/D]

Description SUBST creates a new logical drive and associates it with the specified drive and directory. DOS treats it as if it were a real drive. For example after you type

SUBST Z: C:\DOSSUTIL

then typing DIR Z: lists the contents of C:\DOSSUTIL. Running

SUBST without parameters or switches display a list of the drives defined with the SUBST command.

switches

SET CONFIGURATION SWITCHES

Syntax SWITCHES = [/K] [/W] [/N] [/F]

Description SWITCHES is a catch-all directive that will probably be expanded in future versions of DOS. The /D switch causes DOS to ignore keys such as F11 and F12 on 101 and 102 key keyboards. The /W switch enables you to move WINA20.386, the file that SETUP placed in the root directory of your hard disk to another drive or directory. /N switch disables the F5 and F8 key interactive startup features, which allows you to skip all or parts of your CONFIG.SYS file. /F switch eliminates the pause which DOS takes after displaying "Starting MS-DOS ...".

sys

TRANSFER SYSTEM FILES

Syntax SYS [d:] [path] d:

Description For a disk to be bootable it must contain the system files IO.SYS, MSDOS.SYS and COMMAND.COM. SYS transfers these files to a hard disk or floppy that does not already contain them.

If you omit the d: and path parameters, DOS looks to the root directory of the current drive for the system files.

time

SET SYSTEM TIME

Syntax TIME [time]

Description TIME sets the current system time. Time is entered in the format hours[:minutes[:seconds[:hundredths]]] [A/P] where A and P specify whether the time is am or pm. The default is am unless hours is greater than 12. If you do not specify a time, TIME displays the current time and prompts you to enter a new one.

tree

DISPLAY DIRECTORY TREE

Syntax TREE [d:[path]] [/A] [/F]

Description TREE graphically depicts the structure of the specified drive from the specified directory down listing all the subdirectories it encounters. If you use /F switch, it also displays the names of the files inside those subdirectories. Use /A when you direct the output from TREE to a printer that does not support the upper half of the IBM character set.

type

TYPE TEXT FILE

Syntax: TYPE [d:] [path] filename

Description: The TYPE command lists the contents of a file to the screen. It is designed to be used with text files, and it stops at the first occurrence of an ASCII Ctrl-Z character. TYPE does not accept wildcards in filename. You can pause long listing as they scroll by pressing Ctrl+S, and continue scrolling by pressing another key.

undelete

UNDELETE FILE

Syntax: UNDELETE [[d:] [path] filename] [/LIST /ALL] [/DOS /DT]

Description: UNDELETE recovers files deleted with DEL or ERASE commands. For added protection against deletions, you can use the MIRROR command to create delete-tracking file. If UNDELETE finds a delete-tracking file when restoring files, it uses it; if there is no delete-tracking file, then it restores file using information left behind in the disk's FAT and directory entries. If you use the /ALL switch, DOS supplies a # character as the first letter in the file name.

unformat

UNFORMAT DISK

Syntax: To restore hard disk partition table [UNFORMAT / PARTN [/L]

To unformat a hard or floppy

UNFORMAT d: [/U] [/L] [/TEST] [/P]

To verify that a disk contains a mirror file

UNFORMAT d: /J

Description: The UNFORMAT command has two distinct uses. The first is to restore a hard disks partition tables if they become corrupted. Partition tables are saved to a floppy with the MIRROR command.

The second use for UNFORMAT is to unformat a formatted disk. UNFORMAT searches the disk for a mirror file (a file created by the FORMAT or MIRROR command that contains a copy of the disk's FAT and root directory) and, if it finds it, uses it to perform the unformat. If there is no mirror file, or if UNFORMAT was started with a /U or /L switch, UNFORMAT attempts to unformat the disk using the information left behind after the format.

This is less reliable and much more time consuming than an unformat performed with the aid of a mirror file.

ver

DISPLAY DOS VERSION

Syntax	VER
Description	It displays the version number of DOS that is running.

vol

DISPLAY VOLUME INFORMATION

Syntax	VOL [d:]
Description	VOL displays the volume label and serial number of the specified drive. If you omit the drive specifier VOL defaults to the current drive.

vsafe

VIRUS PROTECTION FOR COMPUTER

Syntax	VSAFE [/options[+/–] ...] [/NE] [/NX] [/AX] [/CX] [/IN] [/D] [/U]
Description	VSAFE is a memory resident program that provides on going protection against viruses invading your system. If VSAFE finds a virus, it will inform you. With VSAFE installed, however, some programs may cause warning messages that do not necessarily indicate the presence of a virus.

xcopy

COPIES FILE OR FILES

Syntax	XCOPY source [destination] [/A] [D:date] [/E] [/M] [/P] [/S] [/V] [/W]
Description	The XCOPY command is similar to copy except that is uses all available memory rather than single 64K segment and it can copy several files at once without requiring you to swapdisks when copying from floppy to floppy. It also offers a wider selection of options and with /S switch it will even perform a reclusive copy. XCOPY will not copy hidden or system files.

Revision

1. A computer: cannot think, it has vast capabilities of calculations like addition, substraction, etc. and It is totally under the control of the user.
2. Though the first fully operational electronic computer was introduced to the world in 1946, but the historian assumes the starting of a computer age from 1951, when first commercial computer UNIVAC was introduced.
3. Computer is vastly used for Airlines booking, Banking business, Professional Business, Cartoons creations, Cinema editing, Defence applications, Desk Top Publishing, Education books and teaching, Home videos and games, Library management of books, Medicine records, Space Technology and Weather reporting.
4. The main parts of the computer are: Monitor, Central Processing Unit and Keyboard.

5. The block diagram shows all the parts of the computer.
6. Over the years personal computers have gone through various changes and have been named as XT, AT, etc.
7. There are various types of memories which are used by computers.
8. RAM, Random Access Memory and ROM, Read Only Memory are the most common.
9. ROM can be of the type: PROM, EPROM, and EEPROM.
10. Personal computers are known for their speed, reliability and accuracy.
11. The Central Processing Unit has: Primary Storage Unit, Arithmetic Logic Unit, Control Unit and Output Unit.
12. The development of computers have been classified in the form of generations.
13. There are five generation of computers.
14. Computers can of various types: Super Computers, Mainframe Computers, Super Mini Computers and Mini Computers.
15. Laptop computers are also very popular these days.
16. When the computer is put on, the first thing that it needs is the operating system.
17. An operating system consists of a set of instructions that coordinates all the activities of the hardware devices.
18. The main operations of operating systems are: Input/Output Operations, Handling File Systems, Execution of Programs, Allocation of Resources, Detection of Errors and Information Resource Protection.
19. Among the various type of operating systems are: Single Program Operating System, Multiple Program Operating System, Time Sharing Operating System, Real Time Operating System and Microprocessing Operating System.
20. Among the popular operating system are Disk Operating System (DOS).
21. Microsoft Windows is an operating system which can handle graphics easily.
22. UNIX operating system is more popular with large systems.
23. OS/2 operating system was devised for main frames.
24. Linux operating system is more popular with users of Internet.
25. DOS has internal and external commands.
26. Internal commands can be given from anywhere.
27. In DOS the filename is of 8 + 3 format.
28. Root directory is the main directory of the hard disk.
29. DIR command gives the listing of files in directory.
30. DIR/P allows you to view the files on screen page by page.
31. DIR/W gives the listing widthwise.
32. MD command allows you to create directory.
33. CD command is used for changing directory.
34. RD command is used for removing directory.
35. A file can be copied on to another drive or another directory.
36. Xcopy command can be used to copy various files.
37. Backup is used to copy several files at a time for storing.
38. An existing file can be deleted too.
39. Using Date and Time commands, you can see the system date and time.
40. Prompt command allows you to change the command prompt.
41. You can give a file a new name by using the REN command.
42. Restore command allows you to restore the backed up files.

43. Attribute command allows you to change the attributes of the file.

Multiple Choice Questions

1. RAM stands for:
   (a) Random Allowed Memory (b) Ready Access Memory
   (c) Random Access Memory
2. RAM consists of binary numbers 1s and :
   (a) 0s (b) 2s (c) 3s
3. CPU contains Primary Storage, Arithmetic Logic Unit and
   (a) Control Unit (b) Data Unit (c) Alpha Unit
4. Data stored in ROM cannot be changed:
   (a) Yes (b) No
5. A copy of the current instruction is stored in:
   (a) Instruction Register (b) Working Register (c) General Register
6. Computers are classified into ______ generations:
   (a) 7 (b) 3 (c) 5
7. The three main units of computer are: Keyboard, Central Processing Unit and :
   (a) Monitor (b) Mouse (c) Motherboard
8. Which of the following does not belong to the Intel's Processor's series:
   (a) 8086 (b) 80186 (c) 80486
   (d) 8051
9. Which command is used to shift the command from one directory to another?
   (a) CD (b) MD (c) RD
10. Which command would you use to create a new directory?
    (a) CD (b) MD (c) RD
11. The main directory of the hard disk is:
    (a) Main directory (b) Root directory (c) Final directory
12. Which command will always transfer to the root directory?
    (a) CD\ (b) CD/ (c) CD
13. For listing the files widthwise, we give the command as?
    (a) DIR/P (b) DIR/W (c) DIR
14. The files in DOS are named in which format ?
    (a) 9 + 2 (b) 10 + 1 (c) 8 + 3
15. A directory whithin a directory is called:
    (a) Sub directory (b) Part directory (c) Junior directory
16. Prompt command is used to change the command prompt from:
    (a) c:\ (b) c: (c) c
17. Backup files can be restored using the command called:
    (a) Prompt (b) Restore (c) Cleanup
18. Time shows the time in hh:mm and ___ format:
    (a) ss (b) nn (c) pp
19. To rename a file, you give the command as:
    (a) name (b) REN (c) re
20. You can change the status of the file using the command:
    (a) Status (b) Change (c) Atrib

True/False Questions

1. The main parts of the computer are: Mouse, Central Processing Unit and Keyboard.
2. The block diagram shows all the parts of the computer.
3. Over the years personal computers have gone through various changes and have been named as XT, AT, etc.
4. There are various types of memories which are used by computers.
5. RAM is Random Access Memory .
6. ROM is Read Over Memory.
7. ROM can be of the type: PROM, EPROM, and EEPROM.
8. Personal computers are known for their speed, reliability and accuracy.
9. The Central Processing Unit has: Primary Storage Unit, Arithmetic Logic Unit, Control Unit and Output Unit.
10. The development of computers have been classified in the form of generations.
11. There are seven generation of computers.
12. Laptop computers are also very popular these days.
13. Microprocessor is a semiconductor chip consist billions of transistors.
14. 80287 processor is used on PC-AT.
15. DRAM is a type of primary memory.
16. Operating system is a must for every computer.
17. Operating system is a program.
18. Operating system cannot control the working of input/output.
19. UNIX is a popular operating system for PCs.
20. DOS can handle graphics easily.
21. In DOS a filename consists of 2 parts of 8 and 3 characters.
22. Root directory is the main directory of the hard disk.
23. MD command is used to change the directory.
24. RD command is used to create a directory.
25. DIR/W lists the directory page wise.
26. Xcopy does not copy any file.
27. Backup is used for backing up the files.
28. REN is used to rename a file.
29. Using Prompt command you can change the command prompt of DOS.
30. Using Attrib you can change the attributes of the DOS file.

Descriptive Questions

1. What is Random Access Memory? Explain its construction.
2. What is BIOS?
3. Describe the personal computer.
4. Which are the main parts of computers?
5. What is Central Processing Unit?
6. What changes have been brought about in computer over the ages?
7. Describe the various peripherals used in PC, PC-XT and PC-AT.
8. Which type of memories are used by personal computers?
9. Describe the various generations of computers.
10. Describe the various classifications of computers.

11. Draw the block diagram of computer and give its working.
12. Give difference between ROM and RAM.
13. What is microprocosser? Explain its working?
14. What is an operating system?
15. Describe the various functions of the operating system.
16. Describe the various types of operating systems.
17. List out the various popular operating systems.
18. What is DOS used for?
19. Describe the Rename command.
20. What is the command to remove all files in a directory?
21. Is it possible to remove the root directory of your hard disk by using the RD command? If yes, how?
22. Type the command to remove a directory. Where must the cursor be to remove a directory or subdirectory?
23. What are the different options of the DIR command?
24. What is the command to display a directory pagewise?
25. What is the command to display a directory widthwise?
26. What is the root directory?
27. What does the symbol \(backslash) stand for?
28. What display does your monitor show when you type CD?
29. What does the command Backup do?
30. How would you restore the backuped files?
31. How is it possible to see the system date?
32. Is it possible to see the system time, how?
33. What is prompt command used for?

Answers to Objective Type Questions

Multiple Choice Questions

1.	c	2.	a	3.	a	4.	b
5.	a	6.	c	7.	a	8.	d
9.	a	10.	b	11.	b	12.	a
13.	b	14.	c	15.	a	16.	a
17.	b	18.	a	19.	b	20.	c

True False Questions

1.	F	2.	T	3.	T	4.	T
5.	T	6.	F	7.	T	8.	T
9.	T	10.	T	11.	F	12.	T
13.	T	14.	F	15.	T	16.	T
17.	T	18.	F	19.	F	20.	F
21.	T	22.	T	23.	F	24.	F
25.	F	26.	F	27.	T	28.	T
29.	T	30.	T				

2 Microprocessors

Personal Computer Motherboards

Motherboard is the main component inside the main system unit. This is the biggest electronic circuit board inside the computer system, on which many other board are attached. The boards that attach to the motherboard are known as daughterboard or expansion board.

The motherboard contains following :

1. **Processor Support:** The motherboard dictates directly your choice of processor for use in the system.
2. **Peripheral Support:** The motherboard determines, what types of peripherals you can use in your PC.
3. **Performance:** The motherboard is a major determining factor in system's performance, the motherboard determines what types of processors, memory, system buses, and hard disk interface speed your system can have, and these components dictate directly your system's performance.
4. **Upgradability:** The capabilities of motherboard dictate to what extent you will be able to upgrade your machine.

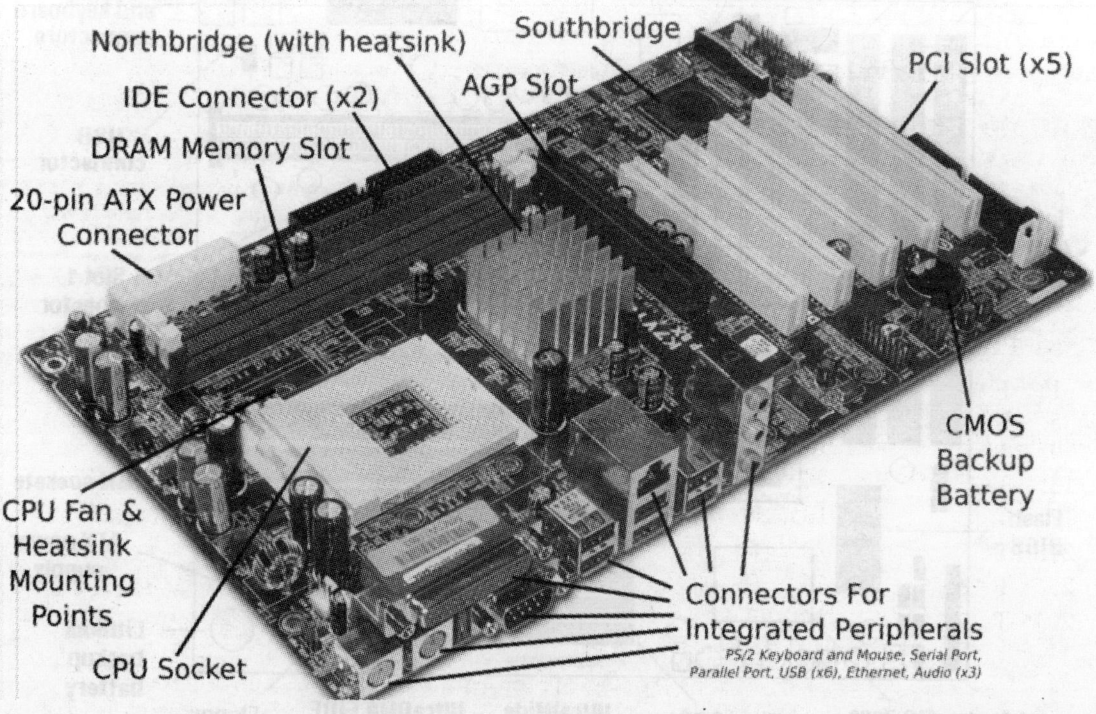

5. **Organization:** The way that the motherboard is designed and laid out dictates how the entire computer is going to be organized.
6. **Control:** The motherboard contains the chipset and BIOS program, which control most of the data flow within the computer.
7. **Communication:** All communication between the PC and its peripherals, other PCs, and user, goes through the motherboard.

Various Motherboard Types

PC/XT

It is series of personal computers based on the Intel 8088 processor, introduced by IBM in 1983. XT stands for eXtended Technology.The PC/XT was the first personal computer to offer a built-in hard disk and the capability to expand memory 640K on the motherboard. The original PC/XT used an Intel 8088 running at a clock speed of 4.77 MHz . The system was largely intended for business users. It came with 128 kB of memory, a 360 kB double-sided 5 1/4" full-height floppy disk drive, and a 10 MB hard drive, a serial port, eight 8-bit

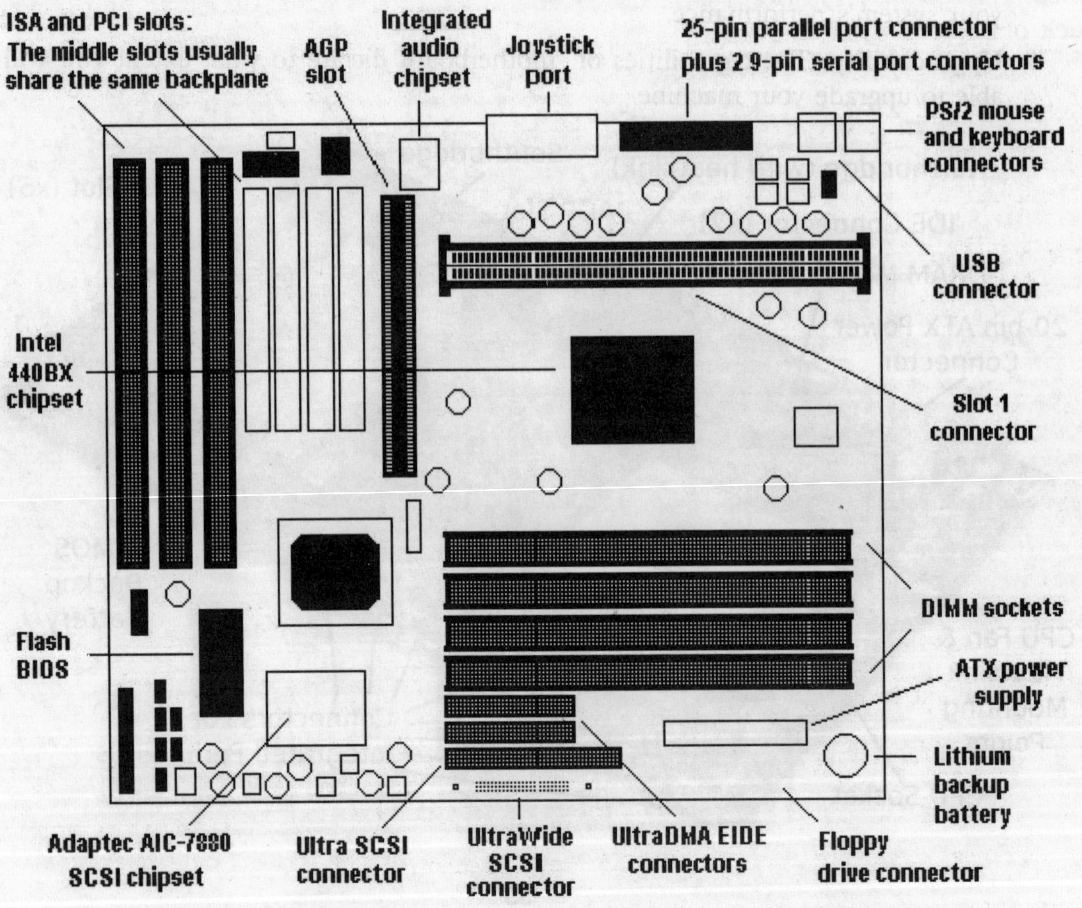

ISA expansion slots, and an Intel 8088 microprocessor running at 4.77 MHz. The eight slots were an increase over the five in the IBM PC, although three were taken up by the floppy drive adapter, the hard drive adapter, and the serial card. Like the original PC, the XT came with a BASIC interpreter in PC and XT keyboards are not compatible with more modern PC.

PC/AT

PC/AT, was IBM's second-generation PC, designed around the Intel 80286 microprocessor running at 6 MHz and released in 1984. AT originally stood for Advanced Technology .The AT represented a significant performance increase over previous computers, up to 75 percent faster than the PC/XT, and the AT bus standard is used in many clones or IBM compatible computers.

It was the most advanced machine in the PC line and featured a new keyboard, a higher-capacity 5.25" floppy (1.2MB) and a 16-bit data bus. AT-class machines ran considerably faster than the earlier 8088-based XT PCs. The motherboard includes connectors for two serial ports, a parallel port, floppy drive, and two IDE chains (for IDE devices such as hard disks and CD-ROM drives). Located just to the left of the keyboard connector, but not pointed out in the photo, is a PS/2 mouse connection on the motherboard.

These connectors will have ribbon cables connected to them that attach to ports on the back of the computer, the floppy drive(s), and hard drives/CD-ROM drives.

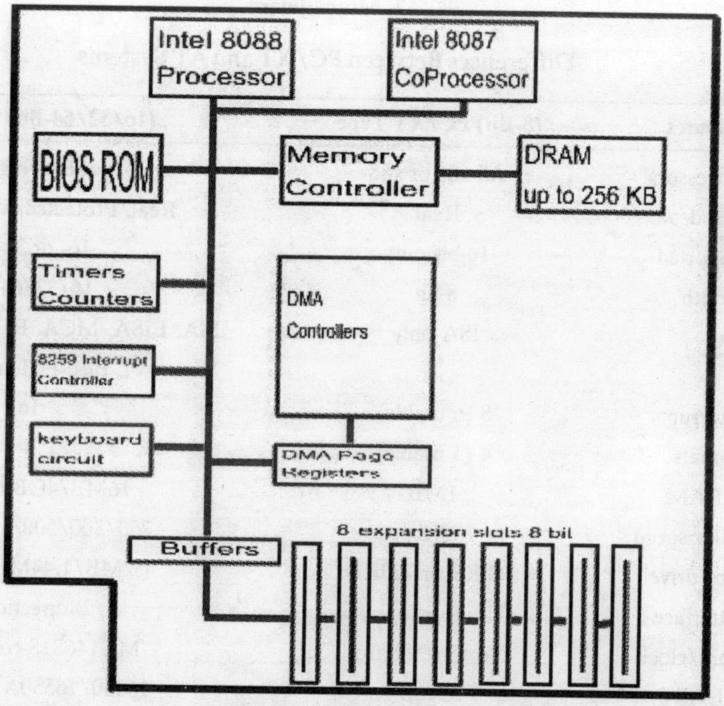

PC-XT Block Diagram

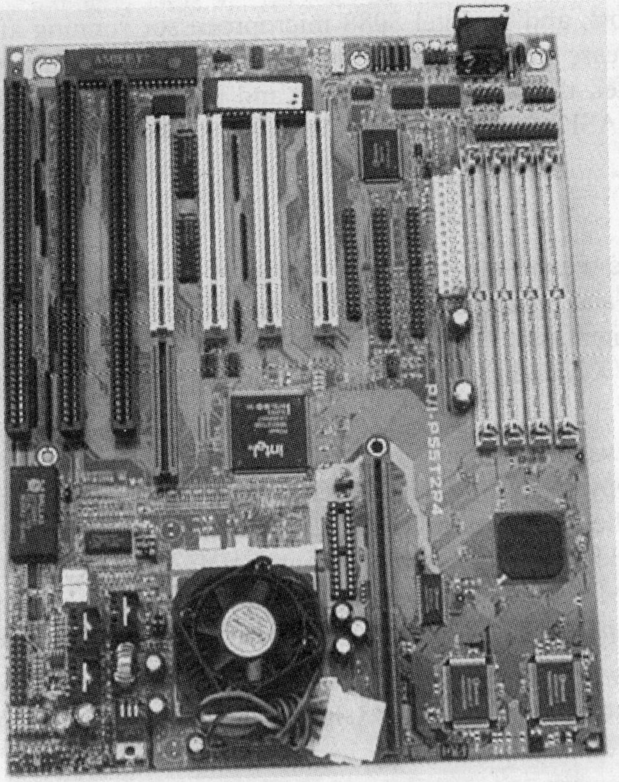

PC-AT Motherboard

Differences Between PC/XT and AT Systems

System Attributes	(8-Bit) PC/XT Type	(16/32/64-Bit) AT Type
Supported processors	All x86 or x88	286 or higher
Processor modes	Real	Real/Protected/Virtual Real
Software supported	16-bit only	16- or 32-bit
Bus slot width	8-bit	16/32/64-bit
Slot type	ISA only	ISA, EISA, MCA, PC-Card, Cardbus, VL-Bus, PCI, and AGP
Hardware interrupts	8 (6 usable)	16
DMA channels	4 (3 usable)	8
Maximum RAM	1MB	16MB/4GB or more
Floppy controller speed	250Kbps	250/300/500/1,000 Kbps
Standard boot drive	360KB or 720KB	1.2MB/1.44MB/2.88MB
Keyboard interface	Unidirectional	Bidirectional
CMOS memory/clock	None standard	MC146818-compatible
Serial-port UART	8250B	16450/16550A or greater

Pentium Motherboard

ATX motherboard

Intel, the primary manufacturer of PC CPUs, has proposed a new motherboard layout called the ATX.

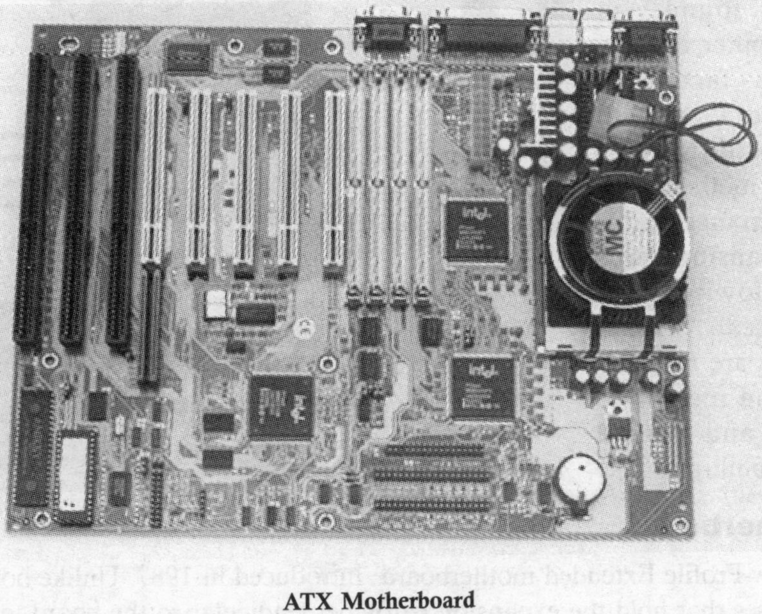

ATX Motherboard

The bus slots are parallel to the short side of the motherboard. Instead of the long side of the motherboard running front to back in the PC, the short side runs front to back. The bus slots are located in the same general location, and the adapters still install in these slots and mount to the back of the computer's chassis. The serial, parallel, keyboard, and mouse connectors are built right onto the motherboard and stick out the back of the chassis when the motherboard is installed. One of the main reasons for the ATX design is to move the

CPU closer to the power supply fan for better cooling, which means the CPU will last longer and suffer fewer faults.

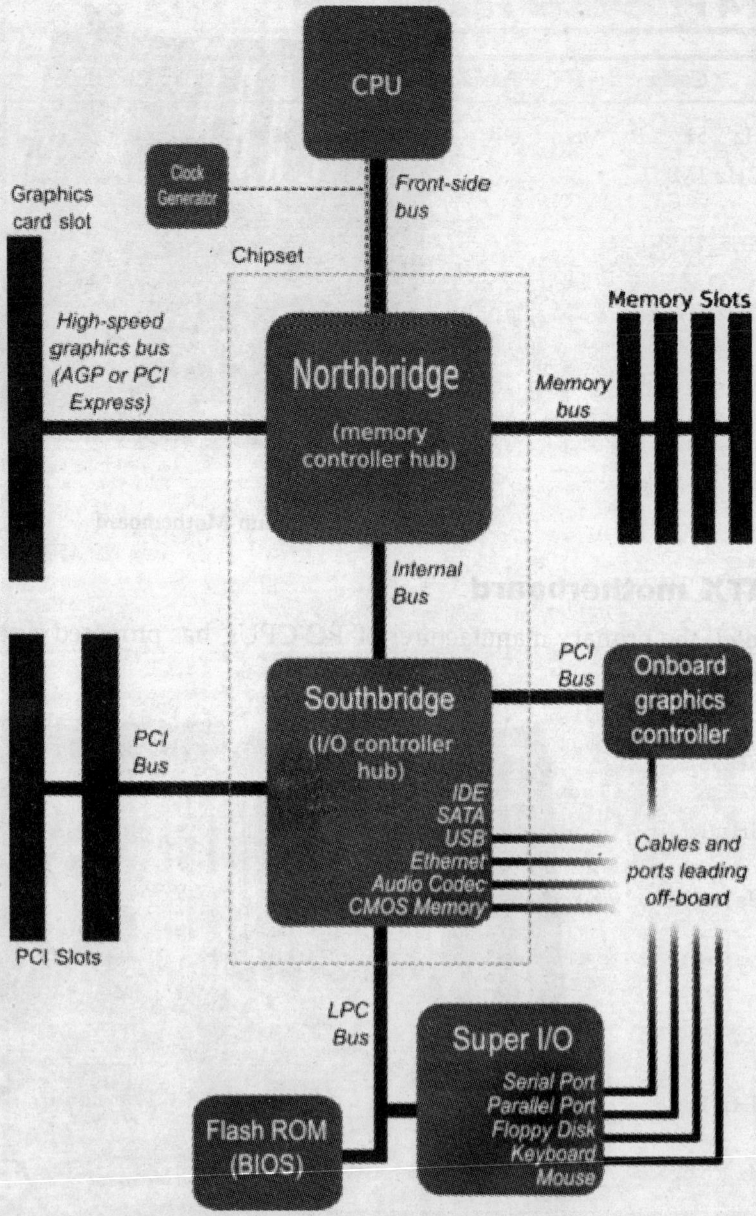

LPX motherboard

It is Low-Profile Extended motherboard introduced in 1997 by Western Digital. Unlike boards for desktop and tower cases that hold the expansion cards perpendicular to the board, cards plug into a riser card on the LPX and are parallel with the board. The LPX form factor is not a standard one but a non-standard proprietary one sometimes found in desktop computer models. This form factor is characterized by an expansion board that runs parallel to the motherboard. A riser card arrangement is used for expansion cards thereby allowing for smaller cases. LPX motherboards are typically integrated and most have the video and sound components built-in.

NLX motherboard

It is New Low-Profile Extended motherboard introduced in 1987. Unlike boards for desktop and tower cases that hold the expansion cards perpendicular to the board, cards plug into a riser card on the NLX and are parallel with the board. NLX has been a form factor in use with desktops for quite some time. It is a compact form factor, often referred to as a "low-profile application". NLX motherboards are easily distinguished by the riser card to which the expansion cards connect. The riser cards allow from two to four expansion cards to be plugged in. These expansion cards sit parallel to the motherboard. The benefit of the NLX form factor is that the bulk of a traditional server is reduced to a space-saving smaller server.

Intel 4 Processor Family

Speed	Cache Size	HT	Speed Step	EM64TF	System Bus	Package	Product Name
2.40 GHz	512 KB	No	No	No	400 MHz	mPGA478	Pentium 4 orocessor 2.40 GHz
2.40A GHz	1MB L2	No	No	No	533 MHz	mPGA478	Pentium 4 processor 2.40A GHz
2.40B GHz	512 KB	No	No	No	533 MHz	mPGA478	Pentium 4 processor 2.40B GHz
2.40C GHz	512 KB	Yes	No	No	800 MHz	mPGA478	Pentium 4 processor with 2.40C GHz
2.60 GHz	512 KB	No	No	No	400 MHz	mPGA478	Pentium 4 processor with 2.60 GHz
2.60C GHz	512 KB	Yes	No	No	800 MHz	mPGA478	Pentium 4 processor with HT 2.60C GHz
2.66 GHz	512 KB	No	No	No	533 MHz	mPGA478	Pentium 4 processor with 2.66 GHz
2.80 GHz	1 MB	Yes	No	No	800 MHz	FCLGA775	Pentium 4 processor 520 GHz with HT
2.80 GHz	512 KB	No	No	No	533 MHz	mPGA478	Pentium 4 processor 2.80 GHz
2.80A GHz	1 MB	No	No	No	533 MHz	mPGA478	Pentium 4 processor 2.80A GHz
2.80C GHz	512 KB	Yes	No	No	800 MHz	mPGA478	Pentium 4 processor with HT 2.80 GHz
2.80E GHz	1 MB	Yes	No	No	800 MHz	mPGA478	Pentium 4 processor with HT 2.80 GHz
3.00 GHz	1 MB	Yes	No	No	800 MHz	FCLGA775	Pentium 4 processor 530 with HT
3.00 GHz	2 MB	Yes	Yes	Yes	800 MHz	FCLGA775	Pentium 4 processor 630 with HT
3.00 GHz	512 MB	Yes	No	No	800 MHz	mPGA478	Pentium 4 processor with HT 3 GHz
3.00E GHz	1 MB	Yes	No	No	800 MHz	mPGA478	Pentium 4 processor with HT 3E GHz
3.06 GHz	512 KB	Yes	No	No	533 MHz	mPGA478	Pentium 4 processor with HT 3.06 GHz
3.20 GHz	1 MB	Yes	No	No	800 MHz	FCLGA775	Pentium 4 processor 540 with HT
3.20 GHz	2 MB	Yes	Yes	Yes	800 MHz	FCLGA775	Pentium 4 processor 640 with HT
3.20 GHz	512 KB	Yes	No	No	800 MHz	mPGA478	Pentium 4 processor with HT 3.20 GHz
3.20E GHz	1 MB	Yes	No	No	800 MHz	mPGA478	Pentium 4 processor with HT 3.20E GHz
3.40 GHz	1 MB	Yes	No	No	800 MHz	FCLGA775	Pentium 4 processor 550 with HT

3.40 GHz	2 MB	Yes	Yes	Yes	800 MHz	FCLGA775	Pentium 4 processor 650 with HT
3.40 GHz	512 KB	Yes	No	Yes	800 MHz	mPGA478	Pentium 4 processor with HT 3.40 GHz
3.40 GHz	512 KB L2 cache 2 MB L3 cache	Yes	No	No	800 MHz	FCLGA775	Pentium 4 processor with HT Extreme Edition 3.40 GHz
3.40E GHz	1 MB	Yes	No	Yes	800 MHz	mPGA478	Pentium 4 processor with HT 3.40E GHz
3.46 GHz	512 KB L2 cache 2 MB L3 cache	Yes	No	No	1066 MHz	FCLGA775	Pentium 4 processor with HT Extreme Edition 3.46 GHz
3.60 GHz	1 MB	Yes	No	No	800 MHz	FCLGA775	Pentium 4 processor 560 with HT
3.60 GHz	2 MB	Yes	Yes	Yes	800 MHz	FCLGA775	Pentium 4 processor 660 with HT
3.73 GHz	2 MB	Yes	No	Yes	1066 MHz	FCLGA775	Pentium 4 processor with HT Extreme Edition 3.73 GHz
3.80 GHz	1 MB	Yes	No	No	800 MHz	FCLGA775	Pentium 4 processor 570 with HT

Advancements in Motherboard Technology

Intel NetBurst microarchitecture delivers a number of innovative features including Hyper-Threading Technology, hyper-pipelined technology, 1066, 800, 533 or 400 MHz system bus, and Execution Trace Cache. It also provides a number of enhanced feature such as Advanced Trnaster Cache, Advanced Dynamic Execution, enhanced floating-point and multimedia unit, and Streaming SIMD Extension, enhanced loating-point and mutimedia unit, and Streaming SIMD Extensions 2 (SSE2). Further enhancements in the 90 nm process-based Pentium 4 processor include Steaming SIMD Extension 3 (SSE3).

Many of these innovations and advances were made possible with improvements in processor technology, process technology, and circuit design and could not previously be implemented in high-volume, manufacturable solutions.

The features and resulting benefits of the microarchitecture are defined below:

Hyper-Threading Technology

Hyper-Threading Technology (HT Technology) is a groundbreaking technology to improve processor performance. It allows software programs to "see" two processors and work more efficiently.

This new technology enables the processor to execute two series, or threads, of instructions at the same time, thereby improving performance and system responsiveness. Hyper-Threading Technology requires a computer system with an Intel Pentium 4 processor supporting HT Technology and a HT Technology enabled chipset, BIOS and operating system.

Hyper-Pipelined Technology

The hyper-pipelined technolgy of the Intel NetBurst microarchitecutre increases the pipeline depth delivering increased performance, frequency and scalability of the processor.

Intel Enhanced Memory 64 Technology (Intel EM64T)

Intel EM^$T provides an enhancement to the Intel's 32-bit architecture by enabling the desktop processor platform to access larger amounts of memory. With appropriate 64-bit supporting hardware and software, platforms based on an Intel processor supporting Intel EM64T can enable use of extended virtual and physical memory. EM64T requrires a computer system with a processor, chiset, BIOS, operating system, device drivers and applications enabled for Intel EM64T, Processor will not operate (including 32-bit operation) without an Intel EM64T enabled BIOS.

Integrated 2MB Level 3 Cache on Intel Pentium 4 Processor Extreme Edition 3.46 GHz

The 2-MB L3 cache is available only with the Pentium 4 processor Extreme Edition. The additional third level of cache is located on the processor die and is designed specifically to meet the computer needs of high-end gamers and other power users. The Integrated L3 cache is available in 2 MB and when coupled with either the 1066 MHz or 800 MHz system bus provides a high bandwidth path to memory. The efficient design of the integrated L3 cache proveds a faster path to large data sets stored in cache on the processor. This results in reduced average memory latency and increased throughput for larger workloads.

Integrated 2MB Level 2 Cache on Intel Pentium 4 Processor Extreme Edition 3.73 GHz and 6xx

The 2-MB Advanced Transfer Cache (on-die, full speed Level 2 cache) with 8-way associative and Error Correcting Code (ESS) can improve overall performance by allowing the processor to have faster access to a larger amount of the most often used data.

Advanced Dynamic Execution

The Advance Dynamic Execution engine is a very deep, out-of-order speculative execution engine that keeps the execution units executing instructions. It also includes an enhanced branch prediction algorithm that has the net effect of reducing the number of branch mis-predictions.

Chipsets for the Pentium and Beyond

Pentium chipsets (referred to as fifth-generation chipsets) were more closely tied to the design of the processor than were the 486 chipsets. When Intel created the Pentium processor, it also developed the PCI bus and a chipset to support and integrate the capabilities of these two developments. This PCIset, as it became known, was developed as an exact match for the Pentium processor. Intel chipsets are designated in numbered series: the 420 for 486 chipsets, the 430 for Pentium chipsets, the 440 series for Pentium II and the 450 series for Pentium Pr chipsets (along with the 400FX). The newer 460 and 800 series chipsets just being announced are designed to support the IA-64 (Intel Architecture – 64 bits) processors, such as the Itanium, now emerging.

Here are some of the more common Intel Pentium and above chipsets:

430LX (Mercury): The 430LX was the first Pentium chipset developed to support the 60MHz and 66MHz 5V processors. The Mercury chipset included the PCI bus and supported up to 128MB of RAM. This chipset was made absolute by the chipsets that supported the 90MHz and 100MHz 3.3V processors.

430NX (Neptune): The 430NX was developed to support Intel's second generation Pentium chips. It supported Pentium processors running at 90MHz to 133MHz. Some of the improvements offered over he 430LX chipset are support for dual processors, 512MB of RAM and 512KB of L2 cache.

430FX (Triton I): This was first of the Triton chipsets. It featured support for EDO RAM pipelined burst and synchronous cache, Plug-and-Play and PCI level 2.0 compliance. However, it only supported 128MB of RAM (down from the 512MB supported by the Neptune chipset) and did not have dual processor capabilities.

430MX (Mobile Triton): This is a version of the 430FX designed for laptop, notebook and other portable PCs.

430HX (Triton II): This chipset supported EDO RAM and concurrent PCI buses and was designed for use in business-level servers. It was the next generation of the 430NX and included support for 512MB of RAM and L2 cache.

430VX (Triton III): This chipset was developed to support the home PC market. It featured support for USB, SDRAM and PCI interfaces.

430TX: With this chipset, Intel dropped the Triton label for its chipsets. The 430TX was adaptable for both desktop and mobile use and provided CPI, USB, DMMA and other interfaces.

440LX: Designed for the Pentium II, this AGPset chipset provides support for the LS-120 "superdisk," Ultra DMA, AGP, USB, SDRAM, ECC RAM and the PC97 power management specification. Figure 5-5 shows this chipset.

440LXR: A low-end version of the 440LX chipset.

440BX: Another Pentium II chipset that supports 100MHz bus, dual processors, FireWire and up to 1GB of RAM.

440GX: This chipset is designed for midrange workstations and supports dual CPU and up to 2GB of SDRAM along with dual AGP interfaces. This is an AGPset.

440FX (Natoma): This chipset supported both the Pentium II and the Pentium Pro processors with USB, EDO RAM, ECC memory, dual processors and PCI.

450GX (Orion server): The 450GX chipset and the 450KX share the same basic design. However, the GX version is optimized for the Pentium Pro and supports four processors and 8GB of RAM but FPM memory only.

450KX (Orion workstation): The workstation version of the Orion chipset supports dual processors and 1GB of RAM.

450NX: This is a high-powered chipset designed for Xeon workstations and servers. It supports up to four CPUs, 2MB of L2 cache, 8GB of EDO memory & two 32-bit or one 64-bit PCI interface.

460GX (Merced): This chipset supports very high-end servers and workstations with supports for four CPUs and other high-performance features. You will see this chipset linked to the new high powered Itanium processor.

810: This chipset is designed for value-priced PCs. It includes support for integrated 3-D graphics (AGP) with MPEG-2, 100MHz system bus, two USB ports and the Intel Accelerated Hub, which features a 266MB per second bus speed between memory and peripherals.

810e: This chipset is an extended version of the 810 chipset based on the 440BX chipset and intended for home market and office PCs. Its features are the same as the 9\810 chipset, with added support for 133MHz system bus and the ATA-66 interface.

815: The Intel 815 chipset is specifically designed to work with the Pentium III processor, but it also provides backward compatibility to other Intel processors.

820: Another extension of the 810 chipset designed to support high-end desktops and workstations.

850: The Intel 850 chipset was designed in tandem with the Pentium 4 processor and supports, among many high-performance innovations and features, a 400 MHz system bus that provides over 3 times the bandwidth of previous chipset and processor technologies.

Various Cards on the Motherboards

As we have seen and studied in this chapter, so far, motherboard has various cards. Let us now go through the various cards and their functioning.

1. A Display /video card, is card in computer whose function is to generate and output images to a display. The term is usually used to refer to a separate, dedicated expansion card that is plugged into a slot on the computer's motherboard. A video card consists of a printed circuit board on which the components are mounted. These include:

(*i*) **The GPU:** It is a microprocessor dedicated to manipulating and rendering graphics according to the instructions received from the computer's operating system and the software being used. At their simplest level, GPUs include functions for manipulating two-dimensional graphics, such as blitting. Modern and more advanced GPUs also include functions for generating and manipulating three-dimensional graphics elements, rendering objects with shading, lighting, texture mapping and other visual effects.

(*ii*) **Video Memory:** Unlike integrated video controllers, which usually share memory with the rest of the computer, most video cards have their own separate onboard memory, referred to as video RAM (VRAM). If the video card is integrated in the motherboard, it will use the computer RAM memory (lower throughput). If it is not integrated, the video card will have its own video memory which is called Video RAM or VRAM. The VRAM capacity of most modern video cards range from 128 to 768 MB. In 2006, the VRAM was based on DDR technology, standing out DDR2, GDDR3 and

GDDR4. The memory clock rate is between 400 MHz and 1.6 GHz. A very important element of the video memory is the Z-buffer, which manages the depth coordinates in 3D graphics.

Video Cards over the Years

	Year	Text Mode	Graphics Mode	Colors	Memory
MDA	1981	80*25	-	1	4 KB
CGA	1981	80*25	640*200	16	16 KB
HGC	1982	80*25	720*348	1	64 KB
EGA	1984	80*25	640*350	16	256 KB
IBM 8514	1987	80*25	1024*768	256	-
MCGA	1987	80*25	320*200	256	-
VGA	1987	720*400	640*480	256	256 KB
SVGA	1989	80*25	1024*768	256	2 MB
XGA	1990	80*25	1024*768	65,536	1 MB

(*iii*) **Video BIOS** chip is a chip that contains the basic program that governs the video card's operations and provides the instructions that allow the computer and software to interface with the card. The video BIOS or firmware chip is a chip that contains the basic program that governs the video card's operations and provides the instructions that allow the computer and software to interface with the card. It contains information on the memory timing, operating speeds and voltages of the processor and ram and other information. It is possible to re-flash a bios although this is typically only done by video card overclockers.

Type	**Clock rate (MHz)**	**Bandwidth (GB/s)**
DDR	166 - 950	1.2 - 30.4
DDR2	533 - 1000	8.5 - 16
GDDR3	700 - 1800	5.6 - 54.4
GDDR4	1600 - 2400	64 - 86.4

(*iv*) **PCI Express** is the newest slot that most new cards fit into. It comes in a variety of speeds which vary in size proportionate to the speed. Depending on what speed interface used, PCI Express video cards may have a higher speed interface than AGP, leading to increased performance on the high end cards. PCI Express may be up to twice the speed of the AGP interface.

Pin No.	**Function**
1	Red Video
2	Green Video
3	Blue Video
4	Monitor ID bit-2
5	Ground
6	Red Return (Ground)
7	Green Retrun (Ground)
8	Blue Return (Ground)
9	Composite Sync.
10	Sync. Return (Ground)
11	Monitor ID bit-0
12	Monitor ID bit-1
13	Horiz. Sync.
14	Vert. Sync.
15	Reserverd

2. A sound card is a computer expansion card that can input and output sound under control of computer programs. Typical uses of sound cards include providing the audio component for multimedia applications such as music

Display Card

composition, editing video or audio, presentation/education, and entertainment (games). Many computers have sound capabilities built in, while others require these expansion cards if audio capability is desired. Typical sound card includes a sound chip, usually featuring a digital-to-analog converter, that converts recorded or generated digital waveforms of sound into an analog format. This signal is led to a (typically 1/8-inch earphone-type) connector where an amplifier, headphones, or similar sound destination can be plugged in. More advanced designs usually include more than one sound chip to

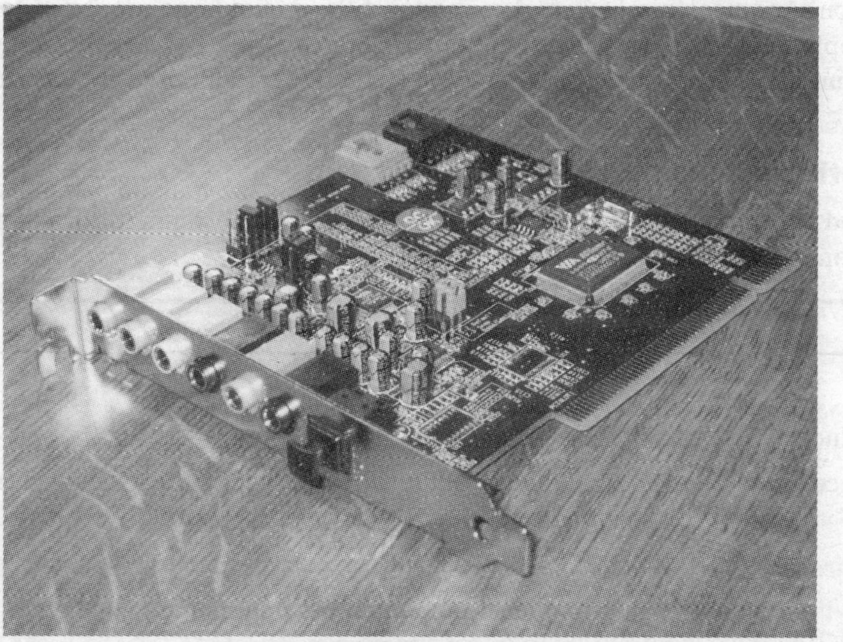

Sound Card

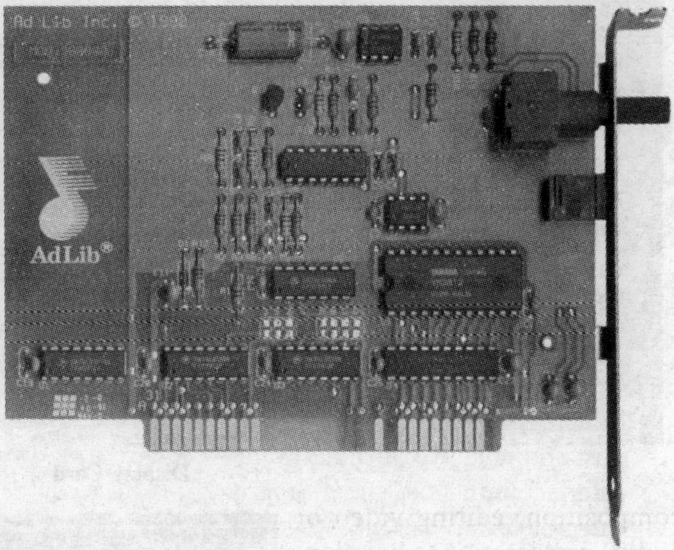

separate duties between digital sound production and synthesized sounds (usually for real-time generation of music and sound effects utilizing little data and CPU time.

Digital sound reproduction is usually achieved by multi-channel DACs, able to play multiple digital samples at different pitches and volumes, optionally applying real-time effects like filtering or distortion. Multi-channel digital sound playback can also be used for music synthesis if used with a digitized instrument bank of some sort, typically a small amount of ROM or Flash memory containing samples corresponding to the standard MIDI instruments. (A contrasting way to synthesize sound on a PC uses "audio codecs", which rely heavily on software for music synthesis, MIDI compliance and even multiple-channel emulation. This approach has become common as manufacturers seek to simplify the design and the cost of the sound card itself most sound cards have a **line in** connector where the sound signal from a cassette tape recorder or similar sound source can be input. The sound card can digitize this signal and store it (controlled by the corresponding computer software) on the computer's hard disk for editing or further reproduction. Another typical external connector is the **microphone** connector, for connecting to a microphone or other input device that generates a relatively lower voltage than the **line in** connector. Input through a microphone jack is typically used by speech recognition software or Voice over IP applications.

Connections

Most sound cards since 1999 conform to Microsoft's PC 99 standard for color coding the external connectors as follows:

Color	Function
Pink	Analog microphone input.
Light blue	Analog line level input.
Lime green	Analog line level output for the main stereo signal (front speakers or headphones).
Black	Analog line level output for rear speakers.
Silver	Analog line level output for side speakers.
Orange	S/PDIF digital output (sometimes used as an analog line output for a center speaker and subwoofer instead)

3. A network card, **network adapter** or **NIC** (network interface controller) is a piece of computer hardware designed to allow computers to communicate over a computer network. It is both an OSI layer 1 (physical layer) and layer 2 (data link layer) device, as it provides physical access to a networking medium and provides a low-level addressing system through the use of MAC addresses. It allows users to connect to each other either by using cables or wirelessly. Every network card has a unique 48-bit serial number called a MAC address, which is stored in ROM carried on the card. Every computer on a network must have a card with a unique MAC address. No two cards ever manufactured share the same address. This is accomplished by the Institute of Electrical and Electronics Engineers (IEEE), which is responsible for assigning unique MAC addresses to the vendors of network interface controllers.

Whereas network cards used to be expansion cards that plug into a computer bus, the low cost and ubiquity of the Ethernet standard means that most newer computers have a network interface built into the motherboard. These motherboards either have Ethernet capabilities integrated into the motherboard chipset, or implemented via a low cost dedicated Ethernet chip, connected through the PCI (or the newer PCI express bus).

A separate network card is not required unless multiple interfaces are needed or some other type of network is used. Newer motherboards may even have dual network (Ethernet) interfaces built-in.

The card implements the electronic circuitry required to communicate using a specific physical layer and data link layer standard such as Ethernet or token ring. This provides a network card typically has a twisted pair, BNC, or AUI socket where the network cable is connected, and a few LEDs to inform the user of whether the network is active, and whether or not there is data being transmitted on it. The Network Cards are typically available in 10/100/1000 Mbits/s(Mbps).

4. A modem (from **mod**ulate and **dem**odulate) is a device that modulates an analogue carrier signal to encode digital information, and also demodulates such a carrier signal to decode the transmitted information. The goal is to produce a signal that can be transmitted easily and decoded to reproduce the original digital data. Modems can be used over any means

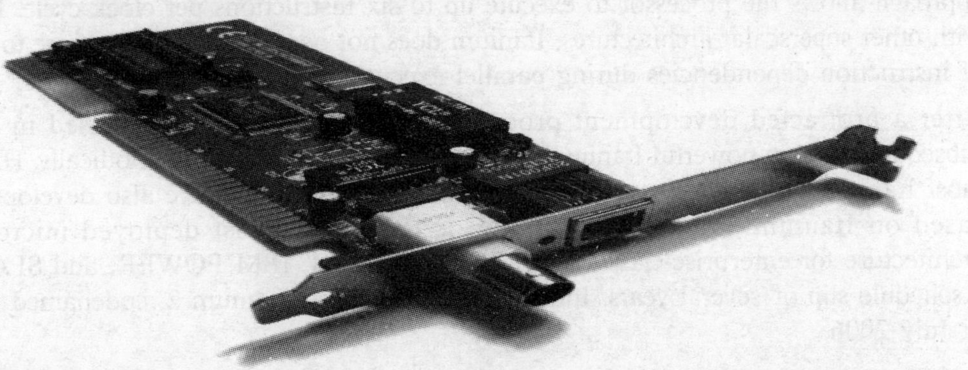

Network Card

of transmitting analog signals, from driven diodes to radio. Experiments have even been performed in the use of modems over the medium of two cans connected by a string. The most familiar example is a voiceband modem that turns the digital '1s and 0s' of a personal computer into sounds that can be transmitted over the telephone lines of Plain Old Telephone Systems (POTS), and once received on the other side, converts those sounds back into 1s and 0s. Modems are generally classified by the amount of data they can send in a given time, normally measured in bits per second, or "bps".Faster modems are used by Internet users every day, notably cable modems and ADSL modems. In telecommunications, "radio modems" transmit repeating frames of data at very high data rates over microwave radio links. Some microwave modems transmit more than a hundred million bits per second. Optical modems transmit data over optic fibers. Most intercontinental data links now use optic modems transmitting over undersea optical fibers. Optical modems routinely have data rates in excess of a billion ($1x10^9$) bits per second.

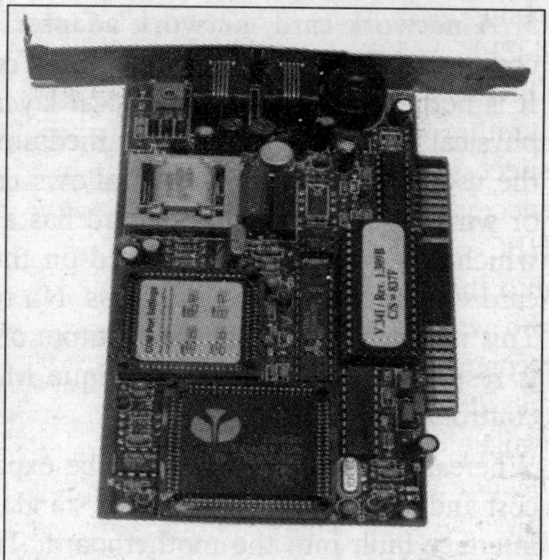

Modem

Itanium Processor

Itanium is the brand name for 64-bit Intel Microprocessors that implement the Intel Itanium architecture (formerly called IA-64). Intel has released two processor families using the brand: Itanium and Itanium 2. The processors are marketed for use in enterprise servers and high-performance computing systems. The architecture originated at Hewlett-Packard (HP) which was then later developed by HP and Intel together.

Itanium's architecture differs dramatically from the x86 and x86-64 architectures used in other Intel processors. The architecture is based on explicit instruction-level parallelism, with the compiler making the decisions about which instructions to execute in parallel. This approach allows the processor to execute up to six instructions per clock cycle. By contrast with other superscalar architectures, Itanium does not need elaborate hardware to keep track of instruction dependencies during parallel execution.

After a protracted development process, the first Itanium was released in 2001, and subsequently more powerful Itanium processors have been released periodically. HP produces most Itanium-based systems, but several other manufacturers have also developed systems based on Itanium. As of 2007 Itanium is the fourth-most deployed microprocessor architecture for enterprise-class systems, behind x86-64, IBM POWER, and SPARC. After a schedule slip of several years, Intel released its newest Itanium 2, codenamed Montecito, in July 2006.

Itanium processor: 2001–2002

By the time Itanium was released in June, 2001, it was no longer superior to contemporaneous RISC and CISC processors. Itanium competed at the low-end (primarily 4-CPU and smaller systems) with servers based on x86 processors, and at the high end with IBM's POWER architecture and Sun Microsystems' SPARC architecture. Intel repositioned Itanium to focus on high-end business and HPC computing, attempting to duplicate x86's successful "horizontal" (i.e., single architecture, multiple systems vendors) market. Its success was limited to replacing PA-RISC and Alpha in HP systems and MIPS in SGI's HPC systems. POWER and SPARC remained strong, while the 32-bit x86 architecture grew into the enterprise space. With economies of scale fueled by its enormous installed base, x86 was the preeminent "horizontal" architecture in enterprise computing. HP and Intel recognized that Itanium was not competitive and replaced it with Itanium 2 a year later, as they had planned. Only a few thousand of the original Itaniums were sold, due to limited availability caused by poor yields, relatively poor performance, and high cost. However, these machines were useful for software development for the Itanium 2 processors that followed. IBM delivered a supercomputer based on this processor.

Itanium 2 processors: 2002–present

The Itanium 2 was released in 2002, and was marketed for enterprise servers rather than for the whole gamut of high-end computing. The initial Itanium 2 was codenamed McKinley. McKinley used a 180 nm process, but it relieved many of the performance problems of the original Itanium. In 2003, AMD released the Opteron, which implemented its x86-64 64-bit architecture. Opteron gained rapid acceptance in the enterprise server space because it provided an easy upgrade from x86. Intel responded by implementing x86-64 in its Xeon microprocessors in 2004. Intel released a new Itanium 2 family member, codenamed Madison, in 2003. Madison used a 130 nm process and was the basis of all new Itaniums until Montecito was released in June 2006.

Intel Itanium processor

Central processing unit

Itanium processor

Produced:	From June 2001 to June 2002
Manufacturer:	Intel
CPU Speeds:	733 MHz to 800 MHz
FSB Speeds:	266 MT/s to 266 MT/s
Instruction Set:	**Itanium**
Socket:	PAC418
Core Name:	Merced

In March, 2005, Intel announced that it was working on a new Itanium device, codenamed Tukwila, to be released in 2007. Tukwila would have four processors and would replace the Itanium bus with a new Common System Interface, which would also be used by a new Xeon. Intel later said that Tukwila would be delivered in late 2008.

In November 2005, the major Itanium server manufacturers joined with Intel and a number of software vendors to form the Itanium Solutions Alliance to promote the architecture and accelerate software porting. The Alliance announced that its members would invest $10 Billion in Itanium solutions by the end of the decade. As of June 2007, Intel has released seven additional versions of the Itanium 2, and another is expected in late 2007.

Xeon Processors Family

The Xeon brand refers to Intel's x86 multiprocessing CPUs targeted at server and workstation computers. The brand has been maintained over several generations of x86 and x86-64 processors. Older models added the Xeon moniker to the end of the name of their corresponding desktop processor, but more recent models used the name Xeon on its own. The Xeon CPUs generally have more cache than their desktop counterparts in addition to multiprocessing capabilities. Intel's non-x86 IA-64 processors are called Itanium, not Xeon.

Pentium II Xeon

The first Xeon processor was released in 1998 as the Pentium II Xeon (codenamed "Drake") as the replacement of the Pentium Pro. It was based on the 0.25 μm, P6 microarchitecture "Deschutes" Pentium II (sharing its 80523 product code) and used either a 440GX (a dual-processor workstation chipset) or 450NX (quad-processor, or oct with additional logic) chipset, and differed from the desktop Pentium II in that its off-die L2 cache ran at full speed. It also used a larger slot known as slot 2. Cache sizes were 512 KiB, 1 MiB and 2 MiB, and it used a 100 MT/s bus.

Pentium III Xeon

In 1999, the Pentium II Xeon was replaced by the Pentium III Xeon. The initial version, "Tanner", was just like its predecessor except for the addition of Streaming SIMD Extensions (SSE) and a few cache controller enhancements found in the "Katmai" Pentium III. The second version, "Cascades", was based on the "Coppermine" Pentium III core. It was more controversial in that while it had a 133 MT/s bus it only had a 256 KiB on-die L2 cache — in other words, it was the same as the desktop Pentium III whose Slot 1 versions were also capable of dual-processor operation but not quad-processor operation. To improve this situation, Intel released another version, officially also named "Cascades", but often referred to as "Cascades 2 MB". That came in two variants: with 1 MiB or 2 MiB of L2 cache. Its bus speed was fixed at 100 MT/s, though in practice the cache was able to offset this. Product codes for Tanner and Cascades mirrored that of Katmai and Coppermine; 80525 and 80526 respectively.

Xeon & Xeon MP (32-bit)

In mid-2001, the Xeon was introduced ("Pentium" was dropped from the name). The initial variant that used the new NetBurst architecture, "Foster", was slightly different from the desktop Pentium 4 ("Willamette"). It was a decent chip for workstations, but for server applications it was almost always outperformed by the older Cascade 2 MiB core and AMD's Athlon MP. Combined with the need to use expensive Rambus Dynamic RAM, the Foster's sales were somewhat unimpressive.

At most two Foster processors could be accommodated in an SMP system built with a mainstream chipset, so a second version (Foster MP) was introduced with a 1 MiB L3 cache and Jackson Hyper-Threading. This improved performance slightly, but not enough to lift it out of third place. It was also priced much higher than the dual-processor (DP) versions.

In 2002 Intel released a 130 nm version of the Xeon, codenamed "Prestonia". It supported Intel's new Hyper-Threading technology and had a 512 KiB L2 cache. This was based on the "Northwood" Pentium 4 core. A new server chipset, E7500 (which allowed the use of dual-channel DDR SDRAM) was released to support this processor in servers, and soon the bus speed was boosted to 533 MT/s (accompanied by new chipsets: the E7501 for servers and the E7505 for workstations). The new Xeon performed much better than its predecessor and noticeably better than Athlon MP. The support of new features in the E75xx series also gave it a key advantage over the Pentium III Xeon and Athlon MP (both stuck with rather old chipsets), and it quickly became the top-selling server/workstation processor.

The Xeon MP version of the Prestonia was the "Gallatin", which had an L3 cache of 1 MiB or 2 MiB. It also performed much better than Foster MP, and was popular in servers. Later, Intel's experience with the 130 nm process allowed it to port Xeon to the Gallatin core and also create a Xeon MP with 4 MiB cache.

Foster shared the 80528 product code with Willamette; Prestonia and Gallatin Xeons were designated 80532, like Northwood.

Xeon & Xeon MP (64-bit)

Due to a lack of success with Intel's Itanium and Itanium 2 processors, the 90 nm version of the Pentium 4 ("Prescott") was built with support for 64-bit instructions (called Intel 64, Intel's implementation of x86-64), and a Xeon version codenamed "Nocona" was released in 2004. Released with it were the E7525 (workstation), E7520 and E7320 (both server) chipsets, which added support for PCI Express, DDR-II and Serial ATA. The Xeon was noticeably slower than AMD's Opteron, although it could be faster in situations where Hyper-Threading came into play.

A slightly updated core called "Irwindale" was released in early 2005, with twice the L2 cache of Nocona and able to reduce its clockspeeds during low processor demand. However, independent tests showed that AMD's Opteron still outperformed Irwindale.

64-bit Xeon MPs were introduced in April 2005. The cheaper "Cranford" was an MP version of Nocona, while the more expensive "Potomac" was a Cranford with 8 MiB of L3 cache. All these Prescott-derived Xeons have the product code 80546.

Cache Memory

In computer science, a cache (pronounced "cash" /kæʃ]) is a collection of data duplicating original values stored elsewhere or computed earlier, where the original data is expensive to fetch (due to slow access time) or to compute, relative to the cost of reading the cache. In other words, a cache is a temporary storage area where frequently accessed data can be stored for rapid access. Once the data is stored in the cache, future use can be made by accessing the cached copy rather than re-fetching or recomputing the original data, so that the average access time is lower.

Caches have proven to be extremely effective in many areas of computing because access patterns in typical computer applications have locality of reference. There are several kinds of locality, but this article primarily deals with data that are accessed close together in time (temporal locality). The data might or might not be located physically close to each other (spatial locality).

Xeon model	Core 2 Duo model	Speed (GHz)	L2 Cache (MB)	FSB (MHz)
3040	E6300	1.86	2	1066
N/A	E6320	1.86	4	1066
3050	E6400	2.13	2	1066
N/A	E6420	2.13	4	1066
3060	E6600	2.4	4	1066
3070	E6700	2.66	4	1066
3080	X6800	2.93	4	1066
3065	E6550	2.33	4	1333
3075	E6750	2.66	4	1333
3085	E6850	3.00	4	1333

How cache works?

A cache is a block of memory for temporary storage of data likely to be used again. The CPU and hard drive frequently use a cache, as do web browsers and web servers.

A cache is made up of a pool of entries. Each entry has a datum (a nugget of data) which is a copy of the datum in some backing store. Each entry also has a tag, which specifies the identity of the datum in the backing store of which the entry is a copy.

When the cache client (a CPU, web browser, operating system) wishes to access a datum presumably in the backing store, it first checks the cache.

Double Core Processor

The Athlon 64 X2 is the first dual-core desktop CPU manufactured by AMD. It is essentially a processor consisting of two Athlon 64 cores joined together on one die with additional control logic. The cores share one dual-channel memory controller, are based on the E-stepping model of Athlon 64 and, depending on the model, have either 512 or 1024 KiB of L2 Cache per core. The Athlon 64 X2 is capable of decoding SSE3 instructions (except those few specific to Intel's architecture), so it can run and benefit from software optimizations that were previously only supported by Intel chips. This enhancement is not unique to the X2, and is also available in the Venice and San Diego single core Athlon 64s.

In June 2007, AMD released low-voltage variants of their low-end 65 nm Athlon 64 X2, named "Athlon X2". The Athlon X2 processors feature reduced TDP of 45 W

PC—Processor Specifications at a Glance

Processor	Register Size-bit	Data Bus-bit	Address Bus-bit	Int. Cache	Int. FPU	Max. Memory	Trans. Used
8088	16	8	20	No	No	1MB	29,000
8086	16	16	20	No	No	1MB	29,000
286	16	16	24	No	No	16MB	130,000
386SX	32	16	24	No	No	16MB	275,000
386SL	32	16	24	*	No	16MB	855,000
386DX	32	32	32	No	No	4GB	275,000
486SX	32	32	32	8k	No	4GB	1,185,000
486DX	32	32	32	8k	Yes	4GB	1,200,000
486DX2	32	32	32	8k	Yes	4GB	1,100,000
586	32	64	32	8k Data 8k Instr	Yes	4GB	3,100,000
P6	32	64	36	8k Data 8k Instr	Yes	64GB	5,500,000

Multithreading

The main benefit of dual-core processors like the X2 is their ability to process more software threads at the same time. The ability of processors to execute multiple threads simultaneously is called thread-level parallelism (TLP). By placing two cores on the same die, the X2 effectively doubles the TLP over a single-core Athlon 64 of the same speed. The need for TLP processing capability is dependent on situation to a great degree, and certain situations benefit from it far more than others. Certain programs are currently only written with one thread, and are therefore unable to utilize the processing power of the second core.

Programs often written with multiple threads and capable of utilizing dual-cores include many music and video encoding applications, and especially professional rendering programs. High TLP applications currently correspond to server/workstation situations more than the typical desktop. These applications can realize almost twice the performance of a single-core Athlon 64 of the same specifications.

Multi-tasking also runs a sizable number of threads;

intense multi-tasking scenarios have actually shown improvements of considerably more than two times. This is primarily due to the excessive overhead caused by constantly switching threads, and could potentially be improved by adjustments to operating system scheduling code.

In the consumer segment of the market as well, the X2 improves upon the performance of the original Athlon 64, especially for multi-threaded software applications. The overall increase in performance of the entry level Athlon 64 X2 chip (the Athlon 64 X2 3800+) over the single-core Athlon 64 3800+ chip is almost 10%. The spread between the latter and the Athlon 64 X2 5000+ is almost 40%.

One can interpret from these numbers that the majority of applications (at least in the benchmark test) are still largely single thread-dominated, hence the absence of a larger gap between the two 3800+ processors. As software programmers begin to take advantage of multi-core processing, the spread between single- and multi-core processors will increase.

Revision

1. Motherboard is the main component inside the main system unit.
2. It is used for the following: Processor Support, Peripheral Support, Performace, Upgradability, Organization, Contol and Communication.
3. The original PC/XT used an Intel 8088 processor running at a speed of 4.77 MHz.
4. PC/AT, known as Advanced Technology of Personal Computer, used Intel 80286 microprocessor.
5. Among the features of AT were: 16-bit ISA bus, 15 IRQs and 7 DMA channels.
6. It supported 16 MB of memory at the most.
7. ATX motherboard had better cooling capacity.
8. LPX, known as Low Profile Extended, motherboard, has video and sound components built-in.
9. NLX. known as New Low Profile Extended, motherboard has been a form factor in use with desktops for quite some time.
10. Display card generates and sends output images to a display.
11. A Sound card can input and output sound under control of computer programs.
12. A Network card allows computers to communicate over a computer network.
13. Itanium is the brand name for 64-bit Intel Microprocessors that implement the Intel Itanium architecture (formerly called IA-64).
14. The Itanium 2 was released in 2002, and was marketed for enterprise servers rather than for the whole gamut of high-end computing.
15. The first Xeon processor was released in 1998 as the Pentium II Xeon (codenamed "Drake") as the replacement of the Pentium Pro.
16. In computer science, a cache is a collection of data duplicating original values stored elsewhere or computed earlier, where the original data is expensive to fetch (due to slow access time) or to compute, relative to the cost of reading the cache.
17. The Athlon 64 X2 is the first dual-core desktop CPU manufactured by AMD.

Multiple Choice Questions

1. LPX stands for:
   (a) Low Profile Extended (b) Low Period Extended
   (c) Low Profile Extra
2. PC-ATs full form of:
   (a) Personal Computer Area Technology
   (b) Personal Computer Advanced Technology
   (c) Personal Computer Advanced Techniques
3. PC XT ran on Intel ____ processor.
   (a) 8086 (b) 80286
   (c) 8088
4. Maximum memory in PC AT could be ___ MB:
   (a) 8 (b) 16
   (c) 32
5. Display card generates:
   (a) Text (b) Sound
   (c) Graphics
6. What is the new name of IA-64?
   (a) Itanium (b) Pentium
   (c) Athlon

True/False Questions

1. The original PC/XT used an Intel 8088 processor running at a speed of 4.77 MHz.
2. PC/AT, known as Advanced Technology of Personal Computer, used Intel 8088 microprocessor.
3. It supported 16 MB of memory at the most.
4. ATX motherboard had better cooling capacity.
5. NLX. known as New Low Profile Extended, motherboard has been a form factor in use with desktops for quite some time.
6. Display card generates and sends sound to a output.
7. A Sound card can input and output sound under control of computer programs.
8. Itanium is the brand name for 64-bit Intel Microprocessors that implement the Intel Itanium architecture (formerly called IA-64).
9. The first Xeon processor was released in 1998 as the Pentium II Xeon (codenamed "Drake") as the replacement of the Pentium Pro.
10. The Athlon 64 X2 is the first dual-core desktop CPU manufactured by AMD.

Descriptive Questions

1. Describe the various components inside the main computer system.
2. Describe the various uses of the motherboard.
3. How did PC XT worked?
4. Describe the working of PC AT.

5. What all was there on PC AT motherboard?
6. Describe the following: ATX, LPX and NLX motherboards.
7. What do the following cards do: Display card, Sound card, Network card, TV Tuner card, and IDE card?
8. What types of jumper setting are there of Motherboard?
9. What is Itanium Processor?
10. Describe the various processors in the Itanium family.
11. Describe the various processors in the Xeon family.
12. What do you understand by Cache Memory?
13. Describe Double Core processor.

Answers to Objective Type Questions

Multiple Choice Questions

1. a	2. b	3. c	4. b
5. c	6. a		

True False Questions

1. T	2. T	3. T	4. T
5. T	6. F	7. T	8. T
9. T	10. T		

3 Motherboards

Motherboards

After microprocessor the next item considered to be most important for the computer is the motherboard. It's the motherboard that ties all parts of the computer together and turns them into a personal computer.

The motherboard or main board, of a PC is a large printed circuit board that is home to many of the most essential parts of the computer, including the microprocessor, chipset, cache, memory sockets, expansion bus, parallel and serial ports, mouse and keyboard connectors and IDE, EIDE or SCSI controllers, among other components of the PC. The motherboard binds the PC's operational components together. Even devices like printers, hard disks, CD-ROMs and the like, either connect to or are controlled by the devices or controllers on the motherboard.

Motherboard Designs

Not all motherboards are created equal. To begin with, two different design approaches are used for PC mainboards: the motherboard style and the backplane style.

Motherboards: A motherboard aggregates all of the PC's primary system components of a single printed circuit board (PCB). In the motherboard's single board design, all of the PC's electronic circuitry that provides the conduit through which all operations flow is located on the motherboard.

Backplanes: Backplane-style mainboards are less popular today than they were in the mid – to late 1980s, but they are still around. Backplane mainboards are common in large PC network servers and on other computers on which the processor is upgraded frequently.

The following table shows the length and width of the various motherboards over the years.

Form	*Width*	*Length*	*Design Type*	*Case Type*
IBM PC	8.5	13	Motherboard	IBM PC
IBM PC XT	8.5	13	Motherboard	IBM PC XT
AT	12	11-13	Motherboard	AT Desktop or Tower
Baby AT	8.5	10-13	Motherboard	Baby AT Desktop or Tower
LPX	9	11-13	Backplane	Low profile
Micro-AT	8.5	8.5	Motherboard	Baby AT Desktop or Tower
ATX	12	9.6	Motherboard	ATX Desktop or Tower

Mini-ATX	11.2	8.2	Motherboard	Smaller ATX Desktop
Mini-LPX	8-9	10-11	Backplane	Low profile
Micro-ATX	9.6	9.6	Motherboard	Low profile
NLX	8-9	10-13.6	Backplane	Low profile
Flex-ATX	9	7.5	Motherboard	Flexible design

Components of the Motherboard

The following figure shows where the major components are found on a typical motherboard. They are:

CPU slot and socket

The CPU mounts to the motherboard through either a slot or socket mounting.

Chipset

Many of the circuit and CPU level functions are contained in the chipset.

Memory Sockets

Depending upon the age of the PC, its memory is mounted on the motherboard as individual memory chips that fit into separate DIP (Dual Inline Packaging) sockets or memory modules, such as SIMM (Single Inline Memory Module) or a DIMM (Dual Inline Memory Module) that snap into edge connector mountings.

BIOS ROM

The BIOS, Basic Input/Output System, is stored as firmware on a read-only memory (ROM) chip. The BIOS is used to start the PC up when the power is turned on and provides a link for the CPU to the PC's peripheral devices.

CMOS Battery

The configuration of PC at the systems level is stored in a type of memory. CMOS, Complementary Metal Oxide Semiconductor, that requires very little power to hold its contents. The CMOS battery supplies a steady power steady power source to store the system configuration for use during the PC's boot sequence.

Power connector

A connection must be made to the power supply so that power is available to the circuitry on the motherboard. Motherboards use different voltages of power for different components on the board.

I/O connectors

The motherboard includes a variety of external I/O connections that allow external devices to communicate with the CPU.

Expansion slots

External peripherals and internal devices are interconnected into the motherboard and CPU through the expansion bus. The motherboard features a variety of expansion slots that usually include three or more of the different expansion buses available.

Chipsets of PC

Among the components on the motherboard contributing to its importance are the chipset and its associated controllers. This group of devices provides much of a PC's functionality and its ability to accept, display and move data. The logic circuits of the chipset and controllers give the motherboard its intelligence and its ability to function. The chipset and controllers also control the movement of data on the system buses so that data and instructions can move about the PC, between the CPU, cache memory and peripherals. The system chipset plays a major role in a PC's function, feature set and speed. Unless data and instructions are able to flow between one component of the PC and another, there isn't much point to even powering up the PC.

The chipset controls the bits (data, instructions and control signals) that flow between the CPU, system memory and over the motherboard's bus. The chipset also manages data transfers between the CPU, memory and peripheral devices and provides support for the expansion bus and any power management features of the system.

Controller Chips

Generally, a chipset does not incorporate all of the controllers used to direct the actions of every peripheral device on the PC. In addition to the chipset, there are at least two and possibly more, controllers mounted directly on the motherboard. In most cases, the motherboard will have at minimum a keyboard controller and an I/O controller (a.k.a. the Super I/O controller). Some expansion cards, such as video adapters, sound cards, network interface cards (NICs) and SCSI (Small Computer System Interface) adapters, have built-in controller chips.

A controller chip controls the transfer of data to and from a peripheral device, such as a disk drive, the monitor, the keyboard or a printer. All of these devices depend on a device controller to interact with the CPU and the rest of the PC. For the most part, PC users don't ever think about controller chips on their systems. In fact, most users probably don't even know they exist. How data gets to and from the keyboard is not of concern, only that it does.

On a PC, a controller is typically is single chip that either mounts directly on the motherboard or on a card that is inserted in an expansion slot on the motherboard. Because they control the flow of data to and from peripheral devices, controllers must be matched to the bus architecture of the PC.

Sockets and Slots

Microprocessors are attached to the motherboard of the computer. There are two general types of mountings used to connect the processor onto the motherboard: sockets and slots.

Some processors are available in only one mounting type; others, such as the Intel Celerons are available with both types of mountings. Which type is used is largely a matter of preference on the part of the processor manufacturer. The two types look very different, but functionally their differences are small.

Socket Types

Here are ten of the most commonly used socket types:

Socket 0: A 168-pin inline-layout processor connector for 5V 486DX processors.

Socket 1: A 169-pin inline-layout processor connector for 5V 486DX and 486SX processors.

Socket 2: A 238-pin inline-layout processor connector for 5V 486DX, 486SX and 486DX2 processors.

Socket 3: A 237-pin inline-layout processor connector supporting 3 and 5V 486DX, 486SX, 486DX2 and 486DX4 processors.

Socket 4: A 273-pin inline-layout processor connector supporting 5V Pentium 60 and Pentium 66 processors.

Socket 5: A 320-pin staggered-layout connector supporting early 3V

Socket 6: A 235-pin inline-layout processor connector for 3V 486DX4 processors.

Socket 7: A 321-pin staggered-format socket created to support later Pentium processors. It used a common interface between the L2 cache bus and the main system bus. This common interface typically limited the bus's clock speed. AMD K6, Cyrix 6x86 and IDT processors also use this socket format. This design also provided for a Voltage Regulator Module to allow different voltage levels to be implemented by the socket.

Super 7 Socket: An extension of the Socket 7 design to support 100MHz bus speeds on AMD K6-2 and K6-3 processors allowing them to see an almost 50 percent increase in bandwidth and get around the limitations of the Socket 7.

Socket 8: A 386 pin staggered ZIF-socket format for the Pentium Pro processor.

Socket 370: The original Celeron main board connection. This supported the early Celerons in the Plastic Pin Grid Assembly (PPGA) format.

Slot Types

There are four types of slot mountings used to attach microprocessors to motherboards:

Slot 1 (SC-242 connector): A proprietary Intel connector supporting Celeron SEPP, Pentium II SECC (single-edge contact cartridge), Pentium II SECC2 and Pentium III processors. It has a 242 – pin edge interface and allows higher bandwidth than the original socket designs.

Slot 2 (SC-330 connector): Another Intel processor bus connector styles for the high performance Pentium II Xeon and Pentium III Xeon chips. These processors are designed for Symmetric Multiprocessing (multiple processors working together) and this slot style enhances this interaction.

Slot A: Used by the AMD Athlon processors. It is physically the same as a Slot 1 connector but has incompatible pin-outs.

Slot M: Connectors are planned for the upcoming 64-bit Intel Itanium processor.

Chipsets

One of the fundamental design facts of a PC is that its microprocessor is always faster than the peripheral devices to which it must communicate. This fact has forced designed to develop interfaces that serve as buffers between the slower devices and the faster CPU to match up their speeds and help with the timing of the operations. The very first PCs had an individual chip to control each of the various operations.

It was common for an early PC to have the following separate chips:

Math coprocessor interface: This chip the flow of data between the processor and math coprocessor.

Clock generator: This chip controls the timing of the PC's operations.

Bus controller chip: This chip controls the flow of data on the motherboard's buses.

DMA controller: This chip controls the processes that allowed peripheral devices to interact with memory without involving the processor.

Programmable peripheral interface (PPI): This chip supervises some of the simpler peripheral devices.

Floppy disk controller (FDC): This chip controls the PC's diskette and tape drives.

CRT controller: This chip facilities the PC's display.

UART (universal asynchronous receiver transmitter): This chip is used to send and receive synchronous serial data.

The Windows Device Manger's listing for system devices should list the processor to PCI to ISA bridge controllers and the manufacturers. If these are Intel chips, then you can sure you have an Intel chipset. Another way to check out the chipset on your PC is to open the system unit and find the large square chips, which are usually bigger than most everything else on the motherboard except the microprocessor. A chipset can have only one chip or as many as four separate chips.

Chipset Characteristics

The characteristics of a chipset can be broken down into six categories: host, memory, interfaces, arbitration, south bridge support and power management. Each of these categories defines and differentiates one chipset from another. The characteristics defined in each of these categories are as follows:

Host: This category defines the host processor to which the chipset is matched along with its bus voltage, usually GTL + (Gunning Transceiver Logic Plus) or AGTL + (Advanced Gunning Transceiver Logic Plus) and the number of processors the chipset will support.

Memory: This category defines the characteristics of the DRAM support included in the chipset, including the DRAM refresh technique supported, the amount of memory support (in megabits usually) the type of memory supported and whether memory interleave, ECC (error-correcting code) or parity is supported.

Interfaces: This category defines the type of PCI interface implemented and whether the chipset is AGP-compliant, support integrated graphics, PIPE (pipelining) or SBA (side band addressing).

Arbitration: This category defines the method used by the chipset to arbitrate between different bus speeds and interfaces. The two most common arbitration methods are MTT (Multi-Transition timer) and DIA (Dynamic Intelligent Arbiter).

South bridge support: All Intel chipsets and most of the chipsets for all other manufacturers are two processor sets. In these sets, the north bridge is the main chip and handles CPU and memory interfaces among other tasks, while the sough bridge (or the second chip) handles such things as the USB and IDE interfaces, the RTC (real-time clock) and support for serial and parallel ports.

Power management: All Intel chipsets support both the SMM (System Management Mode) and ACPI (Advanced Configuration and Power Interface) power management standards.

Chipset Built-in Controllers

The controllers and devices included in a chipset are typically those that are common to virtually every PC of the type the chipset is designed to support. The controllers and devices usually included in a chipset are as follows:

Memory controller: This is the logic circuit that controls the reading and writing of data to and from system memory (RAM). Other devices on the PC wishing to access memory must interface with the memory controller. This feature also usually includes error handling to provide for parity checking and ECC (error-correcting code) for every memory word.

EIDE controller: Nearly all mid-to upper-range motherboards now include at least one EIDE connector for hard disks, floppy disks, CD-ROMs, DVDs or other types of internal storage drives. The EIDE controller typically supports devices with ISA, ATA and perhaps an ATA-33 or Ultra – DMA (UDMA) interface.

PCI bridge: Like a network bridge that connects two dissimilar networks, this device logically connects the PCI expansion bus on the motherboard to the processor and other non-PCI devices.

Real-time clock (RTC): This clock holds the date and time on your PC; this is the date and time that is displayed to you on the monitor and is used to date-stamp file activities. This should not be confused with the system clock that provides the timing signal for the processor and other devices.

DMA (Direct Memory Access) controllers: The DMA controller manages the seven DMA channels available for use by ISA/ATA devices on most PCs. DMA channels are used by certain devices, such as floppy disk drives, sound cards, SCSI adapters and some network adapters, to move data into memory without the assistance of the CPU.

IrDA controller: IrDa (Infrared Data Association) is the international organization that has created the standards for short-range, line-of-sight, point-to-point infrared devices, such as a keyboard, mouse and network adapters.

Keyboard controller: A chipset may include the keyboard controller and many of the newer ones do. The keyboard controller is the interface between the keyboard and the processor.

PS/2 mouse controller: When IBM introduced the PS/2 system, the controller for the mouse was included in the keyboard controller. This design has persisted and usually wherever the keyboard controller is, so is the PS/2 mouse controller. This device provides the interface between the Ps/2 mouse and the processor.

Secondary (Level 2 or L2) cache controller: Secondary (L2) cache is located on the motherboard, a daughterboard or as on the Pentium Pro, in the processor package and caches the primary memory (RAM) the hard disk and the CD-ROM drives. The secondary cache controller controls the movement of data to and from the L2 cache and the processor.

CMOS SRAM: The PC's configuration settings are stored in what is called the CMOS memory. The chipset contains the controller used to access and modify this special SRAM area.

BIOS

BIOS, in computing, stands for Basic Input/Output System also incorrectly known as Basic Integrated Operating System and occasionally Built In Operating System. BIOS refers to the firmware code run by an IBM compatible PC when first powered on. The primary function of the BIOS is to prepare the machine so other software programs stored on various media (such as hard drives, floppies, and CDs) can load, execute, and assume control of the PC. This process is known as booting up.

BIOS can also be said to be a coded program embedded on a chip that recognizes and controls various devices that make up the PC. The term BIOS is specific to personal computer vendors. Among other classes of computers, the generic terms boot monitor, boot loader or boot ROM are commonly used. Boot is short for bootstrapping.

The term first appeared in the CP/M operating system, describing the part of CP/M loaded during boot time that interfaced directly with the hardware (CP/M machines usually had a simple boot loader in ROM, and nothing else). Most versions of DOS have a file called "IBMBIO.COM" or "IO.SYS" that is analogous to the CP/M disk BIOS.

How the BIOS boots?

#	Layer
0	Hardware
1	System BIOS
2	Operating system
3	Application

The BIOS runs off the PROM, EPROM or, most commonly, flash memory when the computer is powered on. It initializes several motherboard components and peripherals, including:

- the clock generator,
- the processors and caches,
- the chipset (memory controller and I/O controller),

- the system memory,
- all PCI devices (by assigning bus numbers and resources),
- the primary graphics controller,
- mass storage controllers (such as SATA and IDE controllers),
- various I/O controllers (such keyboard/mouse and USB).

Finally, it loads the boot loader for the operating system, and transfers control to it. The entire process is known as Power-on self-test (POST). On the original IBM PC, the hardware only needed minimal configuration and POST was indeed used for testing; on modern systems, most of POST actually consists of hardware configuration.

Once system memory is initialized, the BIOS typically copies/decompresses itself into that memory and keeps executing from it.

Nearly all BIOS implementations can optionally execute a setup program interfacing the nonvolatile BIOS memory (CMOS). This memory holds user-customizable configuration data (time, date, hard drive details, etc.) accessed by BIOS code. The 80x86 source code for early PC and AT BIOS was included with the IBM Technical Reference Manual.

In most modern BIOS implementations, users select which device boots first: CD, hard disk, floppy disk, flash keydrive and the like. This is particularly useful for installing operating systems or booting to Live CDs, and for selecting the order of testing for the presence of bootable media.

Some BIOS's allow the user to select the operating system to load (e.g. load another OS from the second hard disk), though this is more often handled by a second-stage boot loader.

CMOS

Complementary metal–oxide–semiconductor (CMOS) ("see-moss", is a major class of integrated circuits. CMOS technology is used in chips such as microprocessors, microcontrollers, static RAM, and other digital logic circuits. CMOS technology is also used for a wide variety of analog circuits such as image sensors, data converters, and highly integrated transceivers for many types of communication.

CMOS is also sometimes explained as complementary-symmetry metal–oxide–semiconductor. The words "complementary-symmetry" refer to the fact that the typical digital design style with CMOS uses complementary and symmetrical pairs of p-type and n-type MOSFETs for logic functions.

Two important characteristics of CMOS devices are high noise immunity and low static power supply drain. Significant power is only drawn when its transistors are switching between on and off states; consequently, CMOS devices do not produce as much heat as other forms of logic such as TTL (transistor-transistor logic). CMOS also allows a high density of logic functions on a chip.

The triple compound "metal–oxide–semiconductor" is a reference to the nature of the physical structure of early (and interestingly now, the very latest) field-effect transistors, having a metal gate electrode placed on top of an oxide insulator, which in turn is on top of a semiconductor material. Instead of metal, current gate electrodes (including those up to the 65 nanometer technology node) are almost always made from a different material, polysilicon, but the terms MOS and CMOS nevertheless continue to be used for the modern descendants of the original process. (See also MOSFET.) Metal gates have made a comeback with the advent of high-k dielectric materials in the CMOS transistor as announced by IBM and Intel for the 45 nanometer node and beyond [1].

The combination of MEMS sensors with digital signal processors on one single CMOS chip is sometimes known an CMOSens.

SIMM

A SIMM, or single in-line memory module, is a type of memory module used for random access memory in personal computers. It differs from a DIMM (the most predominant form of memory module today) in that the contacts on a SIMM are redundant on both sides of the module.

Most early PC motherboards (8088 based PCs and XTs) used socketed DIP chips. With the introduction of 80286 based PC/ATs, which could use larger amounts of memory, memory modules evolved from the need of saving motherboard space and to ease memory expansion. Instead of plugging in 8 or 9 single DRAM DIP chips, only one additional memory module was needed to increase the memory of the computer. A few 80286-based computers used (often non-standard) memory modules like SIPP memory (single in-line pin package). SIPP's 30 pins often bent or broke during installation, which is why they were quickly replaced by SIMMs which used contact plates rather than pins.

The first SIMMs appeared on the PS/2 in the mid 1980s, having been first proposed by Skip Coppola while at IBM. They solved several problems at the time, including shrinking motherboard real estate (they took up much less board space than socketed chips) as well as the effects of rapidly advancing memory capacities (a motherboard would quickly become obsolete based on its sockets for a particular RAM chip capacity) This also allowed the manufacturer (IBM at this time) to source RAM chips from different vendors and in different packaging, yet still allow them to be interchangeable through this intermediate form (the SIMM).

30- (top) and 72-pin (bottom) SIMMs. Early 30-pin modules commonly had either 256 KB or 1 MB of memory.

The first variant of SIMMs has 30 pins and provides 8 bits of data (9 bits in parity versions). Therefore, systems usually required that 30 pin SIMMs would have to be installed in sets of 4 (because processors such as the 80486 had 32 bit data paths).

The second variant of SIMMs has 72 pins and provides 32 bits of data (36 bits in parity versions). During the mid 90s, 72-pin SIMMs replaced 30-pin SIMMs.

The Macintosh IIfx requires non-standard 64-pin SIMMs.

Due to the differing data bus widths of the memory modules and some processors, sometimes several modules must be installed in identical pairs or in identical groups of four to fill a memory bank. For instance, on 80386 or 80486 systems (data bus width of 32 bits), either four 30-pin SIMMs or one 72-pin SIMM are required for one memory bank. On Pentium systems (data bus width of 64 bits), two 72-pin SIMMs are required.

The earliest SIMM sockets were conventional push-type sockets. These were soon replaced by ZIF (Zero Insertion Force) sockets in which the SIMM was inserted and rotated until it locked into place. To install a SIMM, the module must be placed in the socket at an angle, then rotated (angled) into position. To remove one, the two metal or plastic clips at each end must be pulled to the side, then the SIMM must be tilted back and pulled out. The earlier sockets used plastic retainer clips which were found to break, so steel clips replaced them.

RAM technologies used on SIMMs include EDO and FPM.

SIMM is standardised under JEDEC JESD-21C standard.

DIMM

A DIMM, or dual in-line memory module, comprises a series of random access memory integrated circuits. These modules are mounted on a printed circuit board and designed for use in personal computers. DIMMs began to replace SIMMs (single in-line memory modules) as the predominant type of memory module as Intel's Pentium processors began to control the market.

The main difference between SIMMs and DIMMs is that SIMMs have a 32-bit data path, while DIMMs have a 64-bit data path. Since Intel's Pentium has (as do several other processors) a 64-bit bus width, it required SIMMs installed in matched pairs in order to use them. The processor would then access the two SIMMs simultaneously. DIMMs were introduced to eliminate this inefficiency. Another difference is that DIMMs have separate electrical contacts on each side of the module, while the contacts on SIMMs on both sides are redundant.

The most common types of DIMMs are:

- 72-pin-DIMMs, used for SO-DIMM
- 144-pin-DIMMs, used for SO-DIMM
- 200-pin-DIMMs, used for SO-DIMM
- 168-pin-DIMMs, used for FPM, EDO and SDRAM
- 184-pin-DIMMs, used for DDR SDRAM
- 240-pin-DIMMs, used for DDR2 SDRAM
- 240-pin-DIMMs, used for FB-DIMM

There are 2 notches on the bottom edge of 168-pin-DIMMs, and the location of each notch determines a particular feature of the module.

- The first notch is DRAM key position. It represents RFU (reserved future use), registered, and unbuffered.
- The second notch is voltage key position. It represents 5.0V, 3.3V, and Reserved.
- The upper DIMM in the photo is an unbuffered 3.3V 168-pin DIMM.

A DIMM's capacity and timing parameters may be identified with SPD (Serial Presence Detect), an additional chip which contains information about the module type.

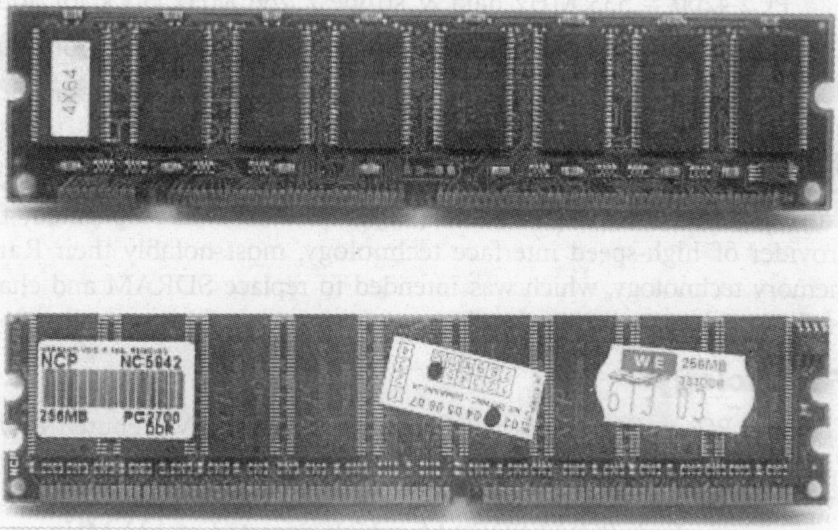

Two types of DIMMs: a 168-pin SDRAM module (top) and a 184-pin DDR SDRAM module (bottom).

ECC DIMMs are those that have extra data bits which can be used by the system memory controller to detect and correct errors. There are numerous ECC schemes, but perhaps the most common is Single Error Correct, Double Error Detect (SECDED) which uses a 9th extra bit per byte.

Speeds

For various technologies, there are certain bus and device clock frequencies that are standardized. There is also a decided nomenclature for each of these speeds for each type.

SDRAM DIMMs - These first synchronous registered DRAM DIMMs had the same bus frequency for data, address and control lines.

PC66 = 66 MHz

PC100 = 100 MHz

PC133 = 133 MHz

DDR SDRAM (DDR1) SDRAM DIMMs - DIMMs based on Double Data Rate (DDR) DRAM have data but not the strobe at double the rate of the clock. This is achieved by clocking on both the rising and falling edge of the data strobes.

PC1600 = 200 MHz data & strobe / 100 MHz clock for address and control

PC2100 = 266 MHz data & strobe / 133 MHz clock for address and control

PC2700 = 333 MHz data & strobe / 166 MHz clock for address and control

PC3200 = 400 MHz data & strobe / 200 MHz clock for address and control

DDR2 SDRAM SDRAM DIMMs - DIMMs based on Double Data Rate 2 (DDR2) DRAM also have data and data strobe frequencies at double the rate of the clock. This is achieved by clocking on both the rising and falling edge of the data strobes. The power consumption of DDR2 is significantly lower than DDR(1) at the same speed.

PC2-3200 = 400 MHz data & strobe / 200 MHz clock for address and control

PC2-4200 = 533 MHz data & strobe / 266 MHz clock for address and control

PC2-5300 = 667 MHz data & strobe / 333 MHz clock for address and control

PC2-6400 = 800 MHz data & strobe / 400 MHz clock for address and control

RIMM

Rambus Inline Memory Module (RIMM) Rambus Incorporated, founded in 1990, is a provider of high-speed interface technology, most notably their Rambus Dynamic RAM memory technology, which was intended to replace SDRAM and challenge DDR SDRAM as the standard memory used in computers.

Technology

The first PC motherboards with support for RDRAM debuted in 1999. They supported PC800 RDRAM, which operated at 800 MHz and delivered 1600 MB/s of bandwidth over a 16 bit bus using a 184 pin RIMM form factor. This was significantly faster than the previous standard, PC133 SDRAM, which operated at 133 MHz and delivered 1066 MB/ s of bandwidth over a 64 bit bus using a 168 pin DIMM form factor.

Some downsides of RDRAM technology, however, included significantly increased latency, heat output, manufacturing complexity, and cost. PC800 RDRAM operated with a latency of 45ns, compared to only 7.5ns for PC133 SDRAM. RDRAM memory chips also put out significantly more heat than SDRAM chips, necessitating heatsinks on all RIMM devices. RDRAM also includes a memory controller on each memory chip, significantly increasing manufacturing complexity compared to SDRAM, which used a single memory controller located on the northbridge chipset. RDRAM was also two to three times the price of PC133 SDRAM due to a combination of high manufacturing costs and high license fees. DDR SDRAM, introduced in 2000, operated at an effective clockspeed of 266 MHz and delivered 2100 MB/s over a 64-bit bus using a 184 pin DIMM form factor.

With the introduction of the i840 chipset, Intel added support for dual-channel PC800 RDRAM, doubling bandwidth to 3200 MB/s by increasing the bus width to 32 bit. This was followed in 2002 by the i850E chipset, which introduced PC1066 RDRAM, increasing total dual-channel bandwidth to 4200 MB/s. Also in 2002, Intel released the E7205 Granitebay chipset, which introduced dual-channel DDR support for a total bandwidth of 4200 MB/s, but at a much lower latency than competing RDRAM. In 2003, Intel released the i875P chipset, and along with it dual-channel DDR400. With a total bandwidth of 6400 MB/s, it marked the end of RDRAM as a technology with competitive performance.

Rambus survived the obsolesence of RDRAM and moved to support DDR and DDR2 in the area of video card technology and in particular, PCI Express. Rambus developed and licensed its XDR RAM technology.

Bus Slots

PCI slots were the first physically-incompatible expansion ports to directly squeeze ISA off of the motherboard. At first, motherboards were largely ISA, including a few PCI slots. By the mid-1990s, the two slot types were roughly balanced, and ISA slots soon were in the minority of consumer systems. Microsoft's PC 97 specification recommended that ISA slots be removed entirely, though the system architecture still required ISA to be present in some vestigial way internally to handle the floppy drive, serial ports, etc. ISA slots remained for a few more years, and it was even possible to see systems with an Accelerated Graphics Port (AGP) sitting near the central processing unit, an array of PCI slots, and one or two ISA slots near the end.

It is also notable that PCI slots are "rotated" compared to their ISA counterparts—PCI cards were essentially inserted "upside-down," allowing ISA and PCI connectors to squeeze together on the motherboard. Only one of the two connectors can be used in each slot at a time, but this allowed for greater flexibility.

8-bit ISA (XT bus architecture)

The XT bus architecture is an eight-bit ISA bus used by Intel 8086 and Intel 8088 systems in the IBM PC and IBM PC XT in the 1980s. The XT bus has four DMA channels, of which three are brought out to the expansion slots. Of these three, two are normally allocated to machine functions:

8 bit ISA or XT bus architecture	
Bus width	8-bit
Compatible with	8 bit ISA
Pins	62
Vcc	+5 V, -5 V, +12 V, -12 V
Clock	4.7727266 MHz

DMA channel	Expansion	Standard function
0	No	Dynamic RAM refresh
1	Yes	Add-on cards
2	Yes	Floppy disk controller
3	Yes	Hard disk controller

The XT bus architecture has single Intel 8259 PIC and eight interrupt lines.

16-bit ISA (AT bus architecture)

The AT bus architecture is an 16-bit version of the ISA bus first in the IBM PC/AT.

PCI Standards

The Peripheral Component Interconnect, or PCI Standard (in practice almost always shortened to PCI) specifies a computer bus for attaching peripheral devices to a computer motherboard. These devices can take any one of the following forms:

- An integrated circuit fitted onto the motherboard itself, called a planar device in the PCI specification.
- An expansion card that fits into a socket.

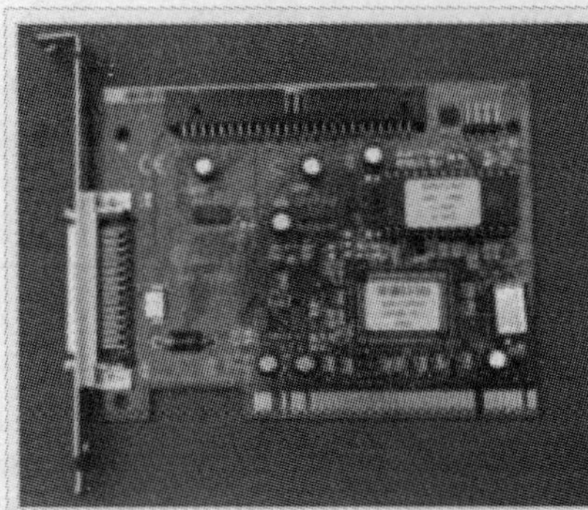

A typical 32-bit PCI card, in this case a SCSI adapter from Adaptec

The PCI bus is common in modern PCs, where it has displaced ISA and VESA Local Bus as the standard expansion bus, but it also appears in many other computer types. The bus will eventually be succeeded by PCI Express, which is standard in most new computers, and other technologies.

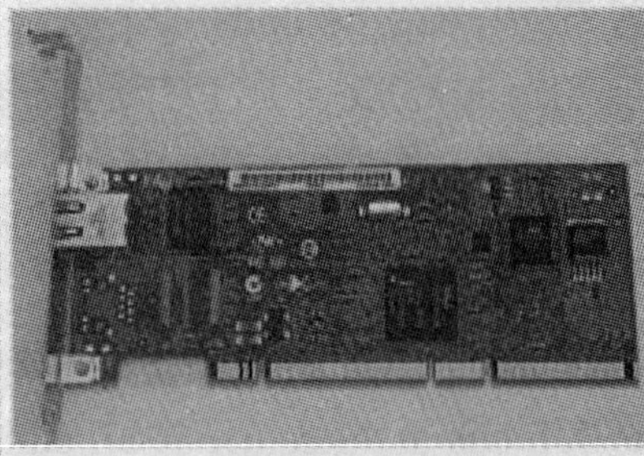

A PCI-X Gigabit Ethernet expansion card

The PCI specification covers the physical size of the bus (including wire spacing), electrical characteristics, bus timing, and protocols. The specification can be purchased from the PCI Special Interest Group (PCISIG).

Conventional Hardware Specifications

These specifications represent the most common version of PCI used in normal PCs.

- 33.33 MHz clock with synchronous transfers
- peak transfer rate of 133 MB per second for 32-bit bus width (33.33 MHz × 32 bits ÷ 8 bits/byte = 133 MB/s)
- peak transfer rate of 266 MB/s for 64-bit bus width
- 32-bit or 64-bit bus width
- 32-bit address space (4 gigabytes)
- 32-bit I/O port space (now deprecated)
- 256-byte configuration space
- 5-volt signaling
- reflected-wave switching

AGI Bus

The Accelerated Graphics Port (also called Advanced Graphics Port, often shortened to AGP) is a high-speed point-to-point channel for attaching a graphics card to a computer's motherboard, primarily to assist in the acceleration of 3D computer graphics. AGP is often referred to as a 'bus', however this is a misnomer - a single AGP controller is only capable of controlling a single device.

This is the main reason that almost all mainboards have only a single AGP slot, although motherboards have been built with multiple independent AGP slots. AGP is currently being phased out in favor of PCI Express.

Advantages over PCI

As computers became increasingly graphically oriented, successive generations of graphics adapters began to push the limits of the PCI bus, leading to the development of AGP, dedicated to graphics adapters. Most motherboards manufactured since the late 1990s include either an on-board integrated AGP adapter, or a physical AGP slot into which a separate AGP-based graphics card can be inserted.

For the needs of modern graphics adapters, AGP is superior to PCI because it provides a dedicated pathway between the slot and the processor rather than sharing the PCI bus, allowing for faster communication. AGP also uses sideband addressing, meaning that addressing for packets is carried outside of the packet, so the entire packet does not need to be read to get addressing information. In addition, to load a texture, a PCI graphics card must copy it from the system's RAM into the card's framebuffer, whereas an AGP card is capable of reading textures directly from system RAM using the Graphics Address Remapping Table (GART). GART reapportions main memory for texture storage, allowing the graphics card to access them directly.

The two main reasons graphics cards with the PCI interface are still produced is that, first, they can be used in nearly any PC; because while some motherboards with built-in graphics adapters lack an AGP slot, few, if any, modern desktop PCs do not have PCI slots. Secondly, a user with an appropriate operating system can use several PCI graphics cards (or several PCI graphics cards in combination with one AGP card) simultaneously — to give many different video outputs (for the use of many screens). This is almost impossible with AGP

1.0 (early AGP 1x and 2x) and AGP 2.0 (AGP 4x) cards, because they do not support more than one AGP Master (video card) per AGP Target (chipset interface); AGP 3.0 (AGP 8x) does support more than one AGP Master per AGP Target, but nonetheless few PC motherboards are equipped with more than one AGP slot. Some server-class computers support having multiple AGP slots in a single system: the HP AlphaServer GS1280 has up to 16 AGP slots, the AlphaServer ES80 up to 4 AGP slots, and the AlphaServer ES47 up to 2 AGP slots.

Versions of AGP

Intel released the first version of AGP; appropriately titled "AGP specification 1.0," in 1997. It included both the 1x and 2x speeds. Specification 2.0 documented AGP 4X and 3.0 documented 8X. Available versions include:

AGP 1x: A 32-bit channel operating at 66 MHz resulting in a maximum data rate of 266 megabytes per second (MB/s), doubled from the 133 MB/s transfer rate of PCI bus 33 MHz / 32-bit; 3.3 V signaling.

AGP 2x: A 32-bit channel operating at 66 MHz double pumped to an effective 133 MHz resulting in a maximum data rate of 533 MB/s; signaling voltages the same as AGP 1x;

AGP 4x: A 32-bit channel operating at 66 MHz quad pumped to an effective 266 MHz resulting in a maximum data rate of 1066 MB/s (1 GB/s); 1.5 V signaling;

AGP 8x: A 32-bit channel operating at 66 MHz, strobing eight times per clock, delivering an effective 533 MHz resulting in a maximum data rate of 2133 MB/s (2 GB/s); 0.8 V signaling.

In addition, AGP Pro cards of various types exist. They require more power and are often longer than standard AGP cards (though they only connect to one AGP slot). These cards are usually used to accelerate professional computer-aided design applications employed in the fields of architecture, machining, engineering, simulations, and similar fields. The AGP Pro slot has a few extra pins which supply extra power to the graphics card.

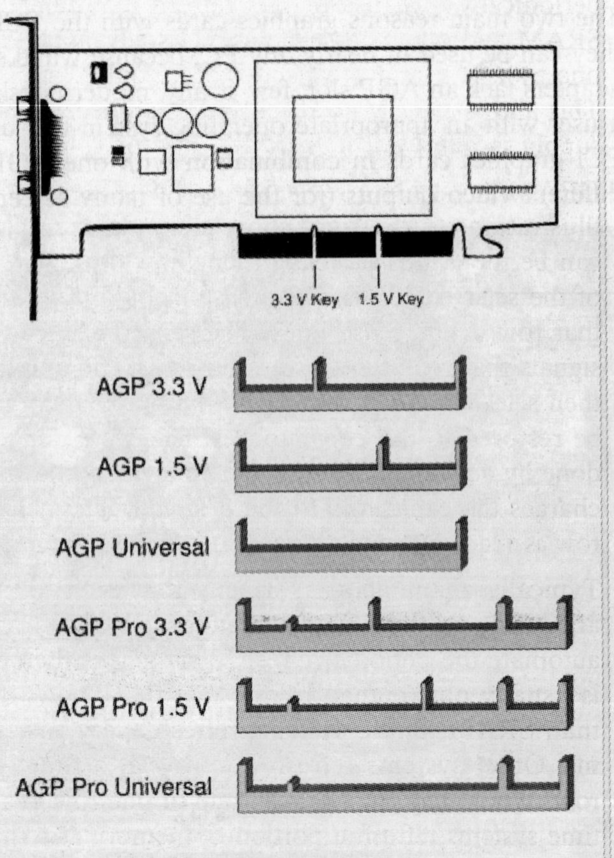

Compatibility, AGP Keys on card (top), on slot (bottom)

However, AGP Pro has not become widely accepted. Instead, modern desktop grade power-hungry video cards are equipped with a separate power source, either through a Molex or peripheral plug for additional power. Generally, there are two types of AGP Pro slots, regarding necessary power: 50 W or 110 W, with or without molex connector on the graphic card (although standard AGP slot is confined to 42 W of power through slot itself).

There are various physical interfaces (i.e. shape of slots), as explained in the Compatibility section below.

AGP version 3.5 is only publicly mentioned by Microsoft under Universal Accelerated Graphics Port (UAGP), which specifies mandatory supports of extra registers once marked optional under AGP 3.0. Upgraded registers include PCISTS, CAPPTR, NCAPID, AGPSTAT, AGPCMD, NISTAT, NICMD. New required registers include APBASELO, APBASEHI, AGPCTRL, APSIZE, NEPG, GARTLO, GARTHI.

DRAM

Dynamic random access memory (DRAM) is a type of random access memory that stores each bit of data in a separate capacitor within an integrated circuit. Since real capacitors leak charge, the information eventually fades unless the capacitor charge is refreshed periodically. Because of this refresh requirement, it is a dynamic memory as opposed to SRAM and other static memory. Its advantage over SRAM is its structural simplicity: only one transistor and a capacitor are required per bit, compared to six transistors in SRAM. This allows DRAM to reach very high density. Since DRAM loses its data when the power supply is removed, it is in the class of volatile memory devices.

DRAM is usually arranged in a square array of one capacitor and transistor per cell. The illustrations to the right show a simple example with only 4 by 4 cells (modern DRAM can be thousands of cells in length/width). A read operation proceeds as follows: the row of the selected cell is activated, turning on the transistors and connecting the capacitors of that row to the sense lines. The sense lines lead to the sense amplifiers, which distinguish signals that represent a stored 0 or 1. The amplified value from the appropriate column is then selected and connected to the output. At the end of a read cycle, the row values must be restored to the capacitors, which were depleted during the read. A write operation is done by activating the row and connecting the values to be written to the sense lines, which charges the capacitors to the desired values. During a write to a particular cell, the entire row is read out, one value changed, and then the entire row is written back int.

Typically, manufacturers specify that each row should be refreshed every 64 ms or less, according to the JEDEC standard. Refresh logic is commonly used with DRAMs to automate the periodic refresh. This makes the circuit more complicated, but this drawback is usually outweighed by the fact that DRAM is much cheaper and of greater capacity than SRAM. Some systems refresh every row in a tight loop that occurs once every 64 ms. Other systems refresh one row at a time — for example, a system with 2^{13} = 8192 rows would require a refresh rate of one row every 7.8 µs (64 ms / 8192 rows). A few real-time systems refresh a portion of memory at a time based on an external timer that governs the operation of the rest of the system, such as the vertical blanking interval that occurs every 10 to 20 ms in video equipment. All methods require some sort of counter to keep track of which row is the next to be refreshed. Some DRAM chips include that counter; other kinds require external refresh logic to hold that counter. (Under some conditions, most of the data in DRAM can be recovered even if the DRAM has not been refreshed for several minutes.)

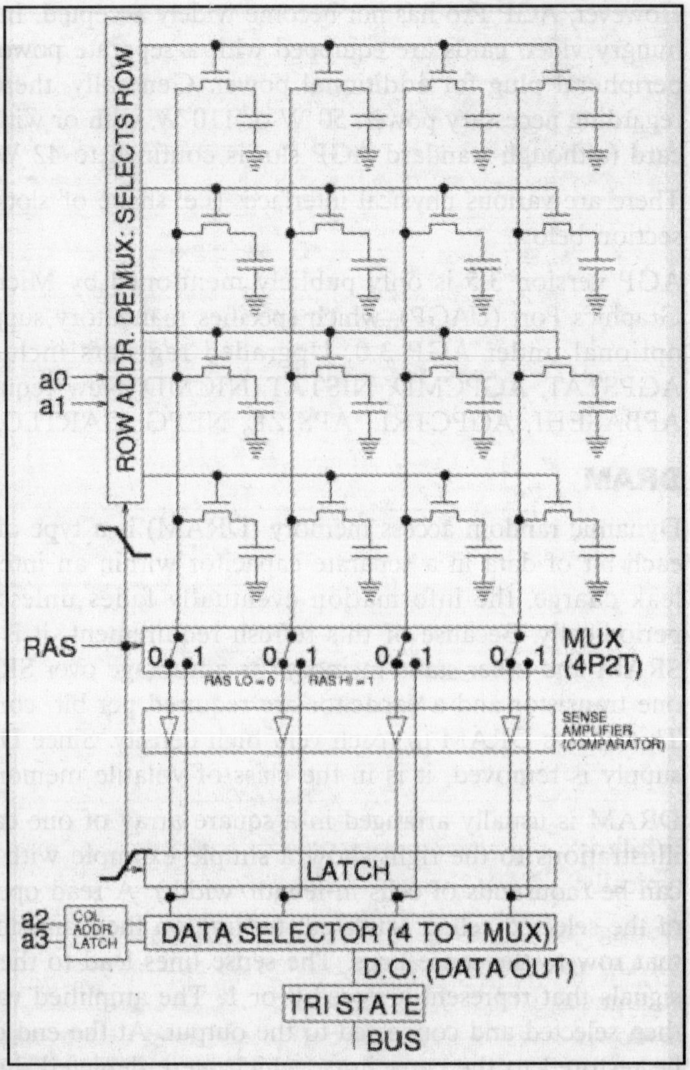

SRAM

Static random access memory (SRAM) is a type of semiconductor memory. The word "static" indicates that the memory retains its contents as long as power remains applied, unlike dynamic RAM (DRAM) that needs to be periodically refreshed (nevertheless, SRAM should not be confused with read-only memory and flash memory, since it is volatile memory and preserves data only while power is continuously applied). SRAM should not be confused with SDRAM, which stands for synchronous DRAM and is entirely different from SRAM, or with pseudostatic RAM (PSRAM), which is DRAM disguised as SRAM.

Random Access

Random access means that locations in the memory can be written to or read from in any order, regardless of the memory location that was last accessed.

Each bit in an SRAM is stored on four transistors that form two cross-coupled inverters. This storage cell has two stable states which are used to denote 0 and 1. Two additional access transistors serve to control the access to a storage cell during read and write operations. It thus typically takes six MOSFETs to store one memory bit.

Access to the cell is enabled by the word line (WL in figure) which controls the two access transistors M_5 and M_6 which, in turn, control whether the cell should be connected to the bit lines: BL and BL. They are used to transfer data for both read and write operations.

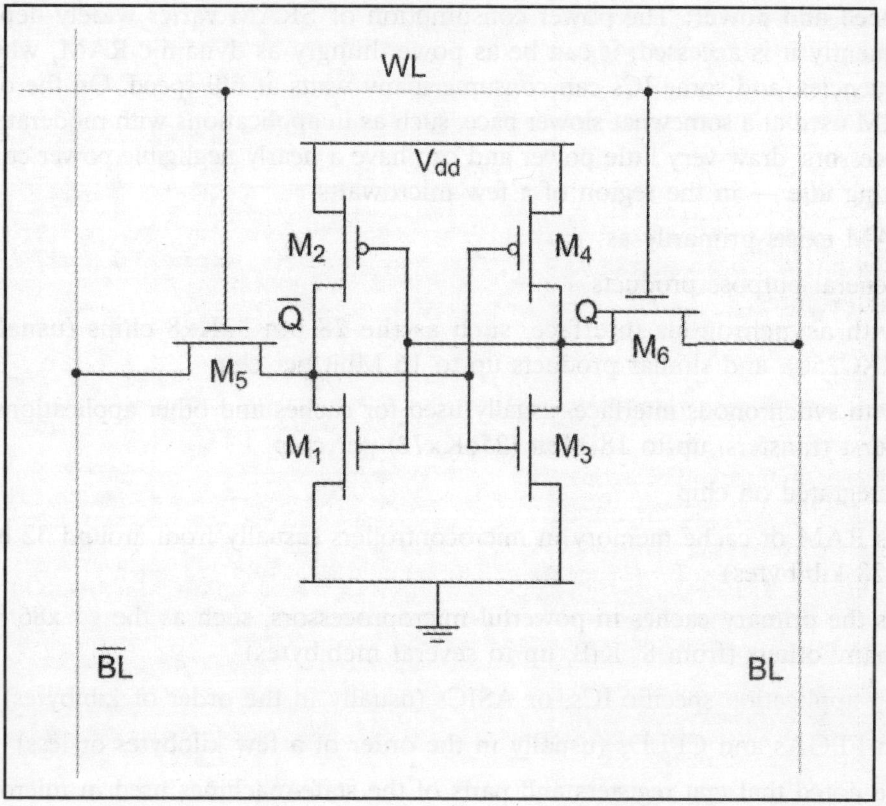

While it's not strictly necessary to have two bit lines, both the signal and its inverse are typically provided since it improves noise margins.

During read accesses, the bit lines are actively driven high and low by the inverters in the SRAM cell. This improves SRAM speed compared to DRAMs—in a DRAM, the bit line is connected to storage capacitors and charge sharing causes the bitline to swing upwards or downwards. The symmetric structure of SRAMs also allows for differential signalling, which makes small voltage swings more easily detectable. Another difference with DRAM that contributes to making SRAM faster is that commercial chips accept all address bits at a time. By comparison, commodity DRAMs have the address multiplexed in two halves, i.e. higher bits followed by lower bits, over the same package pins in order to keep their size and cost down.

The size of an SRAM with m address lines and n data lines is 2^m words, or $2^m \times n$ bits.

Applications and Use

Characteristics: SRAM is a little more expensive, but faster and significantly less power hungry (especially idle) than DRAM. It is therefore used where either speed or low power, or both, are of prime interest. SRAM is also easier to control (interface to) and generally more truly random access than modern types of DRAM. Due to a more complex internal structure, SRAM is less dense than DRAM and is therefore not used for high-capacity, low-cost applications such as the main memory in personal computers.

Clock speed and power: The power consumption of SRAM varies widely depending on how frequently it is accessed; it can be as power-hungry as dynamic RAM, when used at high frequencies, and some ICs can consume many watts at full speed. On the other hand, static RAM used at a somewhat slower pace, such as in applications with moderately clocked microprocessors, draw very little power and can have a nearly negligible power consumption when sitting idle — in the region of a few microwatts.

Static RAM exists primarily as:

- general purpose products
- with asynchronous interface, such as the 28 pin 32Kx8 chips (usually named XXC256), and similar products up to 16 Mbit per chip
- with synchronous interface, usually used for caches and other applications requiring burst transfers, up to 18 Mbit (256Kx72) per chip
- integrated on chip
- as RAM or cache memory in microcontrollers (usually from around 32 bytes up to 128 kibibytes)
- as the primary caches in powerful microprocessors, such as the · x86 family, and many others (from 8 KiB, up to several mebibytes)
- on application specific ICs, or ASICs (usually in the order of kibibytes)
- in FPGAs and CPLDs (usually in the order of a few kilobytes or less)

It may be noted that cpu registers and parts of the state-machines used in microprocessors are also often (not always!) built around static RAM.

Embedded use: Many categories of industrial and scientific subsystems, automotive electronics, and similar, contains static RAM. Some amounts (kibibytes or less) is also embedded in practically all modern appliances, toys, etc that implements an electronic user interface. Several mebibytes may be used in complex products such as digital cameras, cell phones, synthesizers, etc.

SRAM in its dual-ported form is sometimes used for realtime digital signal processing circuits.

In computers: SRAM is also used in personal computers, workstations, routers and peripheral equipment: internal CPU caches and external burst mode SRAM caches, hard disk buffers, router buffers, etc. LCD screens and printers also normally employ static RAM to hold the image displayed (or to be printed). Small SRAM buffers are also found in CDROM and CDRW drives; usually 256 KiB or more are used to buffer track data, which is transferred in blocks instead of as single values. The same applies to cable modems and similar equipment connected to computers. The so called "CMOS RAM" on PC motherboards was originally a battery-powered SRAM chip, but is today more often implemented using EEPROM or Flash.

Hobbyists: Hobbyists often prefer SRAM due to the ease of interfacing. It is much easier to work with than DRAM as there are no refresh cycles and the address and data buses are directly accessible rather than multiplexed. In addition to buses and power connections,

SRAM usually require only three controls: Chip Enable (CE), Write Enable (WE) and Output Enable (OE).

DDR SDRAM

While the access latency of DRAM is fundamentally limited by the DRAM array, DRAM has very high potential bandwidth because each internal read is actually a row of many thousands of bits. To make more of this bandwidth available to users, a Double Data Rate interface was developed. This uses the same commands, accepted once per cycle, but reads or writes two words of data per clock cycle. Some minor changes to the SDR interface timing were made in hindsight.

DDR SDRAM doubles the minimum read or write unit; every access refers to at least two consecutive words.

Typical DDR SDRAM clock speeds are 133, 166 and 200 MHz (7.5, 6, and 5 ns/cycle), generally described as DDR-266, DDR-333 and DDR-400 (3.75, 3, and 2.5 ns per beat). Corresponding 184-pin DIMMS are known as PC2100, PC2700 and PC3200. Speeds up to DDR-550 (PC4400) are available for a price.

DDR2 SDRAM

DDR2 SDRAM is very similar to DDR SDRAM, but doubles the minimum read or write unit again, to 4 consecutive words. The bus protocol was also simplified to allow higher speed operation. (In particular, the "burst terminate" command is deleted.) This allows the bus speed of the SDRAM to be doubled without increasing the speed of internal RAM operations; instead, internal operations are performed in units 4 times as wide as SDRAM. Also, an extra bank address pin (BA2) was added to allow 8 banks on large RAM chips.

Typical DDR2 SDRAM clock speeds are 200, 266, 333 or 400 MHz (5, 3.75, 3 and 2.5 ns/cycle), generally described as DDR2-400, DDR2-533, DDR2-667 and DDR2-800 (2.5, 1/875, 1.5 and 1.5 ns per beat). Corresponding 240-pin DIMMS are known as PC2-3200 through PC2-6400. Speeds up to DDR2-1250 (PC2-10000) are available for a price.

Note that because internal operations are at 1/2 the clock rate, DDR2-400 memory (internal clock speed 100 MHz) has somewhat higher latency than DDR-400 (internal clock speed 200 MHz).

DDR3 SDRAM

DDR3 continues the trend, doubling the minimum read or write unit to 8 consecutive words. This allows another doubling of bandwidth and external bus speed without having to change the speed of internal operations, just the width.

DDR3 memory chips are being made commercially, but computer systems able to use them are not expected until late 2007, with significant usage in 2008. Initial speeds are 400 and 533 MHz, which would be described as DDR3-800 and DDR3-1066, but speeds of 667 and 800 MHz (DDR3-1333 and DDR3-1600) are expected in time. This high speed poses a significant engineering challenge, so the 2008 schedule may be optimistic.

Extended Data Out (EDO) DRAM

EDO DRAM is similar to Fast Page Mode DRAM with the additional feature that a new access cycle can be started while keeping the data output of the previous cycle active. This allows a certain amount of overlap in operation (pipelining), allowing somewhat improved speed. It was 5% faster than Fast Page Mode DRAM, which it began to replace in 1993.

To be precise, EDO DRAM begins data output on the falling edge of /CAS, but does not stop the output when /CAS rises again. It holds the output valid (thus extending the data output time) until either /RAS is deasserted, or a new /CAS falling edge selects a different column address.

Single-cycle EDO has the ability to carry out a complete memory transaction in one clock cycle. Otherwise, each sequential RAM access within the same page takes two clock cycles instead of three, once the page has been selected. EDO's speed and capabilities allowed it to somewhat replace the then-slow L2 caches of PCs. It created an opportunity to reduce the immense performance loss associated with a lack of L2 cache, while making systems cheaper to build. This was also good for notebooks due to difficulties with their limited form factor, and battery life limitations. An EDO system with L2 cache was tangibly faster than the older FPM/L2 combination.

Single-cycle EDO DRAM became very popular on video cards towards the end of the 1990s. It was very low cost, yet nearly as efficient for performance as the far more costly VRAM.

EDO was sometimes referred to as Hyper Page Mode.

Burst EDO (BEDO) DRAM

An evolution of the former, Burst EDO DRAM, could process four memory addresses in one burst, for a maximum of 5-1-1-1, saving an additional three clocks over optimally designed EDO memory. It was done by adding an address counter on the chip to keep track of the next address. BEDO also added a pipelined stage allowing page-access cycle to be divided into two components. During a memory-read operation, the first component accessed the data from the memory array to the output stage (second latch). The second component drove the data bus from this latch at the appropriate logic level. Since the data is already in the output buffer, faster access time is achieved (up to 50% for large blocks of data) than with traditional EDO.

Although BEDO DRAM showed additional optimization over EDO, by the time it was available the market had made a significant investment towards synchronous DRAM, or SDRAM [7]. Even though BEDO RAM was superior to SDRAM in some ways, the latter technology gained significant traction and quickly displaced BEDO.

Multibank DRAM (MDRAM)

Multibank RAM applies the interleaving technique for main memory to second level cache memory to provide a cheaper and faster alternative to SRAM. The chip splits its memory capacity into small blocks of 256 kB and allows operations to two different banks in a single clock cycle.

This memory was primarily used in graphic cards with Tseng Labs ET6x00 chipsets, and was made by MoSys. Boards based upon this chipset often used the unusual RAM size configuration of 2.25 MiB, owing to MDRAM's ability to be implemented in various sizes more easily. This size of 2.25 MiB allowed 24-bit color at a resolution of 1024×768, a very popular display setting in the card's time.

Synchronous Graphics RAM (SGRAM)

SGRAM is a specialized form of SDRAM for graphics adaptors. It adds functions such as bit masking (writing to a specified bit plane without affecting the others) and block write (filling a block of memory with a single colour). Unlike VRAM and WRAM, SGRAM is single-ported. However, it can open two memory pages at once, which simulates the dual-port nature of other video RAM technologies.

SGRAM and SDRAM became the most popular types of DRAM at the end of the 1990s, and well into the first decade of the 2000s.

Battery

The battery inside the PC keeps the clock working when the main power supply to the system is switched off, so that the next time when you switch on the system you will get correct time and date. This battery also provides power to the CMOS memory that keeps the setup information about the system. Usually this battery last for many years, when it eventually fails, your system will lose the setup information saved in the CMOS RAM and also the Real Time Clock (RTC) of your system will stop showing the correct time.

In this condition, every time you switch the correct time and date to the system, to allow the system to show correct time and date as long as machine is on. When the battery inside your system fails you need to replace it with another working battery of the same size and type.

Replacing Battery

To replace the battery, do the following:

1. Switch off system and remove the power supply cable.
2. Remove the main system unit's cover.
3. Remove the battery from the holder and slide in a new battery of the same size and type in the holder.
4. Make sure that it is in correct orientation.
5. Once the battery is replaced, close the cover, switch on the system and run the setup to cofigure the system.

Presently 3V, CR-2030 Lithium battery is commonly used in most of the motherboards.

Super I/O Chip

OnBoard Floppy Controller

Use this item to enable or diable floppy drive controller.

Serial Port Address

Use this item to set the address for the onboard serial port or disable it. Configuration options: [Disabled], [3F8 / IRQ4], [2F8 / IRQ3], [3E8 / IRQ4], [2E8 / IRQ3]

Motherboard Connectors

Several connectors are provided on the motherboard to connect external Reset switche, Power-on LED, Speaker, etc. to the system. When you remove any lead, always remember to note the position and orientation of each of them as some of them are orientation sensitive and will not work when connected in wrong orientation.

Let us see some of these connectors.

External Battery Connector

Pin	Function
1	Battery (+6V DC Input)
2	No Connection
3	Ground
4	Ground

On IBM AT and compatibles, CMOS RAM data is maintained by battery on the motherboard itself and hence do not require any external connection.

Optional Keyboard Connector

Pin	Function
1	Keyboard Clock
2	Keyboard Data
3	No connection
4	Ground
5	+5V

Keyboard connector is a five-pin DIN socket placed towards the rear right hand side of the motherboard.

Power Connector

AT Power Supply

J10	J11
Power Good	Ground

+5V	Ground
+12V	–5V
–12V	+5V
Ground	+5V
Ground	+5V

Power is fed to motherboard from two 6-way non-reversible connectors.

In case you are unsure about which way these two connectors go, always remember that the black wires (ground) of connector J10 and J11 are placed together when connecting them to the motherboard.

ATX Power Supply

Pin	Function	Pin	Function
1	+3.3V	11	+3.3V
2	+3.3V	12	–12V
3	Ground	13	Ground
4	+5V	14	PWR ON
5	Ground	15	Ground
6	+5V	16	Ground
7	Ground	17	Ground
8	PWR GOOD	18	–5V
9	+5V SB	19	+5V
10	+12V	20	+5V

Keylock and Power-on LED Connector

Pin	Function
1	LED+
2	NO CONNECTION
3	LED–
4	KEYLOCK
5	KEYLOCK GROUND

The LED is connected to pin-1 and 3, the keyboard lock switch is connected to pin-4 and 5.

Speaker Connector

Pin	Function
1	+5V
2	Ground
3	Ground
4	SPKR

The loudspeaker is connected by a four-way socket. Only the outer two pins (1 and 4) are used. The loudspeaker is not orientation sensitive and hence it does not matter which way it is connected.

Turbo Mode Selection

Switch Option	System Clock Speed
Open	Turbo
Close	Non-Turbo

"Tubo" switch is nonstandard, so its pin assignments may vary. If you are not sure of its connections, consult the system manual, a wrong connection is unlikely to cause any harm.

Turbo Mode LED Connector

Pin	Function
1	LED
2	LED+

This LED is orientation sensitive and will light only if connected properly.

Reset Connector

Switch Position	Function
Close	Reset the system
Open	Normal operation

The reset button uses a two-pin connector in which pin 1 is the reset line and pin 2 is ground. These two pins are linked when the switch is depressed. The polarization of this switch is unimportant.

Infra-Red (IR) Connector

Pin	Function
1	VCC +5V
2	No Connection
3	IrRx Infrared Receive
4	Ground
5	IrTx Infrared Transmit

This conector provides connection for HP HSDL-1000 compatible infrared (IrDA) transmitter/receiver.

Front Panel Function Connector

Pin		Function	Pin		Function
1		Power LED	14		Ground
2		No connection	15	IDE LED	IDE LED
3	Key Lock	Ground	16		No connection
4		Key lock	17	SW On	GV VR
5		Ground	18		Push on
6		No connection	19	Ground	Standby 5V
7	Ext SMI	Ext SMI	20	Sleep	VCC
8		Ground	21	LED	Sleep LED
9		No connection	22		Ground
10		Speaker	23	Reset	Reset
11	Speaker	No connection	24		No connection
12		Ground	25	Turbo	VCC
13		Vcc	26	LED	+5V

This connector integrates all system front-panel functions into one single 26-pin connector.

CPU Fan Connector

Pin	Function
1	No Connection
2	+12V
3	Ground

CPU fan connector provides +12V DC supply to the CPU cooling fan. This fan is attached on top of the heatsink element.

CD Audio Input Connector

Pin	Function
1	Left Channel Audio
2	Gound
3	Ground
4	Right Channel Audio

Auxiliary Input Connector

Pin	Function
1	Left Channel Audio
2	Gound
3	Ground
4	Right Channel Audio

Telephony Input Connector

Pin	Function
1	Phone
2	Gound
3	Ground
4	Mono

Integrated Function Connector

Pin		Function	Pin		Function
1		USB +5Volt	11		USB +5Volt
2		USB Port1 –	12		USB Port2 –
3	USB1	USB Port1 +	13	USB2	USB Port2 +
4		Ground	14		Ground
5		No connnection	15		No connection
6		PS/2 Data	16		+5V

7	PS/2 Mouse	PS/2 Clock	17		No connection
8		Ground	18	Infrared	IR Receive
9		No connection	19		Ground
10		+5V	20		IR Transmit

Intel 865G Motherboard

The Intel 865G chipset, designed for the Intel Pentium D processor (compatible with the lead free version of Intel 865G Chipsets supporting socket LGA775) and the Intel Pentium 4 processor supporting Hyper-Threading Technology, is a highly flexible and scalable solution that meets a broad range of demanding computing needs. The 865G chipset offers solid performance through a variety of exciting features, including dual-channel DDR 400 main memory, an 800 MHz system bus, and an integrated graphics controller with Intel Extreme Graphics 2 technology.

Chipset Features

Features	*Benefits*
800/533/400 MHz system bus	Platform longevity with support for Intel® Pentium D processor 805 and 820 sequence, delivering improved system bandwidth.
Supports Hyper-Threading Technology	Delivers increased system responsiveness and performance.
Intel Extreme Graphics 2 technology	Fourth-generation graphics architecture supports the latest APIs, allowing software developers to create real-life environments and characters.
Intel Accelerated Hub Architecture	Dedicated data paths deliver maximum bandwidth for I/O-intensive applications.
Dual-Channel DDR 400/333/266 SDRAM	Flexible memory technology allows a full spectrum of DDR usage from incredible performance to more cost-effective systems.
Intel Dynamic Video Output Interface	Two DVO ports offer added display (digital CRT or TV) flexibility through the standard AGP connector.
AGP 8X interface	Increased bandwidth graphics interface enables upgradeability to latest graphics cards.
Integrated high-speed USB 2.0	Eight ports offer up to 40x greater bandwidth over USB 1.1 for a variety of today's demanding high-speed I/O peripherals
Dual independent Serial ATA controllers	Facilitates high-speed storage transfers and easy hard drive upgrades.

Intel RAID technology[PDF 260 KB]	Enables extreme storage performance for Serial ATA hard disks.
Ultra ATA/100	Takes advantage of the existing industry HDD and optical drive interfaces.
AC '97 controller	Supports Dolby* Digital 5.1 surround-sound[1], delivering up to six channels of enhanced sound quality.
Intel® Communication Streaming Architecture	Wire-speed GbE with Dedicated Network Bus (DNB) for performance network connectivity.
Low-power sleep mode	Saves energy.

Intel 910GL Motherboard

The Intel 910GL Express chipset brings compelling new capabilities to the desktop PC. Designed for the Intel Pentium 4 processor supporting Hyper-Threading Technology, the 910GL chipset features a decade's worth of innovation.

Features

Features	*Benefits*
533 MHz system bus	Front Side Bus (FSB) support for high-performance Intel processors and greater system performance.
Supports Hyper-Threading Technology	Increased system responsiveness for multi-tasking.
LGA775 and 478-pin processor package	Supports the highest performance Intel® desktop processors with the flexibility to support 478-pin Intel processors
Intel Graphics Media Accelerator 900	(Intel GMA 900 graphics) Stunning media, incredible visuals and new 3D capabilities. For business users, Intel validates the chipset, processor, graphics and software stack to provide a well-tested platform with support for Microsoft* Windows 2000, Windows XP, Linux (top distributions) and OS/2 (SciTech).
PCI Express* bus architecture	PCI Express x1 I/O offers 500 MB/s concurrently, over 3.5 times more bandwidth than PCI at 133 MB/s.
Dual-channel DDR	Dual-channel DDR400/DDR333 memory configurable up to 2 GB RAM.
Direct Media Interface (DMI)	For I/O intensive applications, new serial point-

	to-point bus delivers up to 2.0 GB/s concurrent bandwidth between the memory and I/O controllers, compared to 266 MB/s with previous generation Intel hub architecture.
Intel High Definition Audio	Support for new consumer audio entertainment formats such as 7.1 surround sound, Dolby* Digital, and DTS*. Audio codec support for 192 kHz quality, multiple streams, and better voice input for speech recognition and voice-over-IP.
Intel® Matrix Storage Technology with ICH6R	Boosts storage performance with RAID 0, while helping to protect your digital memories with RAID 1, on the same disks. Advanced Host Controller Interface (AHCI) further boosts performance with Native Command Queuing (NCQ), and provides native hot plug for drive swaps.
Four Serial ATA ports (SATA/150)	Integrated serial ATA controller facilitates high-speed data transfers at up to 150 MB/s for each of 4 ports. Allows easier hard drive upgrades and expansion for new SATA optical drives.
Ultra ATA/100	Supports legacy hard drives and optical drives.
High-speed USB 2.0 ports	Eight ports offer up to 40X greater bandwidth over USB 1.1, for high-speed I/O peripherals such as digital video cameras.
Intel Serial Digital Video Output (SDVO) ports	Dual SDVO ports offer maximum display (digital CRT or TV) flexibility through the existing PCI Express* x16 connector.

Intel 915 Motherboard

Platforms based on the Intel 915P Express Chipset and Intel Pentium 4 processor supporting Hyper-Threading Technology1 deliver innovative features and new benefits for both home and business users. The Intel 915P Express Chipset was designed to support the capabilities of Hyper-Threading Technology, adding intelligence to help manage and prioritize multiple threads received from the processor. An HT Technology-enabled platform can improve system performance and responsiveness.

The Intel 915P Express Chipset, based on a new architecture, innovative technologies and high-bandwidth interfaces, is the newest discrete graphics chipset for the Intel Pentium 4 processor family. It was designed to enable the convergence of digital entertainment, as well as enhance bandwidth-intensive applications, such as audio, video, photography, and gaming. It also offers corporate users a high-performance stable platform that enables new levels of business collaboration.

This highly flexible and scalable solution meets a broad range of demanding computing needs. The Intel 915P Express Chipset can deliver maximum system performance through its high-bandwidth interfaces, such as dual-channel DDR2 main memory, 800-MHz system bus, PCI Express* Graphics and I/O architecture, and Hi-Speed USB 2.0 connectivity. PCI Express architecture enables increased bidirectional bandwidth to the graphics and I/O interfaces. With up to 500 MB/s concurrent data transfer rate, it delivers more than three and a half times the I/O bandwidth of traditional PCI architecture. And with up to 4 GB/s per direction PCI Express Graphics capability, it provides more than three and a half times the graphics bandwidth of previous generation discrete graphics controllers.

To support the faster memory, increased graphics requirements, and I/O bandwidth, the Intel 915P Express Chipset incorporates a new Memory Controller Hub (MCH) backbone architecture. This new design includes wider internal data buses that support dual-channel DDR2 memory technology at 533 MHz or up to 8.5 GB/s of peak memory bandwidth, for improved platform performance. The new architecture also supports both asynchronous and true isochronous data traffic, with dedicated internal pipelines and specialized arbitration. This enables the Intel 915P Express Chipset to take full advantage of the performance of these new high-speed interfaces.

A high speed serial point-to-point bus architecture, known as Direct Media Interface, links the MCH to the sixthgeneration Intel® I/O Controller Hub (ICH6). This new bus delivers up to 2 GB/s concurrent bandwidth, compared with up to 266-MB/s for the previous Intel® hub architecture. Intel 915P Express Chipset-based platforms also enable system design flexibility, with support for both dual-channel DDR and DDR2 memory, discrete PCI Express graphics, and additional platform capabilities via flexible ICH6 options.

The ICH6 component includes several enhancements and new capabilities, and enables system configuration options for digital home usage and business collaboration. It integrates the Intel® High Definition Audio (Intel® HD Audio) technology, featuring eight independent DMA audio engines that support multiple simultaneous and separate audio input and output streams. This enables high quality integrated audio that rivals the performance of high end discrete solutions. Intel HD Audio is also capable of supporting major consumer entertainment industry formats, such as 7.1 surround sound, Dolby Digital, and DTS. An integrated Serial ATA (SATA) controller supports 4 SATA ports, each providing up to 1.5 GB/s (150 MB/s) transfer rates for SATA optical devices or hard drives. And the Advanced Host Controller Interface (AHCI) provides native hot plug and boosts performance with Native Command Queuing (NCQ) for faster boot times and file transfers. The Intel® ICH6R component elevates SATA storage performance to the next level with Intel® Matrix Storage Technology. Enhanced RAID support allows critical data to be stored on one array that is designed for high reliability, while performance intensive applications like games can reside on separate array designed for maximum performance.

Intel 915P Express Chipset features deliver a compelling solution for both consumer and corporate market segments:

- 800-MHz FSB enables support for today's high-performance Intel Pentium 4 processors.

- Optimized for the Intel Pentium 4 Processor with HT Technology, to enable improved system performance and responsiveness.
- Flexible memory support, with dual-channel DDR2 533/DDR2 400 or DDR400/ DDR333 memory.
- PCI Express up to 4 GB/s per direction for graphics bandwidth and up to 500 MB/ s concurrent data transfers for I/O.
- Intel Matrix Storage Technology, with integrated Raid 0 and Raid 1 capabilities using the latest SATA interface, for accelerated disk I/O performance.
- Intel HD Audio technology's eight independent DMA audio engines can enable multiple separate, simultaneous audio experiences.

Comparision of Various Motherboards

Part #	Description
MB7759	ASUS A8VE-SE, Socket 939 Athlon 64/64 FX, VIA K8T890, PCI Express ATX- Motherboard
MB7758	Asus A8N32-SLI DELUXE Socket 939 for Athlon 64, Athlon 64FX, nVidia nForce4 SLI x16/RAID/2GbE, ATX Motherboard
MB5707	ASUS P5W-DH DELUXE LGA775 CORE2/975X/XFIRE/A/GLAN ATX-Motherboard

SUPERMICRO MOTHERBOARDS

Part #	Description
MB1254	SuperServer 6025B-8R+B - Super X7DB8+ in SC825S2-R700LPB 2U Rackmount(black), Dual 771-pin LGA for Dual-Core Intel Xeon (Woodcrest/ Dempsey), Intel 5000P, Up to 64GB FBDIMM, 8 x SCA SCSI bays, 700W Redundant PS, Low Profile Slots
MB1255	SuperServer 6025B-TR+B - Super X7DBE+ in SC825TQ-R700LPB 2U Rackmount(black), Dual 771-pin LGA for Dual-Core Intel Xeon (Woodcrest/ Dempsey), Intel 5000P, Up to 64GB FBDIMM, 8 x SATA SCSI bays, 700W Redundant PS, Low Profile Slots
MB1271	SuperServer 6025B-3B - Super X7DB3 in SC825TQ-560LPB 2U Rackmount(black), Dual 771-pin LGA for Dual-Core Intel Xeon (Woodcrest/ Dempsey), Intel 5000P, Up to 32GB FBDIMM, 8 x SAS bays, 560W PS, Low Profile Slots
MB1252	SuperServer 6025B-8B - Super X7DB8 in SC823S-550LP 2U Rackmount(black), Dual 771-pin LGA for Dual-Core Intel Xeon (Woodcrest/ Dempsey), Intel 5000P, Up to 32GB FBDIMM, 6 x SCA SCSI bays, 550W PS, Low Profile Slots
MB1253	SuperServer 6025B-TB - Super X7DBE in SC823TQ-550LP 2U Rackmount(black), Dual 771-pin LGA for Dual-Core Intel Xeon (Woodcrest/

	Dempsey), Intel 5000P, Up to 32GB FBDIMM, 6 x SATA bays, 550W PS, Low Profile Slots
MB1279	SuperServer 6015T-TB - Super X7DBT in SC808T-980B 1U Rackmount(black), Dual Node (twin server design) Dual 771-pin LGA for Quad/Dual-Core Intel Xeon and up to 32GB FBDIMM per server, 2 x SATA bays per server, 980W Shared PS
MB1272	SuperServer 6015B-3B - Super X7DBR-3 in SC815TQ-560B 1U Rackmount(black), Dual 771-pin LGA for Dual or Quad-Core Intel Xeon (Clovertown/Woodcrest/Dempsey), Intel 5000P, Up to 32GB FBDIMM, 4 x SAS/SATA bays, 560W PS, PCI-X or PCI Express x8 slot
MB1250	SuperServer 6015B-8+B - Super X7DBR-8+ in SC815S-700 1U Rackmount(black), Dual 771-pin LGA for Dual-Core Intel Xeon (Woodcrest/ Dempsey), Intel 5000P, Up to 64GB FBDIMM, 4 x SCA SCSI bays, 700W PS, PCI-X or PCI Express x8 slot
MB1251	SuperServer 6015B-T+B - Super X7DBR-i+ in SC815TQ-700 1U Rackmount(black), Dual 771-pin LGA for Dual-Core Intel Xeon (Woodcrest/ Dempsey), Intel 5000P, Up to 64GB FBDIMM, 4 x SATA bays, 700W PS, PCI-X or PCI Express x8 slot
MB1262	SuperServer 6015P-8RB - Super X7DBP-8 in SC816S-700 1U Rackmount(black), Dual 771-pin LGA for Quad/Dual-Core Intel Xeon (Clovertown/Woodcrest/Dempsey), Intel 5000P, Up to 32GB FBDIMM, 4 x SCSI bays, 700W Redundant PS
MB1261	SuperServer 6015P-TRB - Super X7DBP-i in SC816A-700 1U Rackmount(black), Dual 771-pin LGA for Quad/Dual-Core Intel Xeon (Clovertown/Woodcrest/Dempsey), Intel 5000P, Up to 32GB FBDIMM, 4 x SATA bays, 700W Redundant PS
MB12752	SuperServer 6015V-MRB - Super X7DVL-E in Black SC512F-520 Mini-1U Rackmount, Intel 5000V chipset, Dual Quad-Core/Dual-Core Xeon support, Up to 16GB, 1 Internal SATA drive bay, 520W PS, Integrated graphics, 2 x Intel Gigabit LAN ports, 1 x PCI-X Slot
MB1148	SuperServer 6014A-8B - Super X6DAR-8G in SC813S-500 1U Rack (black), Dual Xeon EM64T, Intel E7525, Up to 32GB LP ECC Reg. DDR, 4 x SCA bays, 500W Cold Swap PS, VGA, PCI Express x16 and PCI Exp. x8 or PCI-X LP Slot, Dual Gigabit LAN, Dual U320 SCSI
MB1120	SuperServer 7044H-X8RB - Super X6DH8-XG2 in SC743S1-R760 in Rackmountable Tower (black), Dual Xeon EM64T, Intel E7520, 8 x SCA bays, Up to 16GB ECC Reg. DDR2, Tri-Red. 760W PS, 1xPCI Express x8, 5xPCI-X slots, Dual Gigabit LAN, VGA, Dual U320 SCSI
MB1114	SuperServer 6034H-X8RB - Super X6DH8-XG2 in SC833S-R760 in 3U Rackmount (black), Dual Xeon EM64T, Intel E7520, 8 x SCA bays, Up to 16GB ECC Reg. DDR2, Tri-Red. 760W PS, 1xPCI Express x8, 5xPCI-X slots, Dual Gigabit LAN, VGA, Dual U320 SCSI

MB1152 SuperServer 6024H-i2B - Super X6DHE-G2 in SC823i-550LP 2U Rack (black), Dual Xeon EM64T support, Intel E7520, 6xFixed IDE HDD, Up to 16GB ECC Reg. DDR2, 550W PS, 3xPCI Express/3xPCI-X LP Slots, Dual Gigabit LAN, VGA

MB1154 SuperServer 6024H-iB - Super X6DHE-G2 in SC823i-550LP 2U Rack (black), Dual Xeon EM64T support, Intel E7520, 6xFixed IDE HDD, Up to 32GB ECC Reg. DDR, 550W PS, 3xPCI Express/3xPCI-X LP Slots, Dual Gigabit LAN, VGA

MB1130 SuperServer 6024H-82RB - Super X6DH8-G2 in SC823S-R500RC 2U Rack (black), Dual Xeon EM64T, Intel E7520, 6xSCA HDD, Up to 16GB ECC Reg. DDR2, 500W Redundant PS, 3 x PCI-X Slot Riser, Dual Gigabit LAN, VGA, Dual U320 SCSI

MB1150 SuperServer 6024H-8RB - Super X6DH8-G in SC823S-R500LP 2U Rack (black), Dual Xeon EM64T, Intel E7520, 6xSCA HDD, Up to 32GB ECC Reg. DDR, 500W Redundant PS, 2xPCI Express/3xPCI-X/1xPCI LP Slots, Dual Gigabit LAN, VGA, Dual U320 SCSI

MB1158 SuperServer 6024H-TRB - Super X6DHT-G in SC823T-R500LP 2U Rack (black), Dual Xeon EM64T, Intel E7520, 6xSATA HDD, Up to 32GB ECC Reg. DDR, 500W Redundant PS, 2xPCI Express/3xPCI-X/1xPCI LP Slots, Dual Gigabit LAN, SATA RAID, VGA

MB1134 SuperServer 6014H-X8B - Super X6DHR-X8G in SC813S-500 1U Rackmount (black), Dual Xeon EM64T, Intel E7520, Up to 32GB LP ECC Reg. DDR, 4 x SCA bays, 500W Cold Swap PS, VGA, 2 x PCI-X Slots (Full + LP), Dual Gigabit LAN, Dual U320 SCSI

MB1133 SuperServer 6014H-82B - Super X6DHR-8G2 in SC813S-500 1U Rackmount (black), Dual Xeon EM64T, Intel E7520, Up to 16GB LP ECC Reg. DDR2, 4 x SCA bays, 500W Cold Swap PS, VGA, PCI Express x8 or PCI-X Slot, Dual Gigabit LAN, Dual U320 SCSI

MB1144 SuperServer 6014H-8B - Super X6DHR-8G in SC813S-500 1U Rackmount (black), Dual Xeon EM64T, Intel E7520, Up to 32GB LP ECC Reg. DDR, 4 x SCA bays, 500W Cold Swap PS, VGA, PCI Express x8 or PCI-X Slot, Dual Gigabit LAN, Dual U320 SCSI

MB1136 SuperServer 6014H-XiB - Super X6DHR-XiG in SC812i-420 1U Rackmount (black), Dual Xeon EM64T, Intel E7520, Up to 32GB LP ECC Reg. DDR, 3 x IDE bays, 420W Cold Swap PS, VGA, 2 x PCI-X Slots (Full + LP), Dual Gigabit LAN

MB1138 SuperServer 6014H-i2B - Super X6DHR-iG2 in SC812i-420 1U Rackmount (black), Dual Xeon EM64T, Intel E7520, Up to 16GB LP ECC Reg. DDR2, 3 x IDE bays, 420W Cold Swap PS, VGA, PCI Express x8 or PCI-X Slot, Dual Gigabit LAN

MB1146 SuperServer 6014H-iB - Super X6DHR-iG in SC812i-420 1U Rackmount (black), Dual Xeon EM64T, Intel E7520, Up to 32GB LP ECC Reg. DDR, 3 x IDE bays, 420W Cold Swap PS, VGA, PCI Express x8 or PCI-X Slot, Dual Gigabit LAN

MB1140 SuperServer 6014H-TB - Super X6DHR-TG in SC813T-500 1U Rackmount (black), Dual Xeon EM64T, Intel E7520, Up to 32GB LP ECC Reg. DDR, 4 x SATA bays, 500W Cold Swap PS, VGA, PCI Express x8 or PCI-X Slot, Dual Gigabit LAN

MB1141 SuperServer 6014P-8RB - Super X6DHP-8G in SC814S-R560 1U Rackmount (black), Dual Xeon EM64T, Intel E7520, Up to 24GB LP ECC Reg. DDR, 4 x SCA bays, 560W Hot Swap Redundant PS, VGA, PCI Express x8 or PCI-X Slot, Dual Gigabit LAN, Dual U320 SCSI

MB1143 SuperServer 6014P-82RB - Super X6DHP-8G2 in SC814S-R560 1U Rack (black), Dual Xeon EM64T, Intel E7520, Up to 16GB LP ECC Reg. DDR2, 4 x SCA bays, 560W Redundant PS, VGA, PCI Express x8 or PCI-X Slot, Dual Gigabit, Dual U320 SCSI

MB1185 SuperServer 6014P-TRB - Super X6DHP-TG in SC814+T-R560 1U Rackmount (black), Dual Xeon EM64T, Intel E7520, Up to 24GB LP ECC Reg. DDR, 4 x SATA bays, 560W Redundant PS, VGA, PCI Express x8 or PCI-X Slot, Dual Gigabit LAN, Marvell 4-port SATA

MB1118 SuperServer 7044A-82RB - Super X6DA8-G2 in SC942i-R760 Rackmountable Tower (black), Dual Xeon EM64T support, Intel E7525, Up to 16GB ECC Reg. DDR2, Tri-Red. 760W PS, PCI Express x16, Dual Gigabit LAN, Audio, Dual U320 SCSI

MB1035 Super P8SGA, Socket 775 P4, 0/4GB Dual Channel DDR400, Intel 915G Express (Grantsdale), Integrated Intel GMA 900 Graphics, (1)PCI Express x16 Slot (3)PCI Exp. x1 Slots (3)32-bit PCI Slots, Intel 82541GI Gig.LAN, (4) Serial ATA ports, ATX

MB1050 Super X6DA8-G2, Dual Socket 604 for Xeon 800MHz (EM64T), 0/16GB DDR2, 8x240-pin DIMM, Intel E7525 chipset, (1)PCI Express x16 Slot (1)PCI Exp. x4 Slot (3)64-bit PCI-X and (1)32-bit PCI Slots, Dual Gigabit LAN, Audio, Dual U320 SCSI, Ext ATX

MB1051 Super X6DAE-G2, Dual Socket 604 for Xeon 800MHz (EM64T), 0/16GB DDR2, 8x240-pin DIMM, Intel E7525 chipset, (1)PCI Express x16 Slot (1)PCI Exp. x4 Slot (3)64-bit PCI-X and (1)32-bit PCI Slots, Intel 82546GB Dual Gigabit LAN, Integrated Audio, Ext ATX

MB1052 Super X6DA8-G, Dual Socket 604 for Xeon 800MHz (EM64T), 0/32GB DDR, 8x184-pin DIMM, Intel E7525 chipset, Adaptec 2-CH Ultra320 SCSI, Gigabit LAN, Ext. ATX - Motherboard only

MB1055 Super X6DAT-G, Dual Socket 604 for Xeon 800MHz (EM64T), 0/32GB DDR, 8x184-pin DIMM, Intel E7525 chipset, Marvell SATA, Gigabit LAN, Ext. ATX - Motherboard only

MB1058 Super X6DAi-G, Dual Socket 604 for Xeon 800MHz (EM64T), 0/32GB DDR, 8x184-pin DIMM, Intel E7525 chipset, IDE, Gigabit LAN, Ext. ATX - Motherboard only

MB1053 Super X6DAL-TG, Dual Socket 604 for Xeon 800MHz (EM64T), 0/24GB DDR, 6x184-pin DIMM, Intel E7525 chipset, Marvell SATA, Gigabit LAN, ATX - Motherboard only

MB1056 Super X6DAL-XTG, Dual Socket 604 for Xeon 800MHz (EM64T), 0/24GB DDR, 6x184-pin DIMM, Intel E7525 chipset, Marvell SATA, Gigabit LAN, ATX - Motherboard only

MB1057 Super X6DAL-XG, Dual Socket 604 for Xeon 800MHz (EM64T), 0/24GB DDR, 6x184-pin DIMM, Intel E7525 chipset, IDE, Gigabit LAN, ATX - Motherboard only

MB1054 Super X6DAL-G, Dual Socket 604 for Xeon 800MHz (EM64T), 0/24GB DDR, 6x184-pin DIMM, Intel E7525 chipset, 2xSATA ports (RAID), (1)PCI Express x16 Slot (1)PCI Exp. x8 Slot (2)64-bit PCI-X and (2)32-bit PCI Slots, 82541GI Gigabit LAN, Audio, ATX

MB1061 Super X6DHE-G2, Dual Socket 604 for Xeon 800MHz (EM64T), Intel E7520 chipset, IDE, Dual Gigabit LAN, Ext. ATX - Motherboard only

MB1062 Super X6DH8-G2, Dual Socket 604 for Xeon 800MHz (EM64T), Intel E7520 chipset, Adaptec 2-CH Ultra320 SCSI, Dual Gigabit LAN, Ext. ATX - Motherboard only

MB1063 Super X6DHE-XG2, Dual Socket 604 for Xeon 800MHz (EM64T), Intel E7520 chipset, IDE, Dual Gigabit LAN, Ext. ATX - Motherboard only

MB1064 Super X6DH8-XG2, Dual Socket 604 for Xeon 800MHz (EM64T), Intel E7520 chipset, Adaptec 2-CH Ultra320 SCSI, Dual Gigabit LAN, Ext. ATX - Motherboard only

MB1065 Super X6DH8-G, Dual Socket 604 for Xeon 800MHz (EM64T), Intel E7520 chipset, Adaptec 2-CH Ultra320 SCSI, Dual Gigabit LAN, Ext. ATX - Motherboard only

MB1066 Super X6DHE-G, Dual Socket 604 for Xeon 800MHz (EM64T), Intel E7520 chipset, IDE, Dual Gigabit LAN, Ext. ATX - Motherboard only

MB1070 Super X6DVA-EG, Dual Socket 604 for Xeon 800MHz (EM64T), Intel E7320 chipset, IDE, Dual Gigabit LAN, ATX - Motherboard only

MB1071 Super X6DVA-4G, Dual Socket 604 for Xeon 800MHz (EM64T)0, Intel E7320 chipset, SCSI, Dual Gigabit LAN, ATX - Motherboard only

MB1008 Super P4SCA, Socket 478 for P4 (Hyper-Threading), 0/4GB Dual-Channel DDR400, 4xDIMMs, Intel E7210 chipset, 800/533/400MHz FSB, 4xPCI/ 3xISA Slots, Integrated VGA, 2xUSB 2.0, SATA RAID 0, Intel Gigabit LAN, ATX - Motherboard only

TYAN MOTHERBOARDS

Part #	Description
MB7028	Tyan Thunder K8S Pro (S2882G3NR-D) Dual Opteron w/ Dual Core Support, AMD-8131/8111, 0/16GB ECC Reg. DDR333/266, 8x184-pin DIMMs, 4x64-bit PCI-X, 1x32-bit PCI, SATA RAID, Dual Gigabit + 10/100 LAN, Ext. ATX - Motherboard Only
MB7030	Tyan Thunder K8S Pro (S2882UG3NR-D) Dual Opteron w/ Dual Core Support, AMD-8131/8111, 0/16GB ECC Reg. DDR333/266, 8x184-pin DIMMs, 4x64-bit 133MHz PCI-X, 1x32-bit PCI, SATA RAID, Dual Gigabit + 10/100 LAN, AIC7902W U320 SCSI - Motherboard Only

Revision

1. After microprocessor the next item considered to be most important for the computer is the motherboard.
2. A motherboard aggregates all of the PC's primary system components of a single printed circuit board (PCB).
3. The following figure shows where the major components are found on a typical motherboard. They are: CPU slot and socket, Chipset, Memory Sockets, BIOS ROM, CMOS Battery, Power connector, I/O connectors, and Expansion slots.
4. Among the components on the motherboard contributing to its importance are the chipset and its associated controllers.
5. Generally, a chipset does not incorporate all of the controllers used to direct the actions of every peripheral device on the PC.
6. There are two general types of mountings used to connect the processor onto the motherboard: sockets and slots.
7. There are four types of slot mountings used to attach microprocessors to motherboards: Slot 1 (SC-242 connector), Slot 2 (SC-330 connector), Slot A and Slot M.
8. It was common for an early PC to have the following separate chips: Math coprocessor interface, Clock generator, Bus controller chip, DMA controller, Programmable peripheral interface (PPI), Floppy disk controller (FDC), CRT controller and UART (universal asynchronous receiver transmitter).
9. The controllers and devices usually included in a chipset are as follows Memory controller, EIDE controller, PCI bridg, Real-time clock (RTC), DMA (Direct Memory Access) controllers, IrDA controller, Keyboard controller, PS/2 mouse controller, Secondary (Level 2 or L2) cache controller, and CMOS SRAM.
10. BIOS, in computing, stands for Basic Input/Output System also incorrectly known as Basic Integrated Operating System and occasionally Built In Operating System.
11. Two important characteristics of CMOS devices are high noise immunity and low static power supply drain.
12. A SIMM, or single in-line memory module, is a type of memory module used for random access memory in personal computers.

13. The first variant of SIMMs has 30 pins and provides 8 bits of data (9 bits in parity versions).
14. A DIMM, or dual in-line memory module, comprises a series of random access memory integrated circuits.
15. The XT bus architecture is an eight-bit ISA bus used by Intel 8086 and Intel 8088 systems in the IBM PC and IBM PC XT in the 1980s.
16. The Accelerated Graphics Port (also called Advanced Graphics Port, often shortened to AGP) is a high-speed point-to-point channel for attaching a graphics card to a computer's motherboard, primarily to assist in the acceleration of 3D computer graphics.
17. Intel released the first version of AGP; appropriately titled "AGP specification 1.0," in 1997. It included both the 1x and 2x speeds. Specification 2.0 documented AGP 4X and 3.0 documented 8X.
18. Dynamic random access memory (DRAM) is a type of random access memory that stores each bit of data in a separate capacitor within an integrated circuit.
19. Static random access memory (SRAM) is a type of semiconductor memory.
20. DDR2 SDRAM is very similar to DDR SDRAM, but doubles the minimum read or write unit again, to 4 consecutive words.
21. DDR3 continues the trend, doubling the minimum read or write unit to 8 consecutive words. This allows another doubling of bandwidth and external bus speed without having to change the speed of internal operations, just the width.
22. Burst EDO DRAM, could process four memory addresses in one burst, for a maximum of 5-1-1-1, saving an additional three clocks over optimally designed EDO memory.
23. Multibank RAM applies the interleaving technique for main memory to second level cache memory to provide a cheaper and faster alternative to SRAM.
24. The battery inside the PC keeps the clock working when the main power supply to the system is switched off, so that the next time when you switch on the system you will get correct time and date.
25. The Intel 865G chipset, designed for the Intel Pentium D processor (compatible with the lead free version of Intel 865G Chipsets supporting socket LGA775) and the Intel Pentium 4 processor supporting Hyper-Threading Technology, is a highly flexible and scalable solution that meets a broad range of demanding computing needs.
26. The Intel 910GL Express chipset brings compelling new capabilities to the desktop PC. Designed for the Intel Pentium 4 processor supporting Hyper-Threading Technology, the 910GL chipset features a decade's worth of innovation.
27. The Intel 915P Express Chipset, based on a new architecture, innovative technologies and high-bandwidth interfaces, is the newest discrete graphics chipset for the Intel Pentium 4 processor family.

Multiple Choice Questions

1. SIMM stands for :
   (a) Single In-line Memory Module
   (b) Single In-line Memory Mode
   (c) Solo In-line Memory Module
2. DIMM stands for :
   (a) Dual In-line Memory Mode

(b) Dual In-line Memory Module

(c) Duet In-line Memory Module

3. PPI stands for .

(a) Program Peripheral Interface

(b) Programmable Peripheral Interleave

(c) Programmable Peripheral Interface

4. DMA stand for :

(a) Direct Memory Access

(b) Direct Memory Accept

(c) Dual Memory Access

5. UART stand for :

(a) Universal Asynchronous Received Transmitter

(b) Universal Asynchronous Receiver Transistor

(c) Universal Asynchronous Receiver Transmitter

6. DRAM stands for :

(a) Direct Random Access Memory

(b) Dynamic Random Access Memory

(c) Dynamic Random Access Mode

7. RTC stand for :

(a) Real Time Clock

(b) Real Time Clear

(c) Road Time Clock

8. SRAM stands for :

(a) Static Ready Access Memory

(b) Static Random Access Mode

(c) Static Random Access Memory

True/False Questions

1. A motherboard aggregates all of the PC's primary system components of a single printed circuit board (PCB).
2. Among the components on the motherboard contributing to its importance are the chipset and its associated controllers.
3. There are two general types of mountings used to connect the processor onto the motherboard: sockets and slots.
4. There are four types of slot mountings used to attach microprocessors to motherboards: Slot 1 (SC-242 connector), Slot 2 (SC-330 connector), Slot A and Slot M.
5. BIOS, in computing, stands for Basic Input/Output System also correctly known as Basic Integrated Operating System and occasionally Built In Operating System.

6. A SIMM, or single in-line memory module, is a type of memory module used for random access memory in personal computers.
7. The first variant of SIMMs has 30 pins and provides 8 bits of data (9 bits in parity versions).
8. The XT bus architecture is an eight-bit ISA bus used by Intel 8086 and Intel 8088 systems in the IBM PC and IBM PC XT in the 1980s.
9. Intel released the first version of AGP; appropriately titled "AGP specification 1.0," in 1977. It included both the 1x and 2x speeds. Specification 2.0 documented AGP 4X and 3.0 documented 8X.
10. Dynamic random access memory (DRAM) is a type of random access memory that stores each bit of data in a separate capacitor within an integrated circuit.
11. Static random access memory (SRAM) is a type of semiconductor memory.
12. DDR2 SDRAM is very similar to DDR SDRAM, but doubles the minimum read or write unit again, to 4 consecutive words.
13. Burst EDO DRAM, could process four memory addresses in one burst, for a maximum of 5-1-1-1, saving an additional three clocks over optimally designed EDO memory.
14. The battery inside the PC keeps the clock working when the main power supply to the system is switched off, so that the next time when you switch on the system you will get correct time and date.
15. The Intel 910GL Express chipset brings compelling new capabilities to the desktop PC. Designed for the Intel Pentium 4 processor supporting Hyper-Threading Technology, the 910GL chipset features a decade's worth of innovation.

Descriptive Questions

1. Describe Motherboard.
2. Describe the various components of the Motherboard.
3. Describe PC chipset.
4. What is Controller Chip?
5. Describe the various Sockets and Slots.
6. What are the characteristics of Chipsets?
7. Describe the following terms:

BIOS	CMOS
SIMM	DIMM
RIMM	DRAM
SRAM	DDR SDRAM
SSR2 SDRAM	DDR3 SDRAM
EDO DRAM	BEDO DRAM
MDRAM	SGRAM
External Battery Connector	External Battery Connector
Optional Keyboard Connector	Power Connector
AT Power Supply	ATX Power Supply
Keylock and Power-on LED Connector	Speaker Connector

Turbo Mode Selection
Reset Connector
Front Panel Function Connector
CD Audio Input Connector
Telephony Input Connector
BIOS ROM
Expansion slots
Turbo Mode LED Connector
Infra-Red (IR) Connector
CPU Fan Connector
Auxiliary Input Connector
Integrated Function Connector
CMOS Battery

8. Describe the various bus slots.
9. Where is battery placed in the motherboard?
10. What is Super I/O Chip?
11. Describe the various connectors of motherboard.
12. Describe Intel 865G Motherboard
13. What are the features of Intel 910GL Motherboard?
14. Describe Intel 915 Motherboard.

Answers to Objective Type Questions

Multiple Choice Questions

1. a	2. b	3. c	4. a
5. c	6. b	7. a	8. c

True False Questions

1. T	2. T	3. T	4. T
5. F	6. T	7. T	8. T
9. F	10. T	11. T	12. T
13. T	14. T	15. T	

4 Buses

What is a Bus?

Bus is an electronic road along which signals are send from one part of the computer to another.

Thin lines you see on the Motherboard are the buses that take data, address, control signals and power from one place to another on the motherboard.

Depending on their use, bus is divided into three major types:

- Data bus
- Address bus
- Control bus

When someone talks about the bus, without specifying its type, then most probably he is talking about the data bus.

Data Bus

The data bus is used to move data from one place to another. The number of the data lines provided in the bus is very important factor that determines the speed of this data transfer.

Address Bus

The address bus is used to select a particular memory location to read or write the data Maximum memory that CPU can address depends on the size of its address bus.

$$\text{Addressable locations} = 2^{\text{(total address lines)}}$$

If you have 3 address lines total addressable locations will be $2^3 = 8$, 32 bit PCI local bus uses 32 address lines and it can address $2^{32} = 4{,}294{,}967{,}296$ different locations or 4096 Mega Bytes of memory.

Control Bus

The control bus is used to send control and timing signals between various parts of the computer.

Factors Affecting Processing Speed

How Registers Affect Speed

The size of the registers (16-bit register or 32-bit register) which is also called the word size indicate the amount of data with which the computer can work. The bigger the size of register, the faster the computer can process a set of data. Registers retain information on a temporary basis. They are not considered part of main memory. Registers have the ability to receive information, hold it temporarily and then pass it on as directed by supervisory control unit.

There are several type of registers:

1. Instruction Register : It holds the instruction which is being executed.
2. Address Register: It holds the storage location address.
3. Accumulator: It collects results.

Memory and Computing Power

More RAM make the computer run faster. The computer does not necesarily have to load anentire program into memory to run it, but the more ofthe program it can fit into memory, the faster theprogram will run. The computer loads only the most essential parts into memory. Whent it needs access to other parts of the program on the disk, it can unload, or swapout non essential parts and swap in program code or data it needs.

Computer's Internal Clock

Every microcomputer has a system clock made up of quartz crystal. The molecules in the crystal vibrate millions of times per second which is constant. The system uses the vibration of the crystal (quartz) in the system clock to time its processing operations. The clock speed is measured in hertz. Pentium CPU today have clock speed from 75 MHz to 200 MHz.

RISC: More Is Not Always Better

An important aspect of computer system is the design of the instruction set for the processor; because it determines the way, machine language programs are constructed. Early computers had small and simple instruction sets; this was because of the high cost of hardware. With the invention of integrated circuits, computer instruction set tend to increase both in number and complexity. For example, the most common microprocessors found in small computers today viz; 80x86 and 680x0 families uses large (from 100 to 200) instruction sets.

A computer with a large number of instructions is classified as a complex instruction set computer (CISC).

CISC Characteristics

The main reason for provision of a complex instruction set is due to the requirement of the simplification of compilation, and the requirement in the improvement of the overall computer performance. The task of a compiler is to generate a sequence of machine instructions for each high level language statement. The task is simplified if there are machine instructions that implement the statements directly.

The essential goal of a CISC architecture is to attempt to provide a single machine instruction for each statement in a high level language.

Examples of CISC architecture are:

IBM 370 and VAX

Another characteristics of CISC architecture is the incorporation of variable-length instruction formats.

RISC Characteristics

A newer theory in the design of microprocessor holds that, if the instruction set is kept small and simple each instruction will execute much faster, allowing the processor to complete more instructions during a given period. This design results in a faster and less expensive processors. CPUs designed around this methodology are called reduced instruction set computers (RISC). The major characteristics of a RISC methodology are:

1. Relatively few instructions
2. Memory access limited to load and store instructions
3. All operations done within the registers of the CPU
4. Fixed length, easily decoded instruction format

RISC technology is used extensively in mid-size computers such as the IBM RS/6000 and high-end UNIX workstations such as those built by Hewlett Packard & Sun Microsystem.

RISC CPus are also used extensively in printers and other intelligent devices that have their own internal CPUs.

RISC technology are designed and manufactured by the same companies that produce CISC technology.

In 1989, Intel introduced i860 RISC Chip of 64-bit, which contains more than 1 million transistors. Newer RISC chip include the Intel i960, the Motorola 88100. Sun Microsystems are also produced a RISC chip known as SPARC, which it uses in its UNIX workstations.

Revision

1. Bus is an electronic road along which signals are send from one part of the computer to another.
2. Depending on their use, bus is divided into three major types: Data bus, Address bus and Control bus
3. The data bus is used to move data from one place to another. The number of the data lines provided in the bus is very important factor that determines the speed of this data transfer.
4. The address bus is used to select a particular memory location to read or write the data Maximum memory that CPU can address depends on the size of its address bus.
5. The control bus is used to send control and timing signals between various parts of the computer.
6. The size of the registers (16-bit register or 32-bit register) which is also called the word size indicate the amount of data with which the computer can work.
7. There are several type of registers: Instruction Register : It holds the instruction which is being executed; Address Register: It holds the storage location address and Accumulator: It collects results.
8. Every microcomputer has a system clock made up of quartz crystal.
9. An important aspect of computer system is the design of the instruction set for the processor; because it determines the way, machine language programs are constructed.
10. The main reason for provision of a complex instruction set is due to the requirement of the simplification of compilation, and the requirement in the improvement of the overall computer performance.

11. The major characteristics of a RISC methodology are: Relatively few instructions; Memory access limited to load and store instructions; All operations done within the registers of the CPU; and Fixed length, easily decoded instruction format.

Multiple Choice Questions

1. Three types of bus are, Data bus, Address bus and :
   (a) **Control Bus** (b) Cover bus (c) Clear bus
2. CISC stands for :
   (a) Complex Instruction Save Computer
   (b) **Complex Instruction Set Computer**
   (c) Complex Instruction Small Computer
3. RISC stands for .
   (a) Reduced Instruction Save Computers
   (b) Reduced Instruction Small Computers
   (c) **Reduced Instruction Set Computers**

True/False Questions

1. Depending on their use, bus is divided into three major types: Data bus, Address bus and Control bus
2. The address bus is used to select a particular memory location to read or write the data Maximum memory that CPU can address depends on the size of its address bus.
3. The control bus is not used to send control and timing signals between various parts of the computer.
4. There are several type of registers: Instruction Register : It holds the instruction which is being executed; Address Register: It holds the storage location address and Accumulator: It collects results.
5. Every microcomputer does not have a system clock made up of quartz crystal.
6. The main reason for provision of a complex instruction set is due to the requirement of the simplification of compilation, and the requirement in the improvement of the overall computer performance.

Descriptive Questions

1. Describe the vaious buses.
2. What are CISC and RISC?
3. What factors affect the processing speed?

Answers to Objective Type Questions

Multiple Choice Questions

1. a 2. b 3. c

True False Questions

1. T 2. T 3. F 4. T
5. F 6. T

5 Memory

Memory Basics

So far at every stage we have said that computer cannot think on its own and cannot remember anything unless we store in hard disk with save. While working all the information is stored in what is called the memory of the computer till we press the button to save it. Till that point all the information and results are stored in memory. So usually a big memory means a faster and more useful computer.

A PC's memory is made up of electronic components in which the PC temporarily stores data and instructions. Technically, any device that stores data or instructions on the PC can be called memory, including the hard disk, floppy disks, ROM, CMOS, RAM and cache.

However, what is commonly referred to as memory on the PC is its primary storage, which is also known as system memory, temporary storage or RAM. With the exception of ROM, the other forms of storage (hard disk, floppy disk, CD-ROM and the like) are known as secondary storage.

ROM

It's logical then that data stored on read-only memory (ROM) cannot be changed, as its name implies. ROM also has the added feature of being nonvolatile, which means that it can keep its contents even without a power source. This makes it ideal for storing the PC's startup instructions and system BIOS (Basic Input/Output System). While virtually all ROM chips are packed in a DIP (dual inline packaging) form, there are three types of ROM used in a PC:

PROM (programmable read-only memory)

This type of ROM chip is programmed using a special type of programming device called a PROM burner, which permanently stores machine language (binary instructions) code on the PROM chip. A PROM chips is also referred to as OTP (One Time Programmable) memory.

EPROM (erasable programmable read-only memory)

This type of ROM, pronounced "e-prom," is erasable and can be reprogrammed. Unlike a PROM chip that cannot be reused and can only be thrown out when it becomes obsolete, an EPROM chip can be reprogrammed and reused. An EPROM has a quartz window on the face of the chip that exposes the chip's interior circuits. When ultraviolet (UV) light is shined through this window, it causes a chemical reaction that erases the EPROM. In order to reprogram an EPROM, it must be removed from the computer, erased with UV light and then reprogrammed on a PROM programmer.

EEPROM (electronically erasable programmable read-only memory)

Most newer PCs now include an EEPROM (pronounced-e-prom") that can be reprogrammed like an EPROM, but unlike the EPROM doesn't need to be removed from the PC to be reprogrammed. An EEPROM can be reprogrammed, a process called flashing, using specialized software that runs on your PC. An EEPROM is also referred to as flash ROM. Flashing lets you upgrade your computer's BIOS easily without removing and replacing the ROM chip. One thing that all DIP chips suffer from including removable and replaceable PROMs and EPROMs is a condition called chip creep. DIP chips are inserted into what are called through-hole sockets and can and do squirm out of their sockets. Should a ROM chip creep out of its socket, it can cause startup problems. If you have an older motherboard that includes removable DIP ROM or memory chips, you should check them occasionally for creep.

RAM

RAM or Random Access Memory is the main memory inside the computer. It is used to store program, data and results. It is called Random acsess because this memory is organized in such a way that any part of the memory can be accessed without serially going through all the previous memory locations

A better term to describe the RAM would be Read/Write Memory. One can read the information stored inside the RAM as well as write or store information in it.

Two common type of RAM are:

DRAM (Dynamic RAM)
SRAM (Static RAM)

Dynamic RAM (DRAM)

A dynamic RAM (DRAM) is cost wise cheaper than the static RAM (SRAM), and it is the main reason of using the DRAM as the main memory.

DRAM utilizes capacitors to store information, so the problem with the DRAM is once data is stored into it, it can't retain the data for long unless the data is refreshed periodically. Refreshing of a DRAM memory is done by rewriting the entire content of the memory every few millisecond. For this a special refresh circuitry is used.

Unless the DRAM is refreshed every few milliseconds it loses its content.

Static RAM (SRAM)

Unlike the DRAM, SRAM memory retains the information stored inside it, as long as the power supply is provided to the SRAM chip.

One need not refresh the information stored in the SRAM.

Because the SRAM does not require any refresh circuits, the circuitry required to interface SRAM is very simple compared to the interface circuitry for the DRAM chips. Also, the SRAM is much faster than the DRAM.

SRAM generally use flip-flops to store the information.

DDR SDRAM

DDR SDRAM or double-data-rate synchronous dynamic random access memory is a class of memory integrated circuit used in computers. It achieves greater bandwidth than the preceding single-data-rate SDRAM by transferring data on the rising and falling edges of the clock signal (double pumped). Effectively, it nearly doubles the transfer rate without increasing the frequency of the front side bus. Thus a 100 MHz DDR system has an effective clock rate of 200 MHz when compared to equivalent SDR SDRAM, the "SDR" being a retrospective designation.

With data being transferred 64 bits at a time DDR RAM gives a transfer rate of [mbcr x 2 x 64] / 8; annotated it looks like this: (memory bus clock rate) × 2 (for dual rate) × 64 (number of bits transferred) / 8 (number of bits/byte). Thus with a bus frequency of 100 MHz, DDR-SDRAM gives a max transfer rate of 1600 MB/s.

JEDEC has set standards for speeds of DDR SDRAM, divided into two parts: The first specification is for memory chips and the second is for memory modules.

As DDR is superseded by the newer DDR2, the older version is often now referred to as DDR1.

Chip specification

- DDR-200: DDR-SDRAM memory chips specified to operate at 100 MHz
- DDR-266: DDR-SDRAM memory chips specified to operate at 133 MHz
- DDR-333: DDR-SDRAM memory chips specified to operate at 166 MHz
- DDR-400: DDR-SDRAM memory chips specified to operate at 200 MHz

Chip characteristics

- DRAM density. Size of the chip in mebibits. Example: 256 Mibit — 32 MiB chip.
- DRAM organization. Written in the form of 64M x 4, where 64M is a number of storage units (64 million), x4 (pronounced «by 4») — number of bits per chip, which equals the number of bits per storage unit. There are x4 and x8 DDR chips. The former allows the use of advanced error correction features like Chipkill, memory scrubbing and Intel SDDC, while the latter chips are somewhat more expensive.

Stick/module specification

- PC-1600: DDR-SDRAM memory module specified to operate at 100 MHz using DDR-200 chips, 1.600 GB/s bandwidth

- PC-2100: DDR-SDRAM memory module specified to operate at 133 MHz using DDR-266 chips, 2.133 GB/s bandwidth
- PC-2700: DDR-SDRAM memory module specified to operate at 166 MHz using DDR-333 chips, 2.667 GB/s bandwidth
- PC-3200: DDR-SDRAM memory module specified to operate at 200 MHz using DDR-400 chips, 3.200 GB/s bandwidth

Note: All RAM speeds in-between or above these listed specifications are not standardized by JEDEC — most often they are simply manufacturer optimizations using higher-tolerance or overvolted chips.

The package sizes in which DDR SDRAM is manufactured are also standardised by JEDEC.

There is no architectural difference between DDR SDRAM designed for different clock frequencies, e.g. PC-1600 (designed to run at 100 MHz) and PC-2100 (designed to run at 133 MHz). The number simply designates the speed that the chip is guaranteed to run at. Hence DDR SDRAM can be run at lower clock speeds than it was made for (underclocking) or higher clock speeds than it was made for (overclocking).

DDR SDRAM DIMMs have 184 pins (as opposed to 168 pins on SDR SDRAM, or, 240 pins on DDR-2), and can be differentiated from SDRAM DIMMs by the number of notches (DDR SDRAM has one, SDR SDRAM has two). DDR operates at a voltage of 2.5 V, compared to 3.3 V for SDR SDRAM. This can significantly reduce power usage.

Many new chipsets use these memory types in dual-channel or even quad channel configurations, which doubles or quadruples the effective bandwidth.

Variations of 1 GiB PC2100 Registered DDR SDRAM module

Module size	Number of chips	Chip size	Chip organization	Number of rows (ranks)
1 GiB	36	256 Mibit	64M x 4	2
1 GiB	18	512 Mibit	64M x 8	2
1 GiB	18	512 Mibit	128M x 4	1

DDR2 SDRAM

In electronic engineering, DDR2 SDRAM or double-data-rate two synchronous dynamic random access memory is a random access memory technology used for high speed storage of the working data of a computer or other digital electronic device.

It is a part of the SDRAM (synchronous dynamic random access memory) family of technologies, which is one of many DRAM (dynamic random access memory) implementations, and is an evolutionary improvement over its predecessor, DDR SDRAM (double-data-rate synchronous dynamic random access memory).

Its primary benefit is the ability to run its bus at twice the speed of the memory cells it contains, thus enabling faster bus speeds and higher peak throughputs than earlier technologies. This is achieved at the cost of higher latency.

Like all SDRAM implementations, DDR2 stores memory in memory cells that are activated with the use of a clock signal to synchronize their operation with an external data bus. Like DDR before it, DDR2 cells transfer data both on the rising and falling edge of the clock (a technique called double pumping). The key difference between DDR and DDR2 is that in DDR2 the bus is clocked at twice the speed of the memory cells, so four words of data can be transferred per memory cell cycle. Thus, without speeding up the memory cells themselves, DDR2 can effectively operate at twice the bus speed of DDR.

DDR2's bus frequency is boosted by electrical interface improvements, on-die termination, prefetch buffers and off-chip drivers. However, latency is greatly increased as a trade-off. The DDR2 prefetch buffer is 4 bits deep, whereas it is 2 bits deep for DDR and 8 bits deep for DDR3. While DDR SDRAM has typical read latencies of between 2 and 3 bus cycles, DDR2 may have read latencies between 3 and 9 cycles. Because of this higher latency, DDR SDRAM running at the same bus speed as DDR2 is generally considered superior; DDR2 is, however, able to run at substantially higher bus speeds which equates to an overall increase in throughput. Another cost of the increased speed is the requirement that the chips are packaged in a more expensive and more difficult to assemble BGA package as compared to the TSSOP package of the previous memory generations such as DDR and SDRAM. This packaging change was necessary to maintain signal integrity at higher speeds.

Power savings are achieved primarily due to an improved manufacturing process through die shrinkage, resulting in a drop in operating voltage (1.8 V compared to DDR's 2.5 V). The lower memory clock frequency may also enable power reductions in applications that do not require the highest available speed.

Specification standards

Chips

Standard name	Memory clock	I/O Bus clock	Data transfers per second
DDR2-400	100 MHz	200 MHz	400 Million
DDR2-533	133 MHz	266 MHz	533 Million
DDR2-667	166 MHz	333 MHz	667 Million
DDR2-800	200 MHz	400 MHz	800 Million
DDR2-1066	266 MHz	533 MHz	1066 Million

Modules

For use in PCs, DDR2 SDRAM is supplied in DIMMs with 240 pins and a single locating notch. DIMMs are identified by their peak transfer capacity (often called bandwidth).

Module name	Bus clock	Chip type	Peak transfer rate
PC2-3200	200 MHz	DDR2-400	3.200 GB/s

PC2-4200	266 MHz	DDR2-533	4.264 GB/s
PC2-5300	333 MHz	DDR2-667	5.336 GB/s[1]
PC2-6400	400 MHz	DDR2-800	6.400 GB/s
PC2-8500 (planned)	533 MHz	DDR2-1066	8.500 GB/s

DDR2-xxx (or DDR-xxx) denotes effective clockspeed, whereas PC2-xxxx (or PC-xxxx) denotes theoretical bandwidth (though it is often rounded up or down). Bandwidth is calculated by taking transfers per second and multiplying by eight. This is because DDR2 memory modules transfer data on a bus that is 64 data bits wide, and since a byte is comprised of 8 bits, this equates to 8 bytes of data per transfer.

Optionally implement ECC, which is an extra data byte lane used for correcting minor errors and detecting major errors for better reliability. Modules with ECC are identified by an additional ECC in their designation. PC2-4200 ECC is a PC2-4200 module with ECC.

Be "registered", which improves signal integrity (and hence potentially clock speed) by electrically buffering the signals at a cost of an extra clock of increased latency. Those modules are identified by an additional R in their designation, PC2-4200R is a registered PC2-4200 module, PC2-4200R ECC is the same module but with additional ECC.

DD3 SDRAM

DDR3 SDRAM or double-data-rate three synchronous dynamic random access memory is the name of the new DDR memory standard that is being developed as the successor to DDR2 SDRAM.

The memory comes with a promise of a power consumption reduction of 40% compared to current commercial DDR2 modules, due to DDR3's 90 nm fabrication technology, allowing for lower operating currents and voltages (1.5 V, compared to DDR2's 1.8 V or DDR's 2.5 V). "Dual-gate" transistors will be used to reduce leakage of current.

DDR3's prefetch buffer width is 8 bit, whereas DDR2's is 4 bit, and DDR's is 2 bit.

Theoretically, these modules could transfer data at the effective clockrate of 800-1600MHz (for a single clock bandwidth of 400-800MHz), compared to DDR2's current range of 400-1066 MHz (200-533 MHz) or DDR's range of 200-600 MHz (100-300 MHz). To date, such bandwidth requirements have been mainly on the graphics market, where fast transfer of information between framebuffers is required.

DDR3 sticks maintain the 240-pin DIMM interface of DDR2, allowing DDR3 compatible chipsets to host DDR2 modules (though not both types at once).

Prototypes were announced in early 2005, while the DDR3 specification is expected to be publicly available in mid-2007. Supposedly, Intel has preliminarily announced that they expect to be able to offer support for it in mid 2007 with a version of their upcoming Bearlake chipset. AMD's roadmap indicates their own adoption of DDR3 to come in 2008.

The GDDR3 memory, with a similar name but an entirely dissimilar technology, has been in use for several years in high-end graphic cards such as ones from NVIDIA or ATI Technologies, and as main system memory on the Xbox 360. It is sometimes incorrectly referred to as "DDR3".

Spec standards

Chips

- DDR3-800 : DDR3-SDRAM memory chips specified to run at 100 MHz, I/O clock at 400 MHz
- DDR3-1066: DDR3-SDRAM memory chips specified to run at 133 MHz, I/O clock at 533 MHz
- DDR3-1333: DDR3-SDRAM memory chips specified to run at 166 MHz, I/O clock at 667 MHz
- DDR3-1600: DDR3-SDRAM memory chips specified to run at 200 MHz, I/O clock at 800 MHz

Sticks/Modules

- PC3-6400: DDR3-SDRAM memory stick specified to run at 400 MHz using DDR3-800 chips, 6.40 GB/s bandwidth
- PC3-8500: DDR3-SDRAM memory stick specified to run at 533 MHz using DDR3-1066 chips, 8.53 GB/s bandwidth
- PC3-10600: DDR3-SDRAM memory stick specified to run at 667 MHz using DDR3-1333 chips, 10.67 GB/s bandwidth
- PC3-12800: DDR3-SDRAM memory stick specified to run at 800 MHz using DDR3-1600 chips, 12.80 GB/s bandwidth

Features

DDR3 SDRAM Components:

- Introduction of asynchronous RESET pin
- Support of system level flight time compensation
- On-DIMM Mirror friendly DRAM ballout
- Introduction of CWL (CAS Write Latency) per speed bin
- On-die IO calibration engine
- READ and WRITE calibration

DDR3 Modules

- Fly-by command/address/control bus with On-DIMM termination

- High precision calibration resistors

Advantages compared to DDR2

- Higher bandwidth (up to 1600 MHz)
- Performance increase at low power
- Longer battery life in laptops
- Enhanced low power features and thermal design

Disadvantages compared to DDR2

- Commonly higher CAS Latency
- Lower MFIBS per Quad Cycle

DDR1, DDR2 and DDR4 Memory

DDR SDRAM or double-data-rate synchronous dynamic random access memory is a class of memory integrated circuit used in computers. It achieves greater bandwidth than the preceding single-data-rate SDRAM by transferring data on the rising and falling edges of the clock signal (double pumped). Effectively, it nearly doubles the transfer rate without increasing the frequency of the front side bus.

Thus, a system with a 100 MHz front side bus has an effective clock rate of 200 MHz when DDR SDRAM memory is installed. The same system using SDR (single data rate) SDRAM, will not have its front side bus rate doubled and be limited to a 100 MHz front side bus speed.

With data being transferred 64 bits at a time, DDR SDRAM gives a transfer rate of [mbcr x 2 x 64] / 8; annotated it looks like this: (memory bus clock rate) × 2 (for dual rate) × 64 (number of bits transferred) / 8 (number of bits/byte). Thus with a bus frequency of 100 MHz, DDR-SDRAM gives a max transfer rate of 1600 MB/s.

JEDEC has set standards for speeds of DDR SDRAM, divided into two parts: The first specification is for memory chips and the second is for memory modules. As DDR is superseded by the newer DDR2, the older version is often now referred to as DDR1.

Chips and modules

Standard name	*Memory clock*	*Time between signals*	*I/O Bus clock*	*Data transfers per second*	*Module name*	*Peak transfer rate*
DDR-200	100 MHz	10 ns	100 MHz	200 Million	PC-1600	1.600 GB/s
DDR-266	133 MHz	7.5 ns	133 MHz	266 Million	PC-2100	2.133 GB/s
DDR-333	166 MHz	6 ns	166 MHz	333 Million	PC-2700	2.667 GB/s
DDR-400	200 MHz	5 ns	200 MHz	400 Million	PC-3200	3.200 GB/s

All above listed are specified by JEDEC as JESD79. All RAM speeds in-between or above these listed specifications are not standardized by JEDEC — most often they are simply manufacturer optimizations using higher-tolerance or overvolted chips.

The package sizes in which DDR SDRAM is manufactured are also standardised by JEDEC.

DDR SDRAM memory modules have 184 pins and one notch

There is no architectural difference between DDR SDRAM designed for different clock frequencies, e.g. PC-1600 (designed to run at 100 MHz) and PC-2100 (designed to run at 133 MHz). The number simply designates the speed that the chip is guaranteed to run at. Hence DDR SDRAM can be run at lower clock speeds than it was made for (underclocking) or higher clock speeds than it was made for (overclocking).

DDR SDRAM DIMMs have 184 pins (as opposed to 168 pins on SDRAM, or, 240 pins on DDR2 SDRAM), and can be differentiated from SDRAM DIMMs by the number of notches (DDR SDRAM has one, SDRAM has two). DDR SDRAM operates at a voltage of 2.5 V, compared to 3.3 V for SDRAM. This can significantly reduce power usage. Note: some DIMMs have nominal voltage of 2.6 V.

Many new chipsets use these memory types in dual-channel configurations, which doubles or quadruples the effective bandwidth.

Revision

1. A PC's memory is made up of electronic components in which the PC temporarily stores data and instructions.
2. It's logical then that data stored on read-only memory (ROM) cannot be changed, as its name implies.
3. A PROM chips is also referred to as OTP (One Time Programmable) memory.
4. An EPROM has a quartz window on the face of the chip that exposes the chip's interior circuits.
5. EPROM (erasable programmable read-only memory) is the type of ROM, pronounced "e-prom," can be reprogrammed.
6. EEPROM (pronounced-e-prom") that can be reprogrammed like an EPROM, but unlike the EPROM doesn't need to be removed from the PC to be reprogrammed.
7. RAM or Random Access Memory is the main memory inside the computer.
8. DDR SDRAM or double-data-rate synchronous dynamic random access memory is a class of memory integrated circuit used in computers.
9. DDR2 SDRAM or double-data-rate two synchronous dynamic random access memory is a random access memory technology used for high speed storage of the working data of a computer or other digital electronic device.
10. DDR3 SDRAM or double-data-rate three synchronous dynamic random access memory is the name of the new DDR memory standard that is being developed as the successor to DDR2 SDRAM.

Multiple Choice Questions

1. EPROM stands for :
   (a) Erasable Programmable Read Only Memory
   (b) Electric Programmable Read Only Memory
   (c) Erasable Program Read Only Memory
2. DDR SDRAM stands for :
   (a) Double Data Ratio Synchronous Dynamic Random Access Memory

(b) Double Data Rate Synchronous Dynamic Random Access Memory

(c) Double Data Rate Synchronous Dynamic Random Access Mode

3. DDR3 SDRAM stands for .

(a) Double Data Rate Two Synchronous Dynamic Random Access Memory

(b) Double Data Rate To Synchronous Dynamic Random Access Memory

(c) Double Data Rate Three Synchronous Dynamic Random Access Memory

True/False Questions

1. It's logical then that data stored on read-only memory (ROM) cannot be changed, as its name implies.
2. An EPROM has a quartz window on the face of the chip that exposes the chip's interior circuits.
3. RAM or Random Access Memory is not the main memory inside the computer.
4. DDR SDRAM or double-data-rate synchronous dynamic random access memory is a class of memory integrated circuit used in computers.
5. DDR3 SDRAM or double-data-rate three synchronous dynamic random access memory is the name of the new DDR memory standard that is being developed as the successor to DDR2 SDRAM.

Descriptive Questions

1. How is memory used in personal computer?
2. Describe the following terms:

ROM	RAM
DRAM	SRAM
DDR SDRAM	DDR2 SDRAM
DD3 SDRAM	

Answers to Objective Type Questions

Multiple Choice Questions

1. a 2. b 3. c

True False Questions

1. T 2. T 3. F 4. T
5. T

6 HDD

Introduction

It is also called as mass-storage device. Like floppy disks, hard disks store data in tracks that are divided into sectors. A hard disk is a stack of metal platters that spin on one spindle, like a stack of rigid floppy disks. Each platter is coated with iron oxide and the entire unit is encased in a sealed chamber to make it free from dust and other contamination.

The hard disks are sealed inside an airtight vacuum chamber. This allows the heads of the hard disk to fly much closer to the surface of the disk, also allowing much greater precision. In fact, the heads of hard disks fly so close to the surface of the disk that if a dust particle, a human hair or even a fingerprint were placed on the disk it would bridge the gap between the heads and the disk, causing the heads to crash. A head crash, in which the head touches the disk destroys the data stored in the area of the crash and can destroy a read/write head as well.

Because materials such as hair, fingerprints, and dust or smoke particles are much thicker than the gap between the disk and the read/write head, they can cause the head to crash. The increased surface areas provided by multiple platters is the main reasons that hard disk can store so much more data than floppy disks. Waving a magnet past an electric coil like the one in a drive's read/write head causes a current to flow through the coil. The interesting thing is that the faster you move a magnet, the larger the current it generates in the coil. Conversely, the more current you apply to the magnet the stronger its magnetic field becomes.

Hard disk spins at around 3600 RPM instead of a floppy disk's 300 RPM. Some hard drives spin as fast as 5400 RPM. As the hard disk spins faster, the drive's heads can use a lower-intensity current to polarize a spot on the disk. When the drive head reads data from the surface of the disk the fast speed of the disk amplifies the intensity of the current induced in the read head.

Some hard-disk drives hold as many as 12 disks but both sides of disks are not always used. With hard disk, the number of sides that the disk uses in specified by the number of heads. For example, a particular harddisk drive might have six disk platters (12 sides) but only 10 heads, indicating that two sides are not used to store data. Often these are the top side of the top disk and the bottom side of bottom disk.

As hard disks are actually a stack of platters, we use new term cylinder to refer to the same track across all the disk sides. Hard disks generally store 512 bytes of data in a sector, but because of their higher tolerance hard disk can have more sectors per track-54, 63 or more.

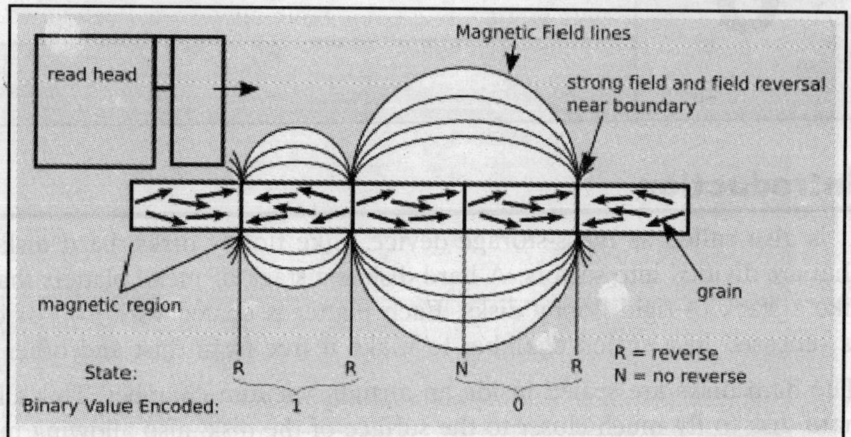

A cross section of the magnetic surface of Hard Disk in action.

When reading from or writing to a hard disk, all access arms are moved to the appropriate cylinder. Although the addressing schemes vary considerably between disks, the address normally will include the cylinder (or track), the recording surface, and the sector number. PC users, who never seem to have enough hard disk storage space, may turn to a removable hard disk cartridge. Once full, a removable hard disk cartridge can be replaced with a fresh one. In effect, a removable cartridge is as portable as a diskette, but the disk cartridge holds much more data.

A concept of using several small disks that work together as a unit is called a redundant array of inexpensive disks or simply RAID. The group of connected disks operates as if it were just one large disk, but it speeds up reading and writing by having multiple access paths. The data file for, say automobile factory tools, may be spread across several disks, thus if the computer is used to look up tools for several workers, the computer need not read the data in turn but instead read them at the same time in parallel.

Working of Hard Disk

Disks are rotated continuously so that read/write heads mounted on movable or fixed arms can read or write programs or data to and from the disk. The Hard Disk Drive can be classified into two sections Mechanical Section and Electronic Section. The Mechanical Section consists of the followings which are explained accordingly.

Spindle Motor : One part of a hard disk, around which the platters rotate.

Disk drive : The motor that actually rotates the disk, plus the read/write heads and associated mechanisms, usually in a mountable housing. Sometimes, it is used synonymously to mean the entire disk subsystem

Platters : The platters are no. of disks made of aluminum or plastic coated with a magnetic material. The data is stored on the platter.

Read/Write Head : The part of the hard disk which writes data to or reads data from a platter It functions like a coiled wire that reacts to a changing magnetic field by producing a minute current that can be detected and amplified by the electronics of the disk drive.

Head Actuator : In a disk drive, the mechanism which moves the read/write head radially across the surface of the platter of the disk drive.

Electronic Section of HDD : The Electronic Section consists of a Logic card which controls

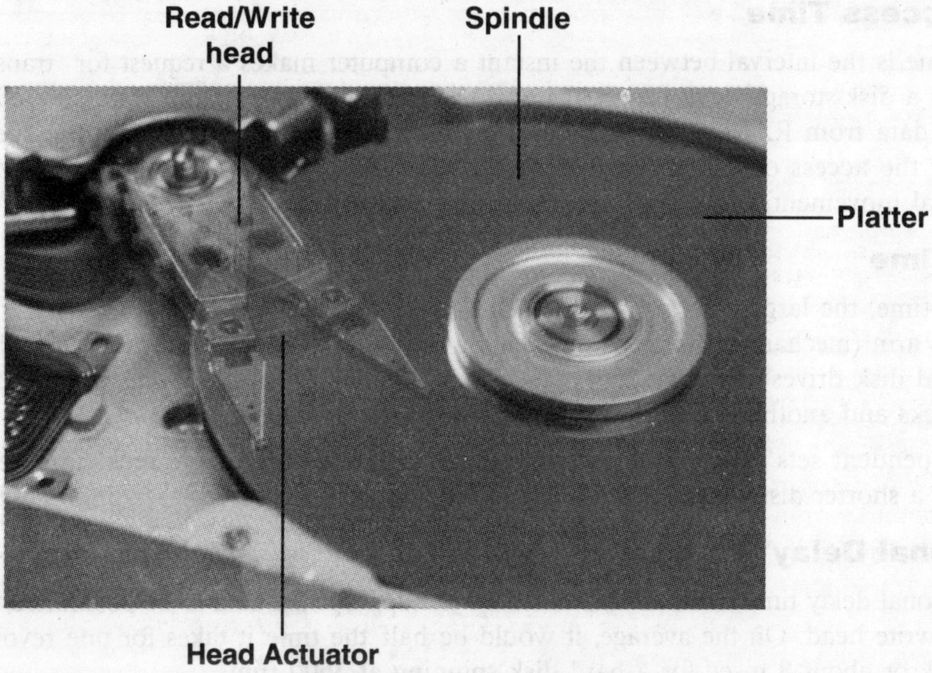

HDD Showing Platters and R/W Heads

the stepper and the spindle motors and the read/write heads of the disk it has 40 pin IDE interface data cable connector and a 4 pin D-type Power supply connector.

Sector : The basic storage unit on a hard disk. On most modern hard disks, sectors are 512

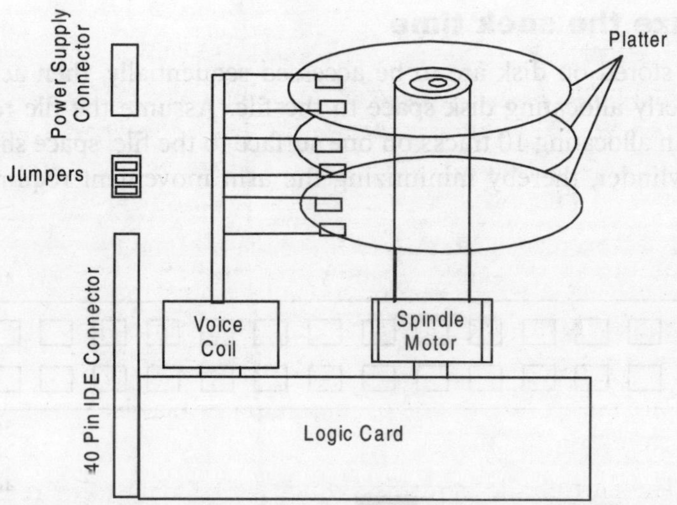

bytes each, four sectors make up a cluster, and there are 17 to 34 sectors in a track although newer drives may have a different number of sectors.

Track : The circular path traced across the spinning surface of a disk platter by the read/write head inside the hard-disk drive. The track consists of one or more clusters.

Disk Access Time

Access time is the interval between the instant a computer makes a request for transfer of data from a disk-storage device to RAM and the instant this operation is completed. The access of data from RAM is performed at electronic speeds-approximately the speed of light. But the access of data from disk storage depends on mechanical apparatus. Any mechanical movement significantly increases the access time.

Seek Time

The seek time, the largest portion of the total access time, consists of how long it takes the access arm (mechanical) to move the read/write head to the desired track or cylinder. Some hard disk drives have two sets of access arms, one for reading and writing on the inside tracks and another for the outside tracks.

Two independent sets of access arms significantly reduce the average seek time because they have a shorter distance to move and can move while the other is reading or writing.

Rotational Delay Time

The rotational delay time is the time it takes for the appropriate data to be positioned under the read/write head. On the average, it would be half the time it takes for one revolution of the disk or about 8 msec for a hard disk spinning at 3600 rpm.

Transmission Time

The transmission time i.e; the time it takes to transmit the data or RAM, is negligible.

Disk Access Time = Seek time + rotational delay time + transmission time

How to minimize the seek time

If records of a file stored on disk are to be accessed sequentially, then access time can be minimized by properly allocating disk space to the file. Assume the file requires 10 tracks of space. Rather than allocating 10 tracks on one surface to the file, space should be allocated to tracks on one cylinder, thereby minimizing the arm movement required to access the records.

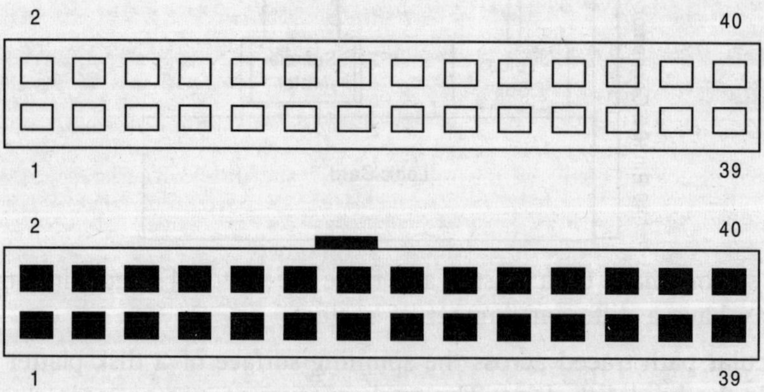

40 PIN MALE and FEMALE at the controller and peripherals.

Advance Technology Attachment

Shown next is the ATA = AT bus Attachment which has been developed by Western Digital, Conner, Seagate and Quantum.

Average Access Time

The time (in milliseconds) that a disk drive takes to find the right track in response to a request (the seek time), plus the time it takes to get to the right place on the track (the latency).

Arial Density

The amount of data which can be stored in one area of a Hard Disk or Floppy.

Interleaving

A hard-disk term which describes a method of arranging disk sectors to compensate for relatively slow computers Spreads sectors apart instead of arranging them consecutively. For example, 3:1 interleaving means your system reads one out of every three tracks on one rotation. The time required for the extra spin lets the read/write head catch up with the disk drive, which might otherwise outrun the head's ability to read the data

Cluster

A cluster is the minimum amount of space used to store a file. If the cluster size for operating system is 256 bytes even a 1-byte file takes up 256 bytes worth of space.

Recording Data on Disk

Data can be recorded on disk tracks with or without the use of keys. A key is a label that is used to identify a particular record. A key is required whenever the location of the record can't be specified exactly. Layout of the fields on a track in disk storage when data is recorded without the use of keys can be as given below:

- BT: beginning of track
- G: fields are separated by a gap
- HA: home address consists of 4 fields
- TC: track condition signals as to whether the track is operative or defective
- CY: cylinder number
- HD: Head number
- EC: Error checking code which tells whether the data is read/write correctly or not.
- TDR: Track descriptor record, serves to indicate an alternative track if the given track is defective.

Many disk systems contain spare tracks that are used as alternates whenever a track becomes defective; this avoids the necessity of terminating a job in the middle or re creating an entire file because of difficulty with one or two tracks.

Record

The data are often consists of hundreds of characters, and thus is much longer than the identification and control fields which preceded it on the track. Data is recorded with associated keys. In many disk systems the length of the key is limited to 255 bytes. Key field makes it possible to check the identification of a record in the disk control unit before it is transferred to the central processor, thus conserving central processor time.

Installation of HDD

The following procedure outlines the installation of a hard disk.

1. Disconnect the power to the computer.
2. Configure the appropriate master/slave settings or SCSI ID for the drive.
3. Insert the drive into an available drive bay. If the drive is too small for the bay, you will need a mounting kit.
4. Screw in the 4 screws - 2 on each side of the bay.
5. If the drive is an IDE disk, connect the IDE cable to the drive. There should be a stripe along 1 edge of the cable. This stripe denotes pin 1. Pin 1 on the drive is usually closest to the power connector on the drive, however, you should consult the manufacturers documentation. Then connect the signal cable to the motherboard ID1 or ID2 interface making sure to note the pin 1 orientation there as well. If the drive is a SCSI drive, a SCSI cable would be connected from the drive to a SCSI controller card.
6. Connect one of the power supply's power connectors to the drive.

Once the drive has been installed it must be configured for use in the following steps:

1. CMOS configuration-Newer BIOSes autodetection features will do this automatically. Otherwise, enter the setup utility during boot up and configure the drive.
2. Certain older drives types must be low-level formatted. Do not do this on IDE drives!
3. Partition the drive-Using the DOS utility FDISK, the drive can be partitioned into logical drives. The disk must contain an active primary partition that will be the C drive. An extended partition may also be created if desired. In Windows NT, the Disk Administrator program is used instead of FDISK. The size of the partitions can be set to a desired size, however, note the following:
    - Windows 95 Rev A(FAT16) only supported partitions up to 2GB in size.
    - Windows 95/98 OSR2(FAT32) supported drives up to 8GB.
    - Even if the OS supports larger partition sizes, the BIOS must also support logical block addressing (LBA) or the maximum partition that you will be able to create will be either 504 or 528 MB.
4. Once the disk has been partitioned, it must then be formatted. This can be done using the DOS format utility.

Due to the magnetic nature of hard disks, they should remain clear of magnetic fields.

Troubleshooting Hard Disk Drives

Symptoms associated with hard disk drive failures include the following:

1. An Invalid Media Type message appears, indicating the controller cannot find a recognizable track/sector pattern on the drive.
2. A No Boot Record Found, a Nonsystem Disk or Disk Error, or an Invalid System Disk message appears, indicating that the system boot files are not located in the root directory of the drive.
3. The video display is active, but the HDD's activity light remains on and no bootup occurs, indicating that the HDD's CMOS configuration information is incorrect.
4. The front panel indicator lights are visible, and the display is present on the monitor screen, but there is no disk drive action and no bootup.
5. The computer boots up to a system disk in the A drive, but not to the hard drive, indicating that the system files on the hard disk drive (HDD) are missing or have become corrupt.
6. The computer does not boot up when turned on.
7. An IBM-compatible 17xx error code is produced on the display.
8. No motor sounds are produced by the HDD while the computer is running.
9. A HDD Controller Failure message appears, indicating a failure to verify hard disk setup by system configuration file error.
10. A C: or D: Fixed Disk Drive error message appears, indicating a hard disk CMOS setup failure.
11. An Out of Disk Space message appears.
12. A Missing Operating System or a Hard Drive Boot Failure message appears.
13. A Current Drive No Longer Valid message appears, indicating that the HDD's CMOS configuration information is incorrect or has become corrupt.

Hard Disk Enhancements

Hard disk drives are accessed over one of a number of bus types, including ATA (IDE, EIDE), Serial ATA (SATA), SCSI, SAS, and Fibre Channel. Bridge circuitry is sometimes used to connect hard disk drives to busses that they cannot communicate with natively, such as IEEE 1394 and USB. Back in the days of the ST-506 interface, the data encoding scheme was also important. The first ST-506 disks used Modified Frequency Modulation (MFM) encoding, and transferred data at a rate of 5 megabits per second. Later on, controllers using 2,7 RLL (or just "RLL") encoding increased the transfer rate by fifty percent, to 7.5 megabits per second; it also increased disk capacity by fifty percent.

Many ST-506 interface disk drives were only specified by the manufacturer to run at the lower MFM data rate, while other models (usually more expensive versions of the same basic disk drive) were specified to run at the higher RLL data rate. In some cases, a disk drive had sufficient margin to allow the MFM specified model to run at the faster RLL data rate; however, this was often unreliable and was not recommended. (An RLL-certified disk drive could run on a MFM controller, but with 1/3 less data capacity and speed.)

Enhanced Small Disk Interface (ESDI) also supported multiple data rates (ESDI disks always used 2,7 RLL, but at 10, 15 or 20 megabits per second), but this was usually negotiated automatically by the disk drive and controller; most of the time, however, 15 or 20 megabit ESDI disk drives weren't downward compatible (i.e. a 15 or 20 megabit disk drive wouldn't run on a 10 megabit controller). ESDI disk drives typically also had jumpers to set the number of sectors per track and (in some cases) sector size.

SCSI originally had just one speed, 5 MHz (for a maximum data rate of 5 megabytes per second), but later this was increased dramatically. The SCSI bus speed had no bearing on the disk's internal speed because of buffering between the SCSI bus and the disk drive's internal data bus; however, many early disk drives had very small buffers, and thus had to be reformatted to a different interleave (just like ST-506 disks) when used on slow computers, such as early IBM PC compatibles and early Apple Macintoshes. ATA disks have typically had no problems with interleave or data rate, due to their controller design, but many early models were incompatible with each other and couldn't run in a master/slave setup (two disks on the same cable). This was mostly remedied by the mid-1990s, when ATA's specification was standardised and the details began to be cleaned up, but still causes problems occasionally (especially with CD-ROM and DVD-ROM disks, and when mixing Ultra DMA and non-UDMA devices).

Serial ATA does away with master/slave setups entirely, placing each disk on its own channel (with its own set of I/O ports) instead. FireWire/IEEE 1394 and USB(1.0/2.0) hard disks are external units containing generally ATA or SCSI disks with ports on the back allowing very simple and effective expansion and mobility. Most FireWire/IEEE 1394 models are able to daisy-chain in order to continue adding peripherals without requiring additional ports on the computer itself.

Acronym	Meaning	Description
SASI	Shugart Associates System Interface	Predecessor to SCSI
SCSI	Small Computer System Interface	Bus oriented that handles concurrent operations.
ST-506		Seagate interface
ST-412		Seagate interface (minor improvement over ST-506)
ESDI	Enhanced Small Disk Interface	Faster and more integrated than ST-412/506, but still backwards compatible
ATA	Advanced Technology Attachment	Successor to ST-412/506/ESDI by integrating the disk controller completely onto the device. Incapable of concurrent operations.

eSATA

Standardized in mid-2004, eSATA defined separate cables, connectors, and revised electrical requirements for external applications:

- Minimum transmit potential increased: Range is 500–600 mV instead of 400–600 mV.

- Minimum receive potential decreased: Range is 240–600 mV instead of 325–600 mV.
- Identical protocol and logical signaling (link/transport-layer and above), allowing native SATA devices to be deployed in external enclosures with minimal modification
- Maximum cable length of 2 m (USB and FireWire allow longer distances.)

Aimed at the consumer market, eSATA enters an external storage market already served by the USB and FireWire interfaces. Most external hard disk drive cases with FireWire or USB interfaces use either PATA or SATA drives and "bridges" to translate between the drives' interfaces and the enclosures' external ports, and this bridging incurs some inefficiency. In the case of USB 2.0, protocol overhead limits the maximum effective bandwidth to a fraction of USB's physical signalling rate. With modern hard disk drives, USB's transfer rate is a bottleneck.

FireWire, with its isochronous transfer mode, is more efficient, such that even in its slower variant, FireWire 400 (IEEE 1394a), the effective transfer rate is significantly faster than that of USB 2.0, but this can still be a bottleneck for fast drives or RAIDs. Some single disks can transfer well over 70 MB/s during real use, well in excess of USB 2.0's or the older FireWire 400's abilities. Finally, some low-level drive features, such as S.M.A.R.T., are not usable through USB or FireWire bridging. eSATA does not suffer from these issues.

eSATA will likely co-exist alongside USB 2.0 and FireWire storage for several reasons. The ubiquity of USB ports on all mass-market computers, and FireWire ports on many consumer electronic appliances, guarantee a large market for USB and FireWire storage. For small form-factor devices (such as external 2.5" disks), a PC-hosted USB or FireWire link supplies sufficient power to operate the device. Where a PC-hosted port is concerned, eSATA connectors cannot supply power, and would therefore be more cumbersome to use.

As of 2007, few computer motherboards have eSATA connectors. Non-equipped desktops can be upgraded with the installation of an eSATA host bus adapter (HBA), while notebooks can be upgraded with Cardbus or ExpressCard versions of an eSATA HBA. Also available are passive eSATA-to-SATA bracket/cable-adapters.

eSATA compared to other buses

	eSATA	SATA 300	PATA 133	FireWire 800	FireWire 400	USB 2.0	Ultra-320 SCSI
Speed (Mbit/s)	2400	2400	1064	786	400	480 (burst)	2560
Max. cable length (m)	2	1	0.46	4.5 (16 cables can be daisy chained up to 72 m)	4.5 (16 cables can be daisy chained up to 72 m)	5 (USB hubs can be daisy chained up to 25 m)	12
Power provided	No	No	No	Yes (12-25 V, 15 W	Yes (12-25 V, 15 W)	Yes (5 V, 2.5 W)	No
Devices per Channel	1 (15 with port multiplier)	1 per line	2	63	63	127	16

With passive-adapters, the maximum cable length is reduced to 1 meter, due to the absence of compliant eSATA signal levels. Full SATA speed for external disks (115 MB/s) have been measured with external RAID enclosures.

eSATA is likely to be ignored by the enterprise and server market, which has already standardized on the separately-developed Serial Attached SCSI (SAS) interface, which has extra features for remote management, link redundancy, and link monitoring.

SATA vs SCSI

SCSI currently offers transfer rates higher than SATA, but is a more complex bus usually resulting in higher manufacturing cost. Some drive manufacturers offer longer warranties for SCSI devices, however, indicating a possibly higher manufacturing quality control of SCSI devices compared to PATA/SATA devices. SCSI buses also allow connection of several drives (using multiple channels, 7 or 15 on each channel) whereas SATA only allows one per channel.

SATA 3.0 Gbit/s offers a maximum bandwidth of 300 MB/s per device compared to SCSI with a maximum of 320 MB/s. Also, SCSI drives provide greater sustained throughput than SATA drives because of disconnect-reconnect and aggregating performance. SATA devices are generally compatible with SAS enclosures and adapters, while SCSI devices cannot be directly connected to a SATA bus.

SCSI hardware is used in enterprises for server purposes, partially due to higher cost of drives and adapters, and partially due to market reasons. The MTBF of SATA drives is usually about 150,000 hours, while SCSI drives are rated for upwards of 1,500,000 hours.

SAS (Serial Attached SCSI) vs Parallel SCSI

- SAS uses Serial transfer protocol to interface multiple devices hence lesser signaling overhead than parallel SCSI, resulting in higher speed.
- No bus contention as SAS bus is point-to-point while SCSI bus is multidrop. Each device is connected by a dedicated bus to the initiator. Connection through expanders may appear to cause some contention, but this is transparent to the initiator.
- SAS has no termination issues and does not require terminator packs like parallel SCSI.
- SAS eliminates clock skew.
- SAS supports higher number of devices (> 16384) while Parallel SCSI limits it to 8, 16, or 32.
- SAS supports higher transfer speed (1.5, 3.0 or 6.0 Gbit/s). The speed is realized on each initiator-target connection, hence higher throughput whereas in parallel SCSI the speed is shared across the entire multidrop bus.
- SAS controllers typically support SATA devices.
- SAS uses SCSI commands to interface with SAS End devices.

SAS vs SATA

- SATA devices are uniquely identified by their port number connected to the Host bus adapter while SAS devices are uniquely identifed by their World Wide Name (WWN).
- Most SAS drives provide Tagged Command Queuing, while most newer SATA drives provide Native Command Queuing, each of which has its pros and cons.
- SATA follows the ATA command set and thus only supports hard drives and CD/DVD drives. In theory, SAS also supports numerous other devices including scanners and printers. However, this advantage could also be moot, as most such devices have also found alternative paths via such buses as USB, IEEE 1394, and Ethernet.
- SAS hardware allows multipath I/O to devices while SATA does not. An effort is underway to use port multipliers to achieve multipathing with SATA II.
- SATA is marketed as a general-purpose successor to Parallel ATA and is now common in the consumer market, while the more expensive SAS is marketed for critical server applications.
- SAS error recovery and reporting are much cleaner than SATA.
- SAS uses higher signaling voltages (800-1600mv TX, 275-1600mv RX) than SATA (400-600mv TX, 325-600mv RX). When SAS is mixed with SATA, the SAS drives run at SATA-voltages. One reason for this higher voltage is so SAS may be used in server backplanes.
- Because of its higher signaling voltages, SAS can use cables up to 8 m (25 ft) long, SATA is limited to 1 m (3 ft).

External SATA

Standardized in mid-2004, eSATA defined separate cables, connectors, and revised electrical requirements for external applications:

- Minimum transmit potential increased: Range is 500–600 mV instead of 400–600 mV.
- Minimum receive potential decreased: Range is 240–600 mV instead of 325–600 mV.
- Identical protocol and logical signaling (link/transport-layer and above), allowing native SATA devices to be deployed in external enclosures with minimal modification
- Maximum cable length of 2m (USB and FireWire allow longer distances.)

Aimed at the consumer market, eSATA enters an external storage market already served by the USB and FireWire interfaces. Most external hard disk drive cases with FireWire or USB interfaces use either PATA or SATA drives and "bridges" to translate between the drives' interfaces and the enclosures' external ports,[citation needed] and this bridging incurs some inefficiency. In the case of USB 2.0, protocol overhead limits the maximum effective bandwidth to a fraction of USB's physical signalling rate. With modern hard disk drives,

USB's transfer rate is a bottleneck. FireWire, with its isochronous transfer mode, is more efficient, such that even in its slower variant, FireWire 400 (IEEE 1394a), the effective transfer rate is significantly faster than that of USB 2.0, but this can still be a bottleneck for fast drives or RAID arrays. Some single disks can transfer well over 90 MB/s during real use, well in excess of USB 2.0's or the older FireWire 400's abilities. Finally, some low-level drive features, such as S.M.A.R.T., are not usable through USB or FireWire bridging. eSATA does not suffer from these issues.

eSATA will likely co-exist alongside USB 2.0 and FireWire storage for several reasons. The ubiquity of USB ports on all mass-market computers, and FireWire ports on many consumer electronic appliances, guarantee a large market for USB and FireWire storage.[citation needed] For small form-factor devices (such as external 2.5" (70 mm) disks), a PC-hosted USB or FireWire link supplies sufficient power to operate the device. Where a PC-hosted port is concerned, eSATA connectors cannot supply power, and would therefore be more cumbersome to use.

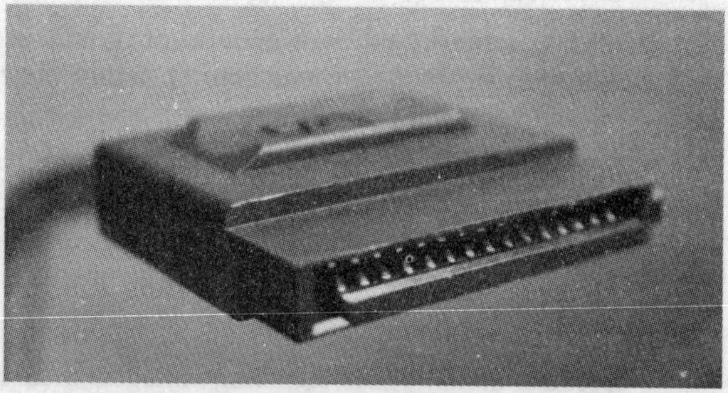

As of 2007, an eSATA external drive enclosure will typically ship with a passive eSATA-to-SATA bracket/cable-adapter to install on desktops that lack an eSATA port or that need another. Desktops can also be upgraded with the installation of an eSATA host bus adapter (HBA), while notebooks can be upgraded with Cardbus or ExpressCard versions of an eSATA HBA. With passive-adapters, the maximum cable length is reduced to 1 meter, due to the absence of compliant eSATA signal levels. Full SATA speed for external disks (115 MB/s) have been measured with external RAID enclosures.

eSATA is likely to be ignored by the enterprise and server market, which has already standardized on the separately-developed Serial Attached SCSI (SAS) interface, which has extra features for remote management, link redundancy, and link monitoring.

Prior to the final eSATA specification, there were a number of products designed for external connections of SATA drives. Some of these use the internal SATA connector or even connectors designed for other interface specifications, such as FireWire. These products are not eSATA compliant. The final eSATA specification features a specific connector designed for rough manipulation. It's similar to the regular SATA connector, but with reinforcements in both the male and female sides, inspired by the USB connector. It's harder to unplug and can withstand a cable being yanked or wiggled. On a SATA connector, this kind of action will break the male side of the connection (the hard drive or host adapter), rendering the device unusable. With an eSATA connector, considerably more force is needed to damage the connector, and even in this situation, only the female side (the cable itself) will break, possibly leaving the male usable.

Cables and connectors

The SATA power and data cables are the most noticeable change from Parallel ATA. Unlike Parallel ATA, the same physical connectors are used on 3.5-in (90 mm) desktop hard disks and 2.5-in (70 mm) notebook disks; this eliminates the need for a mechanical adapter when using a notebook drive in a desktop computer.

Pin #	Function
1	Ground
2	A+
3	A"
4	Ground
5	B"
6	B+
7	Ground

The SATA standard defines a data cable with seven conductors (3 grounds and 4 active data lines in two pairs) and 8 mm wide wafer connectors on each end. SATA cables can be up to 1 m (39 in) long. PATA ribbon cables, in comparison, carry either 40- or 80-conductor wires and are limited to 45 cm (18 in) in length by the PATA specification (however, cables up to 90 cm (36 in) are readily available). Thus, SATA connectors and cables are easier to fit in closed spaces and reduce obstructions to air cooling. However, they are more susceptible to accidental unplugging.

A 7-pin Serial ATA data cable.

Pin #	Function
1-3	3.3V
4-6	Ground
7-9	5V
10	Ground
11	Staggered spinup(in supporting drives)
12	Ground
13-15	12V

The SATA standard also specifies a new power connector. Like the data cable, it is wafer-based, but its wider 15-pin shape prevents accidental misidentification and forced insertion of the wrong connector type. Native SATA devices favor the SATA power-connector over the old four-pin Molex connector (found on all PATA equipment), although some SATA drives retain older 4-pin Molex.

The SATA/power connector has been criticized for its poor robustness—the thin plastic tops of the connectors (see power connector picture at right) can break due to shearing force when the user pulls the plug at a non-orthogonal angle. The seemingly large number of pins are used to supply three different voltages: 3.3 V, 5 V, and 12 V. Each voltage is supplied by three pins ganged together, while ground is provided by five pins. Pin 11 is used in newer drives for staggered spinup. The supply pins are ganged together because the small pins by themselves cannot supply sufficient current for some devices. One pin from each of the three voltages is also used for hotplugging.

Adaptors are available to convert a 4-pin Molex connector to SATA power connector. However, because the 4-pin Molex connectors do not provide 3.3 V power, these adapters provide only 5 V and 12 V power and leave the 3.3 V lines disconnected.

This precludes the use of such adapters with drives that require 3.3 V power. Understanding this, drive manufacturers have largely left the 3.3 V power lines unused. However, without 3.3 V power, the SATA device may not be able to implement hotplugging as mentioned in the previous paragraph.

Revision

1. The hard disks are sealed inside an airtight vacuum chamber.
2. A hard disk is a stack of metal platters that spin on one spindle, like a stack of rigid floppy disks.
3. Access time is the interval between the instant a computer makes a request for transfer of data from a disk-storage device to RAM and the instant this operation is completed.
4. Data can be recorded on disk tracks with or without the use of keys. A key is a label that is used to identify a particular record.
5. The Mechanical Section of hard dis consists of the followings Spindle Motor, Disk drive, Platters, Read/Write Head, Head Actuator, Electronic Section of HDD, Sector and Track.
6. The rotational delay time is the time it takes for the appropriate data to be positioned under the read/write head.
7. A cluster is the minimum amount of space used to store a file.
8. Hard disk drives are accessed over one of a number of bus types, including ATA (IDE, EIDE), Serial ATA (SATA), SCSI, SAS, and Fibre Channel.
9. SCSI originally had just one speed, 5 MHz (for a maximum data rate of 5 megabytes per second), but later this was increased dramatically.
10. Aimed at the consumer market, eSATA enters an external storage market already served by the USB and FireWire interfaces.
11. SCSI currently offers transfer rates higher than SATA, but is a more complex bus usually resulting in higher manufacturing cost.
12. The SATA power and data cables are the most noticeable change from Parallel ATA.

Multiple Choice Questions

1. Hard disk is a _______ device.

   (a) Storage (b) Display

   (c) Removable

2. Spinning speed of each platter of IDE Hard disk is
   (a) 10,000 rpm. (b) 5,000 rpm.
   (c) 7,200 rpm. (d) 6,000 rpm.
3. A Zip drive is used to:
   (a) Storage backup (b) Compress data
   (c) Hide data (d) None of these.
4. Numbers of heads/platter are ....
   (a) 1 (b) 2
   (c) 3
5. Which one is optical storage media:
   (a) HDD (b) Floppy disk
   (c) Pen drive (d) DVD.
6. Formatting is the process of arranging:
   (a) Tracks (b) Sectors
   (c) Both (a) and (b) (d) None of these.

True/False Questions

1. A hard disk is a stack of metal platters that spin on one spindle, like a stack of rigid floppy disks.
2. Data can be recorded on disk tracks with or without the use of keys. A key is a label that is used to identify a particular record.
3. A cluster is the maximum amount of space used to store a file.
4. SCSI originally had just one speed, 5 MHz (for a maximum data rate of 5 megabytes per second), but later this was increased dramatically.
5. Aimed at the consumer market, eSATA enters an external storage market already served by the USB and FireWire interfaces.
6. The SATA power and data cables are the most noticeable change from Parallel ATA.

Descriptive Questions

1. Why SCSI hard disk is costly than IDE hard disk?
2. What is access time of hard disk?
3. What is SCSI hard disk?
4. What do you understand by Access Time?
5. How the hard drive works? Explain its internal working.
6. Explain the types of HDD availlable in the market along with the difference.
7. What are the types of storage devices?
8. Describe the following terms.

   Cluster Record

   eSATA SAS

SCSI SATA

Arial Density Interleaving

Recording data on disk Transmission time

Rotational Delay Time

9. How would you install the hard disk?
10. How would you troubleshoot the hard disk?
11. Describe the cables and connectors of eSATA

Answers to Objective Type Questions

Multiple Choice Questions

1. a	2. c	3. a	4. b
5. d	6. c		

True False Questions

1. T	2. T	3. F	4. T
5. T	6. T		

7 FDD

Introduction

There are two kinds of floppies, 3½" and 5¼" in sizes. These floppies are made of vinyl material and have a plastic coated jacket over them. The vinyl material has a coating of magnetic oxide so that data can be stored on it. Floppy disk can be used both as an input device and an output device meaning that you can both write on it and read from it.

Floppy disk is used for the storage of data which is encoded by electromagnetic means on to tracks on the disk surface. A floppy disk is made of flexible material usually a kind of plastic which has magnetizable particles upon its surface. Floppy disks are supplied within special envelopes which have holes set in them for the drive shaft and read/write heads of the disk drives which are used to operate with the disks. The disks are designed to be handled within the envelope which protects the recording surface.

Floppy disks are used with word processing systems and with PCs and their popularity is related to the ease with which they can be handled and stored off line. They are classed as exchangeable disks. It is also known as diskette.

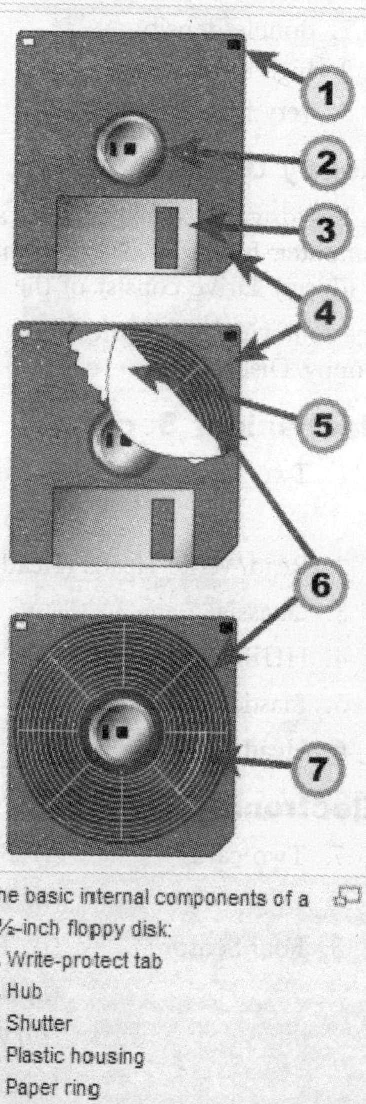

The basic internal components of a 3½-inch floppy disk:
1. Write-protect tab
2. Hub
3. Shutter
4. Plastic housing
5. Paper ring
6. Magnetic disk
7. Disk sector.

Types of Floppy Disks

Floppies come in two physical sizes:

5 1/4 inch and

3 1/2 inch.

The size refers to the diameter of the disk, not to the capacity.

The 5 1/4" type is encased in a flexible vinyl envelope with an oval cutout that allows the read/write head to access the disk.

The density of the disk is a measure of the quantity of the disk surface: the higher the density, the more closely the iron-oxide particles are packed and the more data the disk can store. The disk itself is made of soft flexible mylar plastic with a magnetically sensitive iron oxide coating. The coating is present on both sides, even for single-sided disks that are intended to be recorded on only one side. The second side of a single-sided disk may not have its second side finished, polished and tested but it still has the same coating.

These days 5.25 inch disks (1.2 MB capacity) are used primarily in older computers although some people buy optional 5.25" disk drives for their new PCs to be able to read and write to the old disks. 3.5 inch type is encased in a hard plastic shell with a sliding metal cover. When the disk is inserted into the drive, the cover slides back to expose the disk to the read/write head. The term floppy disk refers to the disk inside, not to the square plastic protector.

The 3.5 inch size floppy disk come in three capacities:

1. double density
2. high density and
3. very high density

Floppy Disk Drives

A disk drive designed to read and write data to a floppy disk for transfer to and from a computer. It can be classified into two sections Mechanical Section and Electronic Section. A Floppy Drive consist of the following:

The following two figures show the block diagram of Floppy Disk Drive and real outlay of Floppy Disk Drive.

Mechanical Section

1. Two Motors : (*i*) Stepper Motor
   (*ii*) Spindle Motor
2. Read/Write Heads (Head zero and head one)
3. Chassis
4. HUB
5. Plastic Jaw
6. Head Actuator

Electronic Section

7. Two cards (*i*) Servo Card
   (*ii*) Logic Card
8. Four Sensor : (*i*) Track Zero Sensor
   (*ii*) Index Hole Sensor
   (*iii*) Write Protect Sensor
   (*iv*) Lock Sensor
9. 34 pin floppy drive connector
10. 4 pin power supply connector

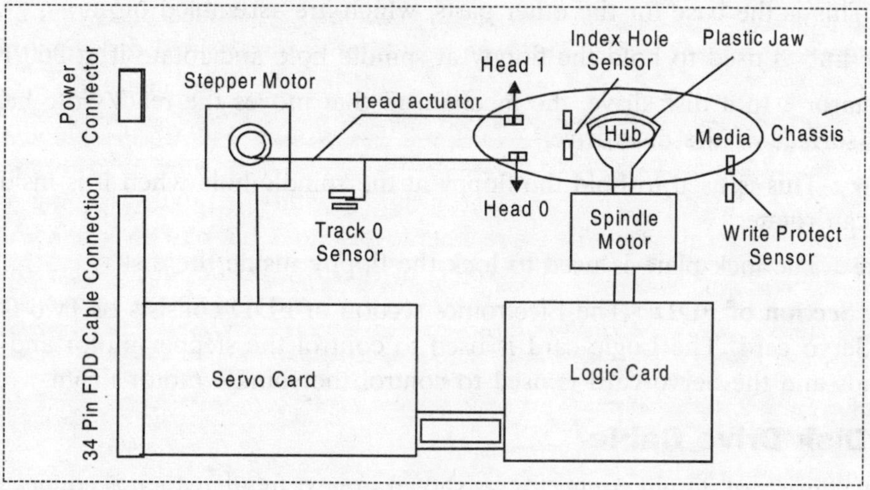

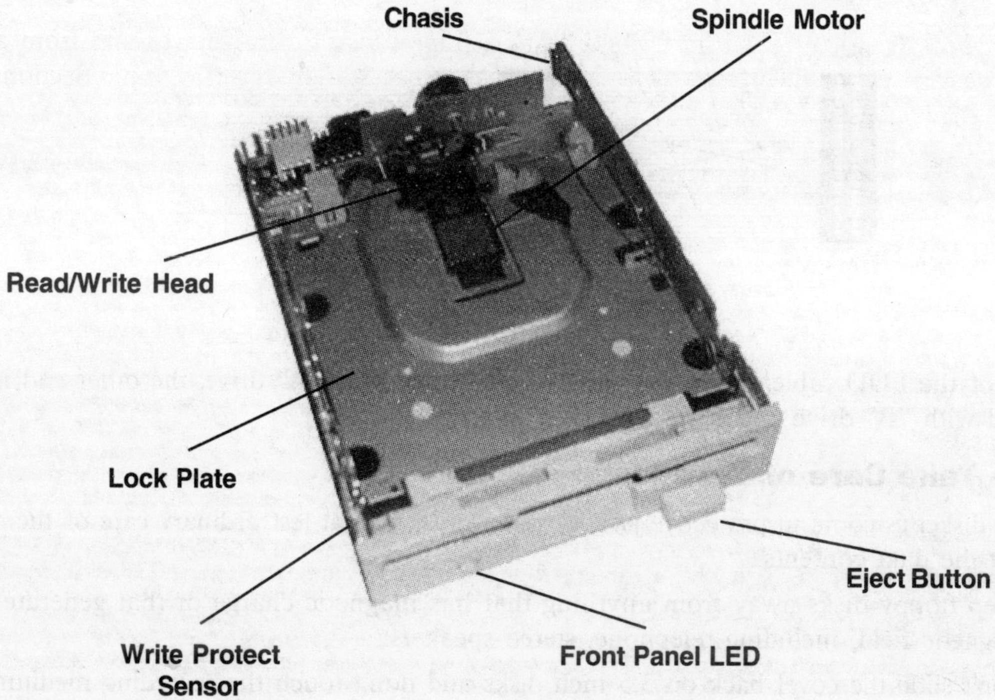

Various parts of the Floppy Disk drive, as shown in the figure are:

Spindle Motor : This motor is used to rotate the floppy disk at 360 revolutions per minute (RPM) so that the sectors can come under the read/write head.

Stepper Motor : This motor is used to move the read/write head over the tracks of the disk, it takes step pulses to move to the next track or previous track.

Read/Write Head : The Read/Write head are used to write and read information on the media *i.e.*, floppy, It works on ,the principle of electromagnetism.

Chassis : This is the base for the other parts, which are assembled on it.

Hub : The hub is used to hold the floppy at spindle hole and rotate it at 360 rpm.

Head Actuator : In a disk drive, the mechanism that moves the read/write head radially across the surface of the disk drive.

Plastic Jaw : This is used to hold the floppy at the spindle hole when it is inside the disk, so that it can rotate.

Lock Plate : The lock plate is used to lock the floppy inside the disk.

Electronic Section of FDD : The Electronics section of FDD consists of Two Cards Logic card and Servo card. The Logic card is used to control the stepper motor and the Read/ Write Heads and the Servo card is used to control the spindle motor's rpm.

Floppy Disk Drive Cable

FDD cable consists of 34 pin connector, as shown in next figure, which is connected between Floppy Drive Controller (FDC) and floppy drive.

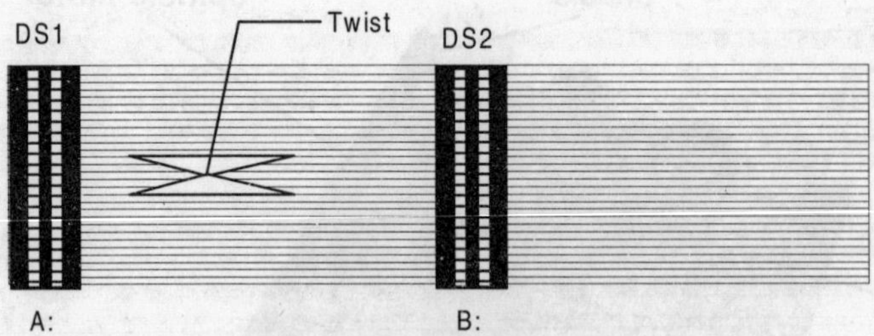

FDD Cable

One end of the FDD cable is twisted which is connected with "A" drive, the other end is connected with "B" drive and FDC controller

How to Take Care of Your Floppy Disks

Although diskettes come in protective jackets, users must take at lest ordinary care of them to protect the data contents:

1. Keep floppy disks away from anything that has magnetic charge or that generates magnetic field, including telephone, stereo speakers.
2. Don't slide the cover back on 3.5 inch disks and don't touch the recording medium of any disk.
3. Never force a disk into a disk drive and never remove a disk from a drive when the drive light is on. The light tells you that the drive is working, and removing the disk is likely to damage the data on it.

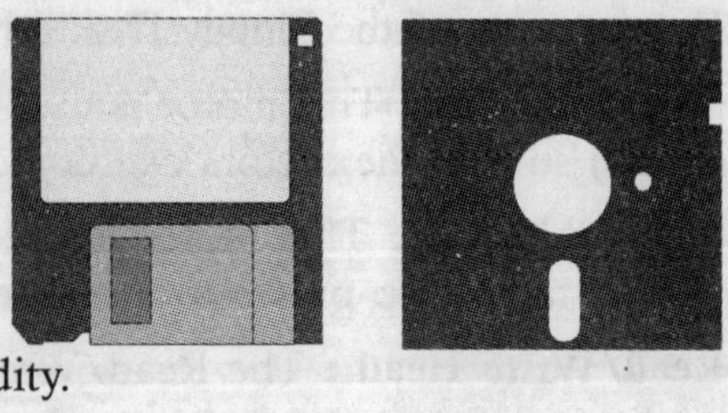

4. Do not expose disks to excessive heat or humidity.

Measuring Drive Performance

When evaluating the performance of common storage devices, you need to be aware of two common measures:

1. The average access time and
2. The data-transfer rate.

Average Access Time

The average access time of a device is the amount of time it takes the device to position its read/write heads over any spot on the recording medium. Access time is the combination of two factors:

1. the speed at which the disk spins (in RPM) and
2. time the read/write head takes to move the heads from one track to another.

Access time is measured in msec. (1/1000 second), so the maximum access time for floppy disks = 60/30 * 1000/1 = 200 m secs.

Average Data Transfer Rate

It implies at which rate drive can transfer data, *i.e.*, how long it takes to read or write data. For data-transfer rates, the unit of time is almost always the second, but units of data may be measured in bytes, KB or MB. Disk controllers coordinate the flow of data to and from the computer and disk drive. They are often connected to the system as an expansion card and can control the flow of data to several drives.

Drive Interface Standards

Another important factor in determining how quickly a drive can read and write data is the type of controller that the drive uses. A disk controller is connected directly to the computer's bus on some computers, the disk controller is an integral part of the computer's main motherboard. On others, the controller is an expansion board that connects to the bus by plugging into one of the computer's expansion slots.

Integrated Drive Electronics (IDE)

The IDE interface places most of the controller's circuitry on the drive itself to provide a simpler interface with the computer. IDE is capable of providing data-transfer rates of about 1 MB per second under ideal conditions.

Enhanced Small Device Interface (ESDI)

It encodes the data on the drive instead of on the controller card. This results in a higher degree of reliability - which in turn allows for higher speeds. ESDI is capable of transferring data at rate of 3 MB per second.

Small Computer System Interface (SCSI)

It takes an approach to interfacing peripheral devices. Because the original concept of SCSI was to provide peripherals access to the computer's bus, one way to think of SCSI is as an extension of the computer's bus. One benefit of SCSI is that bringing the computer's bus directly into the drive improves efficiency greatly. Because a SCSI interface is essentially an extension of a computer's bus, it can accommodate multiple devices — as many as the bus can handle. Most current implementations of SCSI limit the number of devices to seven.

Internal Structure of a Floppy Disk

The outermost track of any disc is called track zero. Track zero is very important for any disk. It is responsible for booting of a computer, for storing the details of directories and files stored inside the disk.

Track zero has four parts:

1. Master Boot Record (MBR): It stores all the information of the operating system through which the floppy disk is formatted.
2. Dos Boot Record (DBR): It is used to store all the system files, which are required for booting of the computer There are three system files, which are required to boot a computer and they are
    i. IO.SYS
    ii. MSDOS.SYS
    iii. COMMAND.COM
3. Directory Structure (DS): It stores the information of all the directories and files stored inside the disk, such as, Directory name, File name, Size of the files and the date and time of the creation or modification of file etc.
4. File Allocation Table (FAT): It is very-very important part of track zero. It stores all the information about the file and directory stored inside the disk such as track number, sector number and side number It is just like an index of a text book.

Installation of Floppy Disk Drives (FDD)

1. Power off and unplug the computer.
2. Detach all devices, *e.g.*, printer, keyboard, monitor.
3. Remove the computer cover. Refer to your computer system manual.
4. If you are replacing an existing drive, note how the drive is connected. For installation of a second drive or a new drive, go to Step 11.
5. Unplug the four pin power cable and the 34 pin flat interface cable.
6. Remove the screws mounting the old drive and carefully remove the unit.
7. Mount the Imation floppy drive using the screws supplied with the kit.
8. Attach the existing flat interface cable making certain that the red wire, Pin 1, is closest to the motor, near the center rear of the drive, as shown in Figure A.
9. Plug the four wire power connector to the drive to complete the installation.
10. Replace the computer cover and reconnect any peripherals.

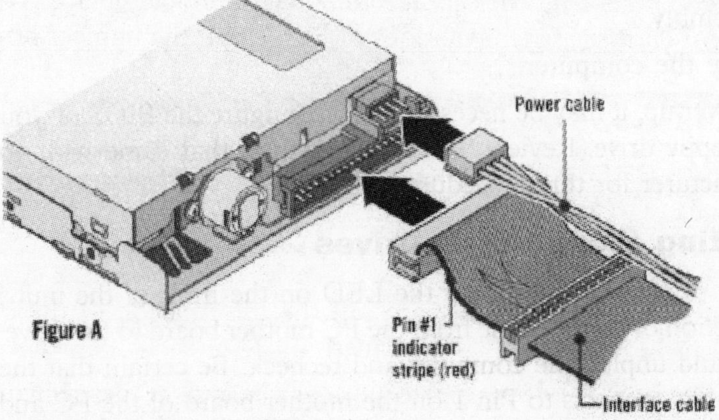

Floppy Drive

11. For a second drive, complete Steps 1 to 3 above.
12. Remove a floppy disk filler panel at the front of the computer unit.
13. Determine that the interface cable to your existing floppy drive has a second connector near the attached drive. If not, substitute the three-connector interface cable shipped with the Imation kit.
14. Using the screws enclosed in the kit, mount the Imation floppy drive in the space in the computer. If your computer does not have an extra floppy bay, you will need to acquire a 5-inch bay adapter panel from your computer supplier.
15. Connect the cable to the floppy drives with the red stripe closest to the motor assembly as shown in Figure A above.
16. The floppy drive attached to the end connector will appear as Drive A in My Computer or Windows Explorer. The drive attached to the second connector from the end will appear as Drive B.
17. Connect the a four wire power plug to the back of each floppy drive.
18. Reassemble the computer and power on.
19. Follow Steps 1 – 3 from the above instructions.
20. Determine if the mother board of the PC has a 34 pin floppy disk connector and that a 4 pin power connector is available. If the PC does not have an unused small power connector, you may need to obtain a standard power connector to mini adapter from your computer store.
21. Locate the floppy bay at the front of the machine and remove the cover.
22. Mount the floppy drive using the screws from the kit.
23. Attach the end of the 34 pin interface cable without the twist to the floppy disk connector on the mother board of your computer being sure to align the red stripe of the cable with Pin 1.

24. Connect the other end of the cable to the floppy drive with the red stripe closest to the motor assembly.

25. Reassemble the computer.

26. During power up, it may be necessary to reconfigure the BIOS of your PC to recognize the new floppy drive. Review the documentation that came with your PC or contact the manufacturer for this procedure.

Troubleshooting Floppy Disk Drives

1. The floppy drive is installed, but the LED on the front of the unit is continually on. The connection of the interface from the PC mother board to the drive may be incorrect. Power off and unplug the computer and recheck. Be certain that the red stripe of the interface cable connects to Pin 1 on the mother board of the PC and also to Pin 1 on the floppy drive. Pin 1 on the drive is closest to the drive motor, at the rear center of the unit.

2. The drive is cabled but is not recognized by the Windows operating system.
   - Go to Control Panel.
   - Click on System.
   - Click on Device Manager.
   - Click the plus sign in front of Floppy Disk Controllers.
   - If there is a yellow exclamation point on the disk controller, highlight the unit and click Remove.
   - Power off the computer and unplug.
   - With the system off, check the cable connections to the floppy drive.
   - Reboot the system and Windows should automatically recognize your drive.

3. After setting up the system BIOS, a message "DISK BOOT FAILURE. INSERT A SYSTEM DISK AND HIT ENTER" appears. After trying several boot disks, the same message keeps appearing. The BIOS is not set up correctly. Obtain the proper settings by contacting your computer manufacturer or the Internet site for the manufacturer of the BIOS of your machine.

Revision

1. There are two kinds of floppies, 3½" and 5¼" in sizes.
2. The 3.5 inch size floppy disk come in three capacities: double density, high density and very high density.
3. A floppy-disk drive is a device that reads and writes data to and from floppy disks.
4. Every new floppy disk must be formatted.
5. Optical disk technology is still emerging and has yet to stabilize; however at present there are three different types of optical disks in common use: read-only, recordable, and erasable.
6. The density of the disk is a measure of the quantity of the disk surface: the higher the density, the more closely the iron-oxide particles are packed and the more data the disk can store.

7. FDD cable consists of 34 pin connector, which is connected between Floppy Drive Controller (FDC) and floppy drive.
8. It implies at which rate drive can transfer data, *i.e.*, how long it takes to read or write data.
9. The IDE interface places most of the controller's circuitry on the drive itself to provide a simpler interface with the computer.
10. ESDI is capable of transferring data at rate of 3 MB per second.
11. The outermost track of any disc is called track zero.

Multiple Choice Questions

1. There are two types of floppies 5¼ and ____:
   (a) 3½ (b) 3¼
   (c) 5½
2. Every new floppy disk has to be _______.
   (a) stored (b) formatted
   (c) labelled
3. .... is used to write protect a floppy.
   (a) Write Protect Notch (b) Write Paper Notch
   (c) With Protect Notch
4. Floppy drive connector is of .... Pins.
   (a) 34 (b) 50
   (c) 72
5. FDC stands for :
   (a) Floppy Disk Controller (b) Floppy Drive Control
   (c) Floppy Drive Controller
6. RPM stands for :
   (a) Resolutions Per Minute (b) Revolutions Per Minute
   (c) Rate Per Minute

True/False Questions

1. There are two kinds of floppies, 3¼" and 5½" in sizes.
2. The 3.5 inch size floppy disk come in three capacities: double density, high density and very high density.
3. New floppy disk need not be formatted.
4. Optical disk technology is still emerging and has yet to stabilize; however at present there are three different types of optical disks in common use: read-only, recordable, and erasable.
5. FDD cable consists of 43 pin connector, which is connected between Floppy Drive Controller (FDC) and floppy drive.
6. It implies at which rate drive can transfer data, *i.e.*, how long it takes to read or write data.
7. ESDI is capable of transferring data at rate of 3 MB per second.

Descriptive Questions

1. How the data is written on the floppy disks?
2. What is floppy disk? Explain contraction and its working?
3. Describe what is there in the mechanical and electronic section of floppy disk drive.
4. How would you take care of your floppy disk drive?
5. How would you install floppy disk drive?
6. Describe troubleshooting of floppy disk drive.

Answers to Objective Type Questions

Multiple Choice Questions

1. a	2. b	3. a	4. a
5. c	6. b		

True False Questions

1. T	2. T	3. F	4. T
5. F	6. T	7. T	

8 CD ROM

CD-ROM

This is not doubt the latest and the best medium for storing data. Though they look very similar to music CDs, so to differentiate from them, the computer ones are called CD-ROMs. They are round in shape and are about 5" in diameter. Till recently they used to be Read Only but now writeable CDs are also available with the relevant drives to write on them. With capacity to write data of about 600 floppies, it has become very popular over the recent times.

In the form of videodisks or compact disks (CDs), optical disks represent a new trend in small, high-capacity storage of images and sound. A single optical disks stores nearly 1 GB of data on one side. To put this storage capacity into perspective, an optical disk can hold 800 television quality images or 60 minutes of high fidelity music.

The explosive growth in storage needs has driven the computer industry to provide cheaper, more versatile storage devices with greater capacity. New storage technologies using optical disks exceed the storage capacities currently available with magnetic disks of the same size. Optical storage techniques used by computers are basically the same as those used to record music on compact disks.

Optical disks differ from magnetic disk storage by the way data is stored and read from the storage media. A laser beam is used to write and read data on these reflective disks, so they are also known as laser disks. In this technology a laser hits a layer of metallic material spread over the surface of a disk. When data is being entered heat from the laser produces tiny spots on the disk surface. To read the data, the laser scans the disk, and a lens picks up different light reflections from the various spots.

Optical disks are becoming a very inviting option for users. They are less sensitive to environmental fluctuations, and they provide more direct-access storage at a cost than is much less per megabyte of storage than the magnetic disk alternative.

Optical disk technology is still emerging and has yet to stabilize; however at present there are three different types of optical disks in common use:

read-only

recordable, and

erasable

Structure of CD-ROM Drive

The CD-ROM has two sections namely Mechanical Section and the Electronics Section.

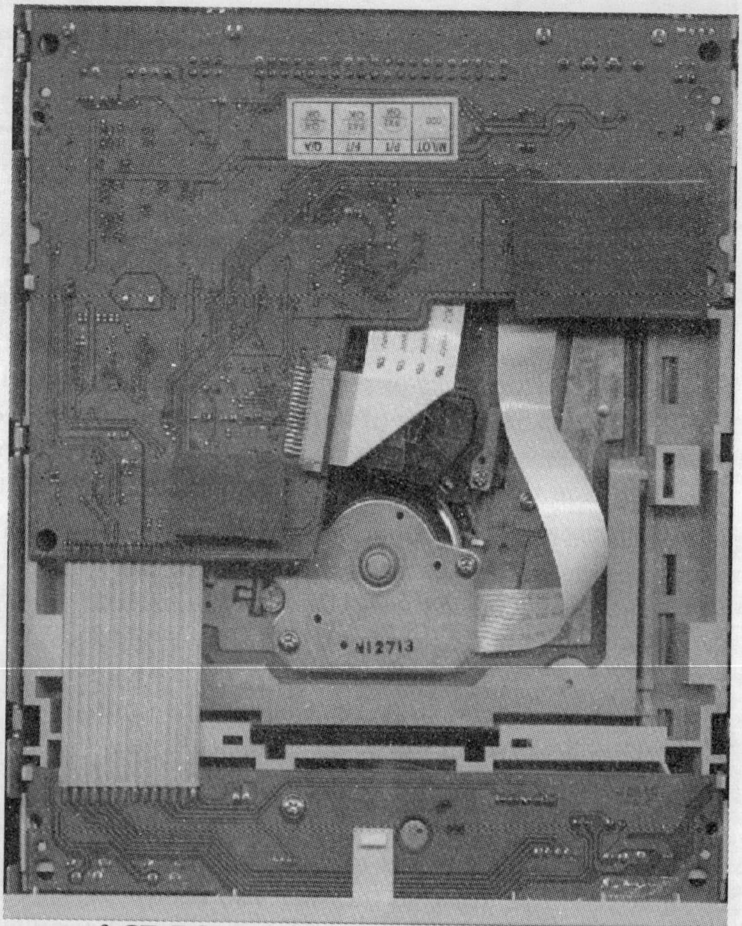

The center of the drive is a cast aluminum or rigid frame assembly. As with other drives, the frame is the single primary structure for mounting the drive's mechanical and electronic components The front panel consists of lid, volume control, and eject button attached to the frame, and offering a fixed reference slot for CD insertion and removal.

The main PC board, handles the drive control and interfacing, and the headphone PC board, which provides an audio jack for headphones. The main CD subassembly called a drive engine, which uses to hold eject, spin, and read the disk. This interchangeability is part of the genius of CD-ROM drives—a single sub-assembly performs 80 percent of the work. Sony, Philips, and Toshiba are the major manufacturers of CD-ROM engines, but other companies, such as IBM and Ikka, are also producing engines.

The engine features a series of mechanisms that accept, clamp, and eject the disk. The foundation of this engine is the BC-7C assembly. It acts as a sub-frame, the sub-frame is shock-mounted with four rubber feet to cushion the engine from minor bumps and ordinary handling as shown in the figure 5.27 below. The slider assembly, loading chassis assembly, and the cover shield provide the mechanical action needed to accept the disk and clamp it into place over the drive spindle, as well as to free the disk and eject it on demand. A motor/gear assembly drives the load unload mechanics. The work of spinning and reading a disk is handled under the engine.

A spindle motor is mounted on the sub-frame and connected to a spindle motor PC board. The most important part of the CD engine is the optical device that contains the 780-nm (nanometer) 0.6-mW gallium aluminum arsenide (GaAIAs) laser diode and detector, along with the optical focus and tracking components. The optical device slides along two guide

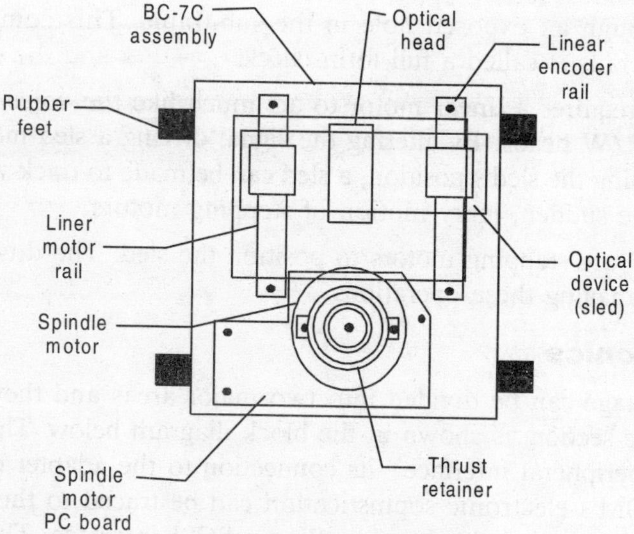

Assembly of CD-ROM Drive

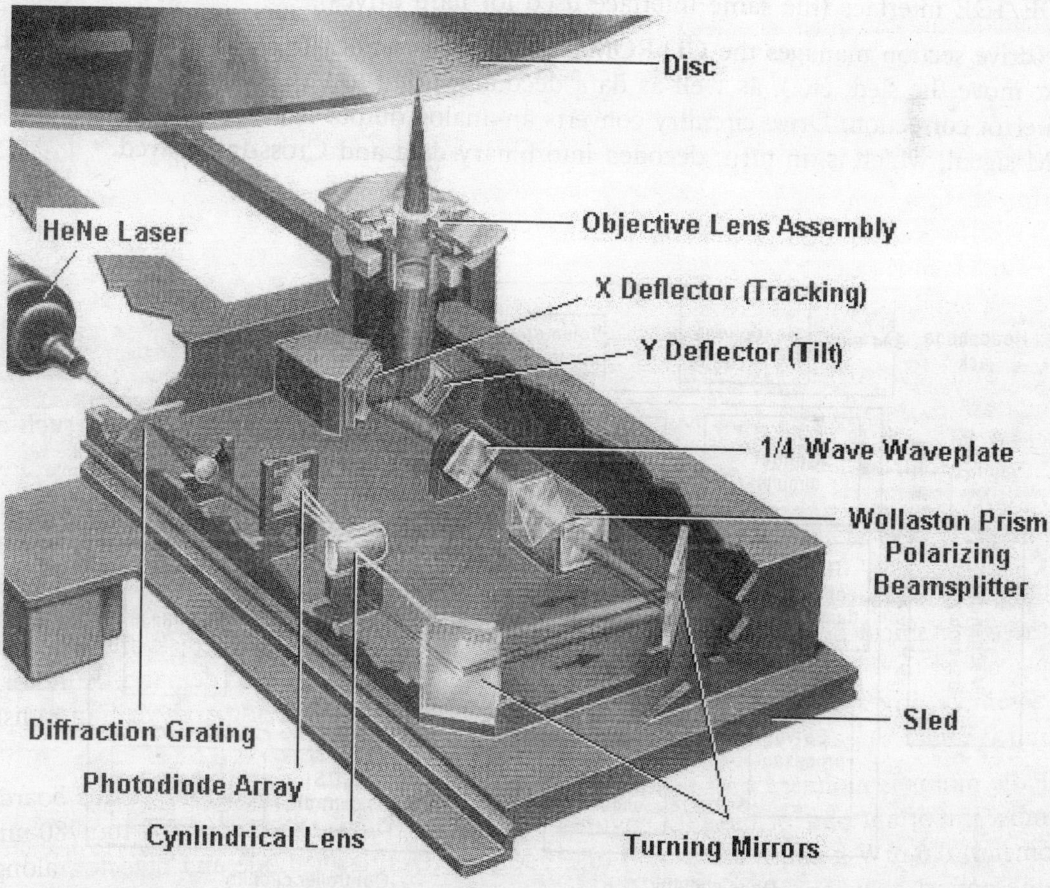

Mechanical Section of CD-ROM Drive

rails and shines through an exposed hole in the sub-frame. This combination of device mounting and guide rails is called a full form check.

A CD drive ideally requires a linear motor to act much like the voice coil motor used to position hard-drive R/W heads. By altering the signal driving a sled motor and constantly measuring and adjusting the sled's position, a sled can be made to track very smoothly along a disk—free from the sudden, jerky motion of stepping motors.

Some CD drives still use stepping motors to position the sled. Thc drive's main PC board is responsible for managing these operations.

CD-ROM Electronics

The electronics package can be divided into two major areas and they are the controller section and the drive section as shown in the block diagram below. The controller section is dedicated to the peripheral interface—its connection to the adapter board. Much of the reason for a CD-ROM's electronic sophistication can be traced to the controller section. The controller circuitry is dedicated to handling a SCSI interface. This allows the unit's "intelligence" to be located right in the drive itself. Most of the CDROM drives use an EIDE/IDE interface (the same interface used for hard drives).

The drive section manages the CD-ROM's physical operations (*i.e.*, load/unload, spin the disk, move the sled, etc.), as well as data decoding Eight-to-Fourteen Modulation (EFM) and error correction. Drive circuitry converts an analog output from the laser diode into an EFM signal, which is, in turn, decoded into binary data and Cross-Interleaved.

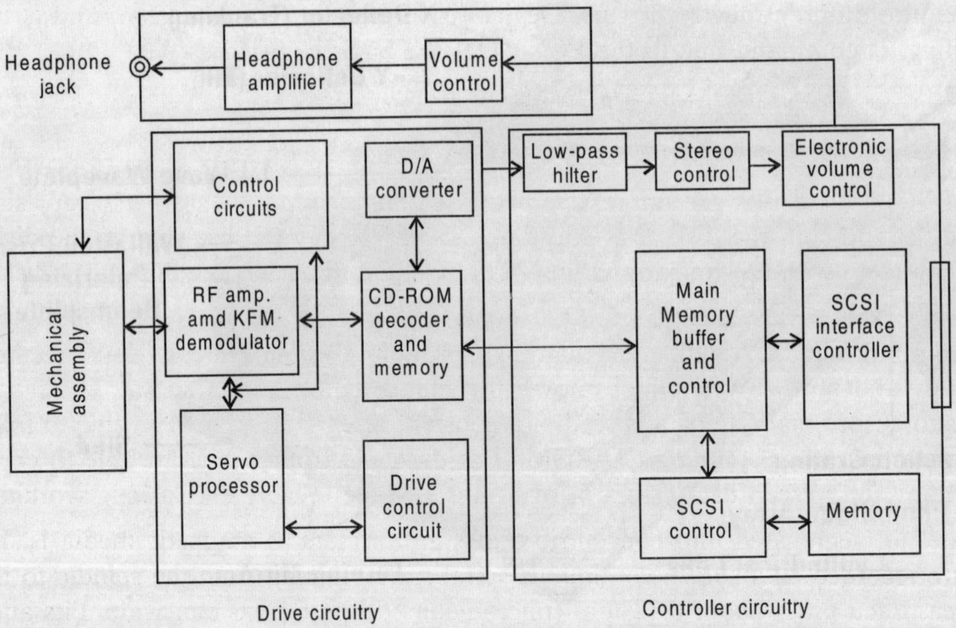

Block diagram of CD-ROM Drive

Reed-Solomon Code (CIRC) Information

A drive-controller IC and servo-processor IC are responsible for directing laser focus, tracking, sled motor control (and feedback), spindle motor control (and feedback), and loading/unloading motor control.

Drive Interface

AT Attachment Packet Interface (ATARI) or IDE Interface. The ATARI connection combines more than adequate performance (CDs hardly strain even the slowest of IDE connections) with low cost and easy wiring. Using the ATARI, the system gets exactly the same degree of control over the CDs as with the more complex SCSI link.

If one already has two IDE hard disks in the PC, a secondary host adapter will give you the connection one needs. Most cables and connectors are keyed to prevent inadvertent mis-insertion. In any case, the red or blue stripe on the edge of the ribbon cable indicates the side of th'e connector holding the lower numbered pins.

Understanding the Software

Hardware alone is not enough to implement a CD-ROM or CD-R drive. BIOS and MS-DOS provide the software support to handle the drive, Manufacturers provide a hardware-specific device driver used to communicate with the CD-ROM and interface. An MS-DOS extension (MSCDEX) provides file handling and logical drive letter support.

Device Drivers

A device driver allows programs to access the CD-ROM or CD-R drive properly at the register (hardware) level. Because most CD-ROM/CD-R drives are designed differently, they require different device drivers. Device driver uses a SYS extension, and is initiated by adding its command line to the PC's CONFIG.SYS file, such as:

```
DEVICE=SSCDROM.SYS/D:MSCD000/N:1/P:300
```

Principles and Working of CD-ROM Drive

CD-ROM/CD-R drives are impressive pieces of engineering. The drive accept standard-sized disks and spin the disk at a Constant Linear Velocity (CLV)—that is, the disk speed varies inversely with the tracking radius. As tracking approaches the disk edge, disk speeds slows, and vice versa.

Keep in mind that CLV is different than the Constant Angular Velocity (CAV) method used by floppy and hard drives, which moves the media at a constant speed. The purpose of CLV is to ensure that CD data is read at a constant rate. A drive must be able to follow the spiral data path on a spinning CD-ROM. The drive electronics must be able to detect and correct any unforeseen data errors in real time, operate reliably over a long working life.

CDs are not segregated into concentric tracks and sectors as magnetic media is. Instead, CDs are recorded as a single, continuous spiral track running from the spindle to the lead out area. Each pit is about 0.12 mm (micrometers deep and 0.6 mm wide. Pits and lands can range from 0.9 to 3.3 mm in length. Approximately 1.6 mm are between each iteration of the spiral. Given these microscopic dimensions, a CDROM disc offers about 16,000 tracks per inch (TPI). During playback, CDs use a highly focused laser beam and laser detector to sense the presence or absence of pits.

The laser/detector pair is mounted on a carriage, which follows the spiral track across the CD. A laser is directed at the underside of the CD, where it penetrates more than 1 mm of clear plastic before shining on the reflective surface. When laser light strikes a land, the light is reflected toward the detector, which, in turn, produces a very strong output signal. As laser light strikes a pit, the light is slightly out of focus. As a result, most of the incoming laser energy is scattered away in all directions, so very little output signal is generated by the detector.

As with floppy and hard drives, the transition from pit to land (and back again) corresponds to binary levels, not the presence or absence of a pit or land. The analog light signal returned by the detector must be converted to logic levels and decoded. A process known as Eight-to-Fourteen Modulation (EFM) is very common with CD-ROMs.

EFM and Data Storage

A complex decoding process is necessary to convert the arcane sequence of pits and lands into meaningful binary information. The technique of EFM is used with CD-ROMs. For hard-disk drives, such techniques as 2.7 RLL encoding can be used to place a large number of bits into a limited number of flux transitions. The same is true for CDs using EFM.

User data, error-correction information, address information, and synchronization patterns are all contained in a bit stream that is represented by pits and lands. Magnetic media encodes bits as flux transitions—not the discrete orientation of any magnetic area. The same concept holds true with CD-ROMs, where binary 1s and 0s do not correspond to pits or lands. A binary 1 is represented wherever a transition (pit to land or land to pit) occurs. The length of a pit or land represents the number of binary 0s.

The EFM encoding technique equates each byte (8 bits) with a 14-bit sequence (called a symbol), where each binary. 1 must be separated by at least two binary 0s.

A CD-ROM frame is composed of 24 synchronization bits, 14 control bits, 24 of the 14-bit data symbols you saw previously, and eight complete 14-bit Error-Correction (EC) symbols. Each symbol is separated by additional three merge bits, bringing the total number of bits in the frame to 588. Thus, 24 bytes of data is represented by 588 bits on a CD-ROM, expressed as a number of pits and lands. There are 98 frames in a data block, so each block carries (98 x 24) = 2048 bytes (2352 with error correction, synchronization, and address bytes).

The basic CD-ROM can deliver 153.6 KB of data (75 blocks) per second to its host controller.

Advantages

1. Instead of using 15 to 20 diskettes an entire suite of programs and data could reside on a single CD-ROM.
2. CD-ROM are not vulnerable to magnetic fields which can destroy the data on a diskette.

3. Optical media are extremely durable and reliable under normal use. Because the surface of the disk (sealed in its plastic coating) is never touched by anything but light and because the medium itself is virtually unaffected by moisture on temperature conditions.
4. One reason optical technology is so reliable is that the read head is several millimeters away from the disk surface.

However there are two main reasons that prevent CD drives from totally displacing hard devices:

One reason is that CD drives are still slow. A drive that meets the multimedia PC2 standard for performance only has to move 900 KB of data per second. A good hard drive, by comparison, transfers 10 MB of data per second. Whereas on time scale the internal hard drive can find the data your application asks for in 10 msec, and on the other side CD-ROM drive takes upto 300 msec for the same task.

The other reason is that you can not write to portions of a writable CD-ROM that already have data written to them. You can add to data that was written to the disk in an earlier session but you can't delete or change what is already there.

Data Transfer Speed in Various CD Drives

Transfer Speed	Megabytes/s	Megabits/s	Mebibits/s
1x	0.15	1.2	1.1444
2x	0.3	2.4	2.2888
4x	0.6	4.8	4.5776
8x	1.2	9.6	9.1553
10x	1.5	12.0	11.4441
12x	1.8	14.4	13.7329
20x	3.0	24.0	22.8882
32x	4.8	38.4	36.6211
36x	5.4	43.2	41.1987
40x	6.0	48.0	45.7764
48x	7.2	57.6	54.9316
50x	7.5	60.0	57.2205
52x	7.8	62.4	59.5093

CD-ROM Capacity

A standard 120 mm CD-ROM holds 650 or 700 MiB of data. To put this storage capacity into context, the average novel contains 60,000 words. Assume that average word length is 10 letters and that each letter occupies one byte.

A novel therefore might occupy 600,000 bytes (600 kB, without layout information). One CD can therefore contain over 1,000 novels. If each novel occupies at least one centimetre of bookshelf space, then one CD can contain the equivalent of over ten metres of bookshelf. However, textual data can be compressed by more than a factor of ten, using compression algorithms, so a CD-ROM can accommodate at least 100 metres of bookshelf space.

In comparison a single layer DVD contains 4.4 GB of data, nearly 7 times the amount of a CD-ROM.

Capacities of Compact Disc types

Type	Sectors	Data max size (MB)	(MiB)	Audio max size (MB)	(MiB)	Time (min)
8 cm	94,500	193.536	~ 184.6	222.264	~ 212.0	21
283,500	580.608	~ 553.7	666.792	~ 635.9	63	
650 MB	333,000	681.984	~ 650.3	783.216	~ 746.9	74
700 MB	360,000	737.280	~ 703.1	846.720	~ 807.4	80
800 MB	405,000	829.440	~ 791.0	952.560	~ 908.4	90
900 MB	445,500	912.384	~ 870.1	1,047.816	~ 999.3	99

Note: Megabyte (MB) and minute (min) values are exact.

CD capacities are always given in binary units, although decimal SI prefixes are usually used: a "700 MB" CD has a nominal capacity of about 700 MiB. DVD capacities, on the other hand, are given in decimal units: a "4.7 GB" DVD has a nominal capacity of about 4.38 GiB.

Installing of CD Drive

The following procedure outlines the installation of a CDROM drive.

1. Disconnect the power to the computer.
2. Configure the appropriate master/slave settings or SCSI ID for the drive.
3. Insert the drive into an available drive bay.
4. Screw in the 4 screws — 2 on each side of the bay.
5. If the drive is an IDE, connect the IDE cable to the drive. There should be a stripe along 1 edge of the cable. This stripe denotes pin 1. Pin 1 on the drive is usually closest to the power connector on the drive, however, you should consult the manufacturers documentation. Then connect the signal cable to the motherboard ID1 or ID2 interface making sure to note the pin 1 orientation there as well. If the drive is a SCSI drive, a SCSI cable would be connected from the drive to a SCSI controller card.
6. Connect one of the power supply's power connectors to the drive.

Troubleshooting CD-ROM Drives

The troubleshooting steps for CD-ROM and DVD drives are nearly identical to those of an HDD system. The connections and data paths are very similar. Basically, three levels of troubleshooting apply to CD-ROM problems. These are the configuration level, the operating system level, and the hardware level.In most systems, the CD-ROM and DVD drives share a controller or host adapter with the hard disk drive. Therefore, verify their Master/Slave jumper settings to ensure they are set correctly. Normally, the CD-ROM or DVD drive should be set up as the master on the secondary IDE channel.

In this manner, each drive has its own communications channel and does not need to share. If three or four IDE devices are installed in the system, you must determine which devices can share the channels most effectively. In many systems, the CD-ROM and DVD drives share a controller or host adapter with the hard disk drive. Therefore, if the hard drive is working and the CD-ROM drive is not, the likelihood that the problem is in the CD-ROM or DVD drive unit is very high.

Recordable Disk:Write Once, Read Many (WORM)

As with the CD, once data have been etched into the surface of a WORM disk they can not be changed. WORM is an ideal medium for making a permanent record of data, *i.e.*, it can be a feasible alternative to magnetic tape for archival storage.

For example, many banks use WORM disks to store a record of each day's transactions. The transactions are written to an optical disk and become a permanent record that can be read but never altered.

Another popular application of WORM disks is in information systems, that require the merging of text and images that do not change for a period of time. A good example is an "electronic catalog".

A customer can pursue a retailer's electronic catalog on a VDT, or perhaps a PC, and see the item while he reads about it and, with a few keystrokes the customer can order the item as well.

Erasable Disks: Magneto-Optical Disks

A hybrid disk, called magneto-optical (MO), combines the best features of magnetic and optical disk technologies. A magneto-optical disk has the high-volume capacity of an optical disk but can be written over as a magnetic disk. The disk surface is coated with plastic and embedded with magnetically sensitive metallic crystals.

To write data, laser beam melts a tiny spot on the plastic surface and a magnet aligns the crystal before the plastic cools. The crystal are placed in such a way that some reflect lights and others do not. Later on, when the data is read by a laser beam, only the crystals that reflect light are picked up.

Disadvantages

1. Magneto-optical disks are too expensive and do not offer anywhere near the kind of reliability that users have come to expect of magnetic media.
2. The access time in magneto-optical disks are relatively slow, about the same as a low-end, Winchester disk.
3. As optical disk technology matures to offer reliable, cost-effective, read/write operation, it eventually may dominate secondary storage in the future as magnetic disks and tape to today.

DVD

DVD stand stands for digital video disc or digital versatile disc, is the next generation of optical disc storage technology. It is bigger, faster CD that can hold cinema-like view, better-than-CD audio, and compatriot CD data. Using a DVD you can have home entertainment, computers, and business information with a single digital format. The DVD will eventually replace audio/video CD, videotape, laserdisc, CD-ROM, and video game cartridges.

There are various variations of DVD; DVD-ROM or DVD-R are physical formats and DVD-Video or DVD-Audio are application formats. DVD-ROM is the base format that holds data. Physical format of DVD-ROM includes recordable variations DVD-R, DVD-RAM, DVD-RW, and DVD-RW. The application formats include DVD-Video, DVD-Video Recording, DVD-Audio, DVD-Audio Recording, DVD Stream Recording, and SACD.

Storage Capacity of DVDs

DVDs are of the same diameter and thickness as CDs, and they are made using some of the same materials and manufacturing methods. Like a CD, the data on a DVD is encoded in the form of small pits and bumps in the track of the disc. A DVD is composed of several layers of plastic, totalling about 1.2 millimeters thick. Each layer is created by injection molding polycarbonate plastic. This process forms a disc that has microscopic bumps arranged as a single, continuous and extremely long spiral track of data.

Once the clear pieces of polycarbonate are formed, a thin reflective layer is sputtered onto the disc, covering the bumps. Aluminium is used behind the inner layers, but a semi-reflective gold layer is used for the outer layers, allowing the laser to focus through the outer and onto the inner layers. After all the layers are made, each one is coated with lacquer, squeezed together and cured under infrared light.

For single-sides discs, the label is silk-screened onto the nonreadable side. Double-sided discs are printed only on the nonredable area near the hold in the middle. If you could lift the data track off a single layer of a DVD, and stretch it out into a straight line, it would be almost 7.5 miles long. A double-sided, double-layer DVD would have 30 miles of data.

Multi-Layer Storage

To increase the storage capacity, a DVD can have up to four layers, two on each side. The laser that reads the disc can actually focus on the second layer through the first layer. Here is a list of the capacities of different forms of DVDs:

DVD disc capacity

Physical size	Single layer capacity		Dual/Double layer capacity	
	GB	GiB	GB	GiB
12 cm, single sided	4.7	4.38	8.5	7.92
12 cm, double sided	9.4	8.75	17.1	15.93
8 cm, single sided	1.4	1.30	2.6	2.42
8 cm, double sided	2.8	2.61	5.2	4.84

Note: GB here means gigabyte, equal to 10^9 (or 1,000,000,000) bytes. Many programs will display gibibyte (GiB), equal to 2^{30} (or 1,073,741,824) bytes.

Example: A disc with 8.5 GB capacity is equivalent to: (8.5 × 1,000,000,000) / 1,073,741,824 H" 7.92 GiB.

Size Note: There is a difference in size between + and - DL DVD formats. For example, the 12 cm single sided disk has capacities:

Disk Type	Sectors	bytes	GB	GiB
DVD-R SL	2,298,496	4,707,319,808	4.7	4.384
DVD+R SL	2,295,104	4,700,372,992	4.7	4.378
DVD-R DL	4,171,712	8,543,666,176	8.5	7.957
DVD+R DL	4,173,824	8,547,991,552	8.5	7.961

Capacity Nomenclature

The four basic types of DVD are referred to by their capacity in gigabytes, rounded up to the nearest integer.

DVD type	Name
Single sided, single layer	DVD-5
Single sided, dual layer	DVD-9
Double sided, single layer	DVD-10
Double sided, dual layer	DVD-18

Another format in limited use is a double sided DVD with one side comprising a single layer of data while the opposite side comprises two layers of data (effectively a DVD-5 on one side bonded to a DVD-9 on the other). This format holds approximately 12.3 GB of data and is known as DVD-14.

Various ROM Drives

According to needs and developments, the ROM has also changed over the years. With the advent of DVDs the option to read and write on it has also added the needed. Various combinations available available are:

CD ROM Drive

It is the simple CD ROM drive which can read all the simple CD ROM formats. But no option of writing to the CD ROM.

DVD ROM Drive

Drive which can read the DVD drive but cannot write DVD but create CD ROM.

DVD Writer

Drive which can read all type of CD ROM including the DVD and write too on DVD ROMs.

Combo Drive

A Combo drive is a type of optical drive that combines CD-R/CD-RW recording capability with the ability to read (but not write) DVD media. The term was popularized by Apple Computer as a name for the low-end substitute for their high-end SuperDrive, which was designed to both read and write DVD and DVD recordable media. The device was created as a mid-range option between a CD burner and a DVD burner, which at the time the combo drive was introduced was generally an expensive option costing in excess of US$300 a unit.

Combo drives are becoming less and less common on new systems, though they do occasionally appear in lieu of CD-only drives on low-end computers to lower production and sale costs. The cost difference between a combo drive and DVD burner has been steadily declining in recent years, so most new PCs (except for the low-end budget computers) have a DVD burner (which also reads and writes CDs).

In Apple computers, only the bottom of the range MacBooks and Mac minis have combo drives.

Super Multi Drive

Super Multi is an informal term used to describe a type of CD and DVD recorder that writes CD-R, CD-RW, DVD-R/DVD-RW, DVD+R/DVD+RW and DVD-RAM formats. Some recorders are also able to write DVD-R DL and DVD+R DL formats.

This term was coined by LG and is now officially protected by LG. It is also used by NEC for some of their products. LiteOn uses the term "Super AllWrite" instead, which essentially has the same meaning.

But these is not the complete list, there can be more.

Revision

1. The CD-ROM has two sections namely Mechanical Section and the Electronics Section.
2. The main CD subassembly called a drive engine, which uses to hold eject, spin, and read the disk.
3. A CD drive ideally requires a linear motor to act much like the voice coil motor used to position hard-drive R/W heads.
4. CDs are recorded as a single, continuous spiral track running from the spindle to the lead out area.
5. A CD-ROM frame is composed of 24 synchronization bits, 14 control bits, 24 of the 14-bit data symbols you saw previously, and eight complete 14-bit Error-Correction (EC) symbols.
6. A hybrid disk, called magneto-optical (MO), combines the best features of magnetic and optical disk technologies.
7. A Combo drive is a type of optical drive that combines CD-R/CD-RW recording capability with the ability to read (but not write) DVD media.
8. CD-ROM (Compact disk-read only memory) are created at a mastering facility.

9. A magneto-optical disk has the high-volume capacity of an optical disk but can be written over as a magnetic disk.
10. DVD stand stands for digital video disc or digital versatile disc, is the next generation of optical disc storage technology.

Multiple Choice Questions

1. DVD stands for:
   (a) Direct Video Disc
   (b) Data Video Disc
   (c) Digital Video Disc
2. CD-ROM stand for:
   (a) Current Disk Read Only Memory
   (b) Compact Disk Read Only Memory
   (c) Close Disk Read Only Memory
3. CD ROM storage is .... MB.
   (a) 650
   (b) 702
   (c) 750
4. WORM stands for:
   (a) Write Once, Read Many
   (b) Write Once, Read Maybe
   (c) Write Over, Read Many

True/False Questions

1. The main CD subassembly called a drive engine, which uses to hold eject, spin, and read the disk.
2. CDs are not recorded as a single, continuous spiral track running from the spindle to the lead out area.
3. A hybrid disk, called magneto-optical (MO), combines the best features of magnetic and optical disk technologies.
4. CD-ROM (Compact disk-read only memory) are created at a mastering facility.
5. A magneto-optical disk has the high-volume capacity of an optical disk but can be written over as a magnetic disk.

Descriptive Questions

1. Why are CDs more command?
2. How would you install the CD Drive?
3. Draw back panel of CD ROM drive?
4. Why are CD-ROM preferred over the floppy disks?
5. What are Optical Disks?
6. Describe the working of DVD.

7. What is WORM?
8. What is an Erasable disk?
9. Define the various storage capacities of the DVD.
10. What is a Combo drive?
11. How would you take care of the CD Drive?
12. Define the various capacities of DVD.

Answers to Objective Type Questions

Multiple Choice Questions

1. c	2. b	3. c	4. a

True False Questions

1. T	2. F	3. T	4. T
5. T			

9 Input Devices

Keyboard

The most common input medium in computer is Keyboard. Without it many consider the computer as incomplete. Let us see how the data is accepted by computer when fed in by the keyboard.

How Computer Accepts Input from the Keyboard

When we press a key on a keyboard key say the letter S, then a tiny computer chip inside either the computer or the keyboard called the keyboard controller, takes a note that a key has been pressed and places a code into part of its memory buffer, indicating which key was pressed. This code is called the key's Scan Code (identifying number). Now without specifying what has happened the keyboard controller signals (*i.e.*, sends interrupt) the computer processing components that something has happened at the keyboard. The keyboard controller sends an interrupt request to the CPU (using the interrupt number 9 assigned to the keyboard interrupt) when it receives a complete keystroke.

Interrupts cause the CPU to put aside what it is doing and jump to an interrupt handling program. In this case the interrupt handles an integral part of the ROM-BIO software. When the computer's processing components receive an interrupt request, the program that is controlling the computer at that moment evaluates the request to determine the appropriate response. In the case of a key press, the program reads the memory location in the keyboard buffer that contains the scan code of the key that was pressed and places the keyboard letter in the computer's main memory.

The keyboard buffer can actually store a number of keystrokes at once. This is necessary

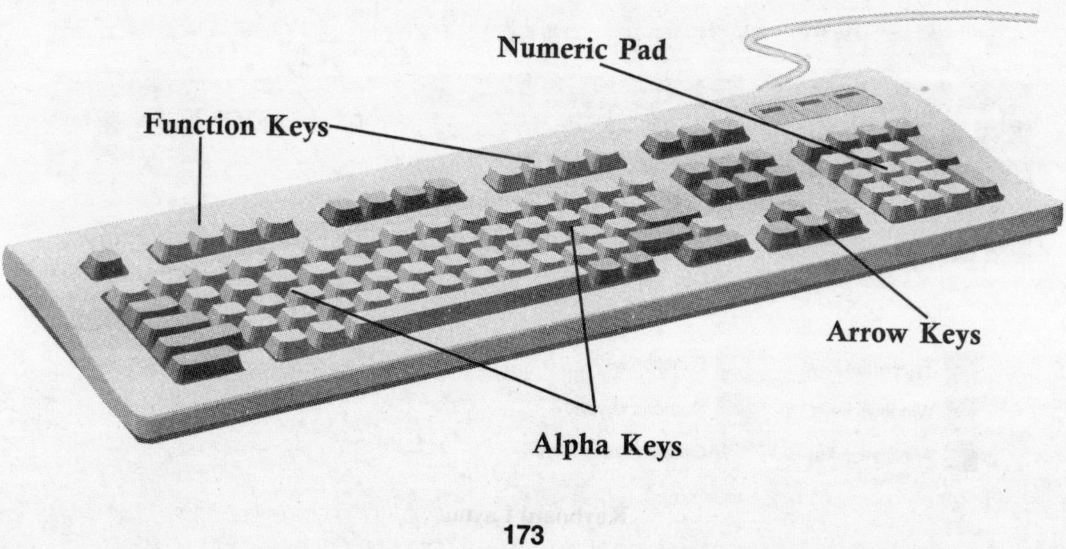

because some time elapses between the pressing of a key and the computer's reading of that key from the keyboard buffer. Also programmers must put instructions into their programs to read keystrokes and program might be doing something else when the key is pressed.

With the keystrokes stored in a buffer the program can react to them when convenient. Because reading the keyboard to get the scan code of a key action is a function of software, we can reassign scan codes to represent different letters or symbols.

Keyboard Keys

There are more keys on computer keyboard than on typewriter. Most commonly used keyboards has **101 keys** and more. With XT, 84 key keyboard was used but it has now become obsolete. The 101 key keyboard has the important keys:

Alphabetic Keys

These are alphabet keys from [A] to [Z]. As in typewriter, you can use [SHIFT] to make them capital, *i.e.*, ABCDE, etc. So if you press a b c d e .... etc. With [SHIFT] key already pressed, you will get A B C D E .... etc. Similar results can be obtained by putting CAPS LOCK key ON.

a = [A]

[SHIFT] + [A] = A

For typing [A], you press [SHIFT] key and then while keeping [SHIFT] key pressed, press the "a". Otherwise for typing a, you don't need to press the [SHIFT] key, just press the a key.

Numeric Keys

The numeric keys (with the characters 0 to 9) are located on the computer's keyboard at two places. You can see them in the top row above the alpha keys (as in typewriter). A

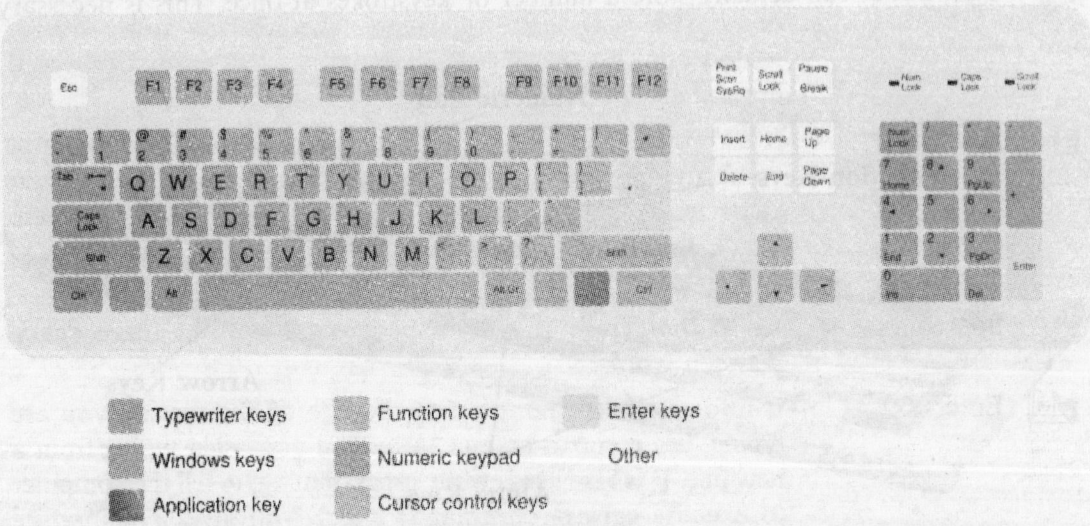

Keyboard Layout

second set of these keys is provided on the right-hand side of the keyboard. The numeric keys in the top row can be used straightaway to type in numeric characters. By simultaneously holding down the Shift key (as in the typewriter), you can also type in special upper characters like ! % $ *, etc. However, to type numeric characters by using the keys on the right side, you will need to press the Num Lock key ON.

Function Keys

These keys are marked [F1] to [F10] in the 84 key format and to [F12] in the 101 format. These keys are used for specific purposes as defined in the computer (a computer program is a set of instructions given to a computer to perform a specific task) which you may be using. For example, in BASIC programming (BASIC is a computer language used for writing programs) [F3] will load the program, [F1] will list the program after loading and [F2] will run the program.

Arrow Keys

On 101 keys keyboard these are placed at two places. The first is called the cursor pad which works independently. The other is the numeric-cum-cursor pad. It is similar to the one on the 84 key keyboard. When the Num Lock key is not in the ON position, pressing the key of the numeric keypad moves the cursor in the direction shown on each key. Otherwise, this portion is used to enter numbers.

Special Keys Including Spacebar

There are several other keys which serve some definite purposes. Some of these keys are available on the typewriter too. The special keys are:

[SHIFT]	Shift Key	It is used for typing capital letters and special characters. In combination with both Control and Alternate keys, it is sometimes used to execute a particular command too.
[CTRL]	Control Key	On its own, this key does not have any purpose. However, combined with different keys, it performs some useful operations. For example, in WordStar software, Control if pressed alongwith B, will make the character Bold.
[←]	Backspace	It allows the cursor to go back by one character. Some types of computer programs allow the backspace to delete the last character. A cursor is usually a blinking line (_), on the screen, which shows where the character you type on your keyboard will appear.
	Spacebar	As in the typewriter, the Spacebar is used to leave space between words.
[ENTER]	Enter Key	It informs the computer that the line of the matter, you are typing, has come to an end. After that you begin typing from a new line. It is also used, while programming, to tell the computer to execute certain commands which you give. Thus, while writing a computer program, you can also use this key to

indicate the end of a given command.

Del Key — If, by mistake, you have typed in something which you did not want to, you can erase the wrong character by pressing the DEL (short for Delete) key.

Various other types of keyboards which are available but very much in use are:

DVORAK Keyboard

The DVORAK Keyboard, named after its inventor August Dvorak, was invented in 1932. Through ergonomic studies of typists, he noticed that the QWERTY layout forces that majority of the work to be done by the weakest finger — the fourth and fifth fingers of the left hand. The stronger, quicker right hand and middle fingers are used only for the least frequently typed characters. The Dvorak keyboard layout, places the most frequently used characters in the center, *i.e.*, on the home row (the vowels plus, d, h, t, n and s).

The next most frequently used characters are placed up one row because it is easier to reach up than down. Because this layout distributes the typing work load among the fingers according to their strengths, awkward strokes are reduced by 90%. Operators who are involved with word processing have found 75% improvement in their production after switching over to Dvorak keyboard.

PC users who want to try the Dvorak layout do not need to replace their QWERTY keyboard. The switch can be made electronically.

AZERTY Keyboard

The AZERTY layout of keyboards are used in some European typewriters. The term describes the sequences of the first six letters in the first row of alphabetic keys.

Troubleshooting Keyboard

Most of the problem faced in keyboard operation can be divided into two categories:

- complete non-operation of the keyboard and .
- broken or stuck keys

First problem could be either because of a broken connection between the keyboard and the system or because of some problem in the keyboard or the main system itself. If you find that your keyboard is not working then to see if the problem is with the keyboard or the main system you can try a different working keyboard on your system.

If the new keyboard is also not working then the problem most probably is with the main system. If the new keyboard is working properly then the problem is with your old keyboard. You can also try your old keyboard on some other machine to make sure that the fault is really with the keyboard.

When the keyboard of a system is not working then some of the points that must be checked are:

- Some old keyboards have a small switch at their bottom side to select the operating mode of the keyboard. Using this switch one can select either XT (8088/8086) or

AT (80286) operating mode.

- Many old computers have a keyboard lock on the front panel. This lock disables the keyboard. Forgetting to unlock this lock, or not properly unlocking this could be one reason of the keyboard not working.
- Another problem could be the connector from lock to the motherboard coming loose at the lock or the motherboard side.
- The keyboard socket on the motherboard—into which the keyboard is plugged—is often one of the reason of keyboard failure. This socket sometimes become loose and may not connect properly with the keyboard. A loose socket may give intermittent problems in the keyboard operation.
- Check the connection between the socket and the motherboard. Check for any loose solder on motherboard.
- Check the keyboard cable. Open the keyboard, remove the cable and using a Multi-meter test each wire for continuity and cross-connection. If some fault is found then replace the cable.

Installing Keyboard

1. Position the keyboard cable over the connector, and pull the keyboard slightly to the right so the cable is not bent. Hold the cable as close as possible to the connector and press straight down. Press the cable firmly into the connector.
2. Flip the keyboard over and insert the small tabs at the bottom of the keyboard into the openings in the PowerBook case.
3. Pull down on the keyboard release tabs (located to the left of the F1 and F9 keys) and then press down on the top portion of the keyboard.
4. Let go of the keyboard release tabs to secure the keyboard in place.
5. Replace the PowerBook battery or plug in the power adapter.
6. Restart the computer.

Removing the Installed Keyboard

1. Place your computer on a clean, flat surface.
2. Shut down your computer, remove the battery from the expansion bay, and disconnect the power adapter, modem, and any other cables connected to the computer.
3. Make sure that the keyboard locking screw is not in the locked position. Your new PowerBook comes with the keyboard unlocked, so unless you or someone else locked the keyboard, you can skip this step.
4. Release the keyboard by pulling down on the keyboard release tabs (located to the left of the F1 and F9 keys) until the top portion of the keyboard pops up.
5. Lift the top portion of the PowerBook keyboard up slightly near the top row of keys and pull it back far enough to release the small tabs that hold the bottom of the keyboard in place.

6. Flip the keyboard over and lay it on the palm rests.
7. Touch a metal surface inside the computer to discharge any static electricity.
8. Grasp the keyboard cable as close as possible to the connector and pull up to disconnect the keyboard from the logic board. Rock the cable carefully if additional leverage is needed.

Mouse

Don't be afraid, it is not a real one. It is so called since it resembling a "Rat". In fact, it is a pointing device. These days it is almost essential for personal computers. Click at any place on the monitor with mouse to point out the location where you want to input the information. All Windows-based programs use mouse, making working with computers easier as you are not required to type commands.

It is a pointing device that lets you move a cursor or pointer on the screen just by moving the mouse around on a flat surface. A mouse also allows you to create graphic elements on the screen, such as lines, curves and freehand shapes and makes using menus and message boxes easier.

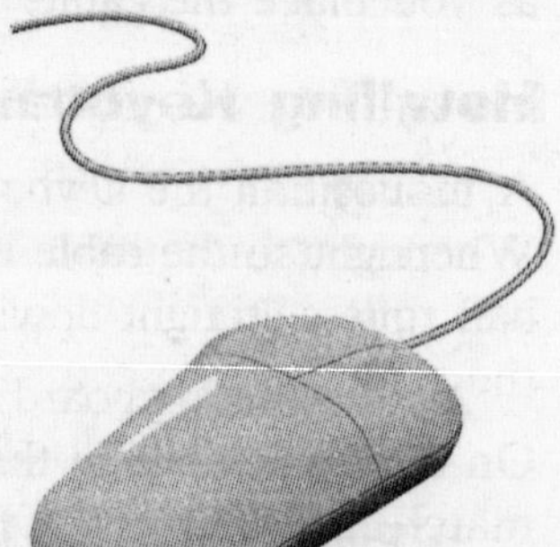

Types of Mouse

There are three basic types of Mouse

1. Mechanical Mouse
2. Optomechanical Mouse
3. Optical Mouse

Mechanical Mouse

A mechanical mouse has a rubber or metal ball on its underside that can roll in all directions. Mechanical sensors within the mouse detect the direction of the rolling ball and make a movement of the screen pointer accordingly.

Optomechanical Mouse

Optomechanical mouse is also similar to a mechanical mouse except that it uses optical sensors to detect the movement of the ball on the Mouse Pad.

Optical Mouse

Optical mouse uses a laser beam to detect the movement of mouse on specially designed Mouse Pad. We must move the mouse along a special mat with a grid so that optical mechanism has a frame of reference. This type of mouse has no mechanical moving parts. Optical mouse respond more quickly and precisely than any other mouse. These are very expensive.

A mouse can be used for many applications ranging from games to designing products with graphics. It provides an alternative for people who are uncomfortable with a keyboard or it can be used in combination with a keyboard to enhance input operations.

The mouse is also used to draw sketches, diagram, etc., on the CRT screen. It is also moved on graphic tablet for drawing work and the same is also used to edit text. For editing text on the screen the cursor is quickly moved to the desired point of the screen by moving the mouse.

How to use the mouse

There are three simple techniques — clicking, double-clicking and dragging

Clicking

To click on something with the mouse means to move the pointer or cursor to the item on the screen and to press the release the mouse button once.

Double-Clicking

Press and release the mouse button twice in rapid succession.

Dragging

After positioning the mouse pointer over the item, then depress the button and hold it down as you move the mouse.

How Mouse Works

A mouse has a ball inside of it that extends just below the housing of the mouse itself. When you slide the mouse around on a flat surface such as a desktop or mouse pad the ball rolls. Movement of the mouse result in a corresponding movement of the pointer on the screen.

On two sides of the ball at 90 angle each other are two small rollers or wheels that spin to match the speed of the ball. Sensors detect how much each roller spins and send this

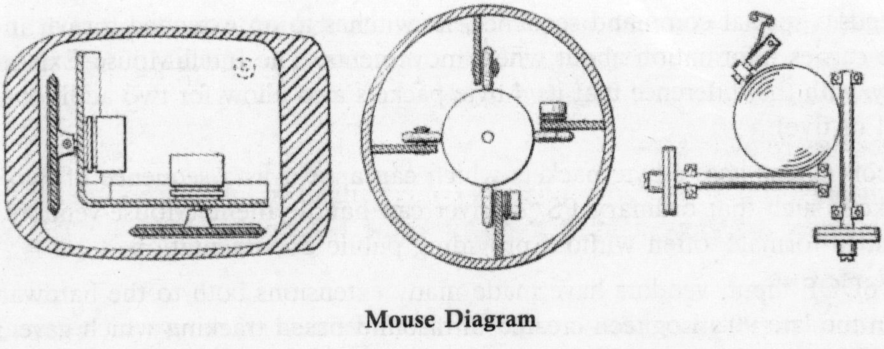

Mouse Diagram

information to the computer in the form of changes to the current pointer position.

Like the keyboard, a mouse does not actually send a message directly to the program that the computer is running. Rather it sends an interrupt request to the CPU. The program that is running checks regularly to see whether a mouse event has occurred or not.

Buttons on the Mouse

A mouse can have one, two or three buttons with a two or three-button mouse the primary or main button is the one on the left because most people are right-handed. We can reconfigure mouse device to make another button primary.

Connectivity and Communication Protocols

To transmit their input, typical cabled mice use a thin electrical cord terminating in a standard connector, such as RS-232C, PS/2, ADB or USB. Cordless mice instead transmit data via infrared radiation or radio (including Bluetooth).

The electrical interface and the format of the data transmitted by commonly available mice has in the past varied between different manufacturers.

Serial interface and protocol

Standard PC mice once used the RS-232C serial standard (released in 1969), via a DB-9 connector. The Mouse Systems Corporation version used a five-byte protocol and supported three buttons. The Microsoft version used an incompatible three-byte protocol and only allowed for two buttons. Due to the incompatibility, some manufacturers sold serial mice with a mode switch: "PC" for MSC mode, "MS" for Microsoft mode.

PS/2 interface and protocol

With the arrival of the IBM PS/2 personal-computer series in 1987, IBM introduced the eponymous PS/2 interface for mice and keyboards, which other manufacturers rapidly adopted. The most visible change was the use of a round 6-pin mini-DIN, in lieu of the former 5-pin connector. In default mode (called stream mode) a PS/2 mouse communicates motion, and the state of each button, by means of 3-byte packets.

Extensions: IntelliMouse and others

A Microsoft IntelliMouse relies on an extension of the PS/2 protocol: the ImPS/2 or IMPS/2 protocol (the abbreviation combines the concepts of "IntelliMouse" and "PS/2"). It initially operates in standard PS/2 format, for backwards compatibility. After the host sends a special command sequence, it switches to an extended format in which a fourth byte carries information about wheel movements. The IntelliMouse Explorer works analogously, with the difference that its 4-byte packets also allow for two additional buttons (for a total of five).

The Typhoon mouse uses 6-byte packets which can appear as a sequence of two standard 3-byte packets, such that ordinary PS/2 driver can handle them. Mouse-vendors also use other extended formats, often without providing public documentation.

For 3D or 6DOF input, vendors have made many extensions both to the hardware and to software. In the late 90's Logitech created ultrasound based tracking which gave 3D input to a few millimeters accuracy, which worked well as an input device but failed as a money making product.

Other input devices, such as PhaseSpace's 3D optical tracking, have served to create VR and AR input devices[citation needed], and experiments in this arena continue at Cambridge, Cardiff, UCSC and other universities as well as in government labs.[citation needed] This type of input device tracks multiple LED sources to provide sub-millimeter tracking for input to control tools and robots in a real or virtual space as well as in computer training.

Advantages

1. It is simple device and very easy to use.
2. It is not that very expensive.
3. It moves the cursor faster than the arrow keys of keyboard do.

Drawbacks of a Mouse

1. The movement of the cursor is not very sensitive to movement of mouse.
2. If the contact between wheels and mouse pad is lost, the cursor does not move.
3. It is not useful in word-processing or in computer programming applications.
4. It requires space on tabletop or other hard surface to roll.
5. It requires serial port for connection with computer system.

A recent development in the wireless mouse or remote mouse, which works on transmission of infrared or radio waves.

Troubleshooting Mouse

If you experience problems with your mouse, the problem could be because of the mouse, mouse driver software, the application software you are using, cables or the main system itself. So, before you throw away your mouse, try the following troubleshooting techniques:

- Make sure the mouse cable is correctly connected to its port.
- Turn your PC's system unit power off and back on and see if the error disappears.
- If you have a second mouse available, turn off your PC's power and connect the new mouse. Power the PC back on to see if the error disappears.
- Try the mouse on some other system where a mouse of the same type is working without any trouble.
- Some software do not support mouse. Try mouse with a program that is known to support the mouse.
- Make sure the mouse device driver being used is correct one and is setup correctly.
- If the mouse is a serial mouse, try using a second serial port. You might need to update the mouse device driver to use the second serial port.
- If you are using a bus mouse, make sure that the mouse adapter card is properly seated in its expansion slot.

Installing Mouse

A mouse connects to one of the serial ports, such as COM1 or COM2 on your computer. This is one of the most simple and commonly used mouse.

To replace or to install a serial mouse, perform these steps.

- First of all check if you have a spare serial port for the mouse. If you do not have a spare serial port, then you need to first install a serial interface board or a multi I/O board into your computer.

If you have a spare serial port or if you are replacing an already available serial mouse then perform the following steps:

- Power off the PC's main system unit.
- Remove the existing mouse by removing the mouse from the serial port.
- Select the new serial port into which you want to install a new mouse, connect the new mouse into the port. Sometime you may require 9 to 25 pin or 25 to 9 pin converter to connect the mouse to the available serial port.
- Power on your system, update your mouse driver and other software as necessary. Test the mouse.

Scanner

Whereas a keyboard, mouse or trackball requires manual input of data, scanners allow input of printed data. A scanner reads text, photographs and graphics from paper which are then converted into bit patterns for processing, storage or output. Scanner is a device that examines a spatial pattern one part after another and generate analog or digital signals corresponding to the pattern. Scanners are often used in mark sensing, pattern recognition or character recognition.

Practically scanner uses light for examining the spatial patterns. In a scanner, as the image is scanned, it is converted into light and dark picture elements, or pixels, similar to newspaper photo. This technique makes the images usable by word processing, desktop publishing, and graphic packages.

There are two main types of scanners, Hand-held scanner and Flat-bed scanner

Hand-held Scanner

These devices read data on price tags, shipping labels, inventory part number, book ISBNs, and the like. Hand-held scanner, sometimes called wand scanners, use either contact or laser technology. It has a set of light emitting diodes. It is placed over the material to be scanned and slowly dragged from the top to the bottom. The light emitted by the diodes are not reflected by black lines and are reflected by whole areas. The material is converted and stored in a bitmap. Typical applications are to store images and reproduce them in publications.

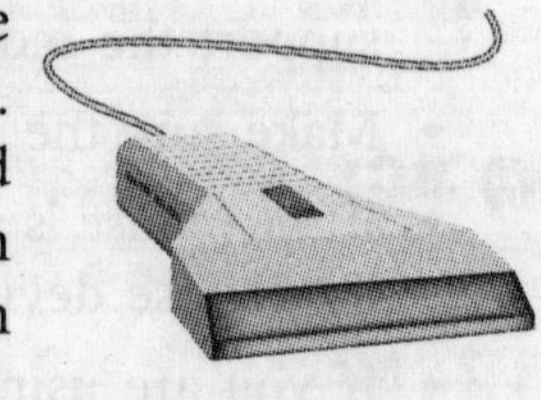

Flat-bed Scanner

It consists of a box with glass plate on top, which is used for placing the document to be scanned. The light beam is situated below the glass plate and is moved from left to right horizontally. After scanning one line the beam moves up little and scans the next line. The scanner can also store colour images.

Other types of scanners are:

Drum Scanners

These scanners use photo multiplier (PM) tubes and are expensive, sensitive devices that can capture information at a higher resolution and higher pixel-depth than flatbed scanners, which are based on charge coupled devices (CCDs). A PM tube is a light-sensing device with a much higher sensitivity and lower noise-to-signal-ration than a CCD. A drum scanner can capture shadow information that is not visible to the human eye. It can transform that information into the visible region and improve the image. This is particularly useful in scanning transparencies. However, drum scanners are too slow and expensive to use for OCR or document management applications.

Sheetfed Scanners

These scanners take up less desk space and are easier to install. But most of these can only scan loose sheets. Sheetfed scanners have been made more compact in size by turning the scanner design inside out. Instead of the head moving over the paper, tiny rubber wheels pull the paper over the scan head. The wheels, however, do not track perfectly, so pages at times get skewed, resulting in a crooked scan. Sheetfed scanners focus more on managing paper flow than on getting an optimal scan.

Installing Scanner

To install a scanner follow the steps below:

(*i*) Parallel Port Scanner

1. Shutdown system.
2. Hook parallel connector to printer port of your computer. If you have a SCSI scanner, or USB simply hook into one of those ports.
3. Unlock scanner head. This is usually done underneath scanner of on sides by power switch.
4. Plug in power for scanner boot system up Windows will recognize new device and hardware manager will appear.

(*ii*) SCSI Scanner

1. If you have a SCSI scanner first cover installing the SCSI Adapter Card.
2. Make sure and refer to your adapters documentation for jumper settings. You will want to set the jumpers if any before we install the adapter.
3. Turn Off PC and unplug from outlet.
4. Remove case cover
5. Unscrew a slot on case for adapter card
6. Connect any necessary internal cables. (drives)
7. Align card with Bus slot and seat evenly. Be careful of any catching the cards ports on anything.

8. Tighten down card snug
9. Close case
10. Hook up power

(*iii*) USB Scanner

1. This one is very simple. You will simply plug in with computer running and install a driver for it.
2. Exit all programs running.
3. With only windows running plug in your scanner into the USB port
4. Give windows a few seconds
5. you should be brought to a hardware wizard
6. Now you are ready to load a driver for it.

Scanning The Scanner

A flatbed scanner uses a light source, a lens, a charge coupled device (CCD) array and one or more analog-to-digital converters (ADCs) to collect optical information about the object to be scanned, and transforms it to a computer image file. A CCD is a miniature photometer that measures incident light and converts that measured value to analog voltage.

When an object is placed on a scanner's copy board or glass surface and start scanning, the light source illuminates a thin horizontal strip of the object called a raster line. Thus, when an image is scanned it can scan one line at a time. During the exposure of each raster line, the scanner carriage (optical imaging elements, which is a network of lenses and mirrors) is mechanically moved over a small distance using a motor. The reflected light is captured by the CCD array. Each CCD converts the light to an analog voltage and indicates the gray level for one pixel. The analog voltage is then converted to a digital value by an analog-to-digital converter (ADC), using.8,10 or 12 bits per colour.

The CCDs elements are all in one row, with one element for each pixel in a line. If you have 300 CCD elements for each inch across the scanner, you can have a maximum potential optical resolution of 300 pixels per inch (ppi) also referred to as dots per inch (dpi). In case you have 600 CCD elements for each inch, then the maximum optical resolution will be 600 ppi or 600 dpi.

There are two methods by which the incident white light is sensed by the CCD. The first involves a rapidly rotating light filter that individually filters the red, green and blue components of the reflected light and is sensed bya single CCD device. Here, the colour filter is fabricated into the chip directly. In the second method, a prismatic beam splitter first splits the reflected white light and three individual CCDs sense the red, green and blue light beams. High precision is required in the optics and in the alignment of the sensing mechanisms for this method.

A Scanner for You

How can one identify a first-rate scanner? The answer is not so simple, though it would suffice to say that it is one that combines accuracy and minimal loss with maximum power and ease in compensating for the distortions. One of the most potentially confusing claims for scanners is the number of bits that they offer. You often come across terms like 24, 30, or 36 bit scanners, but what do they actually mean?

Bits are the basic elements of digital data. A single bit is either on or off, usually expressed as 1 or 0 so that there are only two variations. Each pixel of a scanned image has a 'depth' of one to 32 bits. 1-bit images are black and white (for example, line art). A 2-bit pixel contains four variations (00 01 1011) and allows a variation of the colour from, white to light grey to dark grey to black.

An 8-bit pixel can vary anywhere within the full range of 256 grey values. 24-bit images are actually three 8-bit channels, one each for red, green and blue light. A 32-bit image can be an RGB image with a fourth channel (for example an alpha channel in Adobe Photoshop) or, more commonly, a CMYK image with one 8-bit channel for each of cyan, magenta, yellow and black.

A 24-bit scanner divides each of its primary colours-red, green, or blue (RGB) into 8 bits, or 256 (28) shades. (In grey scale mode, a 24-bit scanner captures 256 shades of grey). This 256^3 gives you 16.7 million possible colours. This is the maximum that most high-end graphics boards will display. A 30-bit scanner offers 10 bit or 1,024 shades for each colour, while a 36-bit scanner offers 12 bits or 4,096 shades.

However, even this data is not enough for a perfect picture. Once the seventh and eighth bits are reached, accuracy takes a nosedive. This results in loss or distorted details—especially in the highlight and shadow regions. Further applying tone corrections—adjusting gamma curve results, brightness and contrast-reduces the size of the colour palette, esulting in loss of data. You can still change the colours but you cannot work with what is not there!

The solution lies in adding more bits and making it a 30-bit scanner. A 30-bit scanner offers 10 bits per colour or captures 1,024 shades of red, green, or blue for over a billion colours. The first 8 bits are fairly accurate, so the scanner can just junk the last couple of bits and leave you with superior 24-bit colour.

If the scanner performs tonal corrections of colour at the hardware level, greater advantage can be derived from the larger number of colours. If one expands part of the tonal range of a 24-bit image to bring out, say, the shadow details, one will automatically end up compressing it elsewhere, thus losing midtones and highlight details. A 30-bit scanner can use the instructions imparted to select and deliver the best 24 bits of data for the required needs, giving one the corrected image with much greater detail retention and smoother tonal continuity.

However, 30-bit and 36-bit scanners use the extra bits internally, and generally send only 24 bits to the computer.

Colour Models

Colour models are closely related to bit depth. Greyscale goes up to 8-bit, which renders 256 shades. Colour images are multiples of 8-bit channels. RGB, the normal model for computer graphics, goes up to 24-bit (three 8-bit channels for red, green, and blue). CMYK, the standard for printing colour images, is a 32-bit model.

RGB Colour

Red, green and blue are the primary colours of light. The human eye responds to stimuli from varying RGB wavelengths and renders the appropriate signals to the brain so that we perceive such colours as cherry, mauve and beige. Most of the scanners use an RGB colour model for recording digital image data. RGB colours is called additive because colours throughout the spectrum are created by adding varying intensities of red, green, and blue light to black (no light). These intensities vary from 255 (full intensity) to 0. Each colour channel has 256 variations and their combinations allow creating a total of 16,777,216 colours. A combination of R:255 G:255 B:255 creates white, while R:0 G:0 B:0 is black (no light).

CMYK Colour

Cyan, magenta and yellow are the secondary colours of RGB and are opposites. When RGB light strikes an object, the amount of cyan, magenta and yellow in the object's pigmentation affects how much light is reflected back (it's the reflected light that we see). Cyan absorbs red light, magenta absorbs green light and yellow absorbs blue light. The degree of absorption depends on the amount of pigment or, in printing terms, the amount of CMY ink. This is why CMYK is considered subtractive; the colours displayed by CMYK are the result of subtracting varying amounts of red, green, and blue light.

In the example below, a printed object composed of 39% cyan, 47% magenta, 0% yellow and 1% black (which absorbs all light) would reflect back 60% red light, 52% green light, and 99% blue light.

Resolve the Resolution

A pixel can have many colours (24 bits or as many as 16.7 million colours), while a dot is a special pixel that has two colours (black and white). Scanners capture pixels, hence we say pixels per inch (ppi). Most printers print dots, hence the term dots per inch (dpi). Pixels contain more information than dots. For scans of photographs you do not need to scan at the resolution of the printer because the extra information contained in the pixels is dispersed among the many dots. Even though scanner specifications are mostly mentioned in dpi these are actually in ppi only.

The true optical resolution is the ability of a scanner to resolve fine details in an original. It is actually the optical sampling rate or ppi rating of the scanner. The optical sampling rate is the number of samples captured in the x-axis by the scanner. This is determined by the width of the scanned area and the number of elements in the CCD. This is only one of the crucial components of resolution. There can be several other important factors that determine the final resolution. These include the optics quality (lens, mirrors, filters), mechanical stability of the optical system, motion of the carriage, vibration of the object, CCD, and optical components, focal range and stability of the optical system, impact of temperature and humidity changes on the optical system, frequency response of the electronic system and image processing applied to the images.

Thus, a high optical sampling rating of a scanner does not necessarily guarantee better resolution than one with a lower optical sampling rate. For example, the resolution of a scanner with a high sampling rate of 600 ppi but low-quality optical system may not be as good as a scanner with a 400 ppi sampling rate and a high-quality optical system.

Interpolation

The true optical resolution of the scanner is also referred to as the horizontal resolution while the y-direction sampling rate is also called the mechanical resolution or the vertical resolution, since it indicates the minimum movement of the scanner's mechanics—the number of steps per inch that the scanner takes in the y direction. This figure is typically double the optical resolution. This vertical resolution is interpolated. Interpolation means the scanner or scanning software generates data based on the real, captured data. If you see something saying 'EOO-b, -9,600 ppi optical', this means that it is a 600 ppi scanner, the interpolated number makes no difference—whether, it is 9,600 or 600, or infinity. Also, in most of the cases, some marketing masterminds reverse three specification. You would be on safer grounds assuming that the lower number is the actual optical resolution of the scanner.

Interpolation guesses the values for pixels at a finer level than the scanner samples them, based on the values of nearby pixels. It is easy to interpolate between two measurements on the same scan line because the scanner measures the entire line and has all the information available. It is harder to interpolate in the other direction–to fill in an interpolated line–because the scanner has not scanned the lines after the interpolated line yet. By taking extra steps in the y direction, one eliminate the need to interpolate in the direction.

Scanners that offer higher interpolated resolutions than the scanner's optical and mechanical resolutions so their interpolation for the higher resolutions at the computer. That gives them the luxury of being able to receive later lines in the images before they interpolate between lines.

Unfortunately, both the scanner-based and software-based interpolations can be less sophisticated than the interpolation routines in a sophisticated program such as Adobe Photoshop, one will often get better results by scanning at the maximum optical resolution for the scanner, and then resampling at a higher interpolated resolution image editor.

If one work involves scanning photos for Web pages or output to an inkjet printer, a 300 ppi scanner will capture enough detail for you. But if printing is carried out with high-resolution output devices or scanning small targets like slides and enlarging them, or reproducing line art, then a 600 ppi scanner is a much better option.

Scanner Software

The scanner comes with a TWAIN driver, which functions as a standalone program for scanning, and enable yours scan images directly into most Windows programs. If an application supports TWAIN driver by entering a sear command. If it supports OLE instead of TWAIN, one can use OLE to call up the driver and insert the scanner image. In addition, all scanners today also come with image editing, OCR and sometimes other applications as we.

Image Quality

In the ultimate analysis, the most important issue for any scanner is image quality.

Understanding what affects image quality will not only help you make a more informed buying decision but will also help to take best advantage of whatever scanner are gets.

High on the list is colour balance–the ability to capture neutral colours in neutral form. If you scan a black-and-white photo in colour and the result has a colour tinge one can be sure that the colours will be off on one's colour photos too. A closely related issue is colour accuracy, or the ability to capture colours that closely match the original. Many scanners often impart a pinkish tinge to scans.

For any given scanner at any given setting, both tonal quality and the colour accuracy will vary depending on the screen or printer you are using to look at the result. That is why an easy-to-use calibration feature is critical. It must be borne in mind that images that look good on screen will not necessarily look good when printed, and images that look good while printed may not look good on the screen, one will want to calibrate for both screen and printer; making sure one uses the appropriate calibration file when you scan, typically by telling the TWAIN driver the final destination for the image.

Another important image quality criterion is gamma correction. Gamma correction essentially lets one modify contrast level at different levels of brightness. Changing the gamma setting can make a tremendous difference to an image.

Noise level and the closely related signal-to-noise ratio are important indicators of how much detail one will be able to see in a scan. A signal-to-noise ratio is the ratio of the usable signal, in this case the image to noise in a scan. Noise is a distortion in the image's analog signal. This is an analog problem and is confined to the analog electronics in a scanner. One can change the signal-to-noise level substantially by changing settings in the TWAIN driver. Turning down the brightness settings also reduces the amount of noise in an image.

Colour registration-a measure of how well the three colours line up with each other– is not usually an issue for colour photos but may be an issue if one is scanning line art. If the registration is off, one will see an extra 'halo' of colour at the edges. When one is scanning a Web page, even a full pixel off is generally acceptable in a 600-dpi scan, though it will be noticeable to those who look for it in 300-dpi scan.

Document Processing

The scanning or digitization of paper documents for storage is quite different from the scanning of pictures for reproduction though it uses some of the same technology. While document scanning can be done on general-purpose office scanners, in major operations it is performed on dedicated, specialized scanners, manufactured by companies like Atiz Innovation, Böwe Bell & Howell, Canon, Epson, Fujitsu, HP, Kodak and others.

Document scanners have document feeders, generally larger than those found on copiers or all-purpose scanners. They scan at lower resolution than other scanners, usually in the range 150dpi to 300 dpi, since higher resolution is usually not needed and makes files much larger to store.

A lot of scans can be made at high speed, traditionally in grayscale but now in color as well. Many are capable of duplex (two-sided) scanning at or near full speed (20ppm (pages per minute) to 150ppm). Sophisticated document scanners have either firmware of software that "cleans up" scans as they are produced, eliminating accidental marks and sharpening type. They also usually compress the scan on the fly.

Many document scans are converted using OCR technology into searchable files. Most scanners use ISIS or Twain device drivers to scan documents into TIFF format so that the scanned pages can be fed into a document management system that will handle the archiving and retrieval of the scanned pages.

The biggest issues with document scanning are preparation and indexing. Preparation involves taking the papers to be scanned and making sure that they are in order, unfolded, without staples or anything else that might jam the scanner. This is a manual task and can be time consuming. Indexing involves associating keywords with files so they can be found later. This process can be automated in some cases, but may involve manual labour. One common practice is the use of barcode recognition technology. During the preparation process, barcode sheets are inserted into the document files, folders and document groups. Using automatic batch scanning, the documents are saved into the appropriate folders and an index is created for integration into document management software systems.

A specialized form of document scanning is book scanning. Technical difficulties arise from the books usually being bound and sometimes fragile and irreplaceable, but some manufacturers have developed specialized machinery to deal with this. For instance, Atiz DIY scanner uses a V-shaped cradle and a V-shaped transparent platen to handle brittle books. Often special robotics are used to turn the pages automatically.

Different New Type of Mouse

Inertial mice

Inertial mice use a tuning fork or other accelerometer (US Patent 4787051) to detect movement for every axis supported. Usually cordless, they often have a switch to deactivate the movement circuitry between use, allowing the user freedom of movement without affecting the pointer position. A patent for an inertial mouse claims that such mice consume less power than optically based mice, offer an increased level of sensitivity, and reduced weight and increased ease-of-use.

3D mice

Also known as flying mice, bats, or wands, these devices generally function through ultrasound. Probably the best known example would be 3DConnexion/Logitech's SpaceMouse from the early 1990s.

In the late 1990s Kantek introduced the 3D RingMouse. This wireless mouse was worn on a ring around a finger, which enabled the thumb to access three buttons. The mouse was tracked in three dimensions by a base station. Despite a certain appeal, it was finally discontinued because it did not provide sufficient resolution.

A recent consumer 3D pointing device is the Wii Remote. While primarily a motion-sensing device (that is, it can tell which way it's going and which way it's tilted), Wii Remote can also detect its spatial position by comparing the distance and position of the lights from the IR emitter using its integrated IR camera (since the nunchuk lacks a camera, it can only tell its current heading and orientation). The obvious drawback to this approach is that it can only produce spatial coordinates while its camera can see the sensor bar.

Double mouse

Double mouse allows for two mice to be used by both hands as input devices such as when operating various graphics and multimedia applications.

Connectivity and communication protocols

To transmit their input, typical cabled mice use a thin electrical cord terminating in a standard connector, such as RS-232C, PS/2, ADB or USB. Cordless mice instead transmit data via infrared radiation (see IrDA) or radio (including Bluetooth or WiFi), although many such cordless interfaces are themselves connected through the aforementioned wired serial busses. While the electrical interface and the format of the data transmitted by commonly available mice is currently standardized on USB, in the past it varied between different manufacturers.

Serial interface and protocol

Standard PC mice once used the RS-232C serial standard (released in 1969), via a DB-9 connector. The Mouse Systems Corporation version used a five-byte protocol and supported three buttons. The Microsoft version used an incompatible three-byte protocol and only allowed for two buttons. Due to the incompatibility, some manufacturers sold serial mice with a mode switch: “PC” for MSC mode, “MS” for Microsoft mode.

PS/2 interface and protocol

With the arrival of the IBM PS/2 personal-computer series in 1987, IBM introduced the eponymous PS/2 interface for mice and keyboards, which other manufacturers rapidly adopted. The most visible change was the use of a round 6-pin mini-DIN, in lieu of the former 5-pin connector. In default mode (called stream mode) a PS/2 mouse communicates motion, and the state of each button, by means of 3-byte packets.[27] For any motion, button press or button release event, a PS/2 mouse sends, over a bi-directional serial port, a sequence of three bytes, with the following format:

Revision

1. Keyboard is the main input device of the computer.
2. The main keys on the keyboard are: Alphabetic keys, Numeric keys, Function keys, and Arrow keys.
3. Mouse is a pointing device.
4. There are three basic types of Mouse: Mechanical Mouse, Optomechanical Mouse and Optical Mouse.
5. Mouse can be used by clicking, double-clicking and dragging.
6. Scanner is a device that examines a spatial pattern one part after another and generate analog or digital signals corresponding to the pattern.

7. There are two types of scanners, Hand-held scanner and Flat-bed scanner.
8. Inertial mice use a tuning fork or other accelerometer (US Patent 4787051) to detect movement for every axis supported.
9. A recent consumer 3D pointing device is the Wii Remote.
10. Double mouse allows for two mice to be used by both hands as input devices such as when operating various graphics and multimedia applications.

Multiple Choice Questions

1. The main keys of the Keyboard are Alphabetic, Arrows, Numeric and :
   (a) Function
   (b) Future
   (c) Faulty
2. A male connector for the serial interface can have 9 or __ pin:
   (a) 30
   (b) 20
   (c) 25
3. Mouse is a _______ device.
   (a) Input
   (b) Pointing
   (c) Output
4. The mouse which is now commonly used is:
   (a) Optical
   (b) Optomechanical
   (c) Mechanical
5. Mouse can be used by clicking, double-clicking and :
   (a) biting
   (b) eating
   (c) dragging

True/False Questions

1. Keyboard is the main ouput device of the computer.
2. The main keys on the keyboard are: Alphabetic keys, Numeric keys, Function keys, and Arrow keys.
3. Mouse is an input device.
4. There are three basic types of Mouse: Mechanical Mouse, Optomechanical Mouse and Optical Mouse.
5. Mouse can be used by clicking, double-clicking and dragging.
6. There are two types of scanners, Hand-held scanner and Flat-bed scanner.

Descriptive Questions

1. What is multimedia keyboard?
2. Describe the various type of keys on the keyboard.
3. How would you install a keyboard??
4. Explain the working of Mouse.
5. How mouse works? Explain.
6. Describe the process of troubleshooting the mouse.
7. Describe the working of Flat-bed scanner.
8. Which are the different type of scanners?
9. What is a 3D mice?

Answers to Objective Type Questions

Multiple Choice Questions

1. a 2. b 3. b 4. a
5. c

True False Questions

1. F 2. T 3. F 4. T
5. T 6. T

10 Power Supply

SMPS (Switched Mode Power Supplies)

Power Supplies

Every electronic system, whether it is a laboratory measuring instrument like an oscilloscope or a commercial system like a laser printer, a photocopier or a home entertainment appliance like color TV or personal computer, is invariably powered by a dc source. These dc supplies provide regulated output voltage against mains voltage and load current variations. Commonly power supplies are classified as ac/dc linear power supplies, dc/dc converters and dc/ac inverters, Based on regulation techniques, power supplies are classified as linear and switched mode power supplies.

Linear Power Supplies

ac/dc linear power supply comprises a transformer, rectifier, filter and a regulator. Any change in the output voltage due to change in input voltage or load current will result in a change in voltage drop across the regulator transistor (series type) or a change in the current through the regulator transistor (shunt type) so as to maintain a constant voltage across the load. The transistors in these linear systems dissipate a lot of energy as heat and reduces the efficiency. Elaborate heat sinking provisions are also necessary.

Switched Mode Power Supplies

The primary power received from the ac mains is rectified and filtered as high voltage dc. It is then Chopped at a high frequency (10 to 100 kHz) using a bipolar transistor and fed to the primary side of a step-down transformer. As this transformer is operating at a very high frequency, its size and weight are very small compared to a transformer operating at 50/60 Hz. The transformed chopped waveform is rectified and filtered at the secondary side. A sample of the output voltage is used as feedback signal for driving the switching transistor which provide the regulation.

Most switching power supplies regulate their output using a method called Pulse Width Modulation. The power switch which feeds the primary side of the step-down transformer is driven by a pulse width modulated oscillator, As the load increases, output voltage tends to fall. The PWM control senses the change and increases the torn 'ON' time of the transistor.

Increased turn 'ON' time means increased stored energy i.e. maximum amount of energy will be passed through the transformer and the output voltage will be maintained. Similarly an increase in the output voltage causes a reduction in the 'ON' time and reduces the amount of energy passing through the transformer until the output voltage is maintained at original value.

The width or the 'ON' time of the oscillator is controlled by the voltage feedback from the secondary rectifier output which forms a closed loop regulator, Most switching supplies ate required to produce more than one regulated dc voltage, Example include supplies for television receivers and personal computers.

Switched Mode Power Supply vs Linear Power Supply

Linear power supplies are good at line regulation, load regulation, low output voltage ripples and almost negligible RF interference. The factors in favour of a SMPS are high efficiency as well as small weight and size. High efficiency is obtained because of less wastage of power when supply is regulated. Operations at high frequencies reduce the size of the transformer for the same power operating at mains frequency. RF radiation due to switching of currents and high ripple output are the disadvantages of SMPS. RF radiation can be reduced by shielding the core as well as the entire unit.

The following table shows the comparison.

Sl. No.	*Terms*	*Switched Mode Power Supply*	*Linear Power Supply*
1.	Efficiency	65-75 %	25-50 %
2.	Temperature rise	20-40 deg. cen	50-100 deg cen
3.	Ripple volts	Higher 25 to 50 mV	Even 5 mV possible
4.	Overall regulation	0.3 % is common (% drop of volts)	Even 0.1%possible
5.	RF interference	Can be a problem unless properly shield	None
6.	Magnetic material	Ferrite core	Steel core
7.	Weight	About 60 watts per kg	20-30 watts per kg
8.	Cost	More parts, special ones, increase the cost	Advantage for small units up to 10 W to 15 W, but cost is higher if bigger.
9.	Reliability	Depends on the availability of suitable transistors	More reliable

SMPS for Computers

A PC needs power at two different voltage levels and both positive and negative polarities: +5 V dc, + 12 V dc, -5 V dc and -2 V dc. The power supply has to provide power at ail these 4 voltage levels. Most power is needed at +5 V dc which is needed by most of the electronic circuitry. A fair mount of power is also required at +12 V dc to operate the disk drive motors. The -5 V dc level is designed for dynamic memory bias voltage. The -12 V dc is primarily used by the RS 232C serial port. All four power levels are bused across the system unit expansion slots.

Power Requirements in PCS

The total power requirements of a PC depend upon the components within it. Each component will draw a certain quantity of current at each of the supply voltage it uses. Some components will draw different current depending on what they are doing. For example, a diskette drive will draw more current when die motor is running and when the heads are moving. High capacity disk drives having several platters and heads will draw more current than lower capacity drives.

The following table shows the power requirement in PCs.

Sl. No.	*System Component*	*Power Required*
1.	Motherboard	35 W
2.	Keyboard	2 W
3.	Floppy drive	5 W {during idle)
		10 W (during spinning)
4.	Hard disk drive	35 W
5.	Multi I/O card	4 W
6.	Floppy/Hard disk drive controller	8 W
7.	Display adopter	5 W

AT Power Supply

It outputs a power good signal which is used by the SMPS to indicate the motherboard that all the outputs from power supply are at the correct level and safe for use by the compuer.

ATX Power Supply

It adds two new signals PW_ON (power on) and +5V SB (Standby) for the new generation of computers. Power On signal is used by the motherboard to switch on/off the power supply. This signal allows the motherboard to control the power supply. Motherboard can put the system in stanby by switching off the power supply, and shift back to normal operation by restoring the power.

"+5V standby" is not controlled by the "power on" signal, it is used to provide power to the motherboard when the system is in standby mode and the main voltages from the power supply has been switched off.

Principle

When Power Supply is turned on, it generates a power good signal which indicates that there is adequate power for processing. When the output voltages are above the minimum sense level, a TTL compatible high level (2.4V DC to 5V DC) is generated on the power good line. The power good signal has a turn-on delay of about 100 ms after the output voltages have reached their respective levels.

Revision

1. Every electronic system, is invariably powered by a dc source.
2. ac/dc linear power supply comprises a transformer, rectifier, filter and a regulator.
3. Linear power supplies are good at line regulation, load regulation, low output voltage ripples and almost negligible RF interference.
4. The total power requirements of a PC depend upon the components within it.
5. When Power Supply is turned on, it generates a power good signal which indicates that there is adequate power for processing.

Multiple Choice Questions

1. SMPS stands for :
   (a) Switched Main Power Supply (b) Switching Main Power Supply
   (c) Save Main Power Supply
2. Average power needed by motherboard is :
   (a) 30 W (b) **35 W**
   (c) 25 W

True/False Questions

1. ac/dc linear power supply comprises a transformer, rectifier, filter and a regulator.
2. The total power requirements of a PC depend upon the components within it.
3. Keyboard need 7 W of power supply.

Descriptive Questions

1. What is SMPS used for?
2. Compare SMPS with the main supply.
3. What are AT and ATX power supply?

Answers to Objective Type Questions

Multiple Choice Questions

1. a 2. b

True False Questions

1. T 2. T 3. F

11 Output Devices

Introduction

Output devices are used to get information from the computer. It may be in the form of display on the monitor, or the hard copy print out on the printer. These are the main ones, but, there are others too.

Monitors and Displays

There would be no What You See Is What You Get (WYSIWYG) on PCs, if there were no monitors or displays on which to see what you get. The PC must produce outputs that can be handled by the senses of humans and so far, technology is limited to sight and sound. Given a choice, most of us still prefer sight over sound. You can accomplish a lot on a PC without sound, but not much would get done without the ability to see what you are working on.

The two general categories of PC visual presentation are the monitor and the display. A monitor has a CRT (cathode ray tube) and look something like a traditional television set (without the controls, of course). On the other hand, a display is a flat-panel device that can be attached to a portable PC or hung on the wall. A monitor is largely desk or table-bound, but a display can get up and move about. A flat-panel display is really an adaptation of the monitor, but because it uses different technology, they are treated as two different components.

The PC Monitor

With personal computer technology advancing as fast as it is, it is hard to believe that any part of a PC could be considered an investment. However, the PC monitor is the only part of the personal computer that actually hold its value and has some durability. A good quality monitor will last for years through several generations of the Pc systems. When making a decision about investigating in a PC monitor, a number of things should be considered. Although this entire chapter is about the technologies used in PC displays, here is a quick overview of the decisions you must make:

Type	Although there are variations within each type of monitor, such as color versus monochrome, resolutions, dot pitch etc. the basic choice is between the more traditional CRT display and the state-of-the-art digital flat-panel LCD (liquid crystal display) display.
Size	Size has a lot to do with the monitor's capability, but more importantly, it impacts your comfort in working with it. As is true in many things, bigger is better when it comes to monitors. Many experts recommend that with technology where it is today that you should never use a CRT monitor smaller than 17 inches or an LCD monitor with a resolution lower than 1024 x 768.

Cost Your budget is a very important consideration when shopping for a new monitor. If you cannot spend more than around Rs.6,000, you can probably forget LCD displays until their prices come down a bit more. If you have a relatively unlimited budget, you choices and comparisons are many.

CRT Displays

Until very recently, standard PC system packages only featured CRT displays. Lately, more and more PCs are being offered with flat-panel displays. As prices continue to drop many experts believe the CRT will soon be replaced by the flat-panel display on all standard PC packages and be available only as an option. But then, the floppy disk was supposed to have been obsolete over five years ago.

A CRT display has some advantages over the LCD displays. It is bright, well-lit, economical and produces excellent color and graphic qualities. A CRT display uses the same technology common to the television set. The CRT (cathode ray tube) is a funnel shaped glass tube that uses electron guns to light up (or as it is technically known, excite) phosphor elements on the back of the display glass. The lighted phosphors blend to form images and movements that show through the display of the CRT for the user to view. The user view the phosphors through a single pane of glass, which is why the display is so bright and why it is easily viewed from an angle. There is a lot more to how the phosphor is used to create an image and it is discussed a little later in the chapter.

Flat-Panel Displays

If you have limited space on a desk or workable space and need to have a PC monitor available, a flat-panel display is probably best for your situation. The major selling point of LCD display is their size, meaning their depth. A typical CRT display, especially the larger displays in use today, are at least 12 inches or more from front to back, which can take up a considerable amount of workspace on a desk. Flat-panel LCD displays are typically only a few inches deep including its foot, which makes them perfect for small desks, cubicles or places where a large CRT monitor would negatively impact the aesthetics or décor. Even the new PCs that are integrated into the same package as a flat panel display are only inches in depth.

Flat-panel displays are backlit, which means the light source of the display shines through several layers of filters and glass before you see it. This is why LCD display appear to be less bright than a bright than a CRT-style display and less legible from an angle. However, LCD displays are digital, which means they are able to reproduce images more accurately, especially colors.

CRT Display Sizes

CRT monitor sizes are given in what are called nominal sizes. The most popular monitor sizes are 15-inch, 17-inch, 19-inch and 21-inch. However, is the size of the CRT measured diagonally from a top corner to an opposite bottom corner, case and all (in the same way a television set is measured and marketed). On a CRT monitor, the case of the monitor includes a front bezel (the plastic around the edge of the display) that covers up a small portion of the display in order to hold it in place. The bezel cuts down the area of the CRT that can be viewed by as much as a full-inch all of the way around the edge of the monitor. Most CRT monitor manufacturers are upfront about this and will usually list the viewable size the monitor along with the nominal size.

The viewable size of a 17-inch CRT display is actually a bit less than 16 inches. When comparing monitors, it is good idea to compare the viewable image size rather than the nominal screen size. You may be surprised that a smaller monitor may be a better value for your money when you compare the price-per-inch of viewable screen.

The following Table illustrates this point by listing the average nominal and viewable screen sizes for CRT monitors.

Nominal Size	*CRT Viewable Size*	*LCD Viewable Size*
14"	13.2"	14"
15"	13.8"	15"
17"	15.9"	17"
19"	18"	19"
21"	19.8"	21"

LCD Display Sizes

LCD flat-panel displays may provide a better bargain on a price per viewable inch basis. The nominal size of an LCD display is its viewable area as opposed to the one-inch margin of error used by CRT manufacturers.

Dots and Pixels

The images displayed on a PC's monitor are created from a pattern of dots in much the same way as the photographs in a newspaper. Dots are shaded lighter or darker so that your eyes can form a visual image from them. The CRT creates these dots from the phosphor on the back of its screen using masking methods that isolate each dot so that it can be illuminated by an electron gun.

A monochrome or single color, monitor has phosphor of only one color, so that when the phosphor dots are illuminated, the text and graphic image is a single color on a contrasting background. Typically, the background is black and the display color is green, amber or white.

The image produced on a color monitor is created by illuminated small triangles of phosphor dots called picture elements or pixels for short. In the CRT, one-third of the dots are red dots, one-third are green dots and one-third are blue dots. These different colored dots are interspersed evenly on the screen so that a dot of each color can be grouped with a dot of each of the other colors to form a triangle or pixel.

A color CRT has three electron guns that are used to light up the phosphors in each pixel. The combinations and intensities used to illuminate the phosphors define the image produced on the screen. The electron guns sweep over the pixels from side to side, one row at a time, to create or refresh the displayed image.

LCD displays are of two different types: passive matrix and active matrix. A passive matrix display has a layer of LCD elements on a grid (matrix) of wires. When current is applied to the wire intersections, the diodes (pixels) are lighted.

A passive matrix refreshes the display by applying current to the pixels at a fixed refresh rate. Active matrix displays control each LCD elements (diode) individually with one or more transistors that continually refresh each element of the display.

Resolution

The number of pixels on a monitor, whether CRT or LCD, determine the amount of detail that can be used to create and image. As the number of pixels increases, the better the image resolution a monitor can produce. The number of pixels on a monitor is its resolution, which is expressed in the number of pixels on each row of the display and the number of rows of pixels on the display.

For example, the VGA standard resolution is 640 x 480 which is read as 640 by 480. This means that the monitor has 640 pixels arranged horizontally on each row of pixels and 480 vertical rows of pixels. A monitor with 640 x 480 resolution uses 307,200 (640 times 480) pixels to create displayed images.

The following table shows the resolutions most commonly supported by today's monitors.

Resolution	*Total Pixels Used*
640 x 480	307,200
800 x 600	480,000
1024 x 768	786,432
1280 x 1024	1,310,720
1600 x 1200	1,920,000

Larger size monitors, such as 19- or 21-inch have trouble displaying smaller resolutions and on most smaller monitors, such as a 14- or 15- inch monitor, higher resolutions don't have the image quality you desire. It is always best to match the monitor and its resolution to your needs.

Because of their construction, LCD displays have natural resolutions that are set by the number of pixels on each line of the display. This is why an LCD display must often reduce the size of the display area to reproduce images in resolutions lower than its natural one.

For example, a 12.1 inch LCD monitor (800 x 600 resolution) has 800 pixels on each row of its display. If the resolution to 640 x 480, it is not possible to evenly represent 640 pixels with 800 pixels and produce clear text or images. So, the display image area is reduced to 10.4 inches for the 640 x 480 image.

However, as the natural resolution and the size of the display get larger, reproducing lower resolutions become much easier in the standard screen area. Table 16-3 illustrates how LCD displays adjust for resolutions other than their natural resolution. In the table, small means the display is reduced, full means it is the natural resolution and linear means that the user must scroll up and down and left and right to see all of the displayed image.

Monitor Size and Resolution

As the space available to hold more pixels increases, so does the monitor's ability to handle higher resolutions. This is not a hard and fast rule, but in general it holds true. Another factor in this equation is the age of the monitor. Most newer monitors can display higher resolutions than many older and larger monitors.

Higher resolutions use smaller pixels and when applied on a smaller monitor, may require a magnifying glass to read the screen. A 15 – inch monitor may support 1280 x 1-24 resolution, but you may never actually use it. In fact, you may never actually use the highest resolution available on any monitor smaller than a 19-inch monitor. On the other hand, lower resolutions look better on smaller monitors. Larger monitors display lower resolutions in pixel blocks that can really detract from the image on the screen

Natural Resolution	*640 x 480*	*800 x 600*	*1024 x 768*
640 x 480	Full	Linear	Linear
800 x 600	Small	Full	Linear
1024 x 768	Small	Small	Full

Color Depth

In addition to its resolution, the color depth of a monitor is another very important characteristic, depending on your needs. The color depth of a monitor is the maximum number of colors that it can display. The color depth is represented as the number of bits required to hold the number of colors in the color depth.

For example, an 8 – bit color depth has a maximum of 256 colors, because that is the highest value that can be written in 8-bits. In binary numbers, the range of numbers available in 8 bits is 0000000 to 11111111 or the range in decimal numbers of 0 to 255, which represents different 256 colors. The colors included in the color palette for a particular color depth are represented in the binary values stored in the number of bits available. The following table lists the number of colors associated with each of the color depths, which are also called bit depths, supported on current monitors.

Colour Depth (in bits)	*Colours Available*	*Common Name*
1	2	Monochrome
4	16	VGA Standard
8	256	256-colour
16	65,536	High colour
18	262,144	LCD colour
24	16,777,216	True Colour (24-bit)
32	4,294,967,296	True Colour (32-bit)

Depending on the PC, video card and monitor, either 24-bit or 32-bit is typically designated as True Color setting. The number of colors that 32-bit color, which is popular with 3D video accelerator systems, can develop is perhaps overkill. The human eye cannot distinguish beyond 16 million or so colors. Above that the eye may have difficulty discerning the color distinction of two adjacent pixels.

Checking Out the Color Depth and Resolution

The following is an exercise you can do to check the resolution and color depth on your own Windows Pc or notebook computer.

1. At the Windows Desktop, right-click in an empty space to display the Desktop menu shown on next page.
2. Choose Properties to open the Display Properties window shown in figure on the next page.
3. Select the Settings tab.
4. Towards the bottom of the Settings tab are two side-by-side settings that control the color depth (Colors) and the screen resolution (Screen Area), as shown below.
5. Change the Screen Area setting to its lowest (the slide all of the way to the left) value. It should be 640 x 480. Now change the color depth (Colors) to 256 (8-bit) color. These settings are the VGA standard settings. Click Apply. Do not restart the system when asked and apply the new settings without restarting the PC.

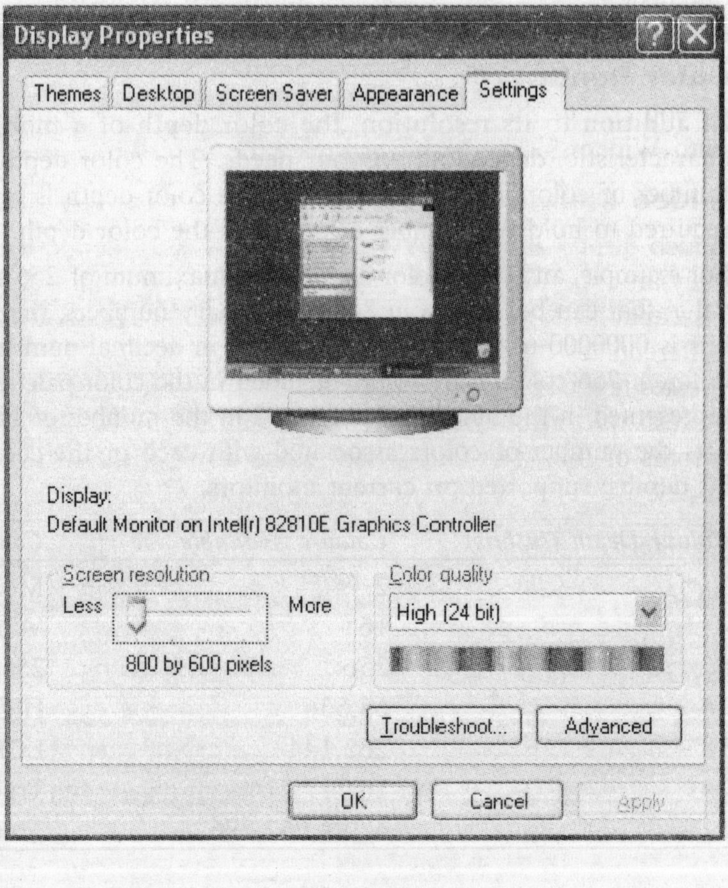

6. Unless these settings were what your monitor was set on to begin with, the displayed image should be constructed of much larger elements and may not fit onto the display.
7. Reopen the Display Properties window and change the resolution (Screen Area) and color depth (Colors) to the highest settings available. Once again, accept the settings

without restarting your PC. The display should be much more detailed and all of the elements should be much smaller than under VGA standard settings.

8. Reset the Display Properties to their original settings, unless you prefer their new values.

Refresh Rate

Another key settings on a video system is its refresh rate or the number of times per second that the screen is entirely redrawn. The refresh rate is actually a function of the video card and indicates how many times per second the data used by the monitor to refresh the displayed image is sent. The phosphor on the CRT's screen begins to dim almost immediately, so the electron gun must sweep back over each pixel a number of times per second to keep the display sharp and bright. A low refresh rate can make the CRT screen flicker and can cause eye fatigue and headaches.

You definitely want a monitor that supports a refresh rate of 75Hz (Hertz) or faster, especially a higher resolutions and color depths. LCD displays do not have refresh rate issues. Because of the way LCD technology works, it can provide stable images at 60Hz and sometimes less. To see the refresh rate on your monitor or to check to see what it is set at, follow the steps used above to display the Display Properties Settings window. Click on the Advanced button to display the Properties window for the video adapter in your PC. Select the Adapter tab. The Refresh rate is selected from a list box that is located about in the middle of the window. On most Windows 9x or Windows 2000 systems, the refresh rate is likely set to Optimal.

If you change the refresh rate and the result is a distorted or blurry image, reboot your PC into Windows Safe Mode and reset the refresh rate.

Video Display Standards

Video display standards are developed more to define the capabilities of video cards than they are for monitors, but by listing the video standards to which the monitor is compatible, its capabilities in terms of color depth and resolution are automatically defined. What differentiates one video display standard from another is the resolution it supports, how it creates text characters, whether it is color or monochrome and its color depth, color palette, refresh rate, scan rates and bandwidth. The following table lists the resolution and color depths of the VGA and SVGA video standards, the two most commonly used standards today.

Standard	*Name*	*Resolution*	*Colour Depth*
VGA	Video Graphics Array	640 x 480	16
		320 x 200	256
SVGA	Super VGA	800 x 600	16
		1024 x 768	256
		1280 x 1024	256
		1600 x 1200	256

Over the years, several video display standards have been used. Here are a few of the more popular ones:

Monochrome Display Adapter (MDA)

This standard displayed only text data in only one color on a solid contrasting background.

Color Graphics Adapter (CGA)

This standard provided the first color graphics support. CGA supports 2 or 4 colors out of a 16- color palette on a 640 x 200 resolution.

Monochrome Graphics Adapter (MGA)

Also known as Hercules Graphics. Developed by Hercules Graphics corporation, this incorporated graphics into the monochrome display. It supported a 720 x 350 resolution for text and a 720 x 348 resolution for graphics, both in monochrome.

Enhanced Graphics Adapter (EGA)

This standard improved the text and graphics display capabilities of the CGA standard. EGA supported graphics with a 640 x 350 resolution and up to 16 colors from 64 – color palette.

Video Graphics Array (VGA)

VGA is now the de facto graphics standard for all monitors, video cards and software. It supports a range of resolutions and color depths, as shown in table 6-5 including 640 x 480 which is commonly known as VGA standard resolution.

Super VGA (SVGA)

SVGA is a collection of standards that defines graphics above the VGA standard. SVGA is commonly linked to the 800 x 600 resolution and 256 colors. Most manufacturers consider SVGA the current standard.

Of the video display standards listed above, only VGA and SVGA are in common use today. The others were part of the video standards evolution and each new standard was an improvement on the last. You may encounter other video display standards, such as XGA (Extended Graphics Array) or UVGA (Ultra VGA), which are loosely defined standards that vary from manufacturer to manufacturer.

The VGA (Video Graphics Array) display standard is considered the base standard for video display systems today. Virtually all current monitors and video cards support the VGA standard. It is the default standard for Windows and almost all other operating systems and device drives that interact directly with the video system.

Video Cards

In general, the video card processes the graphics data produced by software running on the PC and prepares it for use by the monitor for converting it from digital data to an analog signal. The video card also sends out the data needed by the monitor to refresh the image or renew it as it changes.

Video cards, graphics cards and accelerator cards are all names for the adapter card inside the PC that is responsible for generating the signals that tell the monitor what to display. The relationship between the video card and the monitor should be carefully matched. These two device must be compatible in terms of the signal used to communicate to the monitor, the type of connector used to connect them together, the video display standards they support and their speed.

Advantages and Disadvantages of various Displays

Advantages of LCDS

1. Low power consumption and cost
2. Small size

Disadvantages of LCDs

1. LCD do not emit light so the image has very little contrast
2. Resolution is poor
3. Screen is susceptible to glare so the optimum viewing angle is very narrow

Advantages of Plasma Display

1. Resolution is good
2. Glare is less
3. Flickering is absent
4. Images are brighter than CRT

Disadvantages of Plasma Display

1. Uses lot of power
2. The technology is costly
3. Only a single colour is available (reddish orange)

Advantages of Terminals

1. They are relatively inexpensive.
2. Terminals are usually connected on line to a mainframe. This enables users to enter data directly into a processing system, thereby increasing the timeliness of data input and eliminating the need for intermediary storage media viz., floppy disks.
3. User's ability to correct errors or to alter data that has already been typed.
4. Its ability to enter data to computer system from remote sites.
5. Terminals extend the use of the computer to various places of work. They are widely used for such tasks as control, entering orders, updating accounts and seat reservations.

   They can be sited at various points on a factory floor to record and receive information on different stages of an industrial process.

Disadvantages of Terminals

1. Terminal dependency on the main server. If the main server goes down the connected terminals are useless.
2. Long hour work at visual display terminals are unhealthy i.e.; can cause strain in eyes, pain in wrist and back.
3. Terminals can not store data or create backup copies of data input, thereby forcing the user to rekey the original input data if it is lost.

Troubleshooting Monitor

The monitor's glass screen is the component on a PC that should be cleaned the most often the monitor screen produces a lot of static electricity that attracts and hold dust and flying lint. If the screen becomes covered with dust, it can strain your eyes to view the screen for extended periods. The following steps detail how you can safely keep the glass screen and the monitor itself clean and bright:

1. Before cleaning the monitor, switch its power off and unplug it from its power source. There is really no need to disconnect it from the PC. After turning the monitor off, wait a few minutes before beginning to clean it. Do not wear an ESD ground strap when working with a monitor, even to clean it.
2. Using compressed air, clean away any dust on the top of the monitor's case. Point the air stream to blow across the top of the monitor, not directly down on it, to prevent dust from blowing into the monitor's vents. Never open and remove the cover of a monitor! There is an extremely high voltage hazard inside every monitor, regardless of its size.
3. Use a soft cloth and either isopropyl alcohol or a general-purpose no-rinse cleaner to clean the outside of the monitor case. The alcohol is probably a better choice because it will not create a safety hazard if it's inadvertently dripped inside the case.
4. Use and antistatic cleaner of a Scotch-Brite HPEC for electronics cloth to clean the glass of the monitor. Never use an ammonia-based glass cleaner on the monitor glass. The monitor screen is coated with filtering chemicals to help improve the image and reduce eyestrain. Using a harsh cleaner can remove these coatings, harming the monitor and potentially harming you. Never use water or a liquid cleaner to wash the monitor's glass with the power on. Water is an excellent conductor of electricity and if your hand makes sufficient contact with the screen your could be the ground for the electricity in the monitor.
5. Reconnect the monitor and test the video. If nothing displays, check the power switch, the power cord, the video connection and the brightness and contrast settings any of which could have been accidentally disloaded, moved or turned while you were cleaning the case.

Printers

They are hardcopy output devices and can be divided into two distinct categories:

1. Impact Printers
2. Non-impact Printers

Various Features of Printers

Modes

Some printers operate in a number of different modes that trade off print quality for speed. These modes vary with the technology used by the printer.

Three of the most common modes for impact dot matrix printers are draft, near letter quality, and letter quality. Draft mode delivers the highest speed and the lowest quality. To achieve the highest possible speed, in draft mode the printers move their print heads faster than they can fire to print at each dot position on the paper. Typically, in draft mode these printers can blacken only every other dot. The thinly laid dots give text and graphics a characteristic gray look in draft mode. Near letter quality mode slows the print head so that text characters can be rendered without the machine gun, separated dots look of draft mode. Because the dot density is higher, characters appear fully black and are easier to read. Letter quality mode slows printing further, often using two or more passes to give as much detail as possible to each individual character. The printer concentrates on detail work, adding serifs and variable line weights to characters to make them look more like commercially printed text.

Color

Printers start with the primaries when it comes to color. They start with inks corresponding to the three primary colors—red, yellow, and blue. If you want anything beyond those, the printer must find some way of mixing them together. This mixing can be physical or optical. The physical mixing of colors requires that two or more colors of ink actually mix together while they are wet. Printer inks are, however, designed to dry rapidly so the colors to be mixed must be applied simultaneously or in quick succession. Few printers rely on the physical mixing of inks to increase the number of colors they produce.

Optical mixing takes place in either of two ways. One color of ink can be applied over another (that has already dried), or the colors can be applied adjacent to one another.

Applied multiple layers of color require that the inks be to some degree transparent, as a truly opaque ink would obscure the first color to be applied. Most modern printer inks are transparent, which allows them to be used on transparencies for overhead projection as well as paper. The exact hue of a transparent ink is, of course, dependent on the color of the medium it is applied to.

Optical mixing also takes place when dots of two or more colors are intermixed. If the dots are so close together than the eye cannot individually resolve each one, their colors blend together on the retina, blending the individual hues together. Most PC color printers take advantage of this kind of optical mixing by dithering

Print Engines

The actual mechanism that forms an image on paper is called the print engine. Each uses a somewhat different physical principle to put ink on paper. Although each technology has its strengths, weaknesses, and idiosyncrasies, you might not be able to tell the difference between the pages they print. Careful attention to detail has pushed quality up to a level where the paper rather than the printer is the chief limit on resolution, and color comes close to photographic, falling short only on the depth that only a thick gelatin coating makes possible. In making those images, however, the various print engine technologies work differently at different speeds, at different noise levels, and with different requirements. These differences can make one style of print engine a better choice for your particular application than others.

Impact Printers

A printer in which printing is the result of mechanically striking the printing medium. An impact printer makes contact with the paper to produce an image. The impact may be produced by a print hammer character, like that of a typewriter key striking a ribbon against the paper or by a print hammer hitting paper and ribbon against a character.

An impact printer must be used if printing a multiple copy report so that the duplicate copies will receive the imprint.

Impact printers are of following types:

Solid Font

A complete character, such as on a typewriter key, strikes a carbon ribbon or other inked surface against paper to produce an image of the character. The solid-font characters are mounted on one of several types of printing heads such as a ball, wheel or cup.

Advantage

- The advantage of a solid-font over non-solid is that they give the best quality formed character images.

Disadvantage

- Solid-font print heads are usually slower than other types.

Dot Matrix

It is made of separate pinlike (needles) hammers that strike the ribbon against the paper in computer-determined patterns of dots. This type of printer is usually faster than solid-font type, but the image quality is not as good. All of printers print the characters in ASCII character set. This is a set of 128 printable and special control characters. Print speeds are critically important in computer environments because of the volume of output involved. On the basis of speed printers can further be classified as:

Serial or Character Printers

It is the slowest printer. The two major types of character-at-a-time impact printer are:

1. Dot-matrix printers and
2. Daisywheel printer

Dot-Matrix Printer

In it the individual characters are formed by a matrix of wires or styluses. Dot-matrix printers are also called serial printers. The images are formed by a print head that is composed of a series of little print hammers that look like the heads of pins. The print head usually has nine pins or 24 pines. The bottom 2 pins are used to form the descenders of lower case letters viz., p, q, g and y. Many expensive dot-matrix printers do not provide descenders, but print quality is improved when they are used.

The modern minimal printer uses an impact dot matrix print engine. The heart of the machine is a mechanical print head that shuttles back and forth across the width of the paper. A number of thin print wires act as the hammers that squeeze ink from a fabric or Mylar ribbon to paper.

Working Principle of Dot Matrix Printer

In most impact dot matrix printers, a seemingly complex but efficient mechanism controls each of the print wires. The print wire normally is held away from the ribbon and paper, and against the force of a spring, by a strong permanent magnet. The magnet is wrapped with a coil of wire that forms an electromagnet, wound so that its polarity is the opposite of that of the permanent magnet.

To fire the print wire against the ribbon and paper, this electromagnet is energized (under computer control, of course), and its field neutralizes that of the permanent magnet. Without the force of the permanent magnet holding the print wire back, the spring forcefully jabs the print wire out against the ribbon, squeezing ink onto the paper. After the print wire makes its dot, the electromagnet is de-energized and the permanent magnet pulls the print wire back to its idle position, ready to fire again. The Mechanical Section or DMP is shown next.

The two-magnets-and-spring approach is designed with one primary purpose—to hold the print wire away from the paper (and out of harm's way) when no power is supplied to the

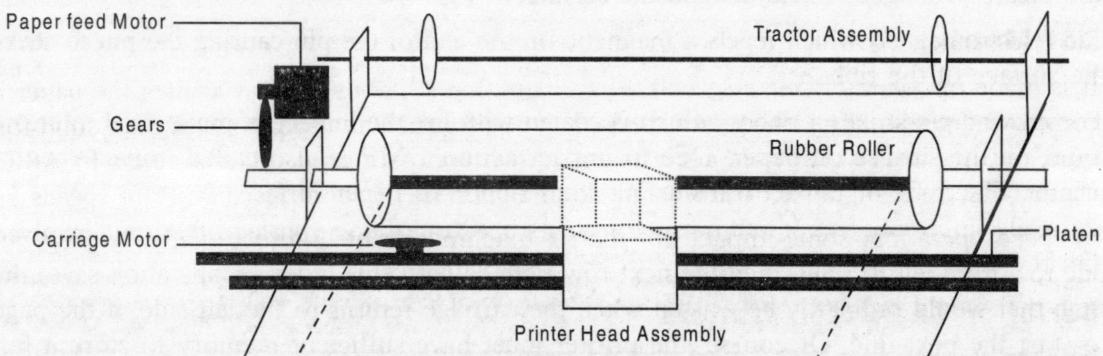

Mechanical Section of DMP

printer and the print head. The complexity is justified .by the protection it affords the delicate print wires.

The print head of a dot matrix printer is made from a number of these print wire mechanisms. Most first generation personal computer printers and many current machines use nine wires arrayed in a vertical column. To produce high quality, the second generation of these machines increased the number of print wires to 18 or 24. These often are arranged in parallel rows with the print wires vertically staggered, although some machines use different arrangements. Because the larger number of print wires fit into the same space (and print at the same character height), they can pack more detail into what they print. Because they are often finer than the print wires of lesser endowed machines, the multitude of print wires also promises higher resolution.

No matter the number of print wires, the print head moves horizontally as a unit across the paper to print a line of characters or graphics. Each wire fires as necessary to form the individual characters or the appropriate dots for the graphic image. The impact of each wire is precisely timed so that it falls on exactly the right position in the matrix. The wires fire on the fly—the print head never pauses until it reaches the other side of the paper.

When computer sends series of hex data in hex format this code type of data represents the character to be printed with the help of printer this data may be punctuation mark tabs, enter and various other types of keyboard words that are sent to the printer by the computer. These codes are first of all stored into buffer Ram or memory because usually printer is a slower device as compare to computer so printer sends this data slowly when the printer Ram is full of the data then printer sends the acknowledgement signals to the computer so that computer can stop sending more data to the printer. The codes stored into the buffer Ram of printer are hexal decimal numbers in the form of binary and these codes represent alphabets like A, B, C in both types of formats capital and small also codes indicate various character and special symbols after storing data the printer microprocessor will send this data to the print head so that a definite print out can be taken. Electrical signals from the microprocessor are amplified and travel to particular circuits to the head which contain 9 pins or 24 pins called printing pins that are erroring in state lines one and of each pins is connected to an electromagnetic the current from the microprocessor activates the magnetic and creates a magnetic field around the so line.

Oid (electromagnet) which repels a magnetic on the end of the pin causing the pin to strike the surface of the ribbon.

The moving pin strikes a ribbon which is coated with ink the impact of pin is used to create a dot on the surface on paper. Due to impact action DMP is also called impact type of printer. The force of impact transfer ink from ribbon to paper surface.

To speed operation, some impact dot matrix machines print bi-directionally, rattling out one row from left to right, then the next row right to left. This mode of operation saves the time that would ordinarily be wasted when the carriage returns to the left side of the page to start the next line. Of course, the printer must have sufficient memory to store a full line of text so that it can be read backwards.

Adding color to an impact dot matrix printer is relatively straightforward. The color the

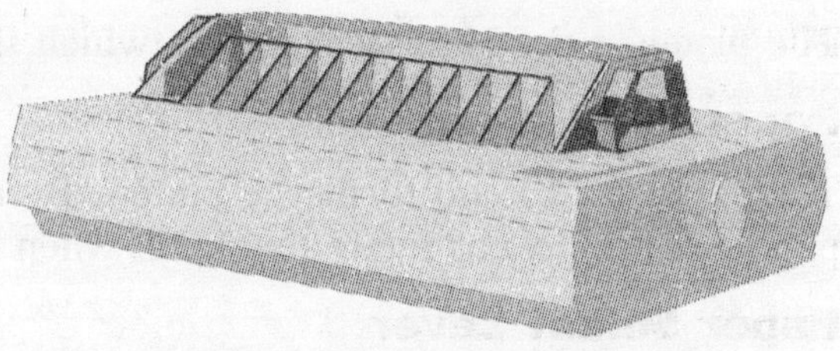

Outlook of Dot Matrix Printer

impact printer actually prints is governed by the ink in or on its ribbon. Although some manufacturers build color impact printer using multiple ribbons, the most successful (and least expensive) designed used special multi-colored ribbons lined with three or four bands corresponding to the primary colors. To change colors, the printer shifts the ribbon vertically so a differently hued band lies in front of the print wires. Most of the time the printer will render a row in one color, shift ribbon colors, then go across the same row in a different color. Of course, the color ribbon costs more and does not last as long as its monochrome equivalent.

As with their typewriter progenitors, all impact dot matrix printers have a number of desirable qualities. Owing to their heritage of more than a century of engineering refinement, they represent a mature technology. Their designs and functions are relatively straightforward and familiar.

Impact technology takes the lead when you share one of the most common business needs, making multi-part forms. Impact printers can hammer an impression not just through a ribbon, but through several sheets of paper as well. Slide a carbon between the sheets or, better yet, treat the paper for non-carbon duplicates, and you get multiple, guaranteed identical copies with a single pass through the mechanism. For a number of business applications—for example the generation of charge receipts—exact carbon copies are a necessity, and impact printing is an absolute requirement. The output from DMP is in the form of dots.

Principal of DMP

The head of DMP works on the basic of electromagnetic induction.

The DOT MATRIX PRINTER (DMP) is an example of Impact printer because while printing the printer head comes in contact with the printing paper. Printer is a simple device consists of mechanical section and Electronic section. It has two sections in electronics.

1. Power Supply Unit (PSU)
2. Logic Card.

Dot Matrix Printer consists of the following:

Power Switch

The power switch is used to turn power to the printer on and off. It is on the left side near the back.

Tractors

The tractors are the sprockets that feed continuous fan-folded paper into the printer and keep the paper properly aligned.

Platen

The platen is the hard steel rod on which the cartridge assembly move.

Paper Feed Knob

The paper feed knob turns the platen. By turning this knob, you can manually feed the paper. Please do not rotate this knob when the printer is powered on.

Paper Select Lever

The paper select lever adjusts the pressure on the platen according to the type and thickness of paper.

Top Cover

The top cover protects the MSP printer from dirt and dust as well as reducing the sound level while printing. The top cover helps hold the paper against the platen when the tractor is installed in the "push" position. The top cover has special beveled edge for tearing off the paper.

Single-Sheet Guide/Paper Separator

The single-sheet guide is used for loading single sheets of paper. It also acts as a paper separator (in the down position) when using continuous paper.

Paper Thickness Lever

The paper thickness lever adjusts the print head to accommodate different paper thickness and types of forms. You can also increase the life of your ribbon by adjusting this lever.

Paper Park Lever

The paper park lever adjusts the printer's tractor mechanism for switching between continuous paper and single sheets, without having to manually remove the continuous paper.

Pressure Release Lever

The pressure release lever is used when you have the tractor mechanism installed in the push position or when you are feeding single sheets. It improves the paper feeding and hence quality of graphics printing.

Control Panel

The control panel is located on the right front of the MSP. It consists of four tactile switches and six lights to indicate the printer status.

On Line Light

The online light is built into the online switch. When this light glows, the printer is online and is ready to work.

Font Lights

The font lights indicate which typeface one is currently using. Selections include: Draft, High sped draft, NLQ Roman, NLQ Sans serif and NLQ Script. By pressing the FONT switch when the printer is OFGFLINE, you can scroll through the options and the lights will indicate, which one is to be selected.

Pitch Lights

These lights indicated the character pitch you are using. By pressing the switch wile the printer is OFFLINE, you can scroll through the options such as Pica Elite and condensed.

ONLINE Switch

Pressing the switch toggles the printer between ONLINE and OFFLINE states.

OFFLINE Mode

Micro line feed (reverse): While holding the ONLINE switch press LF/FF switch. Each time one presses, the printer reverses the paper in micro steps (1/72 Inch).

In MENU mode

Save: Press ONLINE switch to save the current filed selection in the non-volatile memory of the printer. While powering on.

Configuration reset: Hold the ONLINE switch and power on the printer to reset the content's of the non-volatile memory to the factory default settings.

Self-Test Of DMP Printer

1. With the paper loaded on the printer and the power switch- OFF, plug the power cord into an electrical outlet
2. While holding down the LF/FF switch, turn ON the power switch.
3. If you want to interrupt the self-test, press the ONLINE switch.
4. To resume, press ONLINE switch again.
5. If you want to stop the self-test, turn the power switch OFF. The printer will continue printing until you turn the printer OFF.

Connecting Printer with Computer

Computer and Printer communicate by means of a cable, which is usually sold separately. Each computer uses a slightly different cable so you'll need one made specifically for your computer. The cable one needs is called a Centronics parallel printer cable or a parallel printer interface cable as shown in next two figures. It's possible to purchase a cable with the connector attached perpendicular to the cable; this allows you to place the printer close to a wall.

Drawbacks

1. Their speed limitation is slow as compared to line printers.
2. Their print resolutions are inferior to the daisywheel printers.
3. These printers may not be able to print graphic objects adequately but can handle applications such as accounting, personnel and payroll very well.

Daisywheel Printers

A serial impact printer in which the printing element is a plastic hub that has a large number of flexible radial spokes, each spoke having one or more different raised printing characters, the wheel is rotated as it is moved horizontally step by step under computer control, and

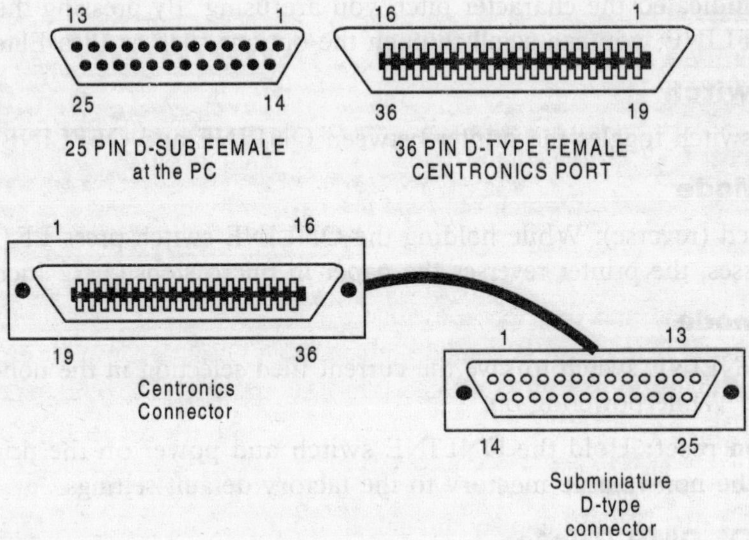

Parallel and Centronics Port

stops when a desired character is in a desired print position so a hammer can drive that character against an inked ribbon.

Daisy Wheel Printers are slower than dot-matrix printers, but they produce a high-resolution output. This high-resolution output is often called letter quality printing because it is suitable for business letters and memos. You can print in as may type fonts or foreign languages on a daisywheel printer as there are print wheels to fit your particular model of machine.

It is also called as a smart printer because of its bi-directional printing and built-in microprocessor control features.

Disadvantages

1. They are noisy
2. They are still too slow for many large volume output situations.
3. To change the typeface style, machine has to be stopped and then the print wheel is changed.
4. They cannot produce graphic output.

Line Printers

It prints an entire line in a single operation without necessarily printing one character at a time. These are generally electro-mechanical devices which print complete lines of print, up to 160 characters in width, at speeds about 300 to 2000 lines per minute. Line printers are used primarily in the mini/mainframe processing environment. Examples of line-at-a-time impact printers are:

1. Chain Printers
2. Band Printers and
3. Drum Printers

Chain Printers

It is a high-speed printer in which the type are carried by the links of a revolving chain. As the characters on the print chain revolve in a horizontal loop, a desired character eventually aligns in a given column. At this instant, the hammer strikes the paper forcing the page into the inked ribbon and the ribbon against the character thus creating the desired symbol on the print page. The chain is cycled continuously until a complete print line has been formed. The print page is then advanced one line and the process is repeated.

Band Printers

On a band printer, several similar sets of fully formed characters are embossed on a horizontal band that is continuously moving in front of the print hammers. In band printer, the paper is momentarily stopped and, as the desired character passes over a given column, the hammer activates, pressing the ribbon against the paper to form the image. It is a line printer that uses band of type characters as its printing mechanism.

Drum printers or (barrel Printers)

A printer in which all the characters for printing are placed round the surface of a cylinder (the barrel) the entire character set being placed round the cylinder at each print position. Print hammers opposite each print position can be activated by the computer striking the paper and bringing it in contact with a continuous ink ribbon between the paper and the surface of the barrel. The barrel rotates at high speed, the appropriate character being selected as it reaches a position immediately opposite the print hammers. A complete line of output is printed for each revolution of the drum since all the characters in each set pass their print stations during revolution.

Non-Impact Printers

Printers that do not strike characters against ribbon or paper when they print, are non-impact printers. Example of non-impact printers include

1. Ink-jet printers
2. Laser printers

These printers makes much less noise than impact printers.

If you are using a non-impact printer, do not try to print on multiple-part carbon forms: because no impact is being made on the paper you will end up with no copies.

A drum printer uses 80 or more character sets embossed on a cylindrical drum. A separate hammer for each character set forces the print page into an inked ribbon and the character when the character aligns at the print position.

Advantages of Non-impact Printers

1. They are faster and quieter

2. They have got the ability to change typefaces automatically and their ability to produce high-quality graphics.

Ink-jet Printers

It uses a technique of projecting droplets of ink at paper to form the required image. Ink-jet printer create an image directly on paper by spraying ink through as many as 64 tiny nozzles. It provides a print resolution of around 360 dots per inch.

The InkJet printers consist of a special nozzle type head. Ink passes through ionic chamber (special) Ink charges in this chamber. The charged ink is passed through the given to electrical field and variation is done in electronic field the charges shape come in the drop.

The ink is passed through the special ink chamber so as to provide it with the charge the changed ink drop when ejected through the nozzle has to pass through various deflection field produced by deflecting coils which are controlled by logic circuit. The charge in drop after passing through this field attains the necessary shape on the paper.

Today's most popular personal printers use inkjet print engines. The odd name "inkjet" actually describes the printing technology. The outlook of inkjet printer is shown here. It sprays droplets of ink onto paper-it works well enough to deliver image sharpness on a par with most other output technologies.

In essence, the inkjet printer is a line printer, little more than a dot matrix printer with the hammer impact removed. Instead of a hammer pounding ink onto paper, the inkjet flings it into place from tiny nozzles, each one corresponding to a print wire of the impact dot matrix printer. The motive force can be an electromagnet or, as is more likely today, a piezoelectric crystal (a thin crystal that bends when electricity is applied across it). A sharp, digital pulse of electricity causes the crystal to twitch and force ink through the nozzle into its flight to paper. The types of inkjet engines are commonplace: thermal, piezoelectric, and phase-change.

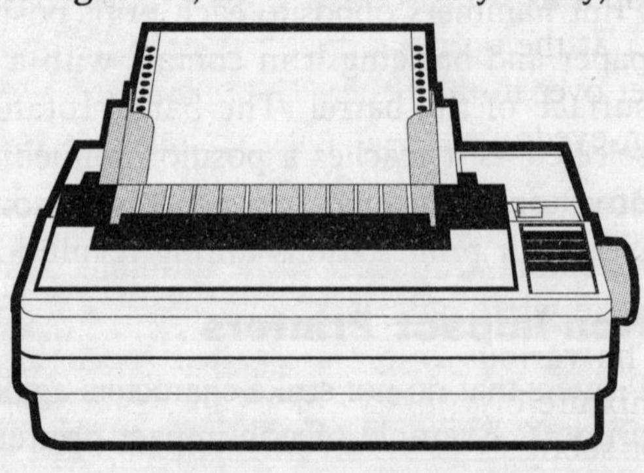

At heart, the basic technology of all three kinds of inkjets is the same. The machines rely on the combination of the small orifice in the nozzle and the surface tension of liquid ink to prevent a constant dibble from the jets. Instead of oozing out, the ink puckers around the hole in the inkjet the same way that droplets of water bead up on a waxy surface. The tiny ink droplets scrunch together rather than spreading out or flowing from the nozzle because the attraction of the molecules in the ink (or water) is stronger than the force of gravity. The inkjet engine needs to apply some force to break the surface tension and force the ink out, and that's where the differences in inkjet technologies arise.

InkJet printers are mostly used medium type of printers between Laser and DMP. These are very small type of printers, which provide higher resolution as compare to DMP cost of inkjet printers is the cost of DMP so we can say that these are the cheaply used printers with respect to DMP but the per page cost of InkJet printer must higher then the DMP.

These printers are void ally used because lost of these printers is best speed is also best and quality is also some much better DMP and Laser. The print out taken with the help of InkJet printer is all most same with that taken with a Laser another quality of inkjet is that these printers print very silently but high amount of noise is associated with DMP so we can say that InkJet printer is the best for there similarly to Laser printers the InkJet printer really works better then a DMP also InkJet have print head that can travel approach the width of page that can print the almost line with one pass.

This mechanical movement puts inkjet printer in the same category as the DMP. As the inkjet printer print character by character so the speed of inkjet printer is specified in character per second. Usually it is 100 to 200 characters per second the main different between resolutions of a printer is defined as number of dots per inch. The main different between inkjet printer and DMP is the inkjet printer head an inkjet printer spits all through ink on the surface of paper to produce a print out but its technology is much better as compare to DMP.

An inkjet is attached to the head which moves across the width of paper which is the colored data is given to the print head contains four ink cartages one for Red, Blue, Yellow, Black and each cartages of printer head is made up of ink filled chambers each attached to a nozzle smaller than hair. An electrical current flows to thin resistances at the bottom of all the color that printer will use to form a small section of a word or picture. A resistance used here is called film type resistance when current passes through the resistance a high amount of heat is produced it will occur. The temperature produced here is more than 900^0f only for a second. The ink jets boiled due to this and forms a bubble of vapor. As the vapor expands it pushes ink through the nozzle. The vapor of printer in the form of a drop jet at the tip of nozzle. The drop jet over comes the pressure of the bubble forces the drop Jet over to the paper. The volume of the ink is above one million of a drop of water from an eyedropper. A typical character is formed by twenty drops across and 30 high.

How printer colors are Created

All colors are made up of different combinations of light we see all the wavelength that make white light through a prism a white light is broken into various color by the prism. The various colors are called spectrum. The spectrum is a mixture of colors. Different mixture of primary color can create any color from the spectrum by either enabling colors or subtracting. Color mixing is of two types additive color mixing subtractive color mixing. Additive color mixing is used to create colors and television. Computer monitors and in movies. Three colors Red, Green, Blue are used to produce all other colors.

Subtractive color Mixing

Reflection properties are used. All color printer use small dots of four inks to make various shades are made by learning dots of unprinted while some printers uses this type of process. Most common color computer can operate up to 3001. But now a day's printer of 700 DPI and 1440 DPI are also used.

Advantages

1. Many of ink-jet printers can also be programmed to print unusual symbols, *e.g.*,

Japanese or Chinese characters.

2. It provide an excellent middle ground between dot-matrix and laser printers.
3. Multiple-nozzle print heads enables them to print in several colours.

Disadvantages

1. They can only create one character at a time and therefore cannot match the print speed of line printers.
2. They are expensive

Laser Printers

The one revolution that has changed the faces of both offices and forests around the world was the photocopier. Trees plummet by the millions to provide fodder for the duplicate, triplicate, megaplicate. Today's non-impact, bi-image laser printer owes its life to this technology. The outlook of Laser Printer shown here.

At heart, the laser printer principle is simple. Some materials react to light in strange ways. Selenium and some complex organic compounds modify their electrical conductivity in response to exposure to light. Both copiers and laser printers capitalize on this photoelectric effect by focusing an optical image on a photo-conductive drum that has been given a static electrical charge. The charge drains away from the conductive areas that have been struck by light but persists in the dark areas. A special pigment called a toner is then spread across the drum, and the toner sticks to the charged areas. A roller squeezes paper against the drum to transfer the pigment to the paper. The pigment gets bonded to the paper by heating or "fusing" it.

The laser printer actually evolved from the photocopier. Rather than the familiar electrostatic Xerox machine, however, the true ancestor of the laser printer was a similar competing process called electro-photography, which used a bright light to capture an image and make it visible with a fine carbon-based toner. The process was developed during the 1960s by Keizo Yamaji at Canon. The first commercial application of the technology, called New Process to distinguish it from the old process (xerography), was a Canon photocopier released in 1968.

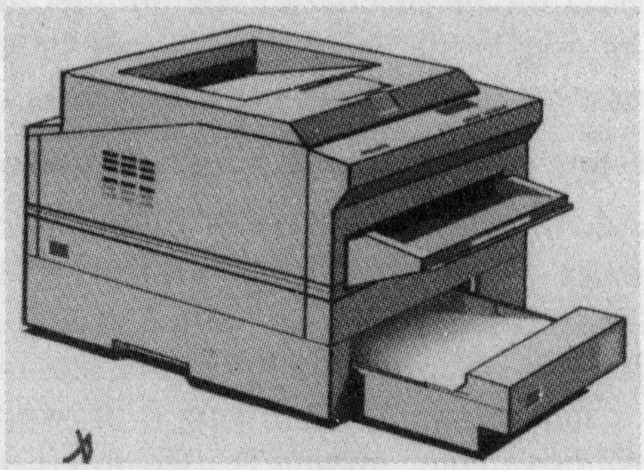

The first true laser printer was a demonstration unit, made by Canon in 1975, that was based on a modified photocopier. The first commercial PC laser printer came in 1984 v/ hen Hewlett-Packard introduced its first LaserJet, which was based on the Canon CX engine. At heart, it and all later lasers use the same process, a kind of heat set, light inspired offset printing.

The magic in a laser printer is forming the image by making a laser beam scan back and forth across the imaging drum. The trick, well known to stage magicians, is to use mirrors.

A small rotating mirror reflects the laser across the drum, tracing each scan line across it. The drum rotates to advance to the next scan line, synchronized to the flying beam of laser light. To make the light and dark pattern of the image, the laser beam is modulated on and off. It's rapidly switched on for light areas, off for dark areas, one minuscule dot at a time to form a bit image.

The major variations on laser printing differ only in the light beam and how it is modulated. LCD-shutter printers, for example, put an electronic shutter (or an array of them) between a constant light source (which need not be a laser) and the imaging drum to modulate the beam. LED printers modulates ordinary Light-Emitting Diodes as their optical source. In any case, these machines rely on the same electro-photographic process as the laser printer to carry out the actual printing process.

The basic laser printer mechanism requires more than just a beam and a drum. In fact, it involves several drums or rollers, as many as six in a single-color printer and more in color machines. Each has a specific role in the printing process. The Mechanical Section of Laser Printer is shown here.

The imaging drum, often termed the OPC for optical photoconductor, must first be charged before it will accept an image. A special roller called the charging roller applies the electrostatic charge uniformly across the OPC.

After the full width of an area of the OPC gets its charge, it rotates in front of the modulated light beam. As the beam scans across the OPC drum and the drum turns; the system creates an electrostatic replica of the page to be printed.

To form a visible image, a developing roller then dusts the OPC drum with particles of

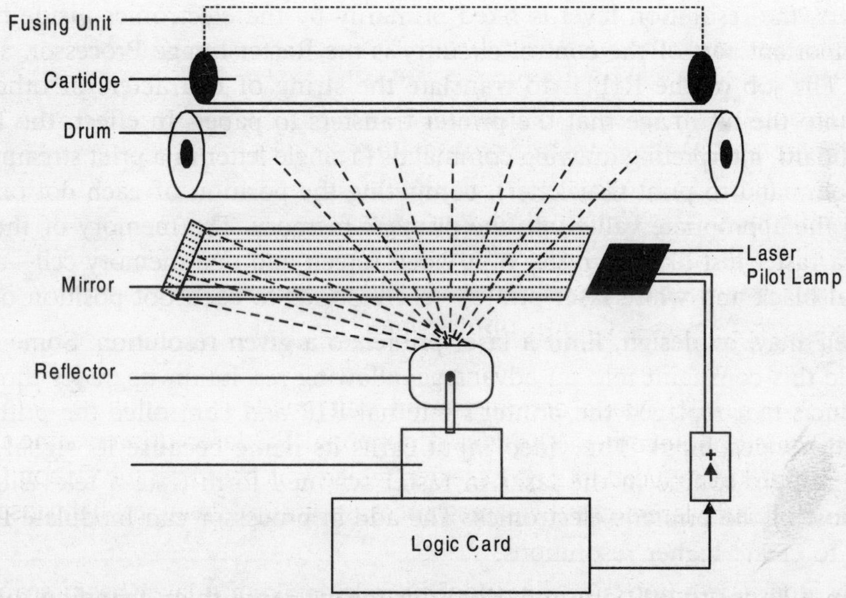

Mechanism of Laser Printer

toner. The light-struck areas with an electrostatic charge attract and hold the toner against the drum. The unexposed parts of the drum do not.

The printer rolls the paper between the OPC drum and a transfer roller, which has a strong electrostatic charge that attracts the toner off the drum. Because the paper is between the transfer roller and the OPC drum, the toner collects on the paper in accord with the pattern that was formed by the modulated laser. At this point only a slight electrostatic charge holds the toner to the paper.

To make the image permanent, the printer squeezes the paper between a fuser and backup roller. As the paper passes through, the printer heats the fuser to a high temperature—on the order of 350 degrees Fahrenheit (200 degrees Celsius). The heat of the fuser and the pressure from the backup roller melt the toner and stick it permanently on the paper. The completed page rolls out of the printer.

Meanwhile, the OPC drum continues to spin, wiping the already-printed area against a cleaning blade that scrapes any leftover toner from it. As the drum rotates around to the charging roller again, the process repeats. Early lasers used OPC drums large enough to hold an entire single-page image. Modern machines use smaller rollers that form the image as a continuous process.

Although individual manufacturers may alter this basic layout to fit a particular package or to refine the process, the technology used by all laser machines is essentially the same. At a given resolution level, the results produced by most mechanisms is about the same, too. You need an eye loupe to see the differences. The major difference is that manufacturers have progressively refined both the mechanism and the electronics to produce higher resolutions Basic laser printer resolution starts at 300 dots per inch. The mainstream is now at the 600 dpi level. The-best PC-oriented laser printers boast 1200 dpi resolution.

In most lasers, the resolution level is fixed primarily by the electronics inside the printer. The most important part of the control circuitry is the Raster Image Processor, also known as the RIP. The job of the RIP is to translate the string of characters or other printing commands into the bit image that the printer transfers to paper. In effect, the RIP works like a video board, interpreting drawing commands (a single letter in a print stream is actually a drawing command to print that letter), computing the position of each dot on the page, and pushing the appropriate value into the printer's memory. The memory of the printer is arranged in a raster just like the raster of a video screen and one memory cell—a single bit in the typical black and white laser printer—corresponds to each dot position on paper.

The RIP itself may, by design, limit a laser printer to a given resolution. Some early laser printers made this constraint into an advantage, allowing resolution upgrades through after-market products that replaced the printer's internal RIP and controlled the printer and its laser through a video input. The video input earns its name because its signal is applied directly to the light source in the laser in raster scanned form (like a television image), bypassing most of the printer's electronics. The add-in processor can modulate the laser at higher rates to create higher resolutions.

Moving from 300 dpi to 600 dpi and 1200 dpi means more than changing the RIP and adding memory, however. The higher resolutions also demand improved toner formulations because, at high resolutions, the size of toner particles limits sharpness much as the size of print wires limits impact dot matrix resolution. With higher resolution laser printers, it becomes increasingly important to get the right toner, particularly if you have toner cartridges refilled. The wrong toner limits resolution just as a fuzzy ribbon limits the quality of impact printer output.

Adding color to a laser printer is more than dumping a few more colors of toner. The laser must separately image each of its three or four primary colors and transfer the toner corresponding to each to the paper. The imaging process for each color requires forming an entire image by passing it past the OPC drum. Forming a complete image consequently requires three or four passes of the drum.

Exactly what constitutes a pass varies among manufacturers. Most color laser printers use three or four distinct passes of each sheet of paper. The paper rolls around the drum and makes four complete turns. Each color gets images separately on the drum, then separately transferred to the sheet. The printer wipes the drum clean between passes.

So-called "one-pass" printing, pioneered by Hewlett-Packard, still requires the drum to make four complete passes as each color gets separately scanned on the drum, and toner is dusted on the drum separately for each color. The paper, however, only passes once through the machine to accept the full color image at once and to have all four colors fused together onto the paper. The first three colors merely transfer to the drum. After the last color—black—gets coated on the drum, the printer runs the paper through and transfers the toner to it. The paper thus makes a single pass through the printer, hence the "one-pass" name.

This single-pass laser technology yields no real speed advantage. The photoconductor drum still spins around the same number of times as a four-pass printer. The speed at which the drum turns and the number of turns it makes determines engine speed, so the one-pass process doesn't make a significant performance increase.

The advantage to one-pass color laser printing comes in the registration of the separate color images. With conventional color laser systems, the alignment of the paper must be critically maintained for all four passes in order for all the colors to properly line up. With the one-pass system, paper alignment is not a problem. Only the drum needs to maintain its alignment, which is easy to do because it is part of the mechanism rather than an interloper from the outside world.

No matter the number of passes, adding color in laser printing subtracts speed. In general, color laser speed falls to one-quarter the monochrome speed of a similar engine because of the requirement of four passes. (With three-pass printing, speed falls to one-third the monochrome rate). For example, a printer rated at 12 pages per minute in monochrome will deliver about 3 ppm in color. Even allowing for this slowdown, however, color lasers are usually faster than other color page printers. They are also often quieter. Compared to thermal wax transfer printers, a popular high quality color technology, they are also economical because a laser uses toner only for the actual printed image. Thermal wax machines need a full page of ink for each page printed no matter the density of the image.

Working of Laser Printer

1. Eraser Lamp clears residual charge from drum
2. Main corona puts-6KV charge on drum surface
3. Laser beam selectively hits parts of the EP drum, making that part conductive. The conductive part loses voltage, dropping from –600V to –100V.
4. Developer Roller Squeezes Toner (represented by the #4 area) into a uniform layer on the EP drum. The parts that are charged to -6KV, however, repel the toner. Toner only remains where the laser has touched, as it is the most positively charged part of the drum.
5. The paper is pulled under the drum, which now contains the desired image written in toner. A second corona, drawing the toner from the drum to the paper.
6. The image now only sits on the paper as fine, dust-like toner. The toner must be fixed to the page. The fuser roller actually melts the toner into the page with heat at a temperature of 180 degrees C.

Cartridges

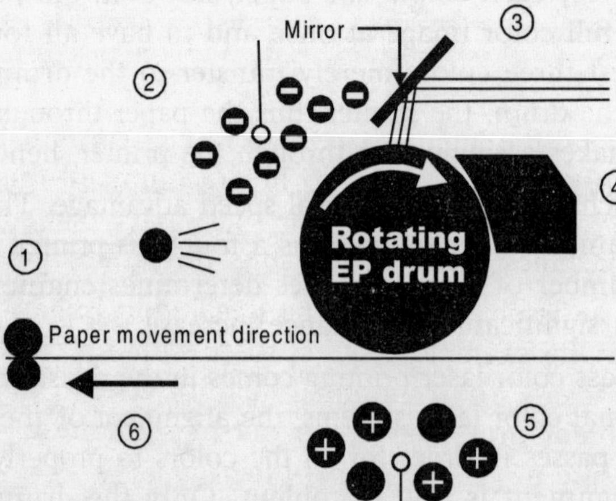

Working of Laser Printer

Laser printers use up a bit of their mechanism with every page they print. The organic photoconductor drum on which images are made gradually wears out. (A new drum material, silicon, is supposed to last for the life of the printer, but few printer models currently use silicon drums.) In addition, the charging corona or other parts may also need to be periodically replaced. And, of course, you need toner.

Laser printer manufacturers have taken various approaches to replacing these consumables. Hewlett-Packard's LaserJets, for example, are designed with one-piece cartridges that contain both the drum and toner. The whole assembly is replaced as a single unit when the toner runs out. Other laser printers are designed so that the toner, drum, and sometimes the fuser, can be replaced individually.

The makers of the latter style of printer contend that the drum lasts for many times more copies than a single shot of toner, so dumping the drum before its time is wasteful. On the other hand, the all-in-one cartridge folks contend that they design their drums to last only as long as the toner.

Surprisingly, from a cost standpoint the choice of technology does not appear to make a difference. (From an ecological standpoint, however, the individual replacement scheme still makes more sense.)

A similar situation reigns among inkjet printers. Some designs incorporate the print head nozzles into the ink cartridge. Others make the nozzles a separately replaceable item. Although the latter should have a cost advantage and a convenience disadvantage, as a practical matter the differences are not significant.

A more important issue to consider with inkjets is single versus separate cartridges for ink colors. Many printers, typically the less expensive models, use a single cartridge for all three primary ink colors. If you use all three colors equally, this is a convenient arrangement. Most of the time, however, one color will run out before another and force you to scrap a cartridge still holding a supply of two colors of rather expensive ink. If you are frugal or simply appalled at the price of inkjet ink, you'll want a separate cartridge for each ink color.

Refilling

One way to tiptoe around the high cost of laser printer consumables is to get toner or ink cartridges refilled. Most manufacturers do not recommend this—because they have no control over the quality of the toner, they can't guarantee that someone else's replacement works right in their machines. Besides, they miss the profits in selling the toner or ink.

Quality really can be an issue, however. The Resolution Enhancement technology of the HP's LaserJet III series, for example, requires toner with a particle size smaller than that of toner used by other printers. You cannot tell the difference in toner just by looking at it—but you can when blotchy gray pages pour out of the printer. When you get cartridges refilled, you must be sure to get the proper toner quality

Printer Control

To make what you see on paper resemble what you preview on your monitor screen, your printer requires guidance from your computer and your software to tell it exactly how to make a printout look. The computer must send the printer a series of instructions, either to control the most intimate operation of the dumb printer or to coax special features from the brainy machine.

The instructions from the computer must be embedded in the character stream because that is the only data connection between the printer and its host. These embedded instructions can take on any of several forms.

Character Mode

In printing text from your PC, a printer receives a stream of ASCII code characters. The printer matches those characters to one of the fonts in its memory, which may be ROM or

RAM. It then uses the pattern from memory to control the placement of bits on paper. All commands to the printer guide the formation and arrangement of these characters.

Because the entire process is oriented toward making characters, the commands to the printer are gauged in terms of characters and lines of text. Most commands deal with fonts and character positioning. For example, the printer may have several fonts in memory and use specific commands to select each one. Other commands tell the printer to emphasize characters or to slant them into italics. Placement commands tell the printer where to put the characters including how to space them.

The printer's interface uses the same signals to carry character data as well as commands. The printer needs some way to distinguish one from the other so that it doesn't print its commands on paper garbled with the text you actually want to see as hard copy. To prevent this confusion, most printers use a combination of two ideas for their commands: special control characters that code commands that also tell the printer not to print the character symbol; and escape sequences, a series of characters preceded by a special command telling the printer not to print the command characters.

Advantages of Laser Printers

1. Very high speed
2. Low noise level
3. Very high image quality
4. Excellent graphics capabilities
5. A variety of type sizes and styles
6. Uses standard, inexpensive copy paper which is loaded into a paper tray.

Thermal Printers

The thermal printers (a non-impact) is an alternative to the other serial printers. Heat elements produce dot-matrix images on heat-sensitive paper. Some fax machines use technique similar to thermal printers to produce documents on heat-sensitive paper. Output on thermal paper fades quickly when exposed to light, but the hardware is often inexpensive.

Advantages

- The advantages include compact size, limited noise, and low purchase price.

Disadvantages

- The major disadvantage is the cost of the heat-sensitive paper.

A thermal printer uses heated dot-matrix wires to print output on specially treated paper.

Electrostatic Printers

Electrostatic printers are devices in which the parts of paper which are to be printed are electrostatically charged, and attract a fine dust which is then fused to the paper by the application of heat. An electrostatic printer may be used in some instances as a plotter. Some properties associated with printers.

Spooling and Printer Buffers

The term spooling is derived from the expression Simultaneous Peripheral Operation On Line. Spooling is a temporary storage of input and output on high-speed input-output devices, which helps in reducing processing delays when transferring data between peripheral equipment and the processors of a computer. The speed of the printers is incredibly slow as compared with the processing speed of the computers to which they are connected. Which makes CPU to sit idle during printing process. To overcome this, two approaches are used.

Spooler Program

It allows the processor to alternate between processing a user's ongoing activity and controlling the printing process. Of course disk space or a dedicated block of primary storage must be available to store the text to be printed by the spooler.

Printer Buffer Hardware

It is an additional storage device that can accept text to be printed as fast as the computer can send it. The buffer then slowly releases the test data to match the printer's speed while the computer is free to do other things.

Printer Installation

Windows Millennium/98/95 Installation Instructions

1. Click the Windows Start button.
2. Choose Settings, and then click Printers.
3. Double-click the Add Printer icon.
4. Click Next.
5. A screen may appear asking you "How is the printer attached to your computer?" Click local, then click Next.
6. Click your printers name brand from the list of Manufacturers then click the model of your printer from the list of printers.
7. Click Next.
8. Click the port the printer is attached to and click Next.
9. Choose whether or not you want the printer to be the default printer and click Next.
10. If the printer is connected and turned on, click Finish. (You may be prompted to insert your Windows installation CD-ROM at this point. Insert the CD-ROM and click OK.)

Windows 2000 Installation Instructions

1. Click the Windows Start button.
2. Choose Settings, then click Printers.
3. Double-click the Add Printer icon.

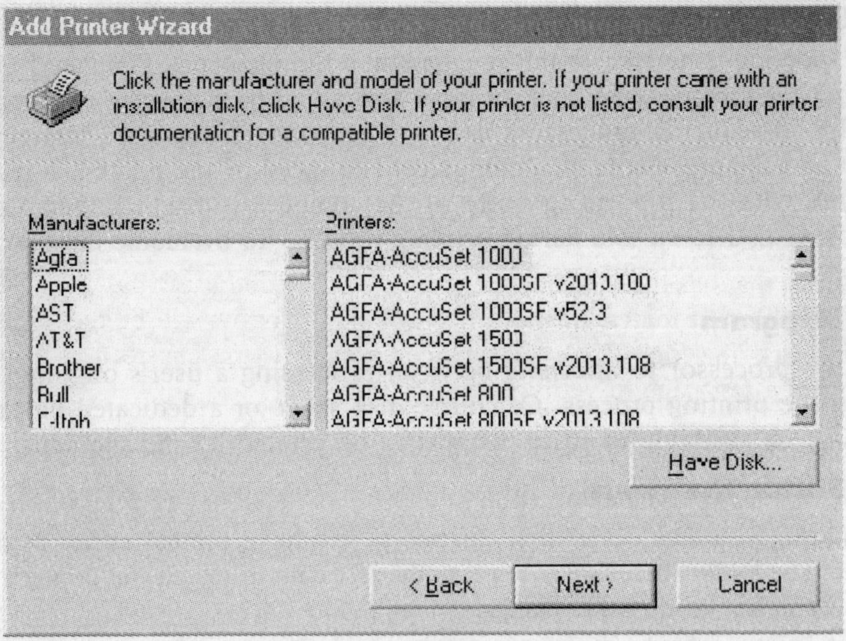

4. Click Next.
5. Click Local or Network printer, then click Next.
6. Click the port the printer is attached to and click Next.
7. Click your printers name brand from the list of Manufacturers then click the model of your printer from the list of printers.

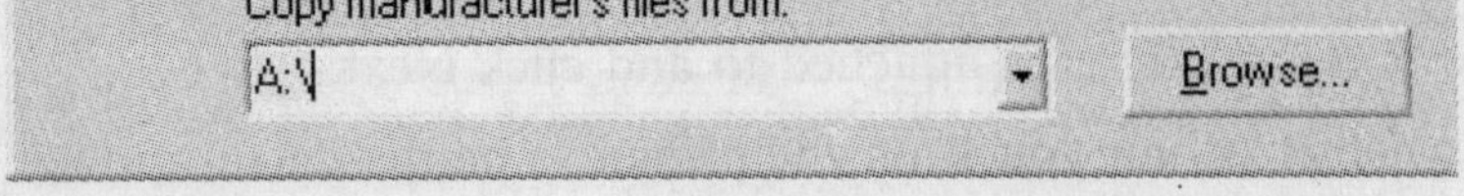

8. Click Next.
9. Choose whether or not you want the printer to be the default printer and click Next.
10. Choose whether or not the printer will be shared. Click Next.
11. If the printer is connected and turned on, click Finish. (You may be prompted to insert your Windows installation CD-ROM at this point. Insert the CD-ROM and click OK.)

Windows requires a 'Printer Driver' to allow communication and the setting up of printer parameters. Windows does have some drivers as standard, but normally the Printer manufacturer will supply a driver disk with the printer.

A printer can be installed one of three ways. Either

- Let Windows 'PLUG and PLAY' install it;
- Run the '*setup*' on the printer driver disk;
- By double clicking on the 'ADD PRINTER' icon in the PRINTERS window. *i.e*, START>SETTINGS>PRINTERS

Once this is done the 'ADD PRINTER WIZARD' will appear click 'NEXT'

Select the drive that has the manufacturer's disk inserted and using the 'FOLDERS' window browse to the relevant folder. In the 'FILE NAME' window will be the correct driver file (Windows selects the file!) Click 'OK' twice and follow the onscreen prompts. Windows will then print a test page to verify that all is OK.

Troubleshooting Printer

Here are a few simple techniques that will solve many printer problems.

1. Reboot your computer. This generally solves most printing problems.

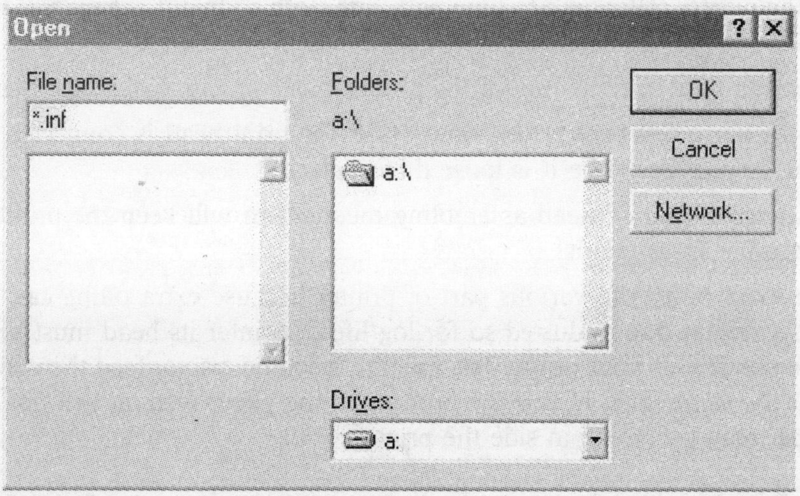

2. If it's not printing, or you're getting a message about the Fax printer, change your default printer: Start — Settings — Printers/Faxes. Right-click the printer you want, and then select (left-click) Set as Default.
3. Check and make sure all connections going to and coming from the printer are firmly in place.
4. Check that the printer is on-line:

   (*i*) Start — Settings — Printers, right-click the printer.

   (*ii*) If there isn't a checkmark by "Set as Default", left-click that option to select it.
5. Print a test page. If that prints and the application you are using doesn't, you probably will need to contact the application's vendor for support.

6. Turn off your printer for 10 seconds and turn it back on. Make a note of any error messages or flashing lights when the printer is turned back on.
7. If your printer is connected directly to another computer, try rebooting that computer. If your printer is connected to a JetDirect box, try unplugging the Jet Direct box for 10 seconds.
8. You may wish to uninstall and then re-install your printer.

Preventive Maintenance

Before starting the troubleshooting we must first examine or check some preventive maintenance steps that can keep our printer in good working condition. The main steps preventive maintenance is.

1. Clean the paper path, ribbon path, and head assembling movement path with a dry soft Cloth we can also use the soft brush for this purpose.
2. Clean the outer surface of printer time to time so that printer; can be kept free from dust.
3. Clean the printer roller time to time with soft cloth so that it is kept free from dust and rust.
4. If you clean time to time and oil the printer then we can avoid expenses repair
5. Check for loose belt because in some DMP the print head is connected to the motor with the help of belt if be it is loose then replace it.
6. Lubricating (oiling) of head assembling mechanism will keep the printer away from heaving unnecessary fault.
7. Do not extra oiling the various part of printer because extra oiling can cause serious fault in a printer due to dusted so for log life of printer its head must be kept cool as can it is possible. If your printer has fraction feed and tractor feed then do not use both these at the same time. If you use both them the paper feeding will not be paper and the paper may get struck in side the printer.

Revision

1. There would be no What You See Is What You Get (WYSIWYG) on PCs, if there were no monitors or displays on which to see what you get.
2. Until very recently, standard PC system packages only featured CRT displays. Lately, more and more PCs are being offered with flat-panel displays.
3. CRT monitor sizes are given in what are called nominal sizes. The most popular monitor sizes are 15-inch, 17-inch, 19-inch and 21-inch.
4. The images displayed on a PC's monitor are created from a pattern of dots in much the same way as the photographs in a newspaper.
5. The number of pixels on a monitor, whether CRT or LCD, determine the amount of detail that can be used to create and image.
6. Another key settings on a video system is its refresh rate or the number of times per second that the screen is entirely redrawn.

7. Printers are used to get the ouput on paper.
8. There are two main types of printers: Impact and Non impact printers.
9. An impact printer makes contact with the paper to produce an image.
10. Dot-matrix printers are also called serial printers.
11. Daisy Wheel Printers are slower than dot-matrix printers, but they produce a high-resolution output.
12. Line printer prints an entire line in a single operation without necessarily printing one character at a time.
13. Chain printer is a high-speed printer in which the type are carried by the links of a revolving chain.
14. On a band printer, several similar sets of fully formed characters are embossed on a horizontal band that is continuously moving in front of the print hammers.
15. Printers that do not strike characters against ribbon or paper when they print, are non-impact printers.
16. The physical properties of LASERS (Light Amplification by Stimulate Emission of Radiation) allows for the very precise positioning of narrow beam of light, transferring a high energy source to a very small area.
17. Electrostatic printers are devices in which the parts of paper which are to be printed are electrostatically charged, and attract a fine dust which is then fused to the paper by the application of heat.

Multiple Choice Questions

1. Printer is a _______ device.
   (a) Input (b) Pointing (c) Output
2. Dot matrix printers are so called because they print characters in terms of :
   (a) Squares (b) Dots (c) Circles
3. Line printers print a ______ at a time.
   (a) character (b) dot (c) line
4. Full form of LASER is:
   (a) Light Amplification by Stimulate Emission of Radiation
   (b) Low Amplification by Stimulate Emission of Radiation
   (c) Light Around by Stimulate Emission of Radiation

True/False Questions

1. Printers are used to get the ouput on paper.
2. There are two main types of printers: Impact and Non impact printers.
3. Dot-matrix printers are also called serial printers.
4. Daisy Wheel Printers are faster than dot-matrix printers, and they produce a high-resolution output.
5. Chain printer is a high-speed printer in which the type are carried by the links of a revolving chain.
6. On a band printer, several similar sets of fully formed characters are embossed on a horizontal band that is continuously moving in front of the print hammers.
7. Printers that do not strike characters against ribbon or paper when they print, are impact printers.
8. Electrostatic printers are devices in which the parts of paper which are to be printed are electrostatically charged, and attract a fine dust which is then fused to the paper by the application of heat.
9. DMP printers can print multiple copies of print output at a time.
10. DMP printers have a good photo quality.
11. Explain the construction of various print heads of DMP printer.

Descriptive Questions

1. Describe the various type of printers.
2. Which are Electrostatic Printers?
3. What are the advantages and disadvantages of Dot Matrix Printers?
4. Describe the working of Daisywheel printers.
5. What are Chain, Band and Drum printers?
6. What are the advantages and disadvantages of using Ink-jet printers?
7. Which are the different type of scanners?
8. Explain the working principal of LASER printer?

Answers to Objective Type Questions

Multiple Choice Questions

1. a	2. b	3. c	4. a

True False Questions

1. T	2. T	3. T	4. T
5. T	6. T	7. T	8. T
9. T	10. T	11. T	

12 I/O Interface

I/O PORTS

Most of the Input-Output (I/O) devices like keyboard, mouse, printers, modems and other devices are connected to the computer system through an interfacing facility called I/O ports. The data communications between devices and the system are established through these ports only.

The keyboard, mouse and speakers are connected through special ports. General-purpose I/O ports include serial port, parallel port and game port. Through these I/O ports an I/O device can be connected to the system.

Serial Port

In the Serial Interface Technique, the data is transmitted as 1-bit at a time through a single wire. The parallel data (byte) from the computer bus is converted into serial data (bits) and sent through the serial cable. It slows down the data transfer rate. It enables to communicate date transfer over a distance.

RS232 is the serial communication standard. The system normally supports two Serial ports COM 1 and COM 2. A 9-pin DB9 connector used with COM 1 and 25 pin DB 25 connector is used with COM 2 for connecting devices. An adapted 9 to 25 pin connector can be used to connect devices either to COM 1 or COM 2.

In modern PCs the serial port interface electronics is included in the motherboard chipset itself. Serial port can be enabled by BIOS set-up. The data transfer rate or the communication speed has to be set to match the speed of the devices connected to the system.

Serial Interface Connectors

A 25-pin or 9-pin D-shell subminiature male connector is used on the system as connector for the serial interface. The 25-pin connector was introduced with the PC system, but as not all the 25-pins are used for data transmission, IBM introduced 9-pin connectors with the AT system.

The parallel port also uses 25-pin D type connector but it can be distinguished from the serial port because the parallel port connector is female, whereas the connector for the serial port are male connectors (connectors with pin).

Old style MDA/CGA/EGA video connectors, which use 9-pin D-shell connectors are also female connectors. If the serial cable for your device contains 25-pin connector and the serial port has only 9-pin connector then many 25-pin to 9-pin converters are available in the market, same is true for conecting 9-pin device to a 25-pin port connector you can get a 9-pin to 25-pin converter.

Parallel Port

In a parallel interface technique the data, i.e. the entire byte is transferred to the devices at once as each bit is transmitted much faster than with a serial communication link. Devices like printers, scanners and plotters are connected to the system through female D25 pin connector. A system normally supports one parallel port LPT1 and it can also support more parallel ports.

Parallel ports are not only used to connect printers but also to connect external CD-ROM drives, external hard disk drive, ZIP drives and other mass storage devices. Recent PCs include two new technology parallel ports called External Parallel Ports (EPP) and Extended Capability Port (ECP). These ports are designed to support data transfer in both directions and also the selection of the direction of data flow can be controlled by software.

Working of Parallel Port

In this interfacing system, the signals travel through data cable, eight bits at a time. Other than the data, some control signals are also passed through the cable between the printer and the computer.

The parallel interface is one of the simplest communication system available, in this eight different lines are provided for the eight data lines, for each signal required to control the communication process a new wire is provided. This makes the circuitry required to drive the parallel signals very simple.

However, this simplicity has one drawback that is the cable required for the transmission. The increased numbers of lines make the cable required for the parallel transmission very thick. The number of lines going together have one more problem of cross-talk. When the electrical signals travel together in a cable, these signals start to affect each other as they travel down the cable. This makes the signal from one wire to change the signal on the other wire or the problem of cross-talk (signal crosses over and start talking with other signals) appears.

To prevent this problem of cross-talk it is recommended to keep the length of the parallel cable limited to maximum 10 feet. If the cable length is more than this, there is a chance of cross-talk appearing in the line.

Uni and Bi-directional Parallel Port

The original parallel interfce provided on the initial IBM computer's were designed as printer output port so they were uni-directional, i.e., they could only send the information to the device connected to the port but they could not receive any information from the device. Later IBM made some changes in the design and made the parallel ports capable of the bi-directional operation.

Enhanced Parallel Port (EPP)

Enhanced Parallel Port or the EPP is a new parallel port specificaion that allows high-speed two-way communication between the computer and the device, other than a printer or scanner.

Extended Capabilities Port (ECP)

Extended Capabilities Port or ECP is also a new high-speed two-way communication parallel port specification, ECP port is mainly used for a printer or scanner.

To connect to a printer to the ECP port you would require:

- EPP/ECP port
- ECP capable printer
- EPP/ECP capable printer cable
- Windows 98/2000/ME/XP operating system

Parallel port provided on the motherboard can be setup as EPP/ECP port using the following procedure

- Enter BIOS setup during computer power on by pressing Del key.
- In the BIOS setup main menu, select Peripheral Setup option.
- Look for Parallel Port Mode.
- Change the mode to EPP/ECP.
- Save and Exit BIOS setup and restart the system.

Game Port

This port in PC is used for connecting game controllers like joystick. The game port adopter is available either in multi I/O cards or in the sound card. Stand alone cards are also available that fit into one of the PC's 8-bit I/O slots.

The game port supports two game controllers at a time using a special split cable. The port is responsible for reporting the X and Y positions of the joystick to the system. It is available through a standard 15-pin D shell connector.

USB Port

Peripheral devices are connected to computers through I/O ports. The devices that support parallel interface standard are connected to parallel ports and devices that support serial interface standard are connected to serial ports.

Normally computers come with one parallel port and two serial ports. Universal Serial Bus (USB) is a peripheral bus standard that allows a variety of peripheral devices to be connected to computers simultaneously. USB is a single, standardized, easy-to-use way to connect upto 127 USB devices to a computer.

USB
Universal Serial Bus

The USB "trident" Icon

Year Created:	January 1996
Width:	1 bits
Number of Devices:	127 per host
Speed:	Up to 480 Mbit/s (USB 2.0)
Style:	Serial
Hotplugging?	Yes
External?	Yes

A USB device is connected to computers by plugging it to the USB connector available at the back of the computer. Type A connector and USB port connect the device to the computer. Type B connector and USB port connect individual devices.

A USB Series "A" plug

Features of USB

1. The computer acts as a host.
2. Up to 127 devices can be connected to the host either directly or by way of USB hubs.
3. USB has a data transfer rate of 480 megabits per second.
4. USB devices are hot swappable—the devices can be connected and disconnected at any time.

USB Hubs

The USB standard supports upto 127 devices and USB hubs are a part of the standard. A hub has four ports commonly. The hub is plugged to the computer and the devices are plugged to the hub. Hubs can be chained to connect more devices. Hubs can be powered hub or unpowered hub.

A USB hub with the plastic cover removed

The USB standard allows the low powered devices like mice to get their power from the bus i.e. from the powered huh. High power devices like printer or scanner will have their own power supply and hence, unpowered hubs can serve these devices.

USB Cable Connection

Inside the USB cable there are four wires for connections, Red wire for + 5V (power) and brown wire for ground (power). The twisted pair yellow and blue is used for data. The four wires are perfectly shielded.

Different Data Transfer Types Used in USB

There are three modes of data transfers.

They are:

1. **Interrupt:** to transfer little date-devices using this type are keyboard or a mouse.
2. **Bulk:** to transfer data in one big pocket-device like a printer use this type.
3. **Isochronous:** Out streams between the device and the host in real time. Devices like speakers use this mode.

The Hardware

A USB cable has four wires: power, ground, D+ and D–. The signal wires usually operate in differential mode. There are two types of USB devices: high speed and low speed. There are differences in the type, length and connectors that can be used with the two types. Generally the requirements are stricter for high speed devices. A high speed device can transfer data at a maximum of 12 Mbs while low speed is limited to 1.5 Mbs. The PIC 16C745 can only operate at low speed standard. The connector at the computer (A End) is a flattened rectangle while at the device (B end) the connector is square with two cut-off corners. Each USB device is able to draw 100 mA from the cable which allows a device to be bus powered. A device can negotiate up to 500 mA once connected to the USB cable but this power may not be available. If the power is unavailable the device must stay in a low power setting. Obviously devices can be powered externally as well.

The Software

When a device is connected, the computer (or a hub) detects the device by a pullup resister. A pullup resister on the D– wire signals a low speed device, while a high speed device has a pullup on the D+ wire. When detected a series of enumeration steps are started. The enumeration process assigns an identifier number to the device (there can be a maximum of 127 devices on a network) and also tells the host computer what sort of capabilities a device has (input, ouput, etc). The device also informs the computer of its name (Vendor, Product, Version and Serial Number). If the device identifies itself as a HID (Human Interface Device) then the device describes how the data should be interpreted.

USB Hub

A USB hub is a device that allows many USB devices to be connected to a single USB port on the host computer or another hub.

USB hubs are often built into equipment, normally keyboards or, more rarely, monitors or printers. Separate USB hubs come in a wide variety of form factors from boxes that look similar to a network hub to small designs intended to be plugged directly into the USB port on a computer (that is, without a connecting cable).

USB History

- USB 0.7: Released in November 1994.
- USB 0.8: Released in December 1994.
- USB 0.9: Released in April 1995.
- USB 0.99: Released in August 1995.
- USB 1.0 Release Candidate: Released in November 1995.
- USB 1.0: Released in January 1996.

  Specified data rates of 1.5 Mbps (Low-Speed) and 12 Mbps (Full-Speed). Did not anticipate or pass-through monitors. Few such devices actually made it to market.
- USB 1.1: Released in September 1998.

  Fixed problems identified in 1.0, mostly relating to hubs. Earliest revision to be widely adopted.

- USB 2.0: Released in April 2000.

  Added higher maximum speed of 480 Mbps (now called Hi-Speed).
- Mini-B Connector ECN: Released in October 2000.

  Specifications for Mini-B plug and receptable. These should not be confused with Micro-B plug and receptable.
- Errata as of December 2000: Released in December 2000.
- Resistor ECN: Released in May 2002.
- Errata as of May 2002: Released in May 2002.
- Interface Associations ECN: Released in May 2003.

  New standard desriptor was added that allows multiple interfaces to be associated with a single device function.
- Rounded Chamfer ECN: Released in October 2003.
- Unicode ECN: Released in February 2005.
- USB On-The-Go Supplement 1.0: Released in December 2001.
- USB On-The-Go Supplement 1.0a: Released in June 2003.
- USB On-The-Go Supplement 1.2: Released in April 2006.
- USB On-The-Go Supplement 1.3: Released in December 2006. This is the current revision

USB Connectors

Connector types

There are several types of USB connectors, and some have been added as the specification has progressed. From the original USB specification:

- Standard-A plug
- Standard-A receptacle
- Standard-B plug
- Standard-B receptacle

Added in the first engineering change noticed to the USB 2.0 specification:

- Mini-B plug
- Mini-B receptacle

Added in the Universal Serial Bus Micro-USB Cables and Connectors Specification:

- Micro-A plug (white)
- Micro-AB receptacle (gray)
- Micro-B plug (black)
- Micro-B receptacle (black)

Adapters, also from the Universal Serial Bus Micro-USB Cables and Connectors Specification (Note that no other adapters are allowed.):

- Standard-A receptacle to Micro-A plug
- Micro-USB is a connector announced by the USB Implementers Forum (USB-IF) on January 4, 2007. It is intended to replace the Mini-USB plugs used in many new smartphones and PDAs. The Micro-USB plug is rated for 10,000 connect-disconnect cycles. It is about half the height of the mini-USB connector in widespread use today but features a similar width.

USB Device Classes

Devices that attach to the bus can be full-custom devices requiring a full-custom device driver to be used, or may belong to a device class. These classes define an expected behavior in terms of device and interface descriptors so that the same device driver may be used for any device that claims to be a member of a certain class. An operating system is supposed to implement all device classes so as to provide generic drivers for any USB device.

Device classes are decided upon by the Device Working Group of the USB Implementers Forum. If the class is to be set for the entire device, the number is assigned to the bDeviceClass field of the device descriptor, and if it is to be set for a single interface on a device, it is assigned to the bInterfaceClass field of the interface descriptor. Both of these are a single byte each, so a maximum of 254 different device classes are possible (values 0x00 and 0xFF are reserved). If bDeviceClass is set to 0x00, the operating system will look at bInterfaceClass of each interface to determine the device class. Each class also optionally supports a SubClass and Protocol subdefinition. These can be used as the main device classes are continuously revised.

The most used device/interface classes (grouped by assigned class ID) are:

0x00 Reserved value - used in the device descriptor to signify that the interface descriptor holds the device class identifier for each interface.

0x01 USB audio device class, sound card-like devices.

0x02 USB communications device class ("CDC"), used for modems, network cards, ISDN connections, Fax.

0x03 USB human interface device class ("HID"), keyboards, mice, etc.

0x06 Still image capture device class, identical to the Picture Transfer Protocol as used across USB

0x07 USB printer device class, printer-like devices.

0x08 USB mass storage device class used for flash drives, portable hard drives, memory card readers, digital cameras, digital audio players etc. This device class presents the device as a block device (almost always used to store a file system).

0x09 USB hubs.

0x0B Smart card readers.

0x0E USB video device class, webcam-like devices, motion image capture devices.

0xE0 Wireless controllers, for example Bluetooth dongles.

0xFF Custom device class - used to establish that a device or interface does not support any standard device class and requires custom drivers.

USB Flash Drivers or Pen Drive

USB flash drives are NAND-type flash memory data storage devices integrated with a USB (universal serial bus) interface. They are typically small, lightweight, removable and rewritable. As of November 2006, memory capacities for USB Flash Drives currently are sold from 32 megabytes up to 64 gigabytes. Capacity is limited only by current flash memory densities, although cost per megabyte may increase rapidly at higher capacities due to the expensive components. (USB Memory card readers are also available, whereby rather than being built-in, the memory is a removable Flash memory card housed in what is otherwise a regular USB flash drive, as described below.)

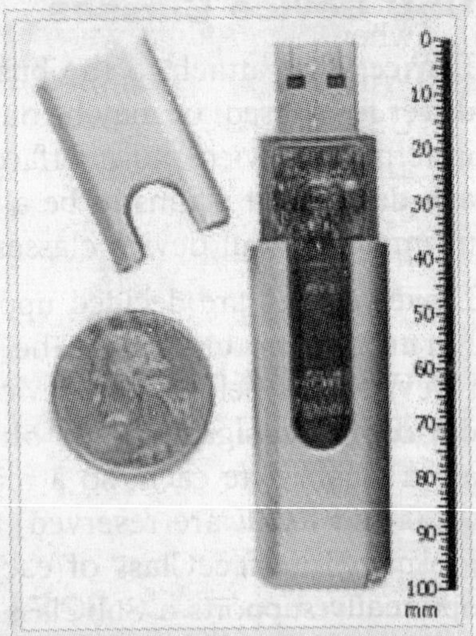

A USB flash drive, shown with a 24 mm U.S. quarter coin for scale.

USB flash drives offer potential advantages over other portable storage devices, particularly the floppy disk. They are more compact, generally faster, hold more data, and are more reliable (due to both their lack of moving parts, and their more durable design) than floppy disks. These types of drives use the USB mass storage standard, supported natively by modern operating systems such as Linux, Mac OS X, Unix, and Windows.

A flash drive consists of a small printed circuit board encased in a plastic or metal casing, making the drive sturdy enough to be carried about in a pocket, as a key fob, or on a lanyard. Only the USB connector protrudes from this protection, and is usually covered by a removable cap. Most flash drives use a standard type-A USB connection allowing them to be connected directly to a port on a personal computer.

To access the data stored in a flash drive, the drive must be connected to a computer, either by plugging it into a USB host controller built into the computer, or into a USB hub. Flash drives are active only when plugged into a USB connection and draw all necessary power from the supply provided by that connection.

However, some flash drives, especially high-speed drives utilizing the USB 2.0 standard, may require more power than the limited amount provided by a bus-powered USB hub, such as those built into some computer keyboards or monitors. These drives will not work unless plugged directly into a host controller (i.e., the ports found on the computer itself) or a self-powered hub.

USB 2.0

Its speed reached a performance level sufficient for consumer equipment while retaining compatibility with older devices. An example of how the popularity of USB displaced FireWire in a commercial device is the Apple iPod. It was originally released with a FireWire connector, which was eventually modified to allow for both USB and FireWire connections when the product was released for Windows. 3rd gcncration iPods used USB and Firewire for data transfer and only allows a FireWire connection to charge the battery from the main adapter. The iPod does charge via both cables when connected to the host computer. With the 4th generation and newer, iPods use USB for data transfer and both USB and Firewire for charging. The Firewire controller chip set has been removed in favour with reduced costs. The iPod Nano and shuffle don't even support Firewire, only supporting USB.

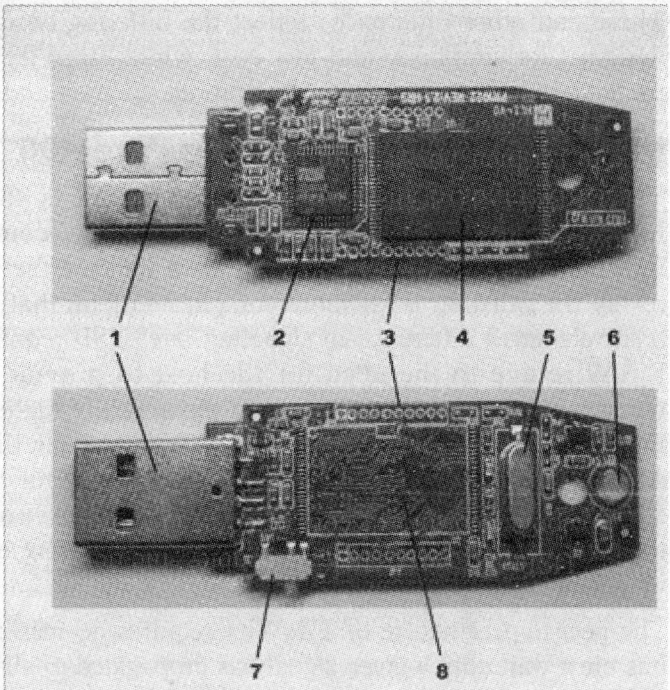

Internals of a typical flash drive (Saitek brand USB1.1 pictured)

1	USB connector
2	USB mass storage controller device
3	Test points
4	Flash memory chip
5	Crystal oscillator
6	LED
7	Write-protect switch
8	Space for second flash memory chip

Today, USB Hi-Speed is used in many consumer products. FireWire, however, retains its popularity in areas such as video and audio production.

Technical differences

The most significant technical differences between FireWire and USB include the following:

- USB networks use a tiered-star topology, while FireWire networks use a repeater-based topology.
- USB uses a "speak-when-spoken-to" protocol; peripherals cannot communicate with the host unless the host specifically requests communication. A FireWire device can communicate with any other node at any time, subject to network conditions.

- A USB network relies on a single host at the top of the tree to control the network. In a FireWire network, any capable node can control the network.

These and other differences reflect the differing design goals of the two buses: USB was designed for simplicity and low cost, while FireWire was designed for high performance, particularly in time-sensitive applications such as audio and video.

USB 2.0 Hi-Speed versus FireWire 400

The signaling rate of USB 2.0 Hi-Speed mode is 480 Mb/s, while the signaling rate of FireWire 400 (IEEE 1394a, the slower, yet more common variant of firewire as of 2007) is 393.216 Mb/s, which would appear to indicate that USB should be slightly faster, but in reality the situation is far more complicated than that and other design factors can dwarf a relatively small difference in signaling rate. USB requires more host processing power than FireWire due to the need for the host to provide the arbitration and scheduling of transactions. USB transfer rates are theoretically higher than FireWire due to the need for FireWire devices to arbitrate for bus access. A single FireWire device may achieve a transfer rate for FireWire 400 as high as 41 MB/s, while for USB 2.0 the rate can theoretically be 55 MB/s (for a single device). In a multi-device environment FireWire rapidly loses ground to USB: FireWire's mixed speed networks and long connection chains dramatically affect its performance.

The peer-to-peer nature of FireWire requires devices to arbitrate, which means a FireWire bus must wait until a given signal has propagated to all devices on the bus. The more devices on the bus, the lower is its peak performance. Conversely, for USB the maximum timing model is fixed and is limited only by the host-device branch (not the entire network). Furthermore, the host-centric nature of USB allows the host to allocate more bandwidth to high priority devices instead of forcing them to compete for bandwidth as in FireWire.

All of the above indicates that USB 2 should be faster than firewire 400 but tests have generally shown that for mass storage using normal consumer equipment firewire is faster often by a significant margin.

Revision

1. Most of the Input-Output (I/O) devices like keyboard, mouse, printers, modems and other devices are connected to the computer system through an interfacing facility called I/O ports.
2. In the Serial Interface Technique, the data is transmitted as 1-bit at a time through a single wire.
3. The parallel port also uses 25-pin D type connector but it can be distinguished from the serial port because the parallel port connector is female, whereas the connector for the serial port are male connectors (connectors with pin).
4. The parallel interface is one of the simplest communication system available, in this eight different lines are provided for the eight data lines, for each signal required to control the communication process a new wire is provided.
5. The game port adopter is available either in multi I/O cards or in the sound card.

6. USB, Universal Serial Bus, is a protocol that allows two way communcation between peripheral devices and a host computer.
7. A USB cable has four wires: power, ground, D+ and D–.
8. A USB hub is a device that allows many USB devices to be connected to a single USB port on the host computer or another hub.
9. There are several types of USB connectors, and some have been added as the specification has progressed.
10. Device classes are decided upon by the Device Working Group of the USB Implementers Forum.
11. USB flash drives are NAND-type flash memory data storage devices integrated with a USB (universal serial bus) interface.

Multiple Choice Questions

1. USB is a _______ device.
   (a) Input
   (b) Output
   (c) Both
2. USB cable has __ wires:
   (a) 3
   (b) 4
   (c) 5
3. USB keyboards are compatible with:
   (a) Windows
   (b) Linux
   (c) DOS
4. Pen drive is based upon:
   (a) Optical technology
   (b) Magnetic Storage Technology.
   (c) Semi conductor technology
   (d) None of these.

True/False Questions

1. A USB cable has four wires: power, ground, D+ and D–.
2. The USB mouse uses the Universal serial bus interface to communicate with computer.
3. An optical mouse is more accurate or precise and has no moving parts.
4. Most of the Input-Output (I/O) devices like keyboard, mouse, printers, modems and other devices are connected to the computer system through an interfacing facility called I/O ports.
5. In the Serial Interface Technique, the data is transmitted as 0-bit at a time through a single wire.
6. The game port adopter is available either in multi I/O cards or in the sound card.

Descriptive Questions

1. What is a USB device?
2. What is USB cable made of?
3. How does USB handle software?
4. Which computer devices are available with USB?
5. What is a serial port?
6. What is a parallel port?
7. Describe the working of pen drive.
8. What are the technical specifications of USB 2.0?
9. What are the features of USB?
10. What sort of software is used for USB?

Answers to Objective Type Questions

Multiple Choice Questions

1. c	2. b	3. a	4. a

True False Questions

1. T	2. T	3. T	4. T
5. F	6. T		

13 Other Peripherals

Zip Drives

A high-capacity floppy disk drive developed by Iomega Corporation, Zip disks are slightly larger than conventional floppy disks, and about twice as thick. They can hold 100 or 250 MB of data. Because they're relatively inexpensive and durable, they have become a popular media for backing up hard disks and for transporting large files.

A Zip drive is a small, portable disk drive used primarily for backing up and archiving personal computer files. The trademarked Zip drive was developed and is sold by Iomega Corporation. Zip drives and disks come in two sizes. The 100 megabyte size actually holds 100,431,872 bytes of data or the equivalent of 70 floppy diskettes. There is also a 250 megabyte drive and disk. The Iomega Zip drive comes with a software utility that lets you copy the entire contents of your hard drive to one or more Zip disks.

The Zip drive can be purchased in either a parallel or a Small Computer System Interface (SCSI) version. In the parallel version, a printer can be chained off the Zip drive so that both can be plugged into your computer's parallel port.

DVD ROM

DVD stand stands for digital video disc or digital versatile disc, is the next generation of optical disc storage technology. It is bigger, faster CD that can hold cinema-like view, better-than-CD audio, and compatriot CD data. Using a DVD you can have home entertainment, computers, and business information with a single digital format. The DVD will eventually replace audio/video CD, videotape, laserdisc, CD-ROM, and video game cartridges.

There are various variations of DVD; DVD-ROM or DVD-R are physical formats and DVD-Video or DVD-Audio are application formats. DVD-ROM is the base format that holds data. Physical format of DVD-ROM includes recordable variations DVD-R, DVD-RAM, DVD-RW, and DVD-RW. The application formats include DVD-Video, DVD-Video Recording, DVD-Audio, DVD-Audio Recording, DVD Stream Recording, and SACD.

Storage Capacity of DVDs

DVDs are of the same diameter and thickness as CDs, and they are made using some of the same materials and manufacturing methods. Like a CD, the data on a DVD is encoded in the form of small pits and bumps in the track of the disc. A DVD is composed of several layers of plastic, totalling about 1.2 millimeters thick. Each layer is created by injection molding polycarbonate plastic. This process forms a disc that has microscopic bumps arranged as a single, continuous and extremely long spiral track of data.

Once the clear pieces of polycarbonate are formed, a thin reflective layer is sputtered onto the disc, covering the bumps. Aluminium is used behind the inner layers, but a semi-reflective gold layer is used for the outer layers, allowing the laser to focus through the outer and onto the inner layers. After all the layers are made, each one is coated with lacquer, squeezed together and cured under infrared light.

For single-sides discs, the label is silk-screened onto the nonreadable side. Double-sided discs are printed only on the nonredable area near the hold in the middle. If you could lift the data track off a single layer of a DVD, and stretch it out into a straight line, it would be almost 7.5 miles long. A double-sided, double-layer DVD would have 30 miles of data.

Multi-Layer Storage

To increase the storage capacity, a DVD can have up to four layers, two on each side. The laser that reads the disc can actually focus on the second layer through the first layer. Here is a list of the capacities of different forms of DVDs:

DVD disc capacity

	Single layer capacity		Dual/Double layer capacity	
Physical size	**GB**	**GiB**	**GB**	**GiB**
12 cm, single sided	4.7	4.38	8.5	7.92
12 cm, double sided	9.4	8.75	17.1	15.93
8 cm, single sided	1.4	1.30	2.6	2.42
8 cm, double sided	2.8	2.61	5.2	4.84

Note: GB here means gigabyte, equal to 10^9 (or 1,000,000,000) bytes. Many programs will display gibibyte (GiB), equal to 2^{30} (or 1,073,741,824) bytes.

Example: A disc with 8.5 GB capacity is equivalent to: (8.5 × 1,000,000,000) / 1,073,741,824 H" 7.92 GiB.

Size Note: There is a difference in size between + and - DL DVD formats. For example, the 12 cm single sided disk has capacities:

Disk Type	Sectors	bytes	GB	GiB
DVD-R SL	2,298,496	4,707,319,808	4.7	4.384
DVD+R SL	2,295,104	4,700,372,992	4.7	4.378
DVD-R DL	4,171,712	8,543,666,176	8.5	7.957
DVD+R DL	4,173,824	8,547,991,552	8.5	7.961

Capacity Nomenclature

The four basic types of DVD are referred to by their capacity in gigabytes, rounded up to the nearest integer.

DVD type	Name
Single sided, single layer	DVD-5
Single sided, dual layer	DVD-9
Double sided, single layer	DVD-10
Double sided, dual layer	DVD-18

Another format in limited use is a double sided DVD with one side comprising a single layer of data while the opposite side comprises two layers of data (effectively a DVD-5 on one side bonded to a DVD-9 on the other). This format holds approximately 12.3 GB of data and is known as DVD-14.

Web Camera

A web camera is basically a low-end digital video camera with low resolution and fixed focus lens. This camera is suited for webcasting, video messaging, etc., applications. One can use the web camera to make low-grade movies and capture still images.

In recent years, source-data automation has expanded to allow the direct entry of graphic information, as well as text-based information via scanners. In a process called imaging, a scanner converts a drawing, a picture, or any document into computer- recognizable form by shinning a light on the image and sensing the intensity of the reflection at each point of the image. That is, the hard-copy image is translated into an electronic format that can be interpreted by and stored on computers. The electronic version of the image can then be stored, probably on disk, and reproduced on the screen when needed.

The image to be stored can be handwritten notes, a photograph, a drawing, an insurance form - anything that can be digitized. Once an image has been digitized and entered to the computer system, it can be retrieved, displayed, altered, merged with text, stored, and sent via data communications to one or several remote locations. Businesses find imaging particularly useful for documents, since they can view an exact replica of the original document at any time. Professional photo agencies are the another area where imaging is useful. Here the film that was shot with a conventional camera is processed onto optical disk instead of prints or slides. Professional photo agencies keep thousands of images on file, ready to be leased for a fee. Typically a couple of dozen small-size images can be displayed on the screen at one time; a particular image can be enlarged to full screen size with a click of a mouse button.

A digital camera can store many more pictures than an ordinary camera. Pictures taken using a digital camera are stored inside its memory and can be transferred to a computer by connecting the camera to it. A digital camera takes pictures by converting the light passing through the lens at the front into a digital image.

It does not by using a grid of tiny light sensors which concert the light that is falling on them into binary patterns of 0s and 1s. Different binary patterns are used to represent the different colours and shades of light that make up a picture. Pictures taken using a digital camera can be easily saved and transferred from one computer to another where they can be edited using special graphics software.

Some digital camera can also capture short clips of moving images but for longer video clips a digital video camera is needed. However both of these types of camera are still quite expensive.

Modem

The modem is a device which allows you to connect your computer to any other computer, anywhere else in the world using a telephone line. This allows you to communicate with the connected person, transfer data, copy software/programs from the connected computer, sent and received mail using e-mail, etc.

Currently, the modem can also be used to sent and receive fax, for this you use modem as fax device. Also you can use modem to connect to the Internet. There are two main types of modems: Internal and External Modems.

Let us see how modem works?

When the computer is switched on and is ready to transmit data, it sends a Data Terminal Ready (DTR) signal to the modem. When the modem is ready to receive data or instruction from the computer, it sends a Data Set Ready (DSR) signal to the computer. Both these signals must be present before the next step can happen. Next, the computer sends a command to the modem to go “Off Hook”, *i.e.*, to open communication with the phone line. Next, the computer issues a command to modem to dial a phone number.

Installing the Modem

There are two ways by which the modem can be installed. One of them is Automatically and the other is Manually.

Automatically

After connecting the modem when you switch on the computer system, Windows 95/98 should automatically detect the modem and ask for the modem driver software. If the auto detection does not work then:

1. Click on the Start/Setting/Controls Panel.
2. In the control panel window double click on Add New Hardware icon.
3. In the next Add New Hardware Wizard screen, to automatically detect new hardware click on Next>option.
4. In the next screen select Yes for Do you want Windows to search for your new hardware? question and click on Next option.
5. Click on Modem to select it.

6. Click on the Next>option, it will start the auto detection process, which may take some time.
7. Finally next screen will appear with an option to click on Details..... button to see the list of detected hardware.
8. Click on Finish option to install the drivers for the detected hardware.

If your modem was not detected during this process then you need to manually install the modem driver software.

Manually

For this, follow the above instructions for step 1 & 2 and in the 3rd, in Add New Hardware Wizard screen, do the following:

1. Click on No, I want to select the hardware for a list, to the Do you want Windows to search for your new hardware? question.
2. Click on Next>option.
3. In the next screen a list of hardware appear, from the list click on Modem.
4. Click on Next>option.
5. Next Windows will try to automatically detect the modem.

To manually install the modem driver,

1. Click on Don't detect my modem; I will select it from a list.
2. Click on Next>option. A list of modem manufacturers and their modem models are shown on the next screen. There is also an option called Have Disk ....., if you have received a modem driver disk or CD with your modem then.
3. Click on the Have Disk . . . . option.
4. Place the driver disk/CD into proper drive and in the next Install From Disk screen select the proper drive. You can also click on Browse . . . . option to search for the driver disk/CD.
5. Once the driver is found on disk, click on OK, this will install the modem driver into the computer system. The driver could be on some sub-directory of the driver disk/CD, check the manual that came with the modem.
6. Restart the computer to make the modem active.

Sometimes the driver disk/CD that comes with the modem contains a SETUP.EXE or INSTALL.EXE program. Running this program will automatically install the modem driver to the Windows.

Flash Disk

A flash drive, related to a solid state drive, is a storage device that uses flash memory rather than conventional spinning platters to store data. Unlike a USB flash drive or keydrive, flash drives tend to physically imitate conventional hard drives in size, shape, and interface so that they may act as a replacement for hard drives.

These products are typically used as low power, rugged replacements for hard drives, especially in installations exposed to extreme conditions. The flash memory cells tend to fail after around a million writes which made early devices unsuitable for storage which is often updated in place, such as swap files. To address this problem, some flash disk vendors have introduced wear-levelling techniques that track usage and transparently relocate the data in highly utilized extents of storage to extents that have been less utilized. Unlike solid state drives, flash drives do not generally require backup battery systems.

Another use for flash drives is running light weight operating systems designed specifically for turning general-purpose PCs into network appliances comparable to more expensive routers and firewalls. In this situation, a write protected flash drive containing the whole operating system is used to boot the system. A similar system could boot from CD, floppy disk or a traditional hard drive but flash memory is a good choice because of very low power consumption and failure rate.

Limited quantities of consumer electronics (such as notebook PCs) have become available including flash drives in place of conventional hard drives. It is widely assumed that this trend will increase over time as the cost of flash drives decreases and the performance needs of consumer electronics continue to increase.

Revision

1. Zip disks are slightly larger than conventional floppy disks, and about twice as thick.
2. A Zip drive is a small, portable disk drive used primarily for backing up and archiving personal computer files.
3. A web camera is basically a low-end digital video camera with low resolution and fixed focus lens.
4. A digital camera can store many more pictures than an ordinary camera.
5. The modem is a device which allows you to connect your computer to any other computer, anywhere else in the world using a telephone line.
6. A flash drive, related to a solid state drive, is a storage device that uses flash memory rather than conventional spinning platters to store data.
7. DVD stand stands for digital video disc or digital versatile disc, is the next generation of optical disc storage technology.
8. DVDs are of the same diameter and thickness as CDs, and they are made using some of the same materials and manufacturing methods.

Multiple Choice Questions

1. A modem performs
   (a) Modulation
   (b) Demodulation
   (c) Analog to digital and digital to analog conversion
   (d) All of these.
2. Web camera is
   (a) a camera
   (b) an input device
   (c) both.

True/False Questions

1. A web camera is basically a low-end digital video camera with low resolution and fixed focus lens.
2. A digital camera cannot store many more pictures than an ordinary camera.
3. A flash drive, related to a solid state drive, is a storage device that uses flash memory rather than conventional spinning platters to store data.
4. DVD stand stands for digital video disc or digital versatile disc, is the next generation of optical disc storage technology.

Descriptive Questions

1. What are Zip disks?
2. Describe zip drive.

3. Describe web camera.
4. How do compare digit camera with web camera?
5. What is a modem?
6. What is flash drive?
7. What is DVD?
8. Describe the various formats of DVD.

Answers to Objective Type Questions

Multiple Choice Questions

1. d 2. c

True False Questions

1. T 2. F 3. T 4. T

14 Computer Installation

Introduction

In this section we shall see how one can assemble a perfect computer. Assembling a computer is a very easy job, one just need to select proper components and then connect them properly. Let us see how to build your dream PC.

First, buy the components required to make the PC and keep them ready.

- Monitor, Main case with Power Supply, keyboard, Mouse
- Motherboard, Procesor, RAM
- Display card, Sound card, Modem card, LAN card
- Floppy drive, Hard Disk drive, CD/DVD drive
- Speaker/Microphone, External, Modem

Keep the following tools handy

- Star/Philips screwdriver set, nose pliers

Before starting the assembly process, touch some metallic grounded object, to make sure that you are free from any static charge. Also, handle the Motherboard, CPU, RAM etc. static sensitive components only from its edges.

Following is a step-by-step procedure to assemble a computer.

Remove Cover of the Main Unit

1. Open the four screws at the back of the system's main unit.
2. Slide the top cover off the main unit.

Remove Base Plate from the Main Unit

1. Remove the screws holding the base plate to the main unit
2. Lift the base plate out of the main unit

Mount the Motherboard to the Base Plate

1. Place the Motherboard on the base plate using the spacers and screws provided (this process is explained later).
2. Tighten the screws provided to fix the Motherboard to the base plate. Do not completely tighten the screws, leave a little room to make any adjustments when some new expansion card is installed.

   Tighten the screws only after you mount all the cards to the Motherboard. One

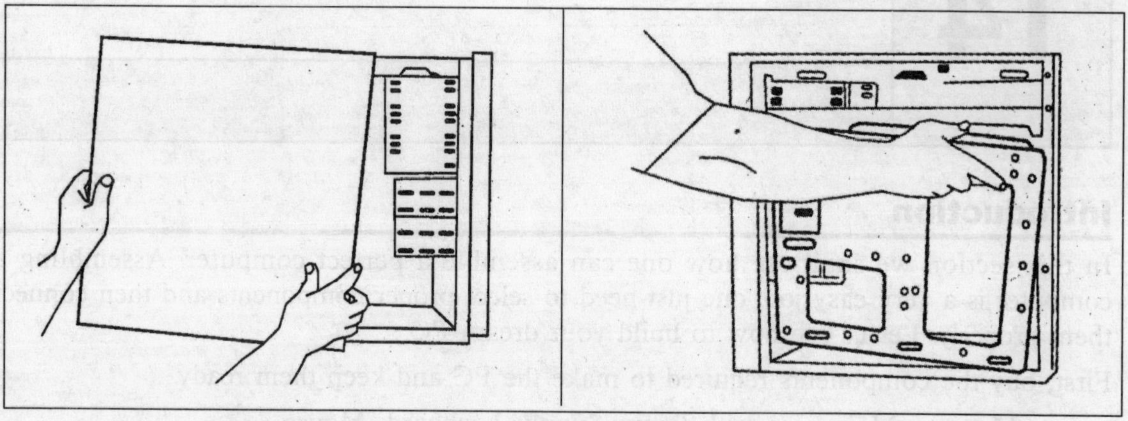

can place foam pieces or old newspaper between Motherboard and base plate, so that Motherboard components will not touch the base plate and short circuit.

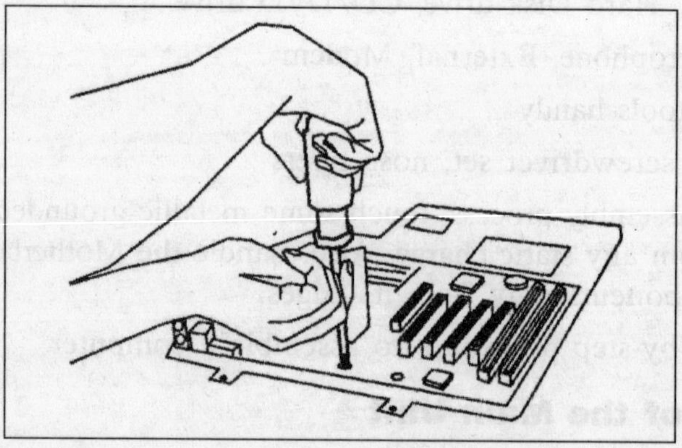

Attach the Processor to the Motherboard

1. Attach the CPU to the Motherboard

   Based on the CPU used, you may use socket-370 or SEC slot socket.

2. Attach CPU fan to the power connector (this is very important, as excessive heat build up may permanently damage the processor)
3. Set any jumpers to configure the Motherboard for the CPU type, this information should be available in the Motherboard manual.

   On most of the new Motherboards, the board automatically detects the processor clock speed and core voltage, without any need for setting up the jumpers

Attach the RAM Modules to the Motherboard

1. To attach RAM module, properly align both ends of the module with the slot given on the Motherboard and push the module into the slot with a smooth push.

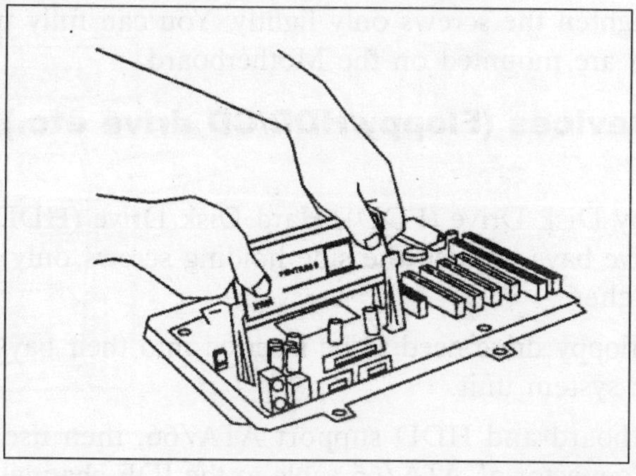

Based on the Motherboard, you may need to install SIMM or DIMM type memory module.

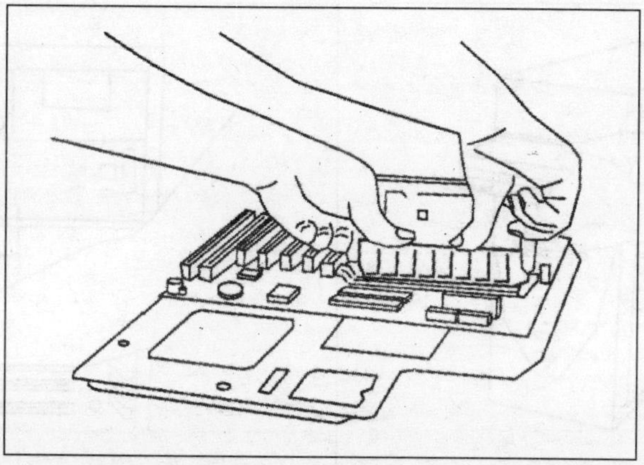

Mount the Motherboard into the Computer Unit

1. Once the CPU and Memory is attached to the Motherboard you can mount the back plate (with the Motherboard) into the main system unit.

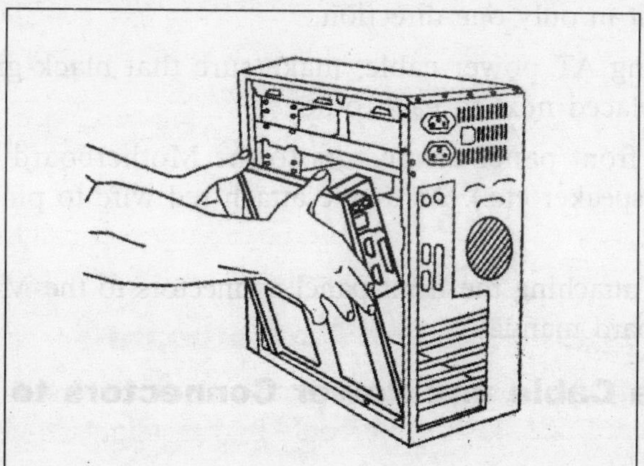

Remember to tighten the screws only lightly. You can fully tighten them after the expansion cards are mounted on the Motherboard.

Attach Storage Devices (Floppy/HDD/CD drive etc.) to the Main Unit

1. Place the Floppy Disk Drive (FDD), Hard Disk Drive (HDD) and CD/DVD etc. to their respective bays, tighten the side holding screws only after power and data cables are attached.

   CD/DVD and floppy drive need to be inserted into their bays from the opening at the front of the system unit.

   If your Motherboard and HDD support ATA/66, then use new ATA/66 cable. Connect Blue Connector of ATA/66 cable to the IDE channel on the Motherboard. Black Connector of this cable should be connected to the master IDE drive, connect White Connector to the slave device.

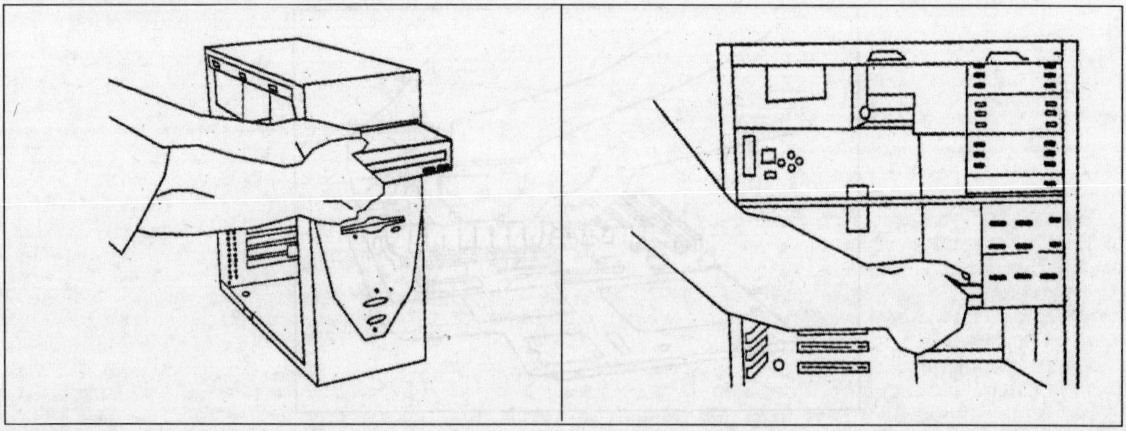

Connect Cables (Reset, Speaker, Power Indicator LED etc.) to the Motherboard

1. Connect power cable to the Motherboard. If you have ATX Power Supply then the connector will fit in only one direction.

   When connecting AT power cable, make sure that black ground lines on both connector are placed next to each other.

2. Attach various front panel connectors to the Motherboard (reset, power/HDD indicator LED, speaker etc.). As a rule attach red wire to pin 1 and black wire to pin 2.

   Information for attaching the front panel connectors to the Motherboard are given in the Motherboard manual.

Attach Drive Data Cable and Power Connectors to the Storage Devices

1. Connect primary IDE channel to the master/boot hard disk drive.

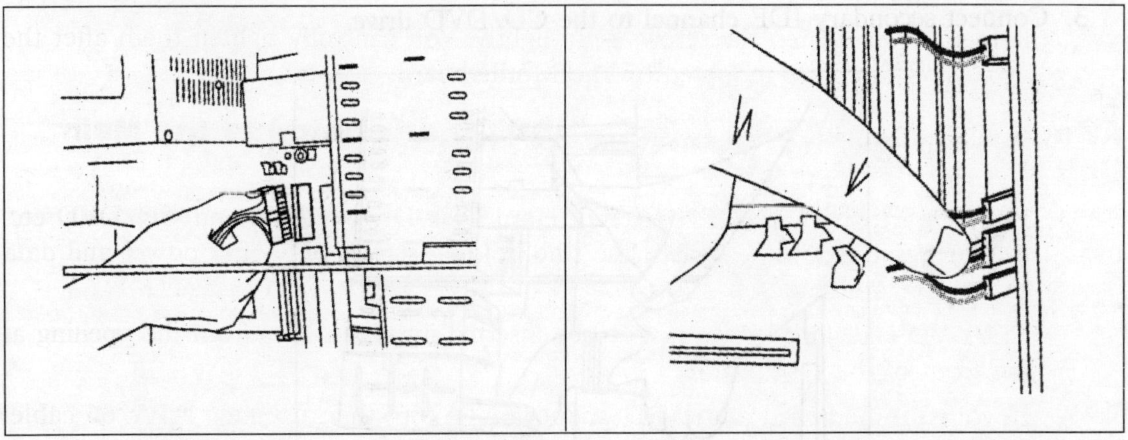

Primary IDE channel is indicated as Pri-Master or IDEO on the Motherboard. When attaching data cable, red/dotted wire on the cable should align with pin-0 on the connector.

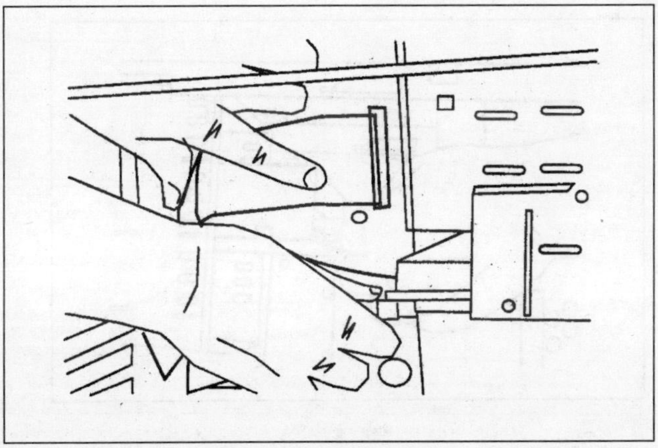

2. Attach power connector to the hard disk drive.

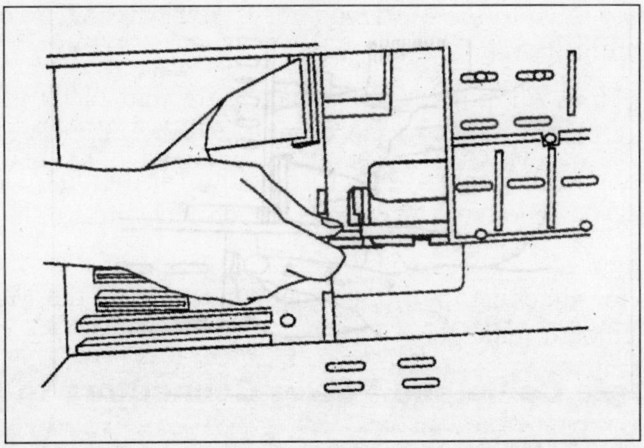

3. Connect secondary IDE channel to the CD/DVD drive.

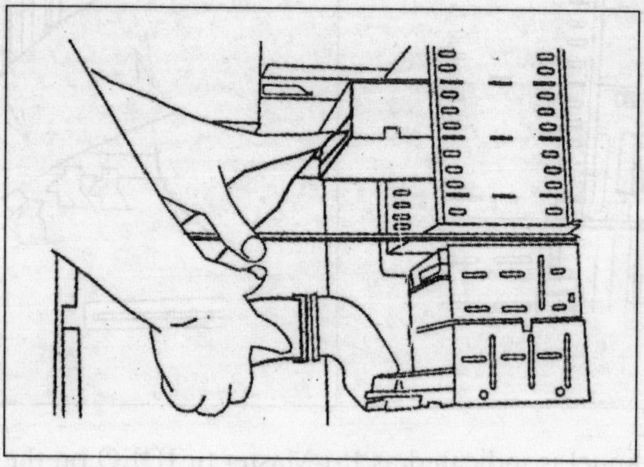

4. Attach power connector the CD/DVD drive.

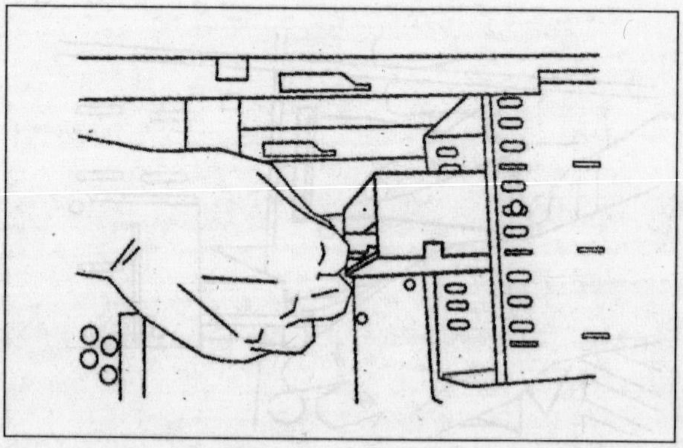

5. Connect floppy drive to the Motherboard connector.

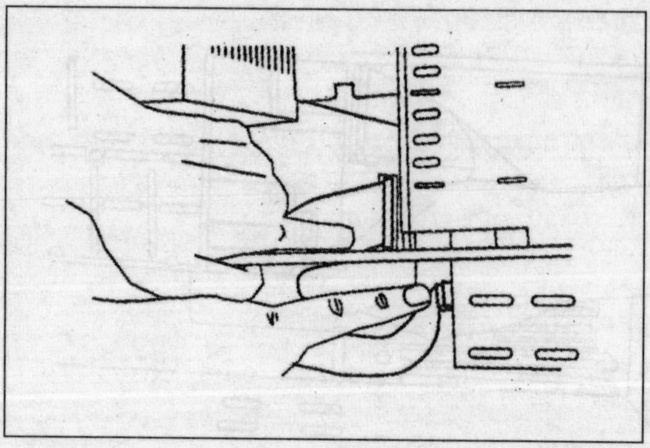

6. Attach power connector to the floppy drive.

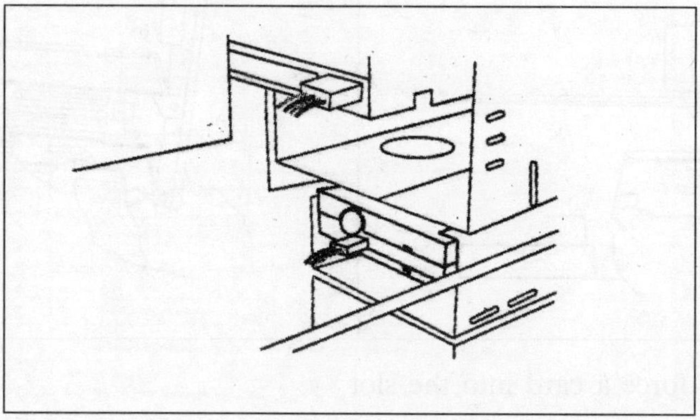

Connecting CD/DVD drive to Secondary IDE channel will improve the speed of the Primary IDE Hard disk drive, compared to connecting the CD/DVD as slave to the Primary IDE channel hard disk drive.

A HDD/CD/DVD can be made master/slave by changing the position of jumper provided on its back.

Once the data cable and power cable is connected to the hard disk and floppy disk drives, use some rubber band or tie-wrap to arrange the data and power cable, so that the air flow inside the system is not blocked.

Connect external port cables

1. Connect Serial, Parallel, Game, Infrared etc. ports to the Motherboard. Connectors for this are provided with the Motherboard. ATX Motherboard does not require this, as these ports are built into the Motherboard itself.

   Position of these connectors, on the Motherboard, is generally provided in the Motherboard manual.

   Arrange these connectors with the help of some rubber band or tie-wrap so that they do not obstruct the airflow inside the system case and keep the system cool.

Connect Display Card and Sound Card

If your Motherboard does not have integrated Display/Sound card then you need to connect these cards to your system.

When handling these cards remember to handle them by edges to prevent any damage due to static charge.

1. To connect the cards find an empty slot
2. Insert the card by first aligning card's edge connectors to the slot on the Motherboard.
3. Slide in the card into the slot by gently rocking the card back and forth and pushing down

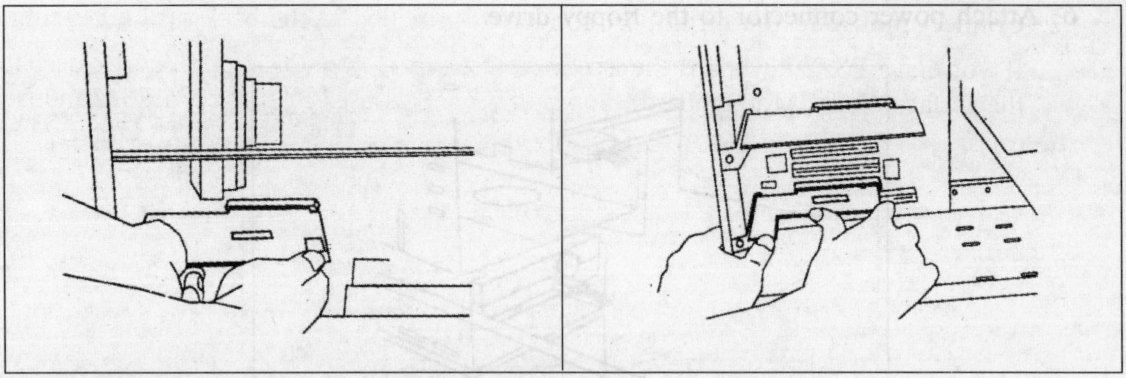

Never try to force a card into the slot

Make sure that the card is firmly seated in the slot

4. Tighten the screw to fix the card to the Motherboard.

Connect CD Audio Cable

1. To use you CD drive to hear Audio CDs, connect Audio Out socket on the CD/DVD drive to the CD-in connector on the Soundcard/Motherboard (if the Motherboard has built in Soundcard)

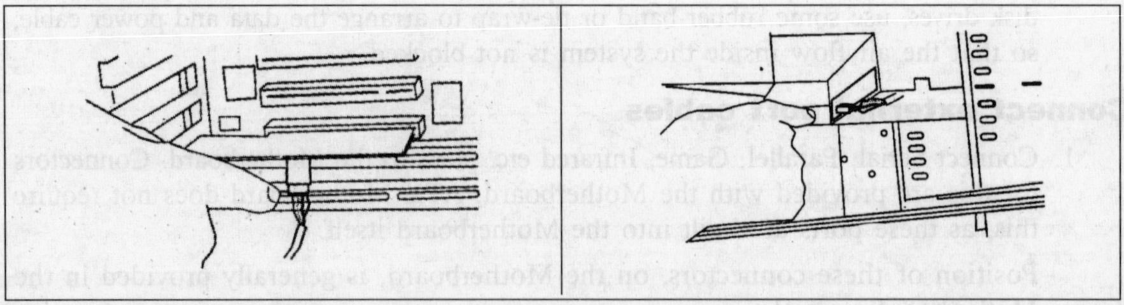

The cable required to make this connection is generally provided with the CD/DVD drive.

Connect Peripherals

1. Connect keyboard to the round opening provided at the back of the system.

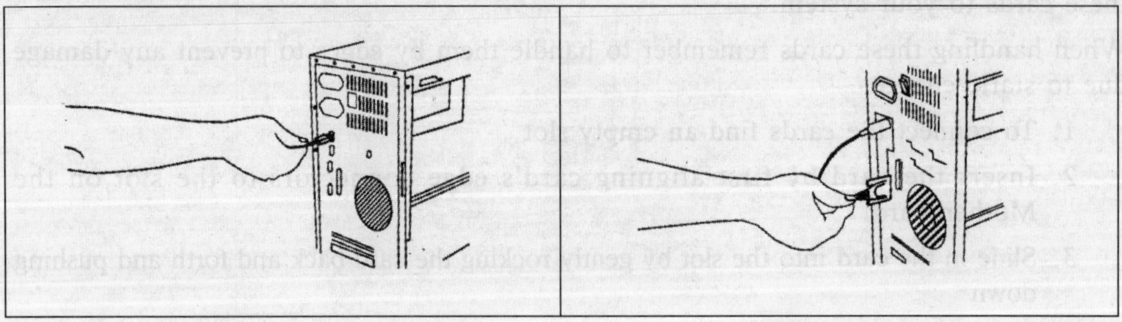

2. Connect mouse to the serial port connector provided at the back of the system.

   If you have PS/2 keyboard then connect it to the lower PS/2 port (port closer to the surface of the Motherboard), upper PS/2 port is used to connect a PS/2 mouse.

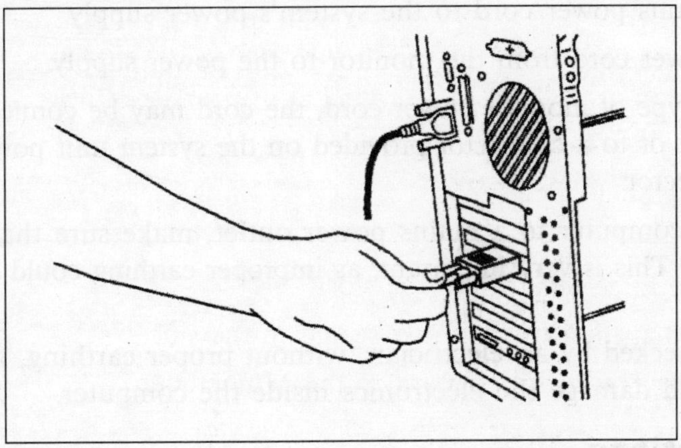

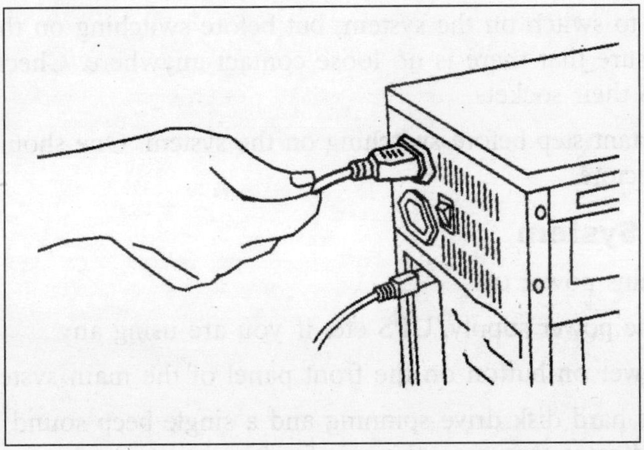

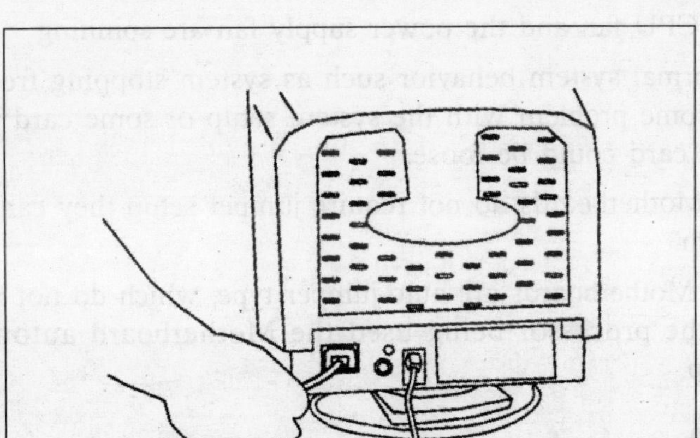

Connect External Cables

1. Connect Data cable from the monitor to the connector at the back of the display card.
2. Connect mains power cord to the system's power supply.
3. Connect power cord from the monitor to the power supply.

Depending on the type of monitor power cord, the cord may be connected directly to the mains power supply or to a connector provided on the system unit power supply near the mains power connector.

Before connecting computer to a mains power outlet, make sure that the power outlet has proper earthing. This is very important, as improper earthing could permanent damage the computer.

Get the earthing checked by an electrician, without proper earthing, floating voltage on the power line could damage the electronics inside the computer.

Check Connections

Now you are ready to switch on the system, but before switching on the system, check all connections; make sure that there is no loose contact anywhere. Check that all cards are seated properly into their sockets.

This is a very important step before switching on the system. One should careful! check all the cards and connectors.

Switch on the System

1. Turn the mains power on
2. Switch on the power supply/UPS etc. if you are using any.
3. Press the power on button on the front panel of the main system unit.

You should hear the hard disk drive spinning and a single beep sound will be heard from the system. This indicates that everything is functioning properly.

Make sure that the CPU fan and the power supply fan are spinning

Check for any abnormal system behavior such as system stopping frequently, this could mean that there is some problem with the system setup or some card may be configured incorrectly or some card could be loose.

Current generation Motherboards do not require jumper setup they can be setup from the BIOS setup program.

Also, most of these Motherboards are auto-jumper type, which do not require any jumper setting. Based on the processor being used the Motherboard automatically required changes in the setup.

Configure BIOS

Ones things are working properly you can make changes in the BIOS Setup to make function in a better way.

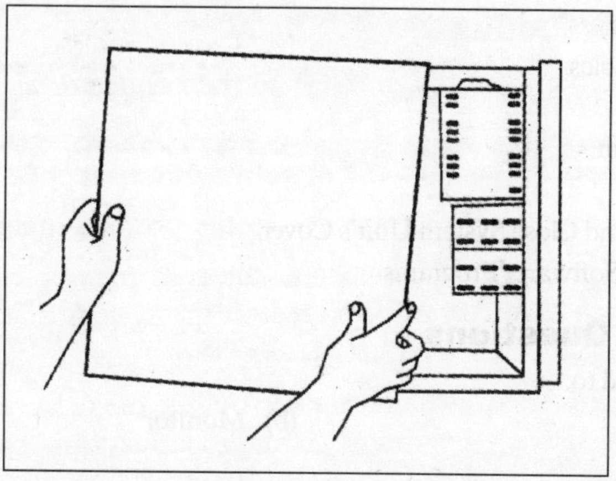

Switch off System and Close System Unit's Cover

Once your system is running without any problem, the system cover can be closed.

1. Before closing the cover, switch off the system.
2. Slide the cover on the system unit and fasten the screws at the back of the unit.

Install the required Software/Programs

Ones your machine is ready, you need to install the operating system (Windows 98/NT/2000/XP, Linux etc.) into your system.

Ones the operating system is installed, install the software required for your work, such as the Microsoft Office, Tally, DTP software such as CorelDraw, PageMaker, Photoshop, etc.

You can also install various regional fonts and their keyboard, if your job requires it.

Revision

1. Various steps involved in installation of the computer are:
   Remove Cover of the Main Unit
   Remove Base Plate from the Main Unit
   Mount the Motherboard to the Base Plate
   Attach the Processor to the Motherboard
   Attach the RAM modules to the Motherboard
   Mount the Motherboard into the computer Unit
   Attach Storage Devices (Floppy/HDD/CD drive etc.) to the Main Unit
   Connect Cables (Reset, Speaker, Power Indicator LED etc.) to the Motherboard
   Attach drive data cable and power connectors to the Storage devices
   Connect external port cables
   Connect Display Card and Sound Card
   Connect CD Audio cable

Connect Peripherals
Connect external cables
Check Connections
Switch on the System
Configure BIOS
Switch off System and Close System Unit's Cover
Install the required Software/Programs

Multiple Choice Questions

1. Processor is attached to:
   (a) Motherboard (b) Monitor
   (c) Keyboard.

True/False Questions

1. For installation you remove cover of the Main Unit
2. You mount the motherboard to the Base Plate
3. Mount the Motherboard into the computer Unit
4. Connect Display Card and Sound Card

Descriptive Questions

1. What all you need for installation of the computer?
2. Describe the complete process of computer installation.

Answers to Objective Type Questions

Multiple Choice Questions

1. a

True False Questions

1. T 2. T 3. T 4. T

15 BIOS

Introduction to BIOS

BIOS stands for Basic Input/Output System also incorrectly known as Basic Integrated Operating System and occasionally Built In Operating System. BIOS refers to the firmware code run by an IBM compatible PC when first powered on. The primary function of the BIOS is to prepare the machine so other software programs stored on various media (such as hard drives, floppies, and CDs) can load, execute, and assume control of the PC. This process is known as booting up.

BIOS can also be said to be a coded program embedded on a chip that recognizes and controls various devices that make up the PC. The term BIOS is specific to personal computer vendors. Among other classes of computers, the generic terms boot monitor, boot loader or boot ROM are commonly used. Boot is short for bootstrapping.

The term first appeared in the CP/M operating system, describing the part of CP/M loaded during boot time that interfaced directly with the hardware (CP/M machines usually had a simple boot loader in ROM, and nothing else). Most versions of DOS have a file called "IBMBIO.COM" or "IO.SYS" that is analogous to the CP/M disk BIOS.

CMOS

Complementary metal–oxide–semiconductor (CMOS) is a major class of integrated circuits. CMOS technology is used in chips such as microprocessors, microcontrollers, static RAM, and other digital logic circuits. CMOS technology is also used for a wide variety of analog circuits such as image sensors, data converters, and highly integrated transceivers for many types of communication.

CMOS is also sometimes explained as complementary-symmetry metal–oxide–semiconductor. The words "complementary-symmetry" refer to the fact that the typical digital design style with CMOS uses complementary and symmetrical pairs of p-type and n-type MOSFETs for logic functions.

Two important characteristics of CMOS devices are high noise immunity and low static power supply drain. Significant power is only drawn when its transistors are switching between on and off states; consequently, CMOS devices do not produce as much heat as other forms of logic such as TTL (transistor-transistor logic). CMOS also allows a high density of logic functions on a chip.

The triple compound "metal–oxide–semiconductor" is a reference to the nature of the physical structure of early (and interestingly now, the very latest) field-effect transistors, having a metal gate electrode placed on top of an oxide insulator, which in turn is on top of a semiconductor material. Instead of metal, current gate electrodes (including those up to the 65 nanometer technology node) are almost always made from a different material, polysilicon, but the terms MOS and CMOS nevertheless continue to be used for the modern descendants of the original process. Metal gates have made a comeback with the advent of high-k dielectric materials in the CMOS transistor as announced by IBM and Intel for the 45 nanometer node and beyond.

The combination of MEMS sensors with digital signal processors on one single CMOS chip is sometimes known an CMOSens.

CMOS Setup

Select the Standard CMOS Setup from the AMIBIOS Setup Main Menu. Various options in this Standard Setup are described below:

Floppy Drive A: and B:

Move the cursor to these fields and select the floppy type. The settings are:

360 KB 5¼ inch

1.2 MB 5¼ inch

720 KB 3½ inch

2.88 MB 3½ inch

Primary Master/Primary Slave/Secondary Master/Secondary Slave

Select these options to configure the drive named in the option. Select Auto Detect IDE to let AMIBIOS automatically configure the drive.

A screen with a list of drive parameters appears

Click OK to configure the drive

Type	How to Configure
SCSI	Select Type. Select Not Installed to the drive parameter screen. The SCSI drivers provided by the SCSI manufacturer should allow you to configure the SCSI drive.
IDE	Select Typ. Select Auto to let AMIBIOS determine the parameters, Click on OK when AMIBIOS displays the drive parameters.
	Select LBA Mode. Select On if the drive has a capacity greater than 540 MB.
	Select Block Mode. Select On to allow block mode data transfers.
	Select 32-bit Mode. Select On to allow 32-bit data transfers.
	Select the PIO Mode. It is best to select Auto to allow AMIBIOS to determine the PIO mode. If you select a PIO mode that is not supported by the IDE drive, the drve will not work properly. If you are absolutely certain that you know the drive's PIO mode, select PIO mode 0-4, as appropriate.

CD-ROM	Select Type. Select CD-ROM.
	Click on OK when AMIBIOS displays the drive parameters.
Standard MFM	Select Type. You must know the drive parameters.
	Select the drive type that exactly matches your drive's parameters.
Non-Standard MFM	Select Type. If the drive parameters do not match the drive parameters listed for drive types 1 - 46, select User and enter the correct hard disk drive parameters.

Entering Drive Parameters

Parameter	Description
Type	The number for a drive with certain identification parameters.
Cyclinders	The number of cylinders in the disk drive.
Heads	The number of heads
Write Precompensation	The actual physical size of a sector gets progressively smaller as the track diameter diminishes. Yet each sector must still hold 512 bytes. Write precompensation circuitry on the hard disk compensates for the physical difference in secor size by booting the right current for sectors on inner tracks. This parameter is the track number on the disk surface where write precompensation begins.
Landing Zone	This number is the cylinder location where the heads normally park when the system is shut down.
Sectors	Sectors is the smallest unit of storage on a disk. It is usually 512 bytes in size.
Capacity	The formatted capacity of the drive is the number of heads time sthe number of cylinders times the number of sectors per track times 512 (bytes per sector). Heads x Cylinders x Sectors/track x 512

Advanced CMOS Setup

Under the advanced section, you can setup the following:

Quick Boot: Set this option to Enabled to instruct AMIBIOS to boot quickly when the computer is powered on.

1st Boot Device: This option sets the type of device for the first boot drivers that the AMIBIOS attempts to boot from after AMIBIOS POST completes. The setting are Disabled, Network, Optical, SCSI, CD-ROM, IDE-0, IDE-1, IDE-2 or IDE-3. The Optimal and Fail-Safe default settings are IDE-0.

2nd Boot Device: This option sets the type of device for the second boot drives that the AMIBIOs attempts to boot after AMIBIOS POST completes. The settings are Disabled, Floppy or IDE-0. The Optimal and Fail-Safe default settings are Floppy.

3rd Boot Device: This option sets the type of device for the third boot drives that the AMIBIOS attempts to boot from after AMIBIOS POST completes. The settings are Disabled, CD-ROM or IDE-0. The optimal and Fail-Safe default settings are CD-ROM.

Try Other Boot Devices: Set this option to Yest to instruct AMIBIOS to attempt to boot from any other drive in the system if it cannot find a boot drive among the drives specified in the 1st Boot Device, 2nd Boot Device, 3rd Boot Device options.

Initial Display Mode: Set this option to BIOS for initial display mode by BIOS. Options are BIOS or Silent.

Display Mode at add-on ROM Nit: Set the display mode at add-on ROM Nit. Settings are Force or Keep Current.

Floppy Access Control: This option specifies the Read/Write access that is set when booting from a floppy drive. The settings are Read/Write or Read-only. The Optimal and Fail-Safe default settings are Read/Write.

Hard Disk Access Control: This option specifies the Read/Write access that is set when booting from a hard disk drive. The settings are Read/Write or Read-Only. The Optimal and Fail-Safe default settings are Read/Write.

S.M.A.R.T. for Hard Disks: Set this option to Enable to permit AMIBIS to use the SMART (System Management and Reporting Technologies) protocol for reporting server system information over a network. The settings are Enabled and Disaled. The Optimal and Fail-Safe default settings are Disabled.

Voot Up Num Lock: Set the option to Off to turn the Num Lock Key off when the computer boots up so you can use the arrow keys on both the numeric keyboard and the keypad. The settings are On or Off. The default settings are On.

PS/2 Mosue Support: Set this option to enable AMIBIOS support for a PS/2 mouse. The settings are Enabled or Disabled. The Optimal and Fail-Safe default settings are Enabled.

Primary Display: This option configures the type of monitor attached to the computer. The settings are Mono, CGA 40x25, cga 80x25, VGA/EGA or Absent. The Optimal and Fail-Safe default settings are VGA/EGA.

Password Check: This option enables password checking when system boots up or when AMIBIOS Setup is run. Settings are Setup or Always.

Boot To OS/2>64MB: Set this option to Enables if running OS/2 operating system and using more than 64 MB of system memory on the motherboard. The settings are Enabled or Disable. The Optimal and Fail-Safe default settings are Disabled.

CPU Serial Number: Set this option to Enabled to display the CPU Serial Number. The settings are Enabled or Disabled. The Optimal and Fail-Safe default settings are Disabled.

System BIOS Cacheable: When set to Enabled, the contents of the F0000h system memory segment can be read from or written to cache memory. The contents of this memory segment are always copied from the BIOS ROM to System RAM for faster execution. The settings are Enabled or Disabled. The Optimal default setting is Enabled. The Fail-Safe default setting is Disabled.

C000, 16K Shadow, C400, 16K Shadow: This option specifies how the 32 KB of Video ROM at C0000h is treated. The settings are:

Setting	Description
Disabled	The contents of the video ROM are not copied to RAM.
Enabled	The contents of the video ROM area from C0000h - C7FFFh are copied (shadowed) from ROM to RAM for faster execution.
Cached	The contents of the video ROM area from C0000h - C7FFFh are copied from ROM to RAM and can be written to or read from cache memory.

C800, 16K Shadow, CC00, 16K Shadow, D000, 16K Shadow, D400, 16K Shadow, D800, 16K Shadow, DC00: These options enable shawoing of the contents of the ROM aread named in the option. The ROM area not used by ISA adapter cards is allocated to PCI adapter cards. The settings are:

Setting	Description
Disabled	The contents of the video ROM are not copied to RAM.
Enabled	The contents of the video ROM area from C0000h - C7FFFh are copied (shadowed) from ROM to RAM for faster execution.
Cached	The contents of the video ROM area from C0000h - C7FFFh are copied from ROM to RAM and can be written to or read from cache memory.

Advanced Chipset Setup

Choose Advanced Chipset Setup on the aMIBIOS Setup Main Menu, all Chipset Setup options are then displayed.

DRAM Tras/Trc Cycle Time <SCLKs>: This option specifies the length of the DRAM TRAS/TRC Cycle time. The settings are 5/7 or 6/8. The Optimal and Fail-Safe default settings are 5/7.

Address Setup Time <SCLKs>: This option specifies the address setup time. The settings are Auto (BIOS automtically decide the optimal delay) or Manual. The Optimal and Fail-Safe default settings are Auto.

CAS# Latency <SCLKs>: This option sets the latency period for the CAS signal. The settings are 2 CLKs or 3 CLKs. The Optimal and Fail-Safe default settings are 3 CLKs.

SDRAM RAS# To CAS# delay <SCLKs>: This option specifies the length of the RAS precharge part of the DRAM system memory access. The settings are 2 CLKs or 3 CLKs. The Optimal and Fail-Safe default settings are 3 CLKs.

SDRAM RAS# Precharge: This option specifies the length of the RAS precharge part of the DRAM system memory access cycle when DRAM system memory is installed in this computer. The settings are 2 CLKs or 3 CLKs or Auto. The Optimal and Fail-Safe default settings are 3 CLKs.

DRAM page closing Policy: This option sets the DRAM Page closing Policy. The settings are Closed or Open.

CPU Latency Timer: This option specifies the latency for the Timer. The settings are Disabled or Enabled. The Optimal and Fail-Safe default settings are Disabled.

Memory Hole: This option specifies the location of an area of memory that cannot be addressed on the PCI bus. The settings are Disabled, 15MB - 16 MB. The Optimal and Fail-Safe default settings are Disabled.

CPU BIST Enable: This option specifies the CPU BIST settings. The settings are Disabled and Enabled. The Optimal and Fail-Safe default settings are Disabled.

ICH Delayed Transaction: This option specifies the ICH Delay Transaction settings. The settings are Disabled and Enabled. The Optimal and Fail-Safe default settings are Disabled.

ICH DCB Enable: This option specifies the ICH DCB Enable settings. The settings are Disabled and Enabled. The Optimal and Fail-Safe default settings are Disabled.

Graphic Mode Select: This option specifies the Graphics Mode settings. The settings are UMA, 1MB or UMA 512 KB. The Optimal and Fail-Safe default settings are UMA 1MB.

Display Cache Window Size: This option specifies the Display Windows Size. The settings are 64MB or 32MB. The Optimal and Fail-Safe default settings are 64MB.

Initialize Display Cache Memory: This option specifies the Initialize Display Cache Memory. The settings are Disabled and Enabled. The Optimal and Fail-Safe default settings are Enabled.

Paging Mode Control: This option specifies the control of Paging Mode. The settings are Close and Open. The Optimal and Fail-Safe default settings are Close.

RAS-to-CAS: This option specifies the RAS-to-CAS settings. The settings are Default or Overdue. The Optimal and Fail-Safe default settings are Default.

CAS Latency: This option specifies the CAS Latency settings. The settings are Slow or Fast. The Optimal and Fail-Safe default settings are Slow.

RAS Timing: This option specifies the RAM Timing settings. The settings are Slow or Fast. The Optimal and Fail-Safe default settings are Slow.

RAS Recharge Timing: This option specifies the RAS Precharge Timing. The settings are Slow or Fast. The Optimal and Fail-Safe default settings are Slow.

BIOS Boot Process

The BIOS runs off the PROM, EPROM or, most commonly, flash memory when the computer is powered on. It initializes several motherboard components and peripherals, including:

- the clock generator,
- the processors and caches,

- the chipset (memory controller and I/O controller),
- the system memory,
- all PCI devices (by assigning bus numbers and resources),
- the primary graphics controller,
- mass storage controllers (such as SATA and IDE controllers),
- various I/O controllers (such keyboard/mouse and USB).

Finally, it loads the boot loader for the operating system, and transfers control to it. The entire process is known as Power-on self-test (POST). On the original IBM PC, the hardware only needed minimal configuration and POST was indeed used for testing; on modern systems, most of POST actually consists of hardware configuration.

Once system memory is initialized, the BIOS typically copies/decompresses itself into that memory and keeps executing from it.

Nearly all BIOS implementations can optionally execute a setup program interfacing the nonvolatile BIOS memory (CMOS). This memory holds user-customizable configuration data (time, date, hard drive details, etc.) accessed by BIOS code. The 80x86 source code for early PC and AT BIOS was included with the IBM Technical Reference Manual.

In most modern BIOS implementations, users select which device boots first: CD, hard disk, floppy disk, flash keydrive and the like. This is particularly useful for installing operating systems or booting to Live CDs, and for selecting the order of testing for the presence of bootable media.

Some BIOS's allow the user to select the operating system to load (e.g. load another OS from the second hard disk), though this is more often handled by a second-stage boot loader.

Boot Disk

A boot disk is a removable digital data storage medium, normally read-only, that can load (boot) an operating system or utility program. Boot disks may create and use a RAM disk for temporary file storage, to eliminate the need to write to the fixed storage media of the computer where the boot disk is used.

Boot disks are used for:

- Operating system installation.
- Data recovery.
- Hardware or software troubleshooting.
- Customizing an operating environment.
- Software demonstration.
- Administrative access in case of lost password (a Windows boot disk does not always permit this, but a Linux or specialist boot disk can sometimes be used for this purpose instead, even if only Windows is installed)

Floppy disks and CD-ROMs are the most common forms of media used, but other media, such as tape drives, zip drives and more recently, USB flash drives can be used. What can be booted depends on whether a computer's BIOS supports booting from that device. For example, some BIOSes do not support booting from a CD-ROM and require a boot floppy to run the software from the CD-ROM.

Boot Floppies

Bootable floppies for PCs usually contain MS-DOS or miniature versions of Linux. The most commonly available floppy disk can hold only 1.44MB of data in its standard format, making it impractical for loading large operating systems. The use of boot floppies is in decline, due to the availability of other higher-capacity options, such as CD-ROMs or USB flash drives.

Booting from a Disk

A modern PC is configured to attempt to boot from various devices in a certain order. If your computer is not booting from the device you desire, such as the floppy drive, you must enter the BIOS setup function, by pressing a special key when the computer is first turned on — Delete, F1, F2, F10 or F12. There will be a menu option for changing the boot order.

Modern Apple computers will boot from an appropriate disk if the user presses the C key while the machine is starting.

Required Files

Windows 95/98, Me, NT/2000/XP/2003 Floppy Boot Disk (MS-DOS)

- COMMAND.COM
- IO.SYS
- MSDOS.SYS

Along with the boot files, usually a Boot sector is also required. This is generally created with the same tool that prepares the boot disk, such as SYS.EXE in early Windows systems.

Disk Partitioning

In computer operating systems, disk partitioning is the creation of logical divisions upon a hard disk that allows one to apply operating system-specific logical formatting.

In layman's terms, partitioning a hard drive can make it appear to be more than one hard drive. Thus, a single physical hard disk drive may host several logical drives.

Partitioning a hard disk drive defines specific areas (the partitions) within the disk. A partition may constitute an entire logical drive or it may form part of a larger virtual drive which could span over several partitions and hard disks.

Within a partition, a file system may be created for the storage of files, or a partition may be used for other purposes, such as swap space for those operating systems that support "swap partitions".

Purpose

Partitioning makes it possible to create several file systems (either of the same type or different) on a single hard disk. This has many benefits, including:

- The use of multi-booting setups, which allow users have more than one operating system on a single computer. For example, one could install Linux, Mac OS X, Microsoft Windows or others onto different partitions of the same hard disk (so they don't conflict) and have a choice of booting into any operating system (supported by the hardware) at power-up.
- Sharing swap partitions between multiple Linux distributions, so such partitions use less hard drive space.
- Protecting or isolating files, to make it easier to recover a corrupted file system or operating system installation.
- Raising overall computer performance. For instance, large hard drives with only one NTFS filesystem typically have a very large Master File Table (MFT), and it generally takes more time to read this MFT than the MFTs of hard drives with multiple partitions (because each partition has fewer files).
- Higher levels of data organization, raising the user efficiency of the system, for example separate partitions dedicated to digital movie processing, photos, email mailboxes or browser cache.

Partitions may be customized to different requirements, for example, allowing for read-only partitions to protect data: if one partition is damaged, none of the other file systems are affected, and the drive's data may still be salvageable.

PC BIOS Partition Types

This section describes partitions as used in MS-DOS, Microsoft Windows and Linux on PC compatible computer systems; for examples of partitioning schemes used in other operating systems, see Slice (disk) and BSD disklabel. Technically, a hard disk should contain either as many as four primary partitions, or one to three primaries along with a single extended partition. Each of these partitions are described by a 16-byte entry in the Partition Table which is located in the Master Boot Record.

The "type" of a partition is identified by a 1-byte code found in its partition table entry. Some of these codes (such as 0x05 and 0x0F) may be used to indicate the presence of an extended partition, but most are used by operating systems that examine partition tables to decide if a partition contains a file system they can mount/access for reading or writing data.

Once a specific partition's type has been identified, additional information about its purpose and probable contents may be found (see: Andries Brouwer. List of partition identifiers for PCs. as one such resource). For example, some type codes are used to hide a partition's contents from various operating systems. However, if an OS or some partitioning tool has been programmed to also examine the boot sectors of any partition, then its file system may no longer remain hidden. There are no officially assigned partition types; thus, more than one kind of file system may lay claim to the same code value.

Primary (or Logical)

A primary (or logical) partition contains one file system. In MS-DOS and earlier versions of Microsoft Windows systems, the first partition (C:) must be a "primary partition". Other operating systems may not share this limitation; however, this can depend on other factors, such as a PC's BIOS.

The "partition type" code for a primary or logical partition can either correspond to a file system contained within (e.g. 0x07 means either an NTFS or an OS/2 HPFS file system) or indicate the partition has a special use (e.g. code 0xBC may mean an Acronis Secure Zone and code 0x82 usually indicates a Linux swap file partition). The FAT16 and FAT32 file systems have made use of quite a number of partition type codes over time due to the limits of various DOS and Windows OS versions. Though a Linux operating system may recognize a number of different file systems (ext2, ext3, reiserfs, etc.), they have all consistently used the same partition type code: 0x83 (Linux native).

Extended

An extended partition is secondary to the primary partition(s). A hard disk may contain only one extended partition; which can then be sub-divided into logical drives, each of which is (under DOS and Windows) assigned additional drive letters. For example, under either DOS or Windows, a hard disk with one primary partition and one extended partition, the latter containing two logical drives, would typically be assigned the three drive letters: C:, D: and E: (in that order).

Extended partitions are useful if you want more than four partitions on a single physical drive. Technically, the number of logical drives is no longer limited in later operating systems, but under Windows there is an effective limit if they are to be assigned drive letters (only 24 letters, C: through Z:, are generally available. Later operating systems may allow more drives to be mounted/accessed by using A-A:, A-B:, A-C:, etc.).

Compressed disks

Hard disks are sometimes compressed to create additional space. Under MS-DOS and early Windows, programs such as STACKER (DR-DOS except 6), SuperStor (DR-DOS 6), DoubleSpace, or DriveSpace (Windows 95) were used. This compression was done by creating a very large file on the partition, then storing the disk's data in this file. At startup, device drivers opened this file and assigned it a separate letter. Frequently, to avoid confusion, the original partition and the compressed drive had their letters swapped, so that the compressed disk is C:, and the uncompressed area (often containing system files) is given a higher name. (SuperStor required a separate device driver to be loaded, DEVSWAP.COM).

Versions of Windows using the NT kernel, including the most recent versions, XP and Vista, contain intrinsic disk compression capability. The use of separate compression utilities has declined sharply.

Partitioning schemes

Microsoft Windows

With Microsoft Windows, the standard partitioning scheme is to create a single active primary partition, the C: drive, where the operating system, user data, applications, and page file all reside. Some users, however, prefer to create multiple partitions so that the operating system can be stored separately from other kinds of data. While this scheme generally results in slightly lower performance due to additional work needing to be done by both the hard drive and the operating system, proponents of multiple partitions generally point to the benefit of being able to erase a single partition (typically the operating system itself) while retaining the other data.

When used in conjunction with 3rd-party partition management programs such as Acronis True Image, Norton PartitionMagic, Norton Ghost, or specialized recovery programs that come with computers manufactured by most major manufacturers, the use of multiple partitions allows computer users to quickly recover from viruses, rootkits, and trojan horses or an otherwise damaged, corrupt or compromised operating system.

Unix

For Unix-based and Unix-like operating systems such as Linux and Mac OS X, the creation of separate partitions for /boot, /home, /tmp, /usr, /var, /opt, swap and all remaining files under the "/" (root directory) is possible. (The same is true for Sun-based operating systems, except their partitions are called slices.) Such a scheme has a number of potential advantages: if one file system gets corrupted, the rest of the data (the other file systems) stay intact, minimizing data loss; partitions can be accessed read-only and the execution of setuid files disabled thus enhancing security; performance may be enhanced due to less disk head travel.

However, this method has the disadvantage of subdividing the drive into fixed-size partitions, so, for instance, a user could run out of hard drive space in his or her /home partition, even though other partitions still have plenty of usable space. A good implementation requires the user to predict how much space each partition will need, which may be a difficult task; especially for new users. Logical Volume Management, often used in servers, introduces a degree of flexibility by allowing data in these volumes to expand into separate physical disks (which can be added when needed); another option is to resize existing partitions when necessary. Typical desktop systems, though, are often comprised of a single "/" (root directory) containing the entire filesystem plus a much smaller swap partition. A separate /home partition, however, can be very useful, since it allows for a clean reinstall of the OS (or a fresh install of another Linux distribution) while leaving the user's data intact.

Partition Recovery

When a partition is deleted, in general, only its partition table entry is removed from a table; and although the data is no longer accessible, it still remains on the disk until it's overwritten. Specialized recovery utilities, (such as TestDisk and gpart), can locate lost file systems and recreate a partition table which includes entries for these recovered file systems. However, some disk utilities may also overwrite a number of beginning sectors of a partition they delete. For example, if Windows Disk Management (Windows 2000/XP, etc.) is used to delete a partition, it will overwrite the first sector (relative sector 0) of the partition before removing it. Hopefully any FAT32 or NTFS partition you wish to recover will still have an available backup boot sector, so the boot sector can be restored.

Disk Formatting

Disk formatting is the process of preparing a hard disk or other storage medium for use, including setting up an empty file system. A variety of utilities and programs exist for this task; pictured to the right is the iconic FORMAT.COM of MS-DOS and PC-DOS.

Large disks can be partitioned, divided into logical sections that are formatted with their own file systems. This is normally only done on hard disks because of the small sizes of other disk types, as well as compatibility issues.

A corrupted operating system can be reverted to a clean state by formatting the disk and reinstalling the OS, as a drastic way of combatting a software problem or malware infection. Obviously, important files should be backed up beforehand.

Two Levels of Formatting

Formatting a disk involves two quite different processes known as low-level and high-level formatting. The former deals with the formatting of disk surfaces and installing characteristics like sector numbers that are visible to, and used by, the disk controller hardware, while the latter deals with file system specific information written by the operating system.

Low-level Formatting of Floppy Disks

The low-level format of floppy disks (and early hard disks) is performed by the disk drive hardware.

The process is most easily described with a standard 1.44 MB floppy disk in mind. Low-level formatting of the floppy normally writes 18 sectors of 512 bytes each on each of 160 tracks (80 on each side) of the floppy disk, providing 1,474,560 bytes of storage on the floppy.

Sectors are actually physically larger than 512 bytes as they include sector numbers, CRC bytes, and other information required in order to identify and verify the sector during reading and writing. These additional bytes do not add to the overall storage capacity of the disk.

To complicate matters, different low-level formats can be used on the same media; for example, large records can be used to cut down on interrecord gap size.

Several freeware, shareware and free software programs (e.g. GParted, FDFORMAT, NFORMAT and 2M) allowed considerably more control over formatting, allowing the formatting of high-density 3 1/2" disks with a capacity up to 2 MB.

Techniques used include:

- head/track sector skew (moving the sector numbering forward at side change and track stepping to reduce mechanical delay),
- interleaving sectors (to minimize sector gap and thereby allowing the number of sectors per track to be increased),
- increasing the number of sectors per track (while a normal 1.44 MB format uses 18 sectors per track, it's possible to increase this to a maximum of 21), and
- increasing the number of tracks (most drives could tolerate extension to 82 tracks – though some could handle more, others jammed).

Linux supports a variety of sector sizes, and DOS and Windows support a large-record-size DMF-formatted floppy format.[citation needed]

Low-level Formatting (LLF) of Hard Disks

User instigated low-level formatting (LLF) of hard disks was common in the 1980s. Typically this involved setting up the MFM pattern on the disk, so that sectors of bytes could be successfully written to it. With the advent of RLL encoding, low-level formatting grew increasingly uncommon, and most modern hard disks are embedded systems, which are low-level formatted at the factory with the physical geometry dimensions and thus not subject to user intervention.

Early hard disks were quite similar to floppies, but low-level formatting was generally done by the BIOS rather than by the operating system. This process involved using the MS-DOS debug program to transfer control to a routine hidden at different addresses in different BIOSs.

Starting in the early 1990s, low-level formatting of hard drives became more complex as technology improved to:

- use RLL encoding,
- store a higher number of sectors on the longer outer tracks (traditionally, all tracks had the same number of sectors, as is still the case with floppy disks),
- encode track numbers into the disk surface to simplify hardware, and
- increase the mechanical speeds of the drive.

Rather than face ever-escalating difficulties with BIOS versioning, disk vendors started doing low-level formatting at the factory. Today, an end-user, in most cases, should never perform a low-level formatting of an IDE or ATA hard drive, and in fact it is often not possible to do so on modern hard drives outside of the factory.

Disk Reinitialization

While it's impossible to perform an LLF on most modern hard drives (since the mid-1990s) outside the factory, the term "low-level format" is still being used (erroneously) for what should be called the reinitialization of an IDE or ATA hard drive to its factory configuration (and even these terms may be misunderstood). Reinitialization should include identifying (and sparing out if possible) any sectors which cannot be written to and read back from the drive, correctly. The term has, however, been used by some to refer to only a portion of that process, in which every sector of the drive is written to; usually by writing a zero byte to every addressable location on the disk; sometimes called zero-filling.

The present ambiguity in the term "low-level format" seems to be due to both inconsistent documentation on web sites and the belief by many users that any process below a "high-level (file system) format" must be called a low-level format. Instead of correcting this mistaken idea (by clearly stating such a process cannot be performed on specific drives), various drive manufacturers have actually described reinitialization software as LLF utilities on their web sites. Since users generally have no way to determine the difference between a true LLF and reinitialization (they simply observe running the software results in a hard disk that must be partitioned and "high-level formatted"), both the misinformed user and mixed signals from various drive manufacturers have perpetuated this error. Note: Whatever possible misuse of such terms may exist (search hard drive manufacturers' web sites for all these terms), many sites do make such reinitialization utilities available (possibly as bootable floppy diskette or CD image files), to both overwrite every byte and check for damaged sectors on the hard disk.

One popular method for performing only the "zero-fill" operation on a hard disk is by writing zero-bytes to the drive using the Unix dd utility (available under Linux as well) with the "/dev/zero" stream as the input file (if=) and the drive itself (either the whole disk, or a specific partition) as the output file (of=).

High-level Formatting

High-level formatting is the process of setting up an empty file system on the disk, and installing a boot sector. This alone takes little time, and is sometimes referred to as a "quick format".

In addition, the entire disk may optionally be scanned for defects, which takes considerably longer, up to several hours on larger harddisks. In the case of floppy disks, both high- and low-level formatting are customarily done in one pass by the software. In recent years, most floppies have shipped preformatted from the factory as DOS FAT12 floppies. It is possible to format them again to other formats, if necessary.

Formatting in DOS

Under MS-DOS and PC-DOS, disk formatting is performed by the FORMAT program. FORMAT usually asks for confirmation beforehand to prevent accidental removal of data, but some versions of DOS had an undocumented /AUTOTEST option; if used, the usual confirmation is skipped and the format begins right away. The WM/FormatC macro virus uses this command to format the C: drive as soon as a document is opened.

There is also the undocumented /U parameter that performs an unconditional format which overwrites the entire partition, preventing the recovery of data through software (but see below).

Recovery of Data from a Formatted Disk

As with regular deletion, data on a disk is not fully destroyed during a high-level format. Instead, the area on the disk containing the data is merely marked as available (in whatever file system structure the format uses), and retains the old data until it's overwritten. If the reformatting is done with a different file system than previously existed in the partition, some data may be overwritten that wouldn't be if the same file system had been used. However, under some file systems (e.g., NTFS; but not FAT), the file indexes (such as $MFTs under NTFS, "inodes" under ext2/3, etc.) may not be written to the same exact locations. And if the partition size is increased, even FAT file systems will overwrite more data at the beginning of that new partition.

From the perspective of preventing the recovery of sensitive data through recovery tools, the data must either be completely overwritten (every sector) with random data before the format, or the format program itself must perform this overwriting; as the DOS FORMAT command did with floppy diskettes, filling every data sector with F6h bytes.

Disk Utility

Disk Utility is the name of a utility created by Apple for performing disk-related tasks in Mac OS X. These tasks include:

- the creation, conversion, compression and encryption of disk images from a wide range of formats read by Disk Utility to .dmg or .cdr, which is identical to the .iso format;
- mounting, unmounting, and ejecting disks (including both · hard disks, removable media and disk images);
- enabling or disabling journaling;
- verifying a disk's integrity, and repairing it if the disk is damaged;
- verifying and repairing permissions;
- disk erasing, formatting and partitioning;
- secure deletion of free space or disk using a 30-pass Gutmann algorithm
- adding or changing partition table between Apple Partition Table and GUID Partition Table;
- creating, destroying, and repairing RAID sets;
- restoring volumes from scanned for ASR images;
- burning disk images to CD or DVD in HFS+ format;
- erasing CD-RWs and DVD-RWs;
- checking the S.M.A.R.T status of a hard disk.

Disk Utility functions may also be accessed from the Mac OS X command line with the diskutil and hdiutil commands.

Disk Utility was updated with Mac OS X v10.3. Prior to v10.3, the functionality of Disk Utility was spread across two applications: Disk Copy and Disk Utility. Disk Copy was used for creating and mounting disk image files, and Disk Utility was used for formatting, partitioning, verifying and repairing file structures. The ability to "zero" all data on a disk was not added until Mac OS X 10.2.3.

Further changes introduced in 10.4.3 allowed Disk Utility to be used to verify the file structure of the current boot drive. However as Apple notes in their public knowledge base doing so can sometimes yield false error messages.

In versions of the Mac OS prior to Mac OS X, similar functionality to the verification features of Disk Utility could be found in the Disk First Aid application. Another application called Drive Setup was used for drive formatting and partitioning, and the application Disk Copy was used for working with disk images.

Computer Software

Computer software, consisting of programs, enables a computer to perform specific tasks, as opposed to its physical components (hardware) which can only do the tasks they are mechanically designed for. The term includes application software such as word processors which perform productive tasks for users, system software such as operating systems, which interface with hardware to run the necessary services for user-interfaces and applications, and middleware which controls and co-ordinates distributed systems.

Terminology

The term "software" is sometimes used in a broader context to describe any electronic media content which embodies expressions of ideas such as film, tapes, records, etc.

Relationship to Computer Hardware

Computer software is so called in contrast to computer hardware, which encompasses the physical interconnections and devices required to store and execute (or run) the software. In computers, software is loaded into RAM and executed in the central processing unit. At the lowest level, software consists of a machine language specific to an individual processor. A machine language consists of groups of binary values signifying processor instructions (object code), which change the state of the computer from its preceding state. Software is an ordered sequence of instructions for changing the state of the computer hardware in a particular sequence. It is usually written in high-level programming languages that are easier and more efficient for humans to use (closer to natural language) than machine language. High-level languages are compiled or interpreted into machine language object code. Software may also be written in an assembly language, essentially, a mnemonic representation of a machine language using a natural language alphabet. Assembly language must be assembled into object code via an assembler.

Types

Practical computer systems divide software systems into three major classes: system software, programming software and application software, although the distinction is arbitrary, and often blurred.

- System software helps run the computer hardware and computer system. It includes operating systems, device drivers, diagnostic tools, servers, windowing systems, utilities and more. The purpose of systems software is to insulate the applications programmer as much as possible from the details of the particular computer complex being used, especially memory and other hardware features, and such accessory devices as communications, printers, readers, displays, keyboards, etc.
- Programming software usually provides tools to assist a programmer in writing computer programs and software using different programming languages in a more convenient way. The tools include text editors, compilers, interpreters, linkers, debuggers, and so on. An Integrated development environment (IDE) merges those tools into a software bundle, and a programmer may not need to type multiple commands for compiling, interpreter, debugging, tracing, and etc., because the IDE usually has an advanced graphical user interface, or GUI.
- Application software allows end users to accomplish one or more specific (non-computer related) tasks. Typical applications include industrial automation, business

software, educational software, medical software, databases, and computer games. Businesses are probably the biggest users of application software, but almost every field of human activity now uses some form of application software. It is used to automate all sorts of functions.

Program and Library

A program may not be sufficiently complete for execution by a computer. In particular, it may require additional software from a software library in order to be complete. Such a library may include software components used by stand-alone programs, but which cannot work on their own. Thus, programs may include standard routines that are common to many programs, extracted from these libraries. Libraries may also include 'stand-alone' programs which are activated by some computer event and/or perform some function (e.g., of computer 'housekeeping') but do not return data to their calling program. Programs may be called by one to many other programs; programs may call zero to many other programs.

Three Layers

Users often see things differently than programmers. People who use modern general purpose computers (as opposed to embedded systems, analog computers, supercomputers, etc.) usually see three layers of software performing a variety of tasks: platform, application, and user software.

Platform Software

Platform includes the firmware, device drivers, an operating system, and typically a graphical user interface which, in total, allow a user to interact with the computer and its peripherals (associated equipment). Platform software often comes bundled with the computer, and users may not realize that it exists or that they have a choice to use different platform software.

Application Software

Application software or Applications are what most people think of when they think of software. Typical examples include office suites and video games. Application software is often purchased separately from computer hardware. Sometimes applications are bundled with the computer, but that does not change the fact that they run as independent applications. Applications are almost always independent programs from the operating system, though they are often tailored for specific platforms. Most users think of compilers, databases, and other "system software" as applications.

User-written Software

User software tailors systems to meet the users specific needs. User software include spreadsheet templates, word processor macros, scientific simulations, and scripts for graphics and animations. Even email filters are a kind of user software. Users create this software themselves and often overlook how important it is. Depending on how competently the user-written software has been integrated into purchased application packages, many users may not be aware of the distinction between the purchased packages, and what has been added by fellow co-workers.

BIOS Features

This program lets your operating system and application programs communicate with computer hardware and peripheral devices such as floppy disk, hard disk, printer, display adapter, etc. Reading the keystroke, displaying on the screen, reading/writing of the serial and parallel port, reading/writing to and from the floppy and hard disk, etc., is done under the control of the BIOS.

The BIOS is a set of insructions or software stored inside a PROM (Programmable Read Ony Memory), PROM is a hardware, so a BIOS is not complete software nor a complete hardware that is the reason a new name "firmware" is used to describe the BIOS.

The term "firmware" is used to describe a software stored in read only memory.

When the user program asks the BIOS to read the keyboard it is the job of the BIOS to read the keyboard in a proper manner, so as the data from the keyboard can be made available to the user program.

If you have two different computers, one having keyboard connection at I/O port 60 and the other having keyboard connection at I/O port 62, you don't have to purchase a different program for each of them.

Your program can just give the "read keyboard" command to the BIOS and it will be the job of the BIOS to read proper I/O port:

port 60 on the first computer and

port 62 on the second computer.

Error Messages BIOS

If a nonfatal error occurs during the POST routine, each time the system is powered on, the error message will appear on the screen in the following format:

ERROR Message Line 1

ERROR Message Line 2

Pres <F1> to RESUME

Note down the error message and press the <F1> key to continue with the bootup procedure. For most of the error messages, generally there is no ERROR Message Line 2.

Generally, for those messags containing a line 2 ERROR Message, the line 2 text will be "RUN SETUP UTILITY". Pressing the <F1> will invoke the BIOS SETUP PROGRAM.

A description of some common error messages appears below:

1. CH-2 Timer Error: Most AT standard system boards include two timers. An error with timer #1 is a fatal error. This error message indicates an error with timer #2.
2. INTR #1 Error: Some problem with the interrupt channel #1.
3. INTR #2 Error: Some error with the interrupt channel #2.
4. CMOS Battery State Low: There is a battery in your system which is used for storing CMOS values. This battery appears to be low in power and needs to be replaced.

5. CMOS Checksum Failure: After the CMOS values are saved, a checksum value is generated to provide for error checking. If the previous value is different from the value currently read, this error message appears. To correct this error, you should run the BIOS SETUP Program.
6. CMOS System Options Not Set: The values tored in the cMOS are either corrupt or nonexistent. Run the BIOS SETUP Program to correct this error.
7. CMOS Display Type Mismatch: The type of video stored in CMOS does not match with the type detected by the BIOS. Run the BIOS SETUP Program to correct this error.
8. Display Switch Not Proper: Some systems require that a video swith/jumper on the motherboard be set to either colour or monochrome, depending on the type of video you are using. To correct this situation, set the switch properly. (Remember to shut down the system first). Se the switch to colour for CGA, EGA, VGA, PGA and to monochrome for other display.
9. Keyboard Is Locked . . . . Inlock It: The keyboard lock on the system is engaged. The system must be unlocked to continue the boot up procedure.
10. Keyboard Error: The BIOS has encountered a timing problem with the keyboard. Make sure you have a main BIOS compatible keyboard BIOS installed in your system. You may also set the "keyboard" option in the BIOS SETUP Program's Standard CMOS Setup option to "Not Installed" which will cause the BIOS to skip the keyboard POST routines.
11. KB/Interface Error: The BIOS has found an error with the keyboard connector on the system board.
12. CMOS Memory Size Mismatch: If the BIOS finds the amount of memory on your system board to be different from the amount stored in CMOS, this error message is generated. Run the BIOS Setup to correct this error.
13. FDD Controller Failure: The BIOS is not able to communicate with the hard disk drive controller. Check all appropriate connections after the system is powered off.
14. HDD Controller Failure: The BIOS is not able to communicate with the hard disk drive controller. Check all appropriate connections after the system is powered down. Also check the drive type in the CMOS setup.
15. C: Drive Error: The BIOS is not receiving any response from hard disk drive C:. It may be necessary to run the Hard Disk Utility to correct this problem. Also, check the type of hard disk selected in the Standard CMOS Setup of the BIOS Setup program.
16. D: Driver Error: The same error has occurred with hard drive D:. Follow the procedures in Error #15 to correct this situation.
17. C: Drive Failure: The BIOS cannot get any response from the hard disk drive C:. It may be necessary to replace the hard disk.
18. D: Drive Failure: The same error as #17 has occurred with hard drive D:.

19. CMOS Time and Date Not Set: Run the Standard CMOS Setup of the BIOS SETUP Program to set the date and time.
20. Cache Memory Bad, Do Not Enable Cache: The BIOS has found the cache memory of the motherboard to be defective.
21. 8042 Gate-A20 Error: The gate-A20 portion of the keyboard controller (8042) has failed to operate correctly. The 8042 chip should be replaced.
22. Address Line Short: An error has occurred in the address decoding circuitry of the motherboard.
23. DMA #2 Error: An error has occurred with the second DMA channel on the motherboard.
24. DMA #1 Error: An error has occurred with the first DMA channel on the motherboard.
25. DMA Error: An error has occurred with the DMA controller on the motherboard.
26. No ROM BASIC: This error occurs when a proper bootable secotr cannot be found on either the floppy diskette drive A: or the hard disk drive C:. The BIOS will try at this point to run ROM BASIC and this error message will be generated when the BIOS does not find it.
27. Diskette Boot Failure: The diskette used to boot-up in floppy drive A: is corrected, you cannot use it to boot-up the system. Use another boot diskette and follow the instructions on the screen.
28. Invalid Boot Diskette: The BIOS can read the diskette in floppy drive A:, but it cannot boot-up the system with it. Use another boot diskette and follow the instructions on the screen.
29. On Board Parity Error: The BIOS has encountered a parity error with some memory installed on the system board. The message will appear as follows:

    ON BOARD PARITY ERROR

    ADDR (HEX) = (XXXX)

    Where XXXX is the address (in hexadecimal) at which the error has occurred. "On Board" means that this memory is part of the memory attached directly to the system board.
30. Off Board Parity Error: The BIOS has encountered a parity error with some memory installed in an I/O (BUS) slot. The message will appear as follows:

    OFF BOARD PARITY ERROR

    ADDR (HEX) = (XXXX)

    Where XXXX is the address (in hexadecimal) at which the error has occurred. "Off Board" means that it is part of the memory installed via an expansion card in an I/O (BUS) slot.
31. Parity Error ????: The BIOS has encountered a parity error with some meory in the system, but it is not able to determine the address of the error. Memory diagnostic

software, such as AMIDIAG or QAPLUS, etc., can be used to find and correct memory problems.

Password Protection

To reset the BIOS you have two options:

- either you can use the BIOS reset jumper provided on your motherboard, check the manual of your PC or motherboard for "Clear CMOS Memory".
- or you can remove the CMOS Setup battery and allow ten minutes for the residual power in the CMOS to drain away. The, reconnect or reinstall the battery.

For both of these steps you would be needing the password, if set by the user in the beginning. Without password you cannot reset the anything in the BIOS.

Optimization of BIOS Parameters

A standard BIOS has the following parameters.

Standard CMOS Setup: Sets time, date, hard diks type, types of floppy drive, monitor type, and if keyboard if installed.

Advanced CMOS Setup: Sets thpematic rate and display, above 1MB memory test, memory test tick sound, hit <del> messae display, system boot up sequence, and many other options.

Advanced Chipset Setup: Sets chipset-specific options and features.

Power Management Setup: Controls power conservation options.

PCI/PnP Setup: Sets options related to PCI bus and Plug and Play options.

Peripheral Setup: Controls I/O Controller-related options.

CPU Configuration Setup: This option selects the type of CPU installed in the motherboard.

Password

A password is a form of secret authentication data that is used to control access to a resource. The password is kept secret from those not allowed access, and those wishing to gain access are tested on whether or not they know the password and are granted or denied access accordingly.

The use of passwords goes back to ancient times. Sentries guarding a location would challenge for a password. They would only allow a person in if they knew the password. In modern times, passwords are used to control access to protected computer operating systems, mobile phones, cable TV decoders, automated teller machines (ATMs), etc. A typical computer user may require passwords for many purposes: logging in to computer accounts, retrieving email from servers, accessing files, databases, networks, web sites, and even reading the morning newspaper online.

Despite the name, there is no need for passwords to be actual words; indeed passwords which are not actual words are harder to guess (a desirable property), but are generally harder for users to remember (an undesirable property). Note that password is often used to describe what would be more accurately called a passphrase. Passcode is sometimes taken to imply that the information used is purely numeric, such as the personal identification number (PIN) commonly used for ATM access. Passwords are generally short enough to be memorized.

Designing a personal, user-friendly password

Passwords vary in the degree of public awareness, security protection and frequency of change. The most public, and therefore least secure, password might be one that is given to members of a group, a committee or some other organization. For instance, "publiclibrary", "internet" or "AAAfinancecommittee" are all examples of easily remembered passwords, more or less publicly known passwords.

Less easily attacked passwords might be built from such a basic form, for instance, "smith12nov34street" or "AAAchairpersonSUE". These are slightly more secure, but being relatively easily predictable should not be relied upon to actually block unauthorized access. Effective access control requires passwords which are more difficult to guess or to find automatically, less publicly known (ideally not at all), and these are the subject of much of the rest of this article.

Security and convenience

In controlling access to anything, trade-offs are made between security and convenience. If a resource is protected by a password, then security is increased with a consequent loss of convenience for users. The amount of security and inconvenience inherent in a particular password system or policy are affected by several factors addressed below. However, there is generally no one universal 'best' way to set a balance between security and convenience for all cases.

Some password protected systems pose little or no risk to a user if compromised, for example a password allowing access to a free information web site with no confidential data. Others pose modest economic or privacy risk, as for instance a password used to access e-mail or a security lock code for a mobile telephone. Still others could have very serious consequences if compromised, such as passwords used to limit access to AIDS treatment records, control a power transmission grid, or access to personnel records (consider the risk of identity theft in this instance).

Factors in the security of a password system

The security of a password-protected system depends on several factors. The system must, of course, be designed for sound overall security, without which no password protection can have any significance. Early passwords on many systems were limited to a few numbers, or upper-case-letters, only often in prescribed patterns limiting the number of possible passwords. Most passwords today usually have fewer such limits. User input is determined by several limiting factors: allowable inputs (numbers / letters, non-visual codes and/or other keys / device inputs), minimum & maximum of time required for input, availability of cut / delete / paste / copy for input, and error/noise tolerance errors in the password or communications input. Some system administrators also enforce other limitations on passwords, such as compulsory change schedules, safe-password analysis feedback, and compulsory length / composition limits.

Here are some password management issues that must be considered:

Rate at which an attacker can try out guessed passwords

The rate at which an attacker can submit guessed passwords to the system is a key factor in determining system security. Some systems impose a long time out (several seconds) after a small number (e.g., a maximum of three) of failed password entry attempts. Absent other vulnerabilities, such systems can be secure with relatively simple passwords, if they are not easily guessed. Examples of passwords that are easily guessed include the name of a relative or pet, an automobile license plate number, and such default passwords as admin, 123456, or letmein.

Other systems store or transmit a cryptographic hash of the password in a manner that makes the hash value accessible to an attacker. When this is done, and it is very common (to most observers' surprise or despair), an attacker can work off-line, rapidly testing candidate passwords against the true password's hash value.

Lists of common passwords are widely available and can further speed the process. (See Password cracking.) A sufficiently complex password used in a system with a good hash algorithm can defeat such attacks as the work factor imposed on such an attacker can be made impossible in practice. Passwords that are used to generate cryptographic keys, e.g. for disk encryption or Wi-Fi security, are also subject to high rate guessing. Stronger passwords are needed in such systems.

Form of stored passwords

Some computer systems store passwords, against which to compare user attempts, as cleartext. If an attacker gains access to such an internal password file, all passwords would be compromised. If some users employ the same password for multiple accounts, those will be compromised as well. More secure systems store each password in a cryptographically protected form, so access to the actual password will be difficult for a snooper who gains internal access to the system, while validation still remains possible.

Email is sometimes used to distribute passwords. Since most email is sent as cleartext, it is available without effort during transport to any eavesdropper. Further, it will be stored on at least two computers as cleartext — the sender's and the receipients's. If it passes through intermediate systems during its travels, it will likely be stored on those as well. Emailed passwords are generally an insecure method of distribution.

A common cryptographically based scheme stores only a "hashed" form of the plaintext password. When a user types in a password on such a system, it is run through the hashing algorithm, and if the hash value generated from the user's entry matches the hash stored in the password database, the user is permitted access. The hash value is created by applying a cryptographic hash function to a string consisting of the submitted password and, usually, another value known as a salt. The salt prevents attackers from building a list of hash values for common passwords. MD5 and SHA1 are frequently used cryptographic hash functions. A modified version of DES was used in early Unix systems.

The UNIX DES function was iterated to make the hash function slow, to further frustrate automated guessing attacks, and used the password candidate as a key to encrypt a fixed value, thus blocking yet another attack on the password hashing system. A more flexible function for iterated hashed passwords is described in PKCS-5.

If the hash function is well designed, it will be computationally infeasible to reverse it to find the plaintext directly. However, many systems do not protect their hashed passwords adequately, and if an attacker can gain access to hashed values he can use widely available tools which compare the encrypted outcome of every word from some collection, such as a dictionary. Long lists of possible passwords in many languages are widely available (eg, on the Internet) and the tools try common variations as well. The existence of these dictionary attack tools demonstrates the relative strengths of different password choices against such attacks. Use of a key derivation function can reduce this risk.

Revision

1. BIOS stands for Basic Input/Output System also incorrectly known as Basic Integrated Operating System and occasionally Built In Operating System.
2. Complementary metal–oxide–semiconductor (CMOS) is a major class of integrated circuits. CMOS technology is used in chips such as microprocessors, microcontrollers, static RAM, and other digital logic circuits.
3. Various options for the floppy drives are: the settings are: 360 KB 5¼ inch, 1.2 MB 5¼ inch, 720 KB 3½ inch and 2.88 MB 3½ inch.
4. Under the advanced section, you can setup the following: Quick Boot, 1st Boot Device, 2nd Boot Device, 3rd Boot Devic, Try Other Boot Devices, Initial Display Mode, Display Mode at add-on ROM Nit, Floppy Access Control, Hard Disk Access Control, S.M.A.R.T. for Hard Disks, Voot Up Num Lock, PS/2 Mosue Support, Primary Display, Password Check, Boot To OS/2>64MB, CPU Serial Number, and System BIOS Cacheable.
5. Advanced Chipset Setup on the aMIBIOS Setup Main Menu are: DRAM Tras/Trc Cycle Time <SCLKs>, Address Setup Time <SCLKs>, CAS# Latency <SCLKs>, SDRAM RAS# To CAS# delay <SCLKs>, SDRAM RAS# Precharge, DRAM page closing Policy, CPU Latency Timer, Memory Hole, CPU BIST Enable, ICH Delayed Transaction, ICH DCB Enable, Graphic Mode Select, Display Cache Window Size, Initialize Display Cache Memory, Paging Mode Control, RAS-to-CAS, CAS Latency, RAS Timing and RAS Recharge Timing.
6. The BIOS turns off the PROM, EPROM or, most commonly, flash memory when the computer is powered on.
7. Boot disks are used for: Operating system installation; Data recovery; Hardware or software troubleshooting; Customizing an operating environment; Software demonstration and Administrative access in case of lost password.
8. A modern PC is configured to attempt to boot from various devices in a certain order.
9. In computer operating systems, disk partitioning is the creation of logical divisions upon a hard disk that allows one to apply operating system-specific logical formatting.
10. Partitioning has many benefits, including: The use of multi-booting setups; Sharing swap partitions between multiple Linux distributions; Protecting or isolating files; Raising overall computer performance and Higher levels of data organization.
11. A primary (or logical) partition contains one file system.
12. An extended partition is secondary to the primary partition(s).
13. Hard disks are sometimes compressed to create additional space.
14. For Unix-based and Unix-like operating systems such as Linux and Mac OS X, the creation of separate partitions for /boot, /home, /tmp, /usr, /var, /opt, swap and all remaining files under the "/" (root directory) is possible.

15. Disk formatting is the process of preparing a hard disk or other storage medium for use, including setting up an empty file system.
16. Formatting a disk involves two quite different processes known as low-level and high-level formatting.
17. Early hard disks were quite similar to floppies, but low-level formatting was generally done by the BIOS rather than by the operating system.
18. High-level formatting is the process of setting up an empty file system on the disk, and installing a boot sector.
19. Computer software, consisting of programs, enables a computer to perform specific tasks, as opposed to its physical components (hardware) which can only do the tasks they are mechanically designed for.
20. Practical computer systems divide software systems into three major classes: system software, programming software and application software.
21. A standard BIOS has the following parameters: Standard CMOS Setup; Advanced CMOS Setup; Advanced Chipset Setup; Power Management Setup; PCI/PnP Setup; Peripheral Setup and CPU Configuration Setup.
22. A password is a form of secret authentication data that is used to control access to a resource.

Multiple Choice Questions

1. BIOS stands for:
   (a) Basic Input/Output System
   (b) Basic Input/Output Software
   (c) Basic Input/Output Solution
2. CMOS stands for:
   (a) Complementary metal–oxygen–semiconductor
   (b) Complementary metal–oxide–semiconductor
   (c) Complementary metal–oxide–semicircle
3. MFT stands for:
   (a) Master Field Table
   (b) Main File Table
   (c) Master File Table
4. PROM stands for:
   (a) Programmable Read Only Memory
   (b) Program Read Only Memory
   (c) Programmable Read Over Memory

True/False Questions

1. Various options for the floppy drives are: the settings are: 360 KB 5¼ inch, 1.2 MB 5¼ inch, 720 KB 3½ inch and 2.88 MB 3½ inch.
2. The BIOS turns off the PROM, EPROM or, most commonly, flash memory when the computer is powered on.
3. A modern PC is configured to attempt to boot from various devices in a certain order.
4. In computer operating systems, disk partitioning is the creation of logical divisions upon a hard disk that allows one to apply operating system-specific logical formatting.
5. A primary (or logical) partition contains two file system.
6. An extended partition is secondary to the primary partition(s).
7. Hard disks never compressed to create additional space.

8. Disk formatting is the process of preparing a hard disk or other storage medium for use, including setting up an empty file system.
9. Formatting a disk involves two quite different processes known as low-level and high-level formatting.
10. High-level formatting is not the process of setting up an empty file system on the disk, and installing a boot sector.
11. Practical computer systems divide software systems into three major classes: system software, programming software and application software.
12. A password is a form of secret authentication data that is used to control access to a resource.

Descriptive Questions

1. What is BIOS?
2. Describe what is available in CMOS.
3. What parameters you have to set in Advanced CMOS Setup.
4. What parameters you have to set in Advanced Chipset Setup.
5. What is a boot disk?
6. What is the purpose of Disk Partitioning?
7. Which are the various forms of formatting?
8. What is Disk Utility?
9. Describe the various BIOS features.
10. Which error messages you get from BIOS?

Answers to Objective Type Questions

Multiple Choice Questions

1. a	2. b	3. c	4. a

True False Questions

1. T	2. T	3. T	4. T
5. F	6. T	7. F	8. T
9. T	10. F	11. T	12. T

16 Operating Systems

Fundamentals of Operating Systems

An operating system (OS) is a set of computer programs that manages the hardware and software resources of a computer. It processes raw data which is given to the computer as input. It then allocates and manages the tasks of the internal system resources of the computer. It is the operating system which performs basic tasks such as controlling and allocating memory, prioritizing system requests, controlling input and output devices, facilitating networking and managing file systems.

Most operating systems come with an application that provides an interface to the operating system managed resources. These applications have had command line interpreters as a basic user interface, but more recently have been implemented as a Graphical User Interface (GUI) for ease of operation.

Operating Systems themselves have no user interfaces; the user of an operating system is an application, not a person.

The operating system forms a platform for other system software and for application software. Windows, Linux, and Mac operating systems are some of the most popular Operating Systems.

Types of Operating Systems

Operating system can be classified into various categories, with respect to the type of processing, it supports. Following are the main types of Operating System:

Batch Operating System

Batch processing requires that a program, its related data and relevant control commands should be submitted together, in the form of a Job. Batch operating system allows no interaction between the users and the executing programs. Thus the programs that have long execution times (like payrolls, forecasting, statistical analysis and large scientific number-crunching programs) and require little operator interaction during execution, were well served by Batch Processing. However, due to long turn-around delays and infeasibility of online debugging, the Batch Processing was not at all suitable for software development.

Batch operating system allows no interaction between the users and the executing programs.

The typical features of a batch operating system are:

1. **Scheduling**. The scheduling of jobs was normally in the order of their arrival, i.e., First Come First Served (FCFS). This criteria provides a fair deal to the jobs, but suffers from long average turn-around time and average waiting time, since some

short jobs may have to wait for unduly long periods to get executed, if some long jobs are laready queued ahead of the short jobs. To overcome this limitation, another criteria known as Shortest Job Next, was evolved, which offered preference to pending shorter jobs over the long jobs. This offered much better average turn around time and average waiting time of the pending jobs.

2. **Memory Management**. Memory used to be divided into two permanent partitions—one permanently occupied by the resident portion of the operating system and the other dynamically used to load the transient programs for execution. When a transient program terminates, it vacates the memory partition occupied by it and the same is assigned to other waiting transient program.
3. **I/O Management**. Since, only one program is used to be under execution at a time, there was no contention for the allocation of I/O Devices. So, a simple program-controlled I/O approach was good enough to access the I/O Devices.
4. **File Management**. Since, these used to only one program accessing the files at a time, there was no need of providing concurrency control.

Thus, in a nutshell the Batch operating system was limited to a Loader and some simple Device Drivers.

Multi-programming Operating System

A multi-programming system permits multiple programs to be loaded into the memory and execute the programs concurrently. A program in execution is called a "Process" or a "Task".

The concurrent execution of programs has a significant potential for improving the utilization of system resources and thus enhancing the system throughout, as compared to batch and serial processing.

This potential is exploited by multi-programming operating system, which multiplexes the computer resources amongst a multitude of concurrent programs. A program in execution is called a Process. When a running process requests one I/O, it goes to "Wait" state. Then another Ready process (i.e., one of the processes from the "Ready" queue) is scheduled to "Run". So, when a process goes for I/O, the CPU is not left idling. When the I/O requested by a Waiting process is completed, it is transferred from "Waiting" to "Ready" state and wait to be scheduled, as per the predecided scheduled criteria.

Time-sharing Interactive Operating System

The time-sharing interactive systems belong to the era of a large mainframe systems, that were made available to a large number of users for accessing concurrently in an interactive mode. Each user used to interact with the system through a separate Video Terminal. A programmer could enter its source code using sophisticated editors, compile the source code, link the object code and run the executable code interactively. At any stage, the user could interact with the execution of its program. Debugging could be performed online. This reduced the time needed for program development, drastically. The operating system served the interactive users, in a round-robin fashion, allowing a fixed time-slice for each user to have control of the CPU. Since, the operators were interacting through slow I/O devices, each user had a feel as if the CPU was available solely to itself. So, the computation capacity of the CPU is multiplexed evenly, amongst the interactive users.

At any stage, the user could interact with the execution of its program. Debugging could be performed online.

So, time-sharing systems were large multi-programmed multi-user systems, designed for program development. One of the major requirements of such a system is good terminal response. It should give an illusion to each user as if the entire computer resources are available to itself, solely. It should provide an equitable share of common resources to each user. For example, when the system is overloaded, the program with higher processing requirements is made to wait longer.

Most time-sharing systems use time-sliced, non pre-emptive scheduling. It has FCFS Queue; and a program requiring service is put at the end of the queue. When the process reaches the front of the queue, it is despatched. If it is not completed within the time slice, it is pre-emptied at the end of the time-slice and put at the end of the queue. Now, it has to wait for the next time-slice, to resume its execution from the point where it left at the end of previous time-slice. A process continues to run in bursts like this, till it terminates.

The main features of a time-sharing interactive operating system are:

1. **Memory Management**. The memory management in time-sharing systems provides for isolation and protection of co-resident programs. Since, the programs are being executed on behalf of different users, they do not involve much of inter-process communication.
2. **I/O Devices Management**. I/O Management must be sophisticated enough to cope with the requirements of multiple users, contending for multiple devices. However, due to relatively slow speed of terminals and users, processing of terminal-interrupts would not be so critical. As in most multi-user environments, allocation and de-allocation of devices must be handled in a manner so as to provide the system integrity, while attempting to optimize the system performance.
3. **File Management**. Since multiple users will be sharing access to multiple files, the file management must provide protection and access control.

Real Time Operating System

It refers to the environment of embedded systems, with a very rigid requirement to complete the processing of input data, in a pre-specified time. The input data, in such systems, is invariably received from real-world sensors. The outputs may be used to control some real-world processes.

For example, an Adir Defence system, receiving information about aircraft movements from radars and control weapons for the elimination of hostile aircraft. For such an application, it can be well appreciated that the processing of data inputs, within specified time limits, is absolutely critical.

So, the real time systems are used in environments, where a large number of events, mostly external to the computer system, must be accepted and processed to a highly time-bound manner (with specified deadlines).

Such applications include process control in indusry (like steel, petro-chemical plants, thermal plants and nuclear plants, etc.), military systems for processing of sensor information and weapon control, telephone switching equipment, flight control, real-time simulations, etc.

1. **Scheduling**. A primary objective fo a real-time system is to provide quick response to external events, so as to meet the specified deadlines of processing. Such systems have to be multi-tasking (may not be multi-user). The scheduling is normally priority-based pre-emptive, in which the processes handling the priority process become ready to run, it pre-empts a lower priority running process. User convenience and resource optimization are of secondary concern. Such systems may be expected to handle thousands of interrupts per second, with a stringent requirement of not missing even a single event.
2. **Memory Management**. The memory management is relatively less demanding, since the process population is more or less static and memory is so designed that most of the processes will always be memory resident, in order to provide a quick response. In fact, the programs are normally ROM resident. But, the processes have closer interaction. This requires features that enable sharing of memory, amongst processes and at the same time provide protection from each other.
3. **I/O Devices Management**. Time critical device management is one of the major requirements of real time systems. The external events and data have to be accepted and processed, in a highly time-bound manner. This is implemented using interrupt mechanism. The system calls allow the users to connect the devices and access Interrupt Service Routines (ISRs) directly, so as to achieve a good response time.
4. **File Management**. The file management is not very critical, since most of the real-time databases will be memory-resident. Some embedded systems may have program and static data on ROM and may not need any online secondary devices at run-time. The dynamic databases are maintained in ROM. If at all any files are to be accessed, as in the case of large real-time systems, the primary objective is fast access.

Category of Real Time Operating Systems

1. **Hard Real Time Operating System**. In Hard Real Time Systems, all critical tasks have to be completed stricly within the specified time limits. Not meeting the deadlines can be catastrophic; like an embedded system controlling the operation of a refinery. In such systems, all code and data must be in RAM/ROM. All kernel delays must be bounded. So, the Operating System should not have any unnecessary frills. Interrupt mechanism must be optimized, so as to respond to the real world inputs, with minimal delays.
2. **Soft Real Time Operating System**. This is less restrictive type of real time system. If the input data is not processed within specifed time intervals, the results

may not be catastrophic, but the output may lose its utility. For example, in a system monitoring flight path of an aircraft, the delayed information will have no utility. In such systems, tasks are divided into two categories—Real Time Tasks and Non-Real Time Tasks. The Real-Time Tasks are accorded priority over the other tasks. Any output from such systems would be useful, only if it is produced within a specified time after receiving the corresponding inputs. So, the kernel delays must be bounded. The soft real time systems are not suitable for industrial and defence use, since the delays are not uncertain.

Combination Operating System

Different types of operating systems are optimized or geared up to serve the needs of specific environments. However, sometimes an environment may be a hybrid of such environments, for example the same computer may be used as software development platform and as a target machine in a real-time environment. For this reason, the commercial operating systems like UNIX, VMS, etc., are designed to provide a large set of services, catering to the need of various environments. If batch and interactive jobs are being run simultaneously, lower priority is assigned to batch jobs. In fact, the batch jobs may be used as filter, executed only when system resources are idling. The processes, handling real-time interrupts to receive real-world events and inputs, will be assigned higher priority. Such systems would normally employ time-sliced, priority-based pre-emptive scheduling. A combination operating system will be one which caters for the needs of a wide spectrum of target environments. For obvious reasons, such operating systems will not be optimized for a specific environment.

If batch and interactive jobs are being run simultaneously, lower priority is assigned to batch jobs.

Distributed Operating System

A distributed operating system caters for a distributed environment, wherein a collection of autonomous computer systems, capable of communicating and cooperating with each other through network, are connected to each other through a LAN/WAN. A distributed operating system governs the operation of such a distributed system and provides a virtual machine abstraction to its users.

Key objective of distributed operating system is transparency, i.e., the resource distribution must be hidden from the users and the application programs, unless they need to determine this information, in which case the information is provided through system services, provided the user has authorization for the same. The distributed operating system provides means for system-side sharing of resources like computational capacity, I/O and files, etc.

A distributed operating system governs the operation of such a distributed system and provides a virtual machine abstraction to its users.

Thus, it should also cater for the following services:

- Global Naming of resources

- Distribution of computations
- Enabling processes to access remote resources
- Enabling processes to communicate with remote processes.

Importance of Operating Systems

As we know the importance of operating system in a computer system. It is there to run the computer and that too without any fault. For this we look at the various needs, goals, services and characteristics of the operating system.

Needs of Operating Systems

Initially the computers were introduced as bare machines. The programs in them were developed by manually translating squeezes of instructions into binary or some other code where base is usually an integer power of 2. Then the instructions and data were entered into computer by means of console switches or through a hexadecimal keyboard. Then address of first instruction was loaded into program counter to start execution of the program.

Results were obtained by examining the contents of the relevant registers and memory locations. Input/output devices were controlled by the executing program itself. There was no concept of any supporting system software at all. User had to do mostly all of sub-controlling jobs manually or through program. The need was of a user who knew each and everything about machine. A general/naive user was not at all able to work on computer.

At that time the following needs gave birth to the system software and development of operating system.

1. **For fast and automatic working:** As the manual entry and working in absence of system software result into the slow speed of processing so a need of such a software was felt which could do most of the intermediate job automatically so that user has to least bother about machines working, resutling into fast and automatic working of the machine. The operating system automates the sequencing of operations involved in program execution.
2. **For better utilization of system Resources:** The bare machine approach was not very efficient. With this approach, running of computer system may require frequent manual loading of programs and data. This results in low utilization of system resources. To overcome this problem operating systems with multiuser environment were developed. In absence of operating system even with the help of editors, debuggers and loaders the program development process was very slow.
3. To realize the resource utilization potential of batch processing, a mounted batch of jobs must be executed automatically, without slow human intervention and their results into the development of operating system.
4. To provide a human interface which could present a communication mode for both of them, the operating system was developed.
5. To match the speed of fast processors and comparatively slow I/O devices the need of operating system was felt.

Goals of Operating Systems

Any operating system should meet the following major goals:

1. Optimize the use of computer resources so as to maximize its throughput.
2. Create a user-friendly computing environment for accessing the computer resources.

To fulfill these two goals operating system started from command mode and travelled upto graphical user interfaces, i.e., the operating system progressed and became more and more friendly. To facilitate the use of hardware resources researches developed different types of operating systems which also consider the user and time requirements. Various types of operating systems are developed over 45 years and they are discussed earlier.

Services of Operating System

An operating system provides an environment for the execution of user programs. Operating System provides certain services to the programs and to the users of those programs for the accessing of system resources.

Some of the common services are:

Program Execution

The main purpose of operating system is to provide an efficient and convenient environment for the execution of programs. So, an operating system must provide various functions for loading of a program into RAM and execute it. Each executing program must terminate, either normally or abnormally.

I/O Operations

A running program would need I/O operations for reading-in of input data and for outputting of results. This I/O may be from/to a file or from/to an I/O device. For each device, some special functions may be necessary (such as rewind a tape, clear screen, etc). All these operations are managed by an operating system.

File Manipulations

Each executing program would need to create, delete and manipulate files, which is managed by the operating system.

Communications

Operating system manages inter-process communication between the processes, executing on the same computer or running on different computers in a distributed/multi-processor environment. An operating system would provide mechanisms for the inter-process communications like mailboxes, shared memory, etc.

Error Detection and Recovery

Errors may occur during execution of a program; like divide by zero, memory access violation, etc. The operating system should provide for detection of such errors (or exceptions) and handle recovery (called Exception Handling).

Resource Allocation

When multiple users are logged onto the system or multiple jobs are runing concurrently, resources would need to be shared amongst them. The operating system would decide on the allocation of resources; like the CPU scheduling algorithm will determine the control of CPU amongst the concurrent processes. Similarly, there will be routines for the allocation and de-allocation of other resources like memory, I/O devices, files, etc.

Accounting

It relates to the accounting of resources used by each user in a multi-user environment. Resource usage statistics may be useful in planning the futuristic requirements of an enterprise.

System Protection

This is also a service provided to ensure that the users and user processes are protected from each other. For example, when a process is having an exclusive access to a device allocated to it, no other process would be granted access to that device during that period. Also, no process would be permitted to access a memory location in a segment not assigned to that process. This service ensures that a process can execute safety.

Characteristics of an Operating System

Characteristics of an Operating System can be discussed under the following heads.

Process Management

Every program running on a computer, be it background services or applications, is a process. As long as a is used to build computers, only one process per CPU can be run at a time. Older microcomputer operating systems such as MS-DOS did not attempt to bypass this limit, with the exception of interrupt processing, and only one process could be run under them (although DOS itself featured TSR as a very partial and not too easy to use solution).

Mainframe operating systems have had multitasking capabilities since the early 1960s. Modern operating systems enable concurrent execution of many processes at once via multitasking even with one CPU. Process management is an operating system's way of dealing with running multiple processes. Since most computers contain one processor with one core, multitasking is done by simply switching processes quickly. Depending on the operating system, as more processes run, either each time slice will become smaller or there will be a longer delay before each process is given a chance to run.

Modern operating systems enable concurrent execution of many processes at once via multitasking even with one CPU.

Process management involves computing and distributing CPU time as well as other resources. Most operating systems allow a process to be assigned a priority which affects its allocation of CPU time. Interactive operating systems also employ some level of feedback in which the task, with which the user is working, receives higher priority. Interrupt driven processes will normally run at a very high priority. In many systems there is a background process, such as the System Idle Process in Windows, which will run when no other process is waiting for the CPU.

Memory Management

Current computer architectures arrange the computer's memory in a hierarchical manner, starting from the fastest registers, CPU cache, random access memory and disk storage. An operating system's memory manager coordinates the use of these various types of memory by tracking which one is available, which is to be allocated or deallocated and how to move data between them. This activity, usually referred to as virtual memory management, increases the amount of memory available for each process by making the disk storage seem like main memory.

There is a speed penalty associated with using disks or other slower storage as memory – if running processes require significantly more RAM than is available, the system may start thrashing. This can happen either because one process requires a large amount of RAM or because two or more processes compete for a larger amount of memory than is available. This then leads to constant transfer of each process's data to slower storage.

An operating system's memory manager coordinates the use of these various types of memory by tracking which one is available.

Another important part of memory management is managing virtual addresses. If multiple processes are in memory at once, they must be prevented from interfering with each other's memory (unless there is an explicit request to utilise shared memory). This is achieved by having separate address spaces. Each process sees the whole virtual address space, typically from address 0 up to the maximum size of virtual memory, as uniquely assigned to it. The operating system maintains a page table that matches virtual addresses to physical addresses. These memory allocations are tracked so that when a process terminates, all memory used by that process can be made available for other processes.

The operating system can also write inactive memory pages to secondary storage. This process is called "**paging**" or "**swapping**" – the terminology varies between operating systems. It is also typical for operating systems to employ otherwise unused physical memory as a page cache; requests for data from a slower device can be retained in memory to improve performance.

The operating system can also pre-load the in-memory cache with data that may be requested by the user in the near future; SuperFetch is an example of this.

Disk and File Systems

All operating systems include support for a variety of file systems. Modern file systems comprise a hierarchy of directories. While the idea is conceptually similar across all general-purpose file systems, some differences in implementation exist. Two noticeable examples of this are the character used to separate directories, and case sensitivity.

Unix demarcates its path components with a slash (/), a convention followed by operating systems that emulated it or at least its concept of hierarchical directories, such as Linux, Amiga OS and Mac OS X. MS-DOS also emulated this feature, but had already also adopted the CP/M convention of using slashes for additional options to commands, so instead used the backslash (\) as its component separator. Microsoft Windows continues with this convention; Japanese editions of Windows use ¥, and Korean editions use © .

Unix and Unix-like operating allow for any character in file names other than the slash, and names are case sensitive. Microsoft Windows file names are not case sensitive. File systems may provide journaling, which provides safe recovery in the event of a system crash. A journaled file system writes information twice: first to the journal, which is a log of file system operations, then to its proper place in the ordinary file system. In the event of a crash, the system can recover to a consistent state by replaying a portion of the journal. In contrast, non-journaled file systems typically need to be examined in their entirety by a utility such as fsck or chkdsk. Soft updates is an alternative to journalling that avoids the redundant writes by carefully ordering the update operations. Log-structured file systems and ZFS also differ from traditional journaled file systems, in that they avoid inconsistencies by always writing new copies of the data, eschewing in-place updates.

A journaled file system writes information twice: first to the journal, which is a log of file system operations, then to its proper place in the ordinary file system.

Many Linux distributions support some or all of ext2, ext3, ReiserFS, Reiser4, GFS, GFS2, OCFS, OCFS2, and NILFS. Linux also has full support for XFS and JFS, along with the FAT file systems, and NTFS. Microsoft Windows includes support for FAT12, FAT16, FAT32, and NTFS. The NTFS file system is the most efficient and reliable of the four Windows file systems, and as of Windows Vista, is the only file system which the operating system can be installed on. Windows Embedded CE 6.0 introduced ExFAT, a file system suitable for flash drives.

Common to all these (and other) operating systems is support for file systems typically found on removable media. FAT12 is the file system most commonly found on floppy discs. ISO 9660 and Universal Disk Format are two common formats that target Compact Discs and DVDs, respectively. Mount Rainier is a newer extension to UDF supported by Linux 2.6 kernels and Windows-Vista that facilitates rewriting to DVDs in the same fashion as what has been possible with floppy disks.

Networking

Most current operating systems are capable of using the TCP/IP networking protocols. This means that one system can appear on a network of the other and share resources such as files, printers, and scanners using either wired or wireless connections. Many operating systems also support one or more vendor-specific legacy networking protocols as well, for example, SNA on IBM systems, DECnet on systems from Digital Equipment Corporation, and Microsoft-specific protocols on Windows. Specific protocols for specific tasks may also be supported such as NFS for file access.

Security

Many operating systems include some level of security. Security is based on the two ideas that:

- The operating system provides access to a number of resources, directly or indirectly, such as files on a local disk, privileged system calls, personal information about users, and the services offered by the programs running on the system;
- The operating system is capable of distinguishing between some requesters of these resources who are authorized (allowed) to access the resource, and others who are not authorized (forbidden). While some systems may simply distinguish between "privileged" and "non-privileged", systems commonly have a form of requester identity, such as a user name. Requesters, in turn, are divided into two categories:
    - Internal security: an already running program. On some systems, a program once it is running has no limitations, but commonly the program has an identity which it keeps and is used to check all of its requests for resources.
    - External security: a new request from outside the computer, such as a login at a connected console or some kind of network connection. To establish identity there may be a process of authentication. Often a username must be quoted, and each username may have a password. Other methods of authentication, such as magnetic cards or biometric data, might be used instead. In some cases, especially connections from the network, resources may be accessed with no authentication at all.

In addition to the allow/disallow model of security, a system with a high level of security will also offer auditing options. These would allow tracking of requests for access to resources (such as, "who has been reading this file?").

Security of operating systems has long been a concern because of highly sensitive data held on computers, both of a commercial and military nature. The United States Government Department of Defense (DoD) created the Trusted Computer System Evaluation Criteria (TCSEC) which is a standard that sets basic requirements for assessing the effectiveness of security. This became of vital importance to operating system makers, because the TCSEC was used to evaluate, classify and select computer systems being considered for the processing, storage and retrieval of sensitive or classified information.

Internal Security

Internal security can be thought of as protecting the computer's resources from the programs concurrently running on the system. Most operating systems set programs running natively on the computer's processor, so the problem arises of how to stop these programs doing the same task and having the same privileges as the operating system (which is after all just a program too). Processors used for general purpose operating systems generally have a hardware concept of privilege. Generally less privileged programs are automatically blocked from using certain hardware instructions, such as those to read or write from external devices like disks. Instead, they have to ask the privileged program (operating system kernel) to read or write. The operating system, therefore, gets the chance to check the program's identity and allow or refuse the request.

An alternative strategy, and the only sandbox strategy available in systems that do not meet the Popek and Goldberg virtualization requirements, is the operating system not running user programs as native code, but instead either emulates a processor or provides a host for a p-code based system such as Java.

Internal security is especially relevant for multi-user systems; it allows each user of the system to have private files that the other users cannot tamper with or read. Internal security is also vital if auditing is to be of any use, since a program can potentially bypass the operating system, inclusive of bypassing auditing.

External Security

Typically an operating system offers (or hosts) various services to other network computers and users. These services are usually provided through ports or numbered access points beyond the operating systems network address. Services include offerings such as file sharing, print services, email, web sites, and file transfer protocols (FTP), most of which can have compromised security.

At the front line of security are hardware devices known as firewalls. At the operating system level, there are a number of software firewalls available. Most modern operating systems include a software firewall, which is enabled by default. A software firewall can be configured to allow or deny network traffic to or from a service or application running on the operating system.

Therefore, one can install and be running an insecure service, such as Telnet or FTP, and not have to be threatened by a security breach because the firewall would deny all traffic trying to connect to the service on that port.

Graphical User Interfaces

Today, most modern operating systems contain Graphical User Interfaces (GUIs, pronounced goo-eez). A few older operating systems tightly integrated the GUI to the kernel—for example, the original implementations of Microsoft Windows and Mac OS. More modern operating systems are modular, separating the graphics subsystem from the kernel (as is now done in Linux, Mac OS X, and to a limited extent in Windows).

Many operating systems allow the user to install or create any user interface they desire. The X Window System in conjunction with GNOME or KDE is a commonly found setup on most Unix and Unix derivative (BSD, Linux, Minix) systems.

Graphical user interfaces tend to evolve over time. For example, Windows has modified its user interface almost every time a new major version of Windows is released, and the Mac OS GUI changed dramatically with the introduction of Mac OS X in 2001.

Device Drivers

A device driver is a specific type of computer software developed to allow interaction with hardware devices. Typically this constitutes an interface for communicating with the device, through the specific computer bus or communications subsystem that the hardware is connected to, providing commands to and/or receiving data from the device, and on the other end, the requisite interfaces to the operating system and software applications. It is a specialized hardware-dependent computer program which is also operating system specific that enables another program, typically an operating system or applications software package or computer program running under the operating system kernel, to interact transparently with a hardware device, and usually provides the requisite interrupt handling necessary for any necessary asynchronous time-dependent hardware interfacing needs.

The key design goal of device drivers is abstraction. Every model of hardware (even within the same class of device) is different. Newer models are also released by manufacturers that provide more reliable or better performance and these newer models are often controlled differently. Computers and their operating systems cannot be expected to know how to control every device, both now and in the future. To solve this problem, OSes essentially dictate how every type of device should be controlled. The function of the device driver is then to translate these OS mandated function calls into device specific calls. In theory a new device, which is controlled in a new manner, should function correctly if a suitable driver is available. This new driver will ensure that the device appears to operate as usual from the operating systems' point of view for any person.

Windows 98

Windows 98 (codenamed Memphis) is a graphical operating system released on June 25, 1998 by Microsoft and the successor to Windows 95. Like its predecessor, it is a hybrid 16-bit/32-bit monolithic product based on MS-DOS.

The first edition of Windows 98 is designated by the internal version number 4.10.1998, or 4.10.1998A if it has been updated with the Security CD from Microsoft. Windows 98 Second Edition is designated by the internal version number 4.10.2222A, or 4.10.2222B if it has been updated with the Security CD from Microsoft. The successor to Windows 98 is Windows Me. Windows 98 Second Edition (SE) is an update to Windows 98, released on May 5, 1999. It includes fixes for many minor issues, improved USB support, and the replacement of Internet Explorer 4.0 with the significantly faster Internet Explorer 5. Also included is Internet Connection Sharing, which allows multiple computers on a LAN to share a single Internet connection through Network Address Translation. Other features in the update include Microsoft NetMeeting 3.0 and integrated support for DVD-ROM drives. However, it is not a free upgrade for Windows 98, but a stand-alone product. This can cause problems if programs specifically request Windows 98 SE, but the user only owns Windows 98

System Requirements

- 486 DX2, 66 MHz or higher processor
- 16MB of RAM (24MB recommended)
- at least 500 MB of space available on HDD. The amount of space required depends on the installation method and the components selected, but virtual memory and system utilites as well as drivers should be taken into consideration.
- Upgrading from Windows 95 (FAT16) or 3.1 (FAT): 140-400 MB (typically 205 MB).
- New installation (FAT32): 190-305 MB (typically 210 MB).
- Both Windows 98 and Windows 98SE can have significant problems associated with hard drives that are over 32 Gigabytes (GB) in size. This issue only occurs with certain

Phoenix BIOS settings. A software update has been made available to fix this shortcoming.

- VGA or higher resolution monitor
- CD-ROM or DVD-ROM drive
- Microsoft Mouse or compatible pointing device.

Editions of Microsoft Windows 98

Release	Version	Release Date	Internet Explorer	USB Support	FAT32 Support	UDMA Support
Windows 98 Retail	4.10.1998	June 25, 1998	4.0	yes	yes	no
Windows 98 Second Edition	4.10.2222	May 5, 1999	5.0	yes	yes	no

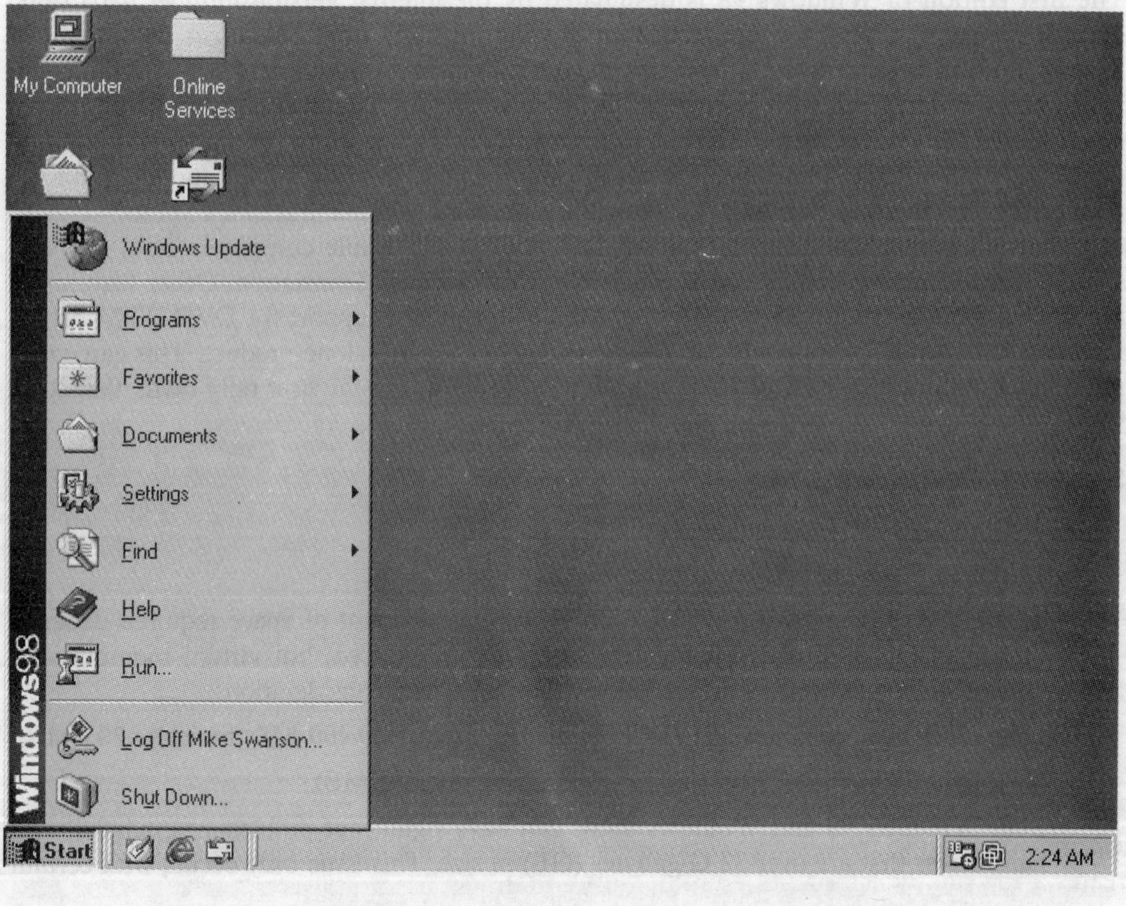

Windows 98 System Tools

- Scandisk - well known program used to maintain the file system. It offers a DOS and a GUI version. Used to check the integrity of the file system and files stored within.
- Defrag - Disk defragmenter, used to counter the negative effects of filesystem fragmentation. It collects fragmented file parts, reconnects them and rearranges all files in optimal order, thus speeding up file access and allowing faster boot times. Note that Microsoft changed the utility shipping with Windows 2000 and XP, which operates faster than the previously used program but can destroy data when partitioning hard disk drives. This happens as, contrary to the old program, the new defragmenter doesn't necessarily put all files on the same sectors, resulting in the deletion of files when an used drive is partitioned.
- Scanreg - used to restore the System registry. It tests the registry's integrity and saves a backup copy each time. The maximum amount of copies is eight. Due to a bug the oldest registry copy available cannot be restored (before restoration, the current configuration is backed up and it erases the oldest registry backup listed). The restoration of a faulty registry can only be done in DOS mode. Important DOS commands: scanreg/opt - optimizes the registry by deleting dead entries; scanreg/fix - repairs registry settings.
- Msconfig - a system utility used to disable programs and services which are not required to run the computer. It is a very efficient tool that can multiply the system's stability and speed.
- Sysedit - a system utility used to modify system configuration files in a text window.
- Regedit - allows manual editing of the registry.

Features of Windows 98

Various features of Windows 98 are listed below:

32-bit Data Link: The Data Link Control (DLC) protocol is used primarily to access IBM Mainframe and IBM AS/400 computers. The 32-bit DLC protocol software built-in to Windows 98 enables a network administrator to add support for 32-bit and 16-bit DLC programs.

ActiveMovie: ActiveMovie is a new media streaming architecture for Windows that delivers high-quality video playback while exposing an extensible set of interface upon which multimedia applications and tools can be built.

Backup Program: Windows 98 backup program now supports SCSI tape devices and has general enhancements so that backing up your data is simpler and faster.

Conversion Utility: For added flexibility, Windows 98 includes a graphical FAT32 conversion utility, which can quickly and safely convert a hard drive from the original version of FAT and FAT32.

Disk Defragmenter Optimization Wizard: Windows 98 uses the process of disk defragmentation to increase the speed with which your applications run. Thus the wizard creates a log file, which identifies your most commonly used programs. Once this log file has been created, it can be used by the disk defragmenter to store the files associated with those programs. By storing all of the files associated with a given application in the same location on your hard disk, this wizard optimizes the speed with which your application runs.

Display Enhancements: Now you can dynamically change your screen resolution and color depth without having to reboot Windows as in earlier versions.

Dr. Watson: This is a tool for capturing information about the system at the time of a program or system malfunction. Dr. Waton reports which program corrupted records the relevant details, such as state of the system and can display it and / or save it on disk for later perusal.

FAT 32: FAT32 is an improved version of the FAT (File Allocation Table) file system that allows disks over two gigabytes to be formatted as a single drive. FAT32 also uses smaller clusters than FAT drives, resulting in a more efficient use of space on large disks.

Intel MMX Processors Support: Provides support so that third parties can build software that exploits the Intel Pentium Multimedia Extensions (MMX) for fast audio and video support on the inter Pentium Processors.

Internet Browsing Functionality: With Windows 98 (via Internet Explorer 4) surfing the Web has become easier due to advanced browsing capabilities such as AutoComplete, enhanced Web searching, improved Favorites list, navigation history on the Forward/Back buttons and improved printing.

Internet Communication: Windows 98 also contains rich tools for online communication including Outlook Express, Microsoft NetMeeting Personal Web Server and the Web Publishing Wizard.

Multilink Channel Aggregation: That means you can connect multiple modems together (assuming you have multiple dial-up phone line available) to get higher transfer speeds to the Internet, other dial-up services or remote computers.

Multiple Display support: Multiple Display Support allows you to use multiple monitors and/or multiple graphics adapters on a single PC. This can be beneficial for doing work such as: desktop publishing, Web development, video editing and for playing computer games.

New Generation of Hardware: Since Windows 95 came out, lots of new types of hardware has come up, e.g. Universal Serial Bus (USB), Accelerated Graphics Port (AGP), Advanced Configuration and Power interface (ACPI) and Digital Video Disc (DVD) and some new video conferencing devices. Windows 98 has drivers, controls and software programs for these new hardware devices.

Point-to-Point Tunneling Protocol (PPTP): The Point-to-Point Tunneling Protocol (PPTP) provides a way to use public data networks, such as the Internet, to create virtual private networks connecting client PCs with servers.

System File Checker Utility: Along the same lines as the Windows System Update, which works on-line. This new utility works off-line when you are not connected to the

Internet to verify if your Windows 98 system files (*.dll, *.com, *.vxd, *.drv, *.ocx, *.inf, *.hlp and so on) are altered, dead or missing.

Windows Scripting: Windows 98 supports direct script execution from the user interface or the command line (a script as a series of commands that can be automatically executed). This support is provided via the Windows Scripting Host (WSH) and allows administrators and / or users to save time by automating many user interface actions such as creating a shortcut, connecting to a network server, disconnecting form a network server, etc.

Windows System Update: This feature ensures you have the latest system software such as drivers and system files that are available. You can access the Microsoft Web-based service over the Internet.

Window Tune-Up Wizard: A new program in the System Tools group keeps the operating system and hard disk in peak condition by defragmenting the hard disk, removing unnecessary startup commands, deleting unnecessary temp, setup and Internet files and checking a hard disk for errors. This result in faster program execution and more disk space.

Running Windows Setup/Installing Windows

To install Windows 98 on a computer with a new or reformatted hard idsk, you start Setup from MS-DOS.

1. Start your computer with the Windows 98 Setup CD in the drive, CD should be a bootable CD.
2. When the Microsoft Windows 98 Startup menu is displayed, select the "Start a computer out CD-ROM support" menu option, and then press Enter.
3. When a command prompt is displayed, type

   Enter
4. When a command prompt is displayed, type

   Setup

   and then press Enter.
5. This command will start the Windows 98 setup.
6. After starting, setup performs a routing check on your computer.
7. It runs the real-mode version of ScanDisk. It creates the Scandisk.log file and checks for errors in the directory strucutre, file allocation table, and the file system.
8. A surface scan is not performed, the disk is not checked for physical errors.
9. If ScanDisk finds errors, it will let you know. You can view the log file by selecting View Log from the ScanDisk screen; otherwise, select Exit.
10. Next, setup program initializes your system and copies the necessary files for installing Windows 98.
11. Afterwards, setup displays the Windows 98 Setup screen. This screen has an information bar on the left-hand side that displays the five steps that Setup will perform and a time that shows the estimated time remaining to complete the installation.

12. To begin the Setup process, click Continue.
13. Setup prepares the Windows 98 Setup Wizard. Then, Setup starts its five-step installation process:

    Step1: Preparing to run Windows 98 Setup.

    Step2: Collecting information about your computer.

    Step3: Copying Windows 98 files to your computer.

    Step4: Restarting your computer.

    Step5: Setting up hardware and finalizing settings.

The folllowing sections describe each one of them.

Preparing to Run Windows 98 Setup

During this step, Setup prepares the Windows 98 Setup Wizard, which guides you through the installation process.

1. Next, Setup displays the Windows 98 Setup dialog box.
2. Creates the Setuplog.txt file in the root directory (C:\).
3. Identifies the drive where Windows 98 is being installed and the source drive where the Windows 98 installation files are located (drive assignment).
4. Creates the C:\Wininst0.400 temporary directory and copies Mini.cab to it. Mini.cab contains the mini-Windows program files required by Setup.
5. Extracts all files in Precopy1.cab and Precopy2.cab to C:\Wininst0.400. These are files necessary to run Setup Wizard.

Collecting Information About Your Computer

During this step, Setup collects information about your computer and prepares it for copying the Windows 98 files through the following phases, where Setup:

1. Presents the License Agreement (License Agreement dialog box).
2. Prompts you to enter the Product Key (Product Key dialog box).
3. Prompts you to select a directory for installing Windows 98 (Select Directory dialog box).
4. Informs you that is preparing the directory where it will install Windows 98 and verifying that there is enough space to install it (Preparing Directory dialog box).
5. Lets you choose the type of Setup you want - Typical, Portable, Compact, or Custom (Setup Options dialog box).
6. Prompts you to enter your name and company name (User Information dialog box).
7. Lets you install the most common components or customize your selection (Windows Components dialog box).
8. Lets you add or remove components (Select Components dialog box).
9. Prompts you to identify your computer on the network (Identification dialog box).

10. Lets you select the location for getting region-specific information from the Internet (Establishing Your Location dialog box).
11. Prompts you to create the Startup Disk (Startup Disk dialog box).
12. Starts copying files (Start Copying Files dialog box).

Copying Windows 98 Files to Your Computer

After Setup has collected the information it needs, it begins copying the Windows 98 files to your computer. During this phase, Windows 98 Setup does not require any input.

Restarting Your Computer

After Setup finishes copying the Windows 98 files to your computer, you ar prompted to restart your computer. You can click the Restart Now button to restart your computer immediately.

If you do not click the button or wait for more than 15 seconds to click it, Setup restarts your computer automatically.

After Setup restarts your computer, the following message appears on your screen:

Getting ready to start Windows 98 for the first time.

Setting Up Hardware and Finalizing Settings

During this phase, Setup configures the following:

1. Control Panel
2. Programs on the Start menu
3. Windows Help
4. MS-DOS program settings
5. Tuning Up Application Start
6. Time Zone
7. System Configuration.

When Setup finishes setting up hardware and configuring settings, Setup restarts your computer and asks you to log on. If your computer is connected to the network, you may be asked for a domain name and a network password. After you log on, Setup does the following:

1. Builds a driver information database
2. Updates system settings
3. Sets up personalized such as settings for the Internet Explorer browsing software, Start menu, Online services, Volume Control, and Channels.

Then, Setup displays the Welcome to Windows 98 dialog box.

This completes the Windows 98 Setup.

Troubleshooting Windows

Windows does not Automatically Power Down my Computer

If you have a fairly recent computer, chances are that you have the newer ATX power supply (when your power button is of the type that doesn't stay in when you press it, chances are it's an ATX system). ATX allows Windows to power of the system, so that when you select Start > Shut Down, the system will switch itself off.

For this to work, you need - besides an ATX type power supply - to have Advanced Power Management enabled in your computers BIOS.

1. Check your motherboard/computer manual on how to enter the BIOS and how to enable APM.
2. You can also change the behavior of your computers power button in Windows:
3. Select Control Panel > Power Management
4. Select the Advanced tab
5. You can choose of having Windows go in to Standby mode, or have Windows Shutdown your computer - when you press the power button

Open and Explore Options on Start Menu are Disabled

You have to check all the drive letters in the TweakUI appelet (My Computer tab) from A: to Z: to re-enable those choices when right clicking on the start button.

1. TweakUI can be found on your CD-ROM in the \tools\reskit\powertoy folder.

Troubleshooting Video Problems

If your having problems with your Video, first make sure you have the latest drivers for your graphics adapter. In Windows 98, graphics hardware acceleration features can be turned off when system performance indicates incompatibility problems:

1. In Control Panel, open System, select the Performance tab, and then click Graphics
2. Drag the slider to change the Hardware acceleration setting, as summarized in the list below. Then click OK
   - The default setting is Full, which turns on all graphics hardware acceleration features available in the display driver
   - The first notch from the right can be set to correct mouse pointer display problems. This setting disables hardware cursor support in the display driver by adding SwCursor=1 to the [Display] section of System.ini
   - The second notch from the right prevents some bit block transfers from being performed on the display card and disables memory-mapped I/O for some display drivers. This setting adds SwCursor=1 and Mmio=0 to the [Display] section of System.ini, and SafeMode=1 to the [Windows] section of Win.ini
   - The last notch from the right (None) can be set to correct problems if your computer

frequently stops responding to input, or has other severe problems. This setting adds SafeMode=2 to the [Windows] section of Win.ini, which removes all driver acceleration support and causes Windows 98 to use only the device-independent bitmap (DIB) engine rather than bit block transfers for displaying images

Problems with Hard Disk Controller after Upgrading to Windows 98

If your computer contains a PCI-IDE hard disk controller that employs serialization between the two IDE channels, you may experience the following problems:

- 32-bit file system access and 32-bit virtual memory are not available
- Device Manager displays an exclamation point in a yellow circle for the primary and secondary IDE channels

Removing and reinstalling the hard disk controller does not resolve the problem.

This can occur if the protected-mode driver for the hard disk controller was not properly initialized when you started Windows 98 previously. When this occurs, a noide entry is placed in the registry, preventing Windows 98 from making future attempts to initialize the protected-mode driver.

This problem can occur with an IDE controller that requires serialization between the primary and secondary IDE channels. The protected-mode drivers for these IDE controllers can fail to be initialized if one of the following situations occurs:

One IDE channel has a supported hard disk, and the second channel has a CD-ROM or other type of drive that requires real-mode drivers to be loaded. Because of the serialization between the two IDE channels, it is impossible to access the hard disk in protected mode and use the other device in real mode. This causes the protected-mode driver to fail initialization, and the noide switch is placed in the registry to prevent future errors. Both disk devices then operate in real-mode

The driver for the IDE controller is manually removed from Device Manager and then reinstalled, or the protected-mode driver is disabled and then re-enabled. Some PCI controller drivers are not designed for dynamic enabling and disabling, and can cause the protected-mode driver to fail initialization. To force Windows 98 to attempt to reinitialize the protected-mode IDE driver you'll have to remove the noide entry from the registry:

1. Select Noide.inf found in the \ tools \ mtsutil folder on the Windows 98 CD
2. Right-Click noide.inf or hold down the Shift key and press the F10 function key
3. Choose Install from the context menu to remove the noide entry

After you update the registry, restart Windows 98. Windows 98 will then attempt to initialize the protected-mode driver for the controller. If no problems are encountered, the file system and virtual memory will operate in 32-bit mode, and Device Manager will not display an exclamation point in a yellow circle for the IDE channels.

If the protected-mode driver is not initialized properly, an error message will be displayed and the NOIDE registry entry will be re-created. Windows 98 will use the MS-DOS compatibility mode file system the next time you start the computer.

Unable to Access CD-ROM Drive After Installing Windows 98

After you install Windows 98, you may be unable to access your CD-ROM drive. This can occur if you have a dual-channel IDE (Integrated Device Electronics) controller installed in your computer. To fix this:

1. Select Start > Settings > Control Panel, and double-click System
2. Select the Device Manager tab
3. Double-click the Hard Disk Controllers branch to expand it, select your IDE controller, and then select Properties
4. Select the Settings tab

In the Dual IDE Channel Settings box, select Both IDE Channels enabled, and then click OK (2 times), and restart your computer

Problems running ScanDisk and Defrag

Many people have problems running ScanDisk and/or Defrag, with the program running 10% or 30% and then stalling. Often with a message that Windows is trying to write to the drive. To run ScanDisk/Defrag successfully:

1. Go to Start > Run and type msconfig in the Open: box
2. On the General tab, uncheck all items listed under Selective startup (make sure that Selective startup is selected)
3. Hit apply and OK and restart Windows
4. This starts Windows with only the basics running; Insures nothing will interfere with ScanDisk and Defrag
5. Run ScanDisk and Defrag, when ready go into msconfig and select Normal startup and restart Windows

How do I know which Windows 98 Updates are Installed?

There are 2 ways to check which updates have been installed on your computer:

Connect to the Windows Update Web site, and when prompted: Windows Update

This program can determine what components are installed on your computer, and whether new components, upgrades, or enhancements are available, specific to your computer. This check is done without sending any information to Microsoft.

Would you like to check now?

click Yes. When the page with updates is displayed, click on Download History to view a complete list of updates on your system, and when they were installed.

Use Windows Explorer, and Open the file \Windows\WULog.txt. The update information is contained in this text file.

The file WULog.txt is a hidden file, so you have to Show all files to be able to see it in Windows Explorer. Microsoft has updated the Windows update, and now a new folder is created under your Program Files called WindowsUpdate. In this folder you will also find the new history file, called wuhistv3.log. You can view entries in this file by richt-clicking on the file, and choosing Open Width..., and selecting Notepad (or you can use this tip to add Notepad to your Send To folder. Once you've done this, you'll have the option to "Send" the file to Notepad, by right-clicking on it, and choosing Send To > Notepad).

Troubleshooting Windows 98 Networking

A lot of people are having problem getting their Windows 9.x home networking to work properly. This document will focus on how to get your networking to work, from the perspective that your hardware is successfully installed.

One of the most commonly reported problems is that you can't get the systems to show up in the Network Neighborhood.

First we need to check the basics to get a system to see other systems in the Network Neighborhood:

- Is File and Printer Sharing for Microsoft Networks installed?

If not, this can be added from the Network aplet in Control Panel. Press Add... on the Configuration tab, and select Service.

- Are the systems part of the same workgroup and have different computer names?

You can check the workgroup of a system from the Network aplet in Control Panel. Select the Identification tab, here the Workgroup name is displayed (and can be changed), as is the Computer name.

You also have to make sure that a computers name is unique on the network.

- Did you share something, a printer or a full disk or a directory?

You can enable sharing by right-clicking on an object (printer, disk or directory) in Windows Explorer, and choosing Sharing... on the Sharing... tab. If you don't have a Sharing... option on your right-click menu, you don't have File and Printer Sharing for Microsoft Networks installed. Only systems with something to share will show up in the Network Neighborhood.

- Check the Bindings of your NIC (Network Interface Card).

You can check the bindings from the Bindings tab on the properties sheet for your NIC. this is done from the Network aplet in Control Panel. Only protocols which are checked are used by the NIC.

If you want to connect to other systems than Win9.x, you may want to use additional/ other protocols & services.

Do you have the same protocol installed on all systems?

Check your system to see if the have the same protocol(s) installed. When installing a NIC on Windows 95, it installs the IPX/SPX-compatible Protocol and NetBEUI protocol's by default, along with clients for both Microsoft- and Netware Networks.

Windows 98 on the other hand only installs the TCP/IP protocol by default, along with the Client for Microsoft Networks.

So to have Windows 98 & 95 machines connecting to each other, you will have to install aditional protocols. NetBEUI is the most easy protocol to get working, along with the IPX/SPX-compatible Protocol. The IPX/SPX protocol has some performance enhancements, and I would recommend it over NetBEUI. As noted above, you will also need to have File and Printer Sharing for Microsoft Networks installed.

USB Devices May Not Work in Windows 98 Second Edition

Universal Serial Bus (USB) devices that are plugged in to a computer running Microsoft Windows 98 Second Edition may not work if the your computer uses the following hardware components:

- An AMD processor (running at 350 MHz or faster)
- A VIA Technologies USB controller

This behavior occurs because there is a timing-specific problem in the Universal Host Controller driver (Uhcd.sys), which may prevent USB devices from enumerating under specific timing conditions. To resolve this issue, download and run the appropriate file for your language version of Windows. The following files are available for download from the Microsoft Download Center:

- English
- German
- Spanish
- French
- Italian
- Japanese
- Portuguese
- Swedish

"Drive W" icons appear in Windows Explorer

When you use Windows Explorer, the icons for Control Panel and Printers may be changed to a Microsoft WordPad icon and their names may be changed to Drive W:. When you double-click either of these icons, you may receive the following error message:

W:\ is not accessible.

This folder was moved or removed.

This is a rather harmless bug, and seems to be related to the combination of Internet Explorer 5.x and Microsoft Office. Hitting F5 (refresh) or clicking Refresh on the View menu in Windows Explorer should restore the normal view.

Virus and Anti-Virus

Have you ever been bitten by a virus. Well the chances are that you have. So, would your comuter say after some time. Computer virus though not very similar to the biological one, is probably more destructive. There are virus which can literally wash your hard disk clean.

Let us try to understand how it gets generated and how it is treated.

Please ignore this article if you are not in a mood for lighter moments. Way back in 60s there was a film called Parakh, made by Mr. Bimal Roy. In this an old lady in her will had left some amount to be given to the best person of the village. So everybody of the village try to impress upon others to show his worthiness. The crux of story is that while trying to prove his worth, the Doctor of the village, introduces a certain type of medicine in the pond of the village. This results in people who are dependent on that water start falling ill and the doctor comes into the picture having the antidote of the same. No doubt his status in the eye of the villagers increases.

The main reason of my telling you this is that there is a saying that most of the Anti-virus software manufactures are the one who introduce the such viruses in the market and then sell their antidotes to make good money. How far is this true, well it is difficult to know but one thing is very clear, the computer virus is a man made thing.

Man does make the virus and he makes the elimination possible too. But, in between the chances of losing data becomes very high. So keeping all this in mind one should be very careful about saving his computer from virus.

History of Virus

The first computer virus for a personal computer was discovered (and created) around 1980. That means we've had about 27 years to get acquainted with them and used to their presence. Computer viruses are not a short-lived curiosity; they are today and will continue to be here for as long as anyone can foresee. They are sufficiently widespread to be a real danger to most computers, requiring people using computers to have at least a basic knowledge of their workings if they want to avoid infections.

So the virus can be said to have the following properties.

1. A virus is a self-replicating program whose main purpose is to propagate itself to as many different places as possible.
2. A virus propagates itself by modifying another program to include itself.
3. A virus can only propagate itself by an (unknowing) act of a user of the system in which it exists.

How viruses actually work?

Virus are created using common programming tools, using knowledge that can be found in any computer book dealing with technical specifications on DOS/Windows. Virus programming demands no special skills. Indeed, many viruses have shown such poor programming skills that it's a wonder they function at all. Yet virus programmers seem to have obtained the reputation of being master programmers.

How does a virus infect a computer?

The computes virus are of many types. There are ones which would effect the boot sector of the computer, some would effect the executable files only, and so on. But, in most cases it is the data which is more likely to be effected since this is what you will have difficulty in creating. The software as such can be loaded again into the computer. Then there are the partition and boot sectors. The partition sector/boot sector is the first part of any disk, hard or floppy. It contains small programs, called the partition record/boot record, which is executed each time the computer is turned on. This program can, like normal files infected by the file infectors, be modified by a virus and thus infected. Viruses targeting the partition or boot sector are called partition-sector virus/boot-sector viruses.

Virus detection

For a virus to propagate, it needs to perform a number of specific actions, such as reading directory entries, opening files, writing to files, etc. Most of these actions are performed all the time by the system itself and other programs alike, although a few would not be performed under ordinary conditions. Detection entails monitoring the system, to watch out for such dubious action. A dubious action could be opening (reading) a COM or EXE file in write mode, as one would not expect executable files to be modified.

All viruses cause some change to the system in which they infect. The change is almost always very easy to spot with normal DOS tools: **increase in file length** (use DOS command dir and a bit of arithmetic), **decrease in memory** (use chkdsk or mem), **change of time/ date stamp** (use dir), etc. For your to detect any change, it is of course required you have the initial state, file length, respectively mem-size before infection, to compare with which is not always possible. If you receive a disk from a friend or a commercial program, the size of the programs on the disk before any possible infection is not known. But even if you do not know if your system is virus free (has the initial state), it is possible to detect any further virus spread, when the virus changes the size of other, until now clean, files. One of the most common virus protection schemes is called Stealth, Stealth is when a crafty virus uses interrupt hooking to run some of its own code that performs according to the virus's wishes. There are numerous ways to use and implement stealth and can, when performed right, be a very cunning way for the virus to hide itself. It is, however, not new thing. One of the earliest viruses, Brain, used some stealth techniques. Brain redirected a request to read the boot sector (now infected) to the original boot sector and thus showed no infection. This would fool an antivirus program using a scan-string search and a checksum search. Stealth is an active defence of the virus and requires that the virus have been run. As such it can easily be defeated using a know clean, uninfected, write protected disk to boot your computer.

Future of Viruses

As far as the computer goes there would always be viruses. So do not worry, take precautions. Have a good anti-virus program loaded into your computer all the time. There is something called Virus shied too, which would warn you when some virus infected is floppy is put. But, remember nothing works better than precaution. Take care and enjoy.

Some popular viruses are listed below:

Scores Virus

These viruses are prevalent in Macintosh computers. Scores virus have a built-in time trigger that activates after two, four and seven days from the data when the disk becomes infected.

The consequences are varied, ranging from printing problems and system crashes to malfunctioning of disk operations. This virus does not directly affect data files but detection of this virus requires detection of all files.

Brain Virus

This is one of the first viruses that come into existence. Also known as the Pakistani virus, it was, developed by Pakistani brothers to keep track of low cost software that were sold out of their outlet in Lahore. The virus pops up a screen saying, "Welcome to the Dungeon". This virus are known to destroy data and are highly contagious.

Lehigh Virus

This virus originated at the Lehigh University Computer Centre. The virus stays in the stack space of COMMAND.COM. When the PC is booted from an infected disk, the virus is spread through commands such as COPY, DIR, TYPE etc. On any other disk with COMMAND.COM the virus code gets copies to another disk and a counter is incremented on the parent. When the counter reaches a value of 4, all files of the disks gets erased. The boot sector gets ruined and the FAT is also corrupted.

Friday the 13th

The virus attacks only COMMAND.COM but also other executable files. When a Com or an EXE file is executed for the first time after booting the virus capture a specific interrupt and inserts its own code. After this whenever any EXE file is executed, the virus code is written to the end of the file, resulting in an enlargement in the size of the file by 1808 bytes. In COM files, the virus code is written to the beginning of the file. The enlargement in the size of the EXE and COM files causes the program to become too large to be loaded into the memory. Also, after a certain interval of time, delays are inserted, resulting in considerable slowing down of the program. The worst disaster occurs when the infected EXE or COM file is executed and when the system date is Friday the 13th; on that day, all the first get deleted.

Sunnuvale Slug

This does a variety of things like displaying a message "Greeting from Sunnyvale. Can you find me?" and sometimes modifies the COPY command resulting in deletion of files instead of copying.

Raindrops

This virus infects COM files. It intercepts the load and executes the function of MS-DOS. It checks whether the file is an EXE file or not. If the file is not an EXE file, the first three bytes of the file are replaced by a jump instruction at the end of the file where it gets attached after encryption. This result is dropping or showering of characters on the screen like raindrops and is also accompanied by appropriate sound effects.

Happy Birthday 30th

This virus gets activated on January 5th, if any of the infected program gets executed and would ask the user to type Happy Birth 30th. It might destroy all the data stored on a disk.

The symptom of this virus are that the computer memory is reported as 6KB lesser than actual; e.g. it would show a memory of 634 KB instead of 640 KB.

Combating Viruses, Worms and Trojan Horses

The first steps to protecting your computer are to ensure your operating system (OS) is up-to-date. This is essential if you are running a Microsoft Windows OS. Secondly, you should have anti-virus software installed on your system and ensure you download updates frequently to ensure your software has the latest fixes for new viruses, worms, and Trojan horses. Additionally, you want to make sure your anti-virus program has the capability to scan e-mail and files as they are downloaded from the Internet. This will help prevent malicious programs from even reaching your computer. You should also install a firewall as well.

A firewall is a system that prevents unauthorized use and access to your computer.

A firewall can be either hardware or software. Hardware firewalls provide a strong degree of protection from most forms of attack coming from the outside world and can be purchased as a stand-alone product or in broadband routers. Unfortunately, when battling viruses, worms and Trojans, a hardware firewall may be less effective than a software firewall, as it could possibly ignore embedded worms in out going e-mails and see this as regular network traffic. For individual home users, the most popular firewall choice is a software firewall. A good software firewall will protect your computer from outside attempts to control or gain access your computer, and usually provides additional protection against the most common Trojan programs or e-mail worms. The downside to software firewalls is that they will only protect the computer they are installed on, not a network.

It is important to remember that on its own a firewall is not going to rid you of your computer virus problems, but when used in conjunction with regular operating system updates and a good anti-virus scanning software, it will add some extra security and protection for your computer or network.

Virus Protection

A more advanced method is the use of simple encryption to encipher the virus. In this case, the virus consists of a small decrypting module and an encrypted copy of the virus code. If the virus is encrypted with a different key for each infected file, the only part of the virus that remains constant is the decrypting module, which would (for example) be appended to the end. In this case, a virus scanner cannot directly detect the virus using signatures, but it can still detect the decrypting module, which still makes indirect detection of the virus possible. Since these would be symmetric keys, stored on the infected host, it is in fact entirely possible to decrypt the final virus, but that probably isn't required, since self-modifying code is such a rarity that it may be reason for virus scanners to at least flag the file as suspicious.

An old, but compact, encryption involved XORing each byte in a virus with a constant, such that a XOR b = c, and c XOR b = a, so that the exclusive or operation had only to be repeated for decryption. It is suspicious code that modifies itself, so the code to do this may be part of the signature in many virus definitions.

Polymorphic code

Polymorphic code was the first technique that posed a serious threat to virus scanners. Just like regular encrypted viruses, a polymorphic virus infects files with an encrypted copy of itself, which is decoded by a decryption module. In the case of polymorphic viruses however, this decryption module is also modified on each infection. A well-written polymorphic virus therefore has no parts that stay the same on each infection, making it very difficult to detect directly using signatures. Anti-virus software can detect it by decrypting the viruses using an emulator, or by statistical pattern analysis of the encrypted virus body.

To enable polymorphic code, the virus has to have a polymorphic engine (also called mutating engine or mutation engine) somewhere in its encrypted body.

Some viruses employ polymorphic code in a way that constrains the mutation rate of the virus significantly. For example, a virus can be programmed to mutate only slightly over time, or it can be programmed to refrain from mutating when it infects a file on a computer that already contains copies of the virus. The advantage of using such slow polymorphic code is that it makes it more difficult for anti-virus professionals to obtain representative samples of the virus, because bait files that are infected in one run will typically contain identical or similar samples of the virus. This will make it more likely that the detection by the virus scanner will be unreliable, and that some instances of the virus may be able to avoid detection.

Metamorphic code

To avoid being detected by emulation, some viruses rewrite themselves completely each time they are to infect new executables. Viruses that use this technique are said to be metamorphic. To enable metamorphism, a metamorphic engine is needed. A metamorphic virus is usually very large and complex. For example, W32/Simile consisted of over 14000 lines of Assembly language code, 90% of it part of the metamorphic engine.

Vulnerability and Countermeasures

The vulnerability of operating systems to viruses

Another analogy to biological viruses: just as genetic diversity in a population decreases the chance of a single disease wiping out a population, the diversity of software systems on a network similarly limits the destructive potential of viruses.

This became a particular concern in the 1990s, when Microsoft gained market dominance in desktop operating systems and office suites. The users of Microsoft software (especially networking software such as Microsoft Outlook and Internet Explorer) are especially vulnerable to the spread of viruses. Microsoft software is targeted by virus writers due to their desktop dominance, and is often criticized for including many errors and holes for virus writers to exploit. Integrated applications, applications with scripting languages with access to the file system (for example Visual Basic Script (VBS), and applications with networking features) are also particularly vulnerable.

Although Windows is by far the most popular operating system for virus writers, some viruses also exist on other platforms.

Any operating system that allows third-party programs to run can theoretically run viruses. Some operating systems are less secure than others. Unix-based OS's (and NTFS-aware applications on Windows NT based platforms) only allow their users to run executables within their protected space in their own directories.

As of 2006, there are relatively few security exploits targeting Mac OS X (with a Unix-based file system); the known vulnerabilities fall under the classifications of worms and Trojans. The number of viruses for the older Apple operating systems, known as Mac OS Classic, varies greatly from source to source, with Apple stating that there are only four known viruses, and independent sources stating there are as many as 63 viruses. It is safe to say that Macs are less likely to be exploited due to their secure Unix base, and because a Mac-specific virus could only infect a small proportion of computers (making the effort less desirable).

Virus vulnerability between Macs and Windows is a chief selling point, one that Apple uses in their Get a Mac advertising.

Windows and Unix have similar scripting abilities, but while Unix natively blocks normal users from having access to make changes to the operating system environment, Windows does not. In 1997, when a virus for Linux was released – known as "Bliss" – leading antivirus vendors issued warnings that Unix-like systems could fall prey to viruses just like Windows.

The Bliss virus may be considered characteristic of viruses – as opposed to worms – on Unix systems. Bliss requires that the user run it explicitly (making it a trojan), and it can only infect programs that the user has the access to modify. Unlike Windows users, most Unix users do not log in as an administrator user except to install or configure software; as a result, even if a user ran the virus, it could not harm their operating system. The Bliss virus never became widespread, and remains chiefly a research curiosity. Its creator later posted the source code to Usenet, allowing researchers to see how it worked.

The Role of Software Development

Because software is often designed with security features to prevent unauthorized use of system resources, many viruses must exploit software bugs in a system or application to spread. Software development strategies that produce large numbers of bugs will generally also produce potential exploits.

Anti-virus Software and other Preventive Countermeasures

There are two common methods that an anti-virus software application uses to detect viruses. The first, and by far the most common method of virus detection is using a list of virus signature definitions. The disadvantage of this detection method is that users are only protected from viruses that pre-date their last virus definition update. The second method is to use a heuristic algorithm to find viruses based on common behaviors. This method has the ability to detect viruses that anti-virus security firms' have yet to create a signature for.

Many users install anti-virus software that can detect and eliminate known viruses after the computer downloads or runs the executable. They work by examining the content heuristics of the computer's memory (its RAM, and boot sectors) and the files stored on fixed or removable drives (hard drives, floppy drives), and comparing those files against a database of known virus "signatures".

Some anti-virus programs are able to scan opened files in addition to sent and received emails 'on the fly' in a similar manner.

This practice is known as "on-access scanning." Anti-virus software does not change the underlying capability of host software to transmit viruses. Users must update their software regularly to patch security holes. Anti-virus software also needs to be regularly updated in order to gain knowledge about the latest threats.

One may also prevent the damage done by viruses by making regular backups of data (and the Operating Systems) on different media, that are either kept unconnected to the system (most of the time), read-only or not accessible for other reasons, such as using different file systems. This way, if data is lost through a virus, one can start again using the backup (which should preferably be recent). If a backup session on optical media like CD and DVD is closed, it becomes read-only and can no longer be affected by a virus.

Likewise, an Operating System on a bootable can be used to start the computer if the installed Operating Systems become unusable.

Another method is to use different Operating Systems on different file systems. A virus is not likely to affect both. Data backups can also be put on different file systems. For example, Linux requires specific software to write to NTFS partitions, so if one does not install such software and uses a separate installation of MS Windows to make the backups on an NTFS partition (and preferably only for that reason), the backup should remain safe from any Linux viruses. Likewise, MS Windows can not read file systems like ext3, so if one normally uses MS Windows, the backups can be made on an ext3 partition using a Linux installation.

How to Install the Windows 98 on a New Hard Disk Drive

There are two ways to install Windows 98 on your hard disk:

- Copy all of the files from the win98 directory on the Windows 98 CD to a directory on your hard disk and install from your hard disk
- Install directly from the CD

Although, I understand Microsoft frowns on the procedure, I prefer the first method for installing Windows 98 on my own hard disk drive. I use the second method when installing Windows on a customer's hard disk. The first method installs faster and every time Windows needs new software or driver from the Windows 98 CD, it will first go to the directory on the hard disk from which it was installed and install the software from there instead asking that you insert the CD. This saves me from having fish-out the Windows 98 CD every time I install new software and hardware, which is often. The advantage of the second procedure is that it saves about 120 MBytes of hard disk space, if in the first method, you leave the files on the hard disk after installation. Furthermore, with the first method, you may still need the CD for some drivers not found in the win98 directory.

Ok, let's install Windows 98:

Method 1

Make a c:\windows\options\cabs directory and copy the files from the win98 directory on the CD-ROM to the cabs directory.

```
a:\> c:
c:>md windows
c:>cd windows (or simply type cd followed by the F3 key)
c:\windows>md options
c:\windows>cd options
c:\windows\options>md cabs
c:\windows\options>cd cabs
c:\windows\options\cabs>copy d:\win98\*.*
```

Where d: is your CD-ROM drive.

The c:/windows/options/cabs directory was a convention established with the standard installation some of the OEM (Original Equipment Manufacturer) versions of Windows 95. You could copy the win98 directory to any desired directory on your hard disk and install from there, but I continue to use the convention so I can remember where the cab files are located.

Cab or cabinet files are files containing one or more compressed files. Most of the Windows 98 files are in cab files on the CD.

```
Install Windows 98.
c:\windows\options\cabs>setup /ie
```

The /ie flag tells Windows 98 not to make a new Startup Floppy during the installation.

Method 2

Change to the win98 directory on the Windows 98 CD and run setup.exe.

```
a:\> d:
```

where d: is your CD-ROM drive letter.

```
d:\> cd win98
d:\win98 > setup /ie
```

Do not run setup from d:\. There is a setup.exe there, but it won't work with this procedure.

Just follow the Windows 98 installation prompts. If setup asks you for a directory in which to install Windows, make sure you tell it to install it in c:\windows (not d:\windows or c:\windows.001, etc.).

If you have moved Windows 3.x to the new drive or if you have the old drive attached with Windows 3.x or 95 on it, the upgrade should install ok. If not, setup will say it can't find an old version of Windows to verify before installing the upgrade. It will then allow you to browse to a drive/directory where the old version of Windows is located. If you have Windows 3.x or 95 on floppy, remove your Startup Floppy, if it is still in A:, insert floppy 1 of the old version of Windows in the floppy drive and point setup to the floppy drive. If you have the old version on CD, remove the Win 98 CD, insert the old Windows CD, and point setup to d:\, where d: is your CD-ROM drive. I have found that setup won't always find what it is looking for the first time you point it at the drive containing the old version of Windows. Point again; you may have to do it several times, but it should eventually take. When verifying Win 3.x floppies, setup will check several of them. I counted five the last time I did it. (The Win 95 upgrade only checks the first one.)

After installation, you may want to install you CD-ROM software on your hard disk drive so you can use it from a direct boot-up to the DOS prompt. Boot to the DOS by holding the Ctrl key as the computer boots or pressing the F8 key just as Windows 98 starts and install form the manufacture's floppy. You may have to boot with the Startup Floppy to install the software from a CD-ROM or install it from Windows. There are many variations. If the installation program asks for the location of the mscdex.exe file, it is located in the c:\windows\command directory.

Likewise, after installation you may have to reinstall the DOS (real mode) software for your sound card, especially older ISA sound cards.

How to Prepare the Hard Disk for the Windows 98 Installation Procedure

The following information applies to preparing an empty hard disk for the installation of Windows 98. If you use the following steps on a hard disk that is not empty, all of the data that is on that hard disk is deleted.

Before you install Windows 98 on an empty hard disk, you must first create a primary partition and then format a file system on that partition. Each allocated space on the hard disk (primary partition or logical drive) is assigned a drive letter. Windows 98 supports the FAT16 and FAT32 file systems. When you run the Fdisk tool on a hard disk that is larger than 512 MB, you are prompted to choose a file system.

The FAT16 file system has a maximum of 2 gigabytes (GB) for each allocated space, or drive letter. For example, if you use the FAT16 file system and you have a 6-GB hard disk, you can have three drive letters (C, D, and E), each with 2 GB of allocated space.

The FAT32 file system supports drives up to 2 terabytes in size and stores files on smaller sections of the hard disk than does the FAT16 file system. This results in more free space on the hard disk. The FAT32 file system does not support drives that are smaller than 512 MB.

How to Partition the Hard Disk

After you decide which file system you want to use, run the Fdisk tool:

1. Insert the Windows 98 Startup disk in the floppy disk drive, and then restart your computer.

2. When the Microsoft Windows 98 **Startup** menu is displayed, choose the Start computer without CD-ROM support option, and then press ENTER.
3. At a command prompt, type fdisk, and then press ENTER.
4. If the hard disk is larger than 512 MB, you receive the following prompt: Your computer has a disk larger than 512 MB. This version of Windows includes improved support for large disks, resulting in more efficient use of disk space on large drives, and allowing disks over 2 GB to be formatted as a single drive.IMPORTANT: If you enable large disk support and create any new drives on this disk, you will not be able to access the new drive(s) using other operating systems, including some versions of Windows 95 and Windows NT, as well as earlier versions of Windows and MS-DOS. In addition, disk utilities that were not designated explicitly for the FAT32 file system will not be able to work with this disk. If you need to access this disk with other operating systems or older disk utilities, do no enable large drive support.Do you wish to enable large disk support (Y/N)? If you want to use the FAT32 file system, press Y, and then press ENTER. If you want to use the FAT16 file system, press N, and then press ENTER.
5. After you press ENTER, the Fdisk **Options** menu is displayed. Press 1 to select the Create DOS partition or Logical DOS Drive option, and then press ENTER.
6. Press 1 to select the **Create Primary DOS Partition** option, and then press ENTER.
7. After you press ENTER, you receive the following prompt: Do you wish to use the maximum available size for primary DOS partition?

FAT32 File System:

a. If you chose the FAT32 file system in step 4 and you want all of the space on the hard disk to be assigned to drive C, press Y, and then press ENTER.
b. Press ESC, and then press ESC to quit the Fdisk tool and return to a command prompt.
c. Skip to step 10.

FAT16 File System:

a. If you chose the FAT16 file system in step 4, and you want the first 2 GB on the hard disk to be assigned to drive C, press Y, and then press ENTER.
b. Press ESC to return to the **Options** menu, and then skip to step i.
c. If you want to customize the size of the partitions (the logical drives) on the hard disk, press N, and then press ENTER.
d. A prompt is displayed for you to type the size that you want for the primary partition in megabytes or percent of disk space. Note that for a Windows 98-based computer, Microsoft recommends that you make the primary partition at least 500 MB. Type the size of the partition that you want to create, and then press ENTER.
e. Press ESC to return to the **Options** menu.
f. Press 2 to select the Set active partition option, and then press ENTER.

g. When you are prompted to type the number of the partition that you want to make the active partition, press 1, and then press ENTER.

h. Press ESC to return to the **Options** menu.

i. To assign drive letters to the additional space on the hard disk:

1. Press 1, and then press ENTER.
2. Press 2 to select the **Create Extended DOS Partition** option, and then press ENTER.
3. The option that appears displays the maximum space that is available for the extended partition. You can adjust the size of the partition or you can use the default size. Note that the default maximum space is recommended, but the space can be divided between multiple drive letters. Type the amount of space that you want, press ENTER, and then press ESC.
4. The Create Logical DOS Drive(s) in the Extended DOS Partition menu is displayed. This is the menu that you use to assign the remaining hard disk space to the additional drive letters. Type the amount of space that you want to assign to the next drive letter at the Enter logical drive size in Mbytes or percent of disk space (%) prompt, and then press ENTER.
5. A table that lists the drive letter that you created and the amount of space that is on that drive is displayed. If there is still free space on the hard disk, it is displayed near the bottom of the table. Repeat steps 1 through 4 until you receive the following message: All available space in the Extended DOS Partition is assigned to local drives
6. After you receive this message, press ESC, and then press ESC to quit the Fdisk tool and return to a command prompt.

8. After you create the partitions, restart you computer with the Windows 98 Startup disk in the floppy disk drive.
9. When the **Windows 98 Startup** menu is displayed, choose the Start computer without CD-ROM support option, and then press ENTER.
10. When a command prompt is displayed, type format c:, and then press ENTER.

    NOTE: If you receive a "Bad command or file name" message, you may need to extract the Format.com utility to your Startup disk. To do this, type the following command at a command prompt, and then press ENTER:

    extract ebd.cab format.com

    After the Format.com utility is extracted to your Startup disk and a command prompt is displayed, type format c:.
11. When you successfully run the Format.com utility, you receive the following prompt:

    WARNING, ALL DATA ON NON-REMOVABLE DISK DRIVE C: WILL BE LOST!

    Proceed with Format (Y/N)? Press Y, and then press ENTER to format drive C.

12. After the format procedure is finished, you receive the following prompt:

    Volume label (11 characters, ENTER for none)? This is an optional feature that you can use to type a name for the hard disk. Type an 11-character name for the drive, or leave it blank, and then press ENTER.

13. Repeat steps 10 through 13 for any additional drive letters that you created in step i.

How to Install Windows 98

After you partition and format your hard disk, you can install Windows 98:

1. Insert the Windows 98 Startup disk in the floppy disk drive, and then restart your computer.
2. When the Windows 98 **Startup** menu is displayed, choose the Start computer with CD-ROM support option, and then press ENTER.
3. If CD-ROM support is provided by the generic drivers on the Startup disk, you receive one of the following messages, where *X* is the drive letter that is assigned to your CD-ROM drive: Drive *X*: = Driver MSCD001Drive *X*: = Driver OEMCD001 **NOTE**: If your CD-ROM drive is not available after you boot from the Windows 98 Startup disk, install the CD-ROM drivers that are included with your CD-ROM drive. For information about how to obtain and install the most current driver for your CD-ROM drive, view the documentation that is included with your device, or contact your hardware manufacturer.
4. Insert the Windows 98 CD-ROM in the CD-ROM drive, type the following command at a command prompt, and then press ENTER *X*:\setupwhere *X* is the drive letter that is assigned to your CD-ROM drive.
5. When you receive the following message, press ENTER, and then follow the instructions on the screen to complete the Setup procedure: Please wait while the Setup initializes. Setup is now going to perform a routine check on your system. To continue press Enter.

Revision

1. An operating system (OS) is a set of computer programs that manages the hardware and software resources of a computer.
2. The operating system forms a platform for other system software and for application software.
3. Batch processing requires that a program, its related data and relevant control commands should be submitted together, in the form of a Job.
4. A multi-programming system permits multiple programs to be loaded into the memory and execute the programs concurrently.
5. The time-sharing interactive systems belong to the era of a large mainframe systems, that were made available to a large number of users for accessing concurrently in an interactive mode.
6. Most time-sharing systems use time-sliced, non pre-emptive scheduling.
7. Different types of operating systems are optimized or geared up to serve the needs of specific environments.

8. A distributed operating system caters for a distributed environment, wherein a collection of autonomous computer systems, capable of communicating and cooperating with each other through network, are connected to each other through a LAN/WAN.
9. An operating system provides an environment for the execution of user programs.
10. Every program running on a computer, be it background services or applications, is a process.
11. Process management involves computing and distributing CPU time as well as other resources.
12. Most current operating systems are capable of using the TCP/IP networking protocols.
13. Internal security can be thought of as protecting the computer's resources from the programs concurrently running on the system.
14. A device driver is a specific type of computer software developed to allow interaction with hardware devices.
15. ATX allows Windows to power of the system, so that when you select Start > Shut Down, the system will switch itself off.
16. If your having problems with your Video, first make sure you have the latest drivers for your graphics adapter.
17. A lot of people are having problem getting their Windows 9.x home networking to work properly.
18. The first computer virus for a personal computer was discovered (and created) around 1980.
19. Virus are created using common programming tools, using knowledge that can be found in any computer book dealing with technical specifications on DOS/Windows.
20. The computes virus are of many types. There are ones which would effect the boot sector of the computer, some would effect the executable files only, and so on.
21. For a virus to propagate, it needs to perform a number of specific actions, such as reading directory entries, opening files, writing to files, etc.
22. A firewall is a system that prevents unauthorized use and access to your computer.
23. To enable polymorphic code, the virus has to have a polymorphic engine (also called mutating engine or mutation engine) somewhere in its encrypted body.
24. Many users install anti-virus software that can detect and eliminate known viruses after the computer downloads or runs the executable.
25. Before you install Windows 98 on an empty hard disk, you must first create a primary partition and then format a file system on that partition.

Multiple Choice Questions

1. Computer Virus is a:
   (a) Hardware
   (b) Computer Device
   (c) **Software program**
2. IDE stands for:
   (a) **Integrated Device Electronics**
   (b) Internal Device Electronics
   (c) Integrated Data Electronics
3. Operating system is:
   (a) Hardware
   (b) Computer Device
   (c) **Software program**

True/False Questions

1. The operating system does not form a platform for other system software and for application software.
2. A multi-programming system permits multiple programs to be loaded into the memory and execute the programs concurrently.
3. Most time-sharing systems use time-sliced, non pre-emptive scheduling.
4. Different types of operating systems are optimized or geared up to serve the needs of specific environments.
5. An operating system does not provide an environment for the execution of user programs.
6. Process management involves computing and distributing CPU time as well as other resources.
7. Most current operating systems are capable of using the TCP/IP networking protocols.
8. A lot of people are having problem getting their Windows 9.x home networking to work properly.
9. The first computer virus for a personal computer was discovered (and created) around 1990.
10. The computes virus are of many types. There are ones which would effect the boot sector of the computer, some would effect the executable files only, and so on.
11. A firewall is a system that prevents unauthorized use and access to your computer.
12. Many users install anti-virus software that can detect and eliminate known viruses after the computer downloads or runs the executable.

Descriptive Questions

1. What is an operating system?
2. What is Window 98?
3. How would you install Windows 98?
4. What precautions would you take to keep Windows 98 working properly?
5. What is a Computer Virus?
6. How would you remove virus?

Answers to Objective Type Questions

Multiple Choice Questions

1. c	2. a	3. c

True False Questions

1. F	2. T	3. T	4. T
5. F	6. T	7. T	8. T
9. F	10. T	11. T	12. T

17 Testing and Maintenance

Power on Self Test

Power-on self-test (POST) is the common term for a computer's, router's or printer's pre-boot sequence. The same basic sequence is present on all computer architectures. It is the first step of the more general process called initial program load (IPL), booting, or bootstrapping. The term POST has become popular in association with and as a result of the proliferation of the PC. It can be used as a noun when referring to the code that controls the pre-boot phase or when referring to the phase itself. It can also be used as a verb when referring to the code or the system as it progresses through the pre-boot phase. Alternatively this may be called "POSTing."

General Internal Workings

On power up, the main duties of POST are handled by the BIOS, which may hand some of these duties to other programs designed to initialize very specific peripheral devices, notably for video and SCSI initialization. These other duty-specific programs are generally known collectively as option ROMs or individually as the video BIOS, SCSI BIOS, etc.

The principal duties of the main BIOS during POST are as follows:

- verify the integrity of the BIOS code itself
- determine the reason POST is being executed
- find, size, and verify system main memory
- discover, initialize, and catalog all system buses and devices
- pass control to other specialized BIOSes (if and when required)
- provide a user interface for system's configuration
- identify, organize, and select which devices are available for booting
- construct whatever system environment that is required by the target OS

The BIOS will begin its POST duties when the CPU is reset. The first memory location the CPU tries to execute is known as the reset vector. In the case of a hard reboot, the northbridge will direct this code fetch (request) to the BIOS located on the system flash memory. For a warm boot, the BIOS will be located in the proper place in RAM and the northbridge will direct the reset vector call to the RAM.

During the POST flow of a contemporary BIOS, one of the first things a BIOS should do is determine the reason it is executing. For a cold boot, for example, it may need to execute all of its functionality. If, however, the system supports power savings or quick boot methods, the BIOS may be able to circumvent the standard POST device discovery, and simply program the devices from a preloaded system device table.

The POST flow for the PC has developed from a very simple, straightforward process to one that is complex and convoluted. During POST, the BIOS must integrate a plethora of competing, evolving, and even mutually exclusive standards and initiatives for the matrix of hardware and OSes the PC is expected to support. However, the average user still knows the POST and BIOS only through its simple visible memory tests and setup screen.

Fundamental Structure

In the case of the IBM PC compatible machines, the main BIOS is divided into two basic sections. The POST section, or POST code, is responsible for the tasks mentioned above, and the environment POST constructs for the OS is known as the runtime code, the runtime BIOS, or the runtime footprint. Primarily these two divisions can be distinguished in that POST code should be flushed from memory before control is passed to the target OS while the runtime code remains resident in memory. This division may be a misleading oversimplification, however, as many Runtime functions are executed while the system is POSTing.

Error reporting

The original IBM BIOS reported errors detected during POST by outputting a number to a fixed I/O port address, 80. Using a logic analyzer or a dedicated POST card, an interface card that shows port 80 output on a small display, a technician could determine the origin of the problem. (Note that once an operating system is running on the computer, the code displayed by such a board is often meaningless, since some OSes, e.g. Linux, use port 80 for I/O timing operations.) In later years, BIOS vendors used a sequence of beeps from the motherboard-attached loudspeaker to signal error codes.

Original IBM POST error codes

- 1 short beep - Normal POST - system is OK
- 2 short beeps - POST error - error code shown on screen
- No beep - Power supply or system board problem
- Continuous beep - Power supply, system board, or keyboard problem
- Repeating short beeps - Power supply or system board problem or keyboard
- 1 long, 1 short beep - System board problem
- 1 long, 2 short beeps - Display adapter problem (MDA, CGA)
- 1 long, 3 short beeps - Enhanced Graphics Adapter (EGA)
- 3 long beeps - 3270 keyboard card

POST AMI BIOS beep codes

1. Memory refresh timer error
2. Parity error in base memory (first 64 KiB block)
3. Base memory read/write test error
4. Mother board timer not operational

5. Processor error
6. 8042 Gate A20 test error (cannot switch to protected mode)
7. General exception error (processor exception interrupt error)
8. Display memory error (system video adapter)
9. AMI BIOS ROM checksum error
10. CMOS shutdown register read/write error
11. Cache memory test failed

POST beep codes on CompTIA A+ Hardware Core exam

These POST beep codes are covered specifically on the CompTIA A+ Core Hardware Exam:

Beeps	Meaning
Steady, short beeps	Power supply may be bad
Long continuous beep tone	Power supply bad or not plugged into motherboard correctly
Steady, long beeps	Power supply bad
No beep	Power supply bad, system not plugged in, or power not turned on
No beep	If everything seems to be functioning correctly there may be a problem with the 'beeper' itself.
One long, two short beeps	Video card failure

IBM POST diagnostic code descriptions

- 100 to 199 - System boards
- 200 to 299 - Memory
- 300 to 399 - Keyboard
- 400 to 499 - Monochrome display
- 500 to 599 - Color/graphics display
- 600 to 699 - Floppy-disk drive or adapter
- 700 to 799 - Math coprocessor
- 900 to 999 - Parallel printer port
- 1000 to 1099 - Alternate printer adapter
- 1100 to 1299 - Asynchronous communication device, adapter, or port
- 1300 to 1399 - Game port
- 1400 to 1499 - Color/graphics printer
- 1500 to 1599 - Synchronous communication device, adapter, or port
- 1700 to 1799 - Hard drive and/or adapter
- 1800 to 1899 - Expansion unit (XT)
- 2000 to 2199 - Bisynchronous communication adapter

- 2400 to 2599 - EGA system-board video (MCA)
- 3000 to 3199 - LAN adapter
- 4800 to 4999 - Internal modem
- 7000 to 7099 - Phoenix BIOS chips
- 7300 to 7399 - 3.5-inch disk drive
- 8900 to 8999 - MIDI adapter
- 11200 to 11299 - SCSI adapter
- 21000 to 21099 - SCSI fixed disk and controller
- 21500 to 21599 - SCSI CD-ROM system

Beep Error Codes

The following error messages are conveyed through a number of short beeps, you can always identify the error by counting the number of short beeps.

All errors listed, with the exception of number 8, are fatal errors.

No. of Beeps	Error
1	Refresh Failure - The memory refresh circuitry of the Motherboard is faulty.
2	Parity Error - A parity error was detected in the base memory (the first block of 64 KB) of the system.
3	Base of 64 KB Memory Failure - A memory failure occurrred in the base memory, i.e., within the first 64 KB of memory.
4	Timer Not Operational - Timer # 1 on the system board has failed to function properly.
5	Processor Error - The CPU (Central Processor Unit) on the system board has generated an error.
6	8042 - Gate A20 Failure - The keyboard controller (8042) contains the Gate A20 switch which allows the CPU to operate in virutal mode. This error message means that the BIOS is not able to switch the CPU into projected mode.
7	Processor Exception Interrupt Error - The CPU on the motherboard has generated an exception interrupt.
8	Display Mmeory Read/Write Error - The system video adapter is either missing or its memory is faulty. This is not a fatal error.
9	ROM Checksum Error - The BIOS ROM checksum value does not match the value encoded in the BIOS.
10	CMOS Shudtdown Register Read/Write Error - The shudown register for the CMOS memory has failed.

Debugging Tools for Windows

Debugging Tools for Windows is a set of extensible tools for debugging device drivers for the Microsoft Windows family of operating systems. Debugging Tools for Windows supports debugging of:

- Applications, services, drivers, and the Windows kernel.
- Native 32-bit x86, native Intel Itanium, and native x64 platforms.
- Microsoft Windows NT 4.0, Windows 2000, Windows XP, Microsoft Windows Server 2003, and Windows Vista.
- User-mode programs and kernel-mode programs.
- Live targets and dump files.
- Local and remote targets.

In addition to Debugging Tools for Windows, effective debugging also requires:

- Special debugging routines, macros, and global variables in the Windows Driver Development Kit (DDK). You can use these routines in your driver code to send messages to a debugger and set breakpoints to aid in debugging.
- Access to Windows symbol files. If you have access to the Internet while debugging, you can set your debugger's symbol path to point to the Windows symbol server. If you do not have access to the Internet while debugging, you can download symbols in advance from the Microsoft website.

Debugging Tools for Windows includes WinDbg, a powerful debugger with a graphical interface and a console interface, as well as the console-based debuggers NTSD, CDB, and KD.

WinDbg

WinDbg provides source-level debugging through a graphical user interface and a text-based interface.

- WinDbg uses the Microsoft Visual Studio debug symbol formats for source-level debugging. It can access any public function's names and variables exposed by modules that were compiled with Codeview (.pdb) symbol files.
- WinDbg can view source code, set breakpoints, view variables (including C++ objects), stack traces, and memory. It includes a command window to issue a wide variety of commands not available through the drop-down menus. For kernel-mode debugging, WinDbg typically requires two computers (the host machine and the target machine). It also allows you to remotely debug user-mode code.

To Prepare for a Debugging Session

1. If you want to debug kernel-mode code, set up a host computer to run the debugger and a target computer to run the code being debugged. Connect the two computers using either an IEEE 1394 cable or a null-modem cable between two serial ports.
2. Download and install the latest version of Debugging Tools for Windows on the

host computer. The tools can also be installed from the Windows DDK, the Platform SDK, or the Customer Support Diagnostics CD.

3. Use Windows Symbol Server to access the symbol files from the host computer.

About the Microsoft Symbol Server

Symbol server technology is built into Debugging Tools for Windows. Microsoft provides access to an Internet symbol server that contains symbol files for the Microsoft Windows Server 2003, Windows XP, and Windows 2000 operating systems, as well as other Microsoft products.

The Internet symbol server is populated with a variety of Windows symbols for Microsoft Windows operating systems, including hot fixes, Service Packs, Security Rollup Packages, and retail releases. Symbols are also available on the server for current Betas and Release Candidates for Windows products, plus a variety of other Microsoft products, such as Microsoft Internet Explorer.

If you have access to the Internet during debugging, you can configure the debugger to download symbols as needed during a debugging session, rather than downloading symbol files separately before a debugging session. The symbols are downloaded to a directory location that you specify and then the debugger loads them from there.

To use the Microsoft Symbol Server

1. Make sure you have installed the latest version of Debugging Tools for Windows.
2. Start a debugging session.
3. Decide where to store the downloaded symbols (the "downstream store"). This can be a local drive or a UNC path.
4. Set the debugger symbol path as follows, substituting your downstream store path for *DownstreamStore*.

   SRV**DownstreamStore****http://msdl.microsoft.com/download/symbols**

   For example, to download symbols to c:\websymbols, you would add the following to your symbol path:

   SRV*c:\websymbols*http://msdl.microsoft.com/download/symbols

   Note: http://msdl.microsoft.com/download/symbols is not browsable and is intended only for access by the debugger. For more information on setting symbol paths and using symbol servers, see the documentation accompanying Debugging Tools for Windows.

Debug Card

A shortcut to all your hardware problems! Just plug into the PCI slot and it will conduct a complete hardware diagnostic test to detect the defective hardware in no time!

The purpose of the debug card is to make the difficult troubleshooting procedure easier and quicker. This debugging card will assist any technicians (from novice to advance users) in accurately and conveniently locating their hardware problems faster, cutting down the troubleshooting time drastically simply by displaying an easy to follow POST (Power On Self Test) code on its display.

Installation

Quick and easy to install into an open PCI slot of your PC motherboard.

Easy to read LED Display on the Display.

Will assist in revealing where problem is while troubleshooting.

Can be used to identify whether CPU or motherboard is defective.

Will help to determine if the memory is faulty.

Able to pinpoint whether the Video card is problematic.

6 LEDs that can hint whether power supply is failing.

Simple to follow POST Code table for problem description.

Drastically reduce troubleshooting time.

Helpful to both Novices and Experienced users alike.

Windows XP Recovery and Console Debugging

When you use the Windows Recovery Console, you can obtain limited access to the NTFS file system, FAT, and FAT32 volumes without starting the Windows graphical user interface (GUI). In the Windows Recovery Console, you can:

- Use, copy, rename, or replace operating system files and folders.
- Enable or disable service or device startup the next time that start your computer.
- Repair the file system boot sector or the Master Boot Record (MBR).
- Create and format partitions on drives.

Only an administrator can obtain access to the Windows Recovery Console so that unauthorized users cannot use any NTFS volume.

Starting the Windows Recovery Console

To start the Windows Recovery Console, use one of the following methods:

- Use the Windows Setup floppy disks or the Windows CD-ROM to start your computer. At the "Welcome to Setup" screen, press F10 or press 'R" to repair.
- Use the Winnt32.exe utility with the **/cmdcons** option to add the Windows Recovery Console to the Windows Startup folder. This procedure requires approximately 7 megabytes (MB) of hard disk space on the system partition to hold the Cmdcons folder and files.

Using the Command Console

After you start the Windows Recovery Console, you receive the following message:

```
Microsoft Windows(R) Recovery Console
```

The Recovery Console provides system repair and recovery functionality.

Type EXIT to quit the Recovery Console and restart the computer.

```
C:\WINDOWS
```

Which Windows Installation would you like to log on to

(To cancel, press ENTER)? After you enter the number for the appropriate Windows installation, Windows will then prompt you to enter the Administrator account password.

If you use an incorrect password three times, the Windows Recovery Console quits. Also, if the Security Accounts Manager (SAM) database is missing or damaged, you cannot use the Windows Recovery Console because you cannot have correct authentication. After you enter your password and the Windows Recovery Console starts, type exit to restart the computer.

When you use Windows XP Professional, you can set group policies to enable automatic administrative logon.

Restrictions and limitations of the Recovery Console

When you use the Windows Recovery Console, you can use only the following items:

- The root folder
- The %SystemRoot% folder and the subfolders of the Windows installation that you are currently logged on to
- The Cmdcons folder
- The removable media drives such as the CD-ROM drive or the DVD-ROM drive

Note If you try to obtain access to other folders, you may receive an "Access Denied" error message. Also, when you are using the Windows Recovery Console, you cannot copy a file from the local hard disk to a floppy disk. However, you can copy a file from a floppy disk or from a CD-ROM to a hard disk, and you can copy a file from one hard disk to another hard disk.

Available commands

HELP

Use the **help** command to list all the following supported commands:

attrib	del	fixboot	more	set
batch	delete	fixmbr	mkdir	systemroot
bootcfg	dir	format	more	type
cd	disable	help	net	
chdir	diskpart	listsvc	rd	
chkdsk	enable	logon	ren	
cls	exit	map	rename	
copy	expand	md	rmdir	

ATTRIB

Use the **attrib** command with one or more of the following parameters to change the attributes of a file or a folder:

-R	+R	-S
+S	-H	+H
-C	+C	

Notes:

+ : Sets an attribute

- : Resets an attribute

R : Read-only file attribute

S : System file attribute

H : Hidden file attribute

C : Compressed file attribute

You must set or clear at least one attribute.

To view attributes, use the **dir** command.

BATCH

batch ***inputfile*** **[*outputfile*]**

Use this command to run commands that are specified in a text file. In the command syntax, *inputfile* specifies the text file that contains the list of commands to be run, and *outputfile* specifies the file that contains the output of the specified commands. If you do not specify an output file, the output appears on the screen.

BOOTCFG

Use this command for boot configuration and recovery. This command has the following options:

```
bootcfg /add
bootcfg /rebuild
bootcfg /scan
bootcfg /list
bootcfg /disableredirect
bootcfg /redirect [portbaudrate] | [useBiosSettings] Examples:
bootcfg /redirect com1 115200
bootcfg /redirect useBiosSettings
```

You can use the following options:

/add : Adds a Windows installation to the boot menu list.

/rebuild :	Iterates through all Windows installations so that you can specify which installations to add.
/scan :	Scans all disks for Windows installations and displays the results so that you can specify which installations to add.
/default :	Sets the default boot entry.
/list :	Lists the entries already in the boot menu list.
/disableredirect :	Disables redirection in the boot loader.
/redirect :	Enables redirection in the boot loader, with the specified configuration.

CD and CHDIR

Use the **cd** and **chdir** commands to change to a different folder. For example, you can use the following commands:

Type cd .. to change to the parent folder.

Type cd drive: to display the current folder in the specified drive.

Type cd without parameters to display the current drive and folder. The **chdir** command treats spaces as delimiters. Because of this, you must put quotation marks ("") around a folder name that contains a space, for example:

cd "\windows\profiles\username\programs\start menu"The **chdir** command works only in the system folders of the current installation of Windows, in removable media, in the root folder of any hard disk partition, or in the local installation sources.

CHKDSK

chkdsk *drive* /p /r

The **chkdsk** command checks the specified drive and repairs or recovers the drive if the drive requires it.The command also marks any bad sectors and it recovers readable information.

You can use the following options:

/p : Does an exhaustive check of the drive and corrects any errors.

/r : Locates bad sectors and recovers readable information.

If you specify the **/r** option, the **/p** option is implied. When you specify the **chkdsk** command without arguments, the command checks the current drive with no options in effect.

When you run the **chkdsk** command, you are required to use the Autochk.exe file. CHKDSK automatically locates this file in the startup folder. If the Command Console was preinstalled, the startup folder is typically the Cmdcons folder. If CHKDSK cannot find Autochk.exe in the startup folder, CHKDSK tries to locate the Windows CD-ROM installation media. If it cannot find the installation media, CHKDSK prompts you for the location of the Autochk.exe file.

CLS

Use this command to clear the screen.

COPY

copy ***source destination***

Use this command to copy a file. In the command syntax, *source* specifies the file to copy and *destination* specifies the folder or file name for the new file. You cannot use wildcard characters indicated by an asterisk (*), and you cannot copy a folder. If you copy a compressed file from the Windows CD-ROM, the file is automatically decompressed at the same time it is copied.

The source of the file can be removable media, any folder in the system folders of the current Windows installation, the root of any drive, the local installation sources, or the Cmdcons folder.

If *destination* is unspecified, the default destination is the current folder. If the file already exists, you are prompted whether you want the copied file to overwrite the existing file. The destination cannot be removable media.

DEL and DELETE

del ***drive*: *path filename***

delete ***drive*: *path filename***

Use this command to delete a file. In the command syntax, *drive*: *path filename* specifies the file that you want to delete. The **delete** command works only in the system folders of the current Windows installation, in removable media, in the root folder of any hard disk partition, or in the local installation sources. The **delete** command does not accept wildcard characters.

DIR

dir ***drive*: *path filename***

Use this command to display a list of files and subfolders in a folder. In the command syntax, *drive*: *path filename* specifies the drive, folder, and files to list. The **dir** command lists all files, including hidden and system files. Files can have the following attributes:

D : Directory

H : Hidden file

S : System file

E : Encrypted

R : Read-only file

A : Files ready for archiving

C : Compressed

P : Reparse point The **dir** command works only in the system folders of the current

Windows installation, in removable media, in the root folder of any hard disk partition, or in the local installation sources.

DISABLE

disable ***servicename***

Use this command to disable a Windows system service or driver. In the command syntax, *servicename* specifies the name of the service or driver that you want to disable.

Use the **listsvc** command to display all services or drivers that are eligible to be disabled. The **disable** command prints the old start type of the service before resetting the start type to SERVICE_DISABLED. Record the old start type if you must enable the service again.

The **disable** command displays the following start_type values:

```
SERVICE_DISABLED
SERVICE_BOOT_START
SERVICE_SYSTEM_START
SERVICE_AUTO_START
SERVICE_DEMAND_START
```

DISKPART

diskpart ***/add /delete device_name drive_name partition_name size***

Use this command to manage the partitions on your hard disk volumes. You can use the following options:

/add :	Creates a new partition.
/delete :	Deletes an existing partition.
device_name:	The name of the device that is used to create a new partition.
drive_name:	A drive-letter-based name, for example D:.
partition_name:	The partition-based name for deleting an existing partition.
size:	The size of the new partition in megabytes.

You can determine the device name from the output of the MAP command, for example, \Device\HardDisk0. You can use the partition name instead of the drive name argument, for example, **\Device\HardDisk0\Partition1**. If you use no arguments, a user interface for managing your partitions appears.

If you use this command, you can damage the partition table if the disk has been upgraded to a dynamic disk configuration. Do not modify the structure of dynamic disks unless you are using the Disk Management tool.

ENABLE

enable ***servicename start_type***

You can use the **enable** command to enable a Windows system service or driver.

Use the **listsvc** command to display all eligible services or drivers to enable. The **enable** command prints the old start type of the service before resetting it to the new value. It is a good idea to note the old value, in case you have to restore the start type of the service.

Valid options for *start_type* are:

```
SERVICE_BOOT_START
SERVICE_SYSTEM_START
SERVICE_AUTO_START
SERVICE_DEMAND_START
```

If you do not specify a new start type, the **enable** command prints the old start type for you.

EXIT

Use the **exit** command to quit the Recovery Console and restart your computer.

EXPAND

expand *source* **[/F:filespec]** *[destination]* **[/y]**

expand *source* **[/F:filespec] /D**

Use this command to expand a file. In the command syntax, *source* specifies the name of the file to be expanded and *destination* specifies the folder for the new file. If you do not specify a destination, the command defaults to the current folder. You cannot include wildcard characters.

You can use the following options:

/y :	Do not prompt before overwriting an existing file.
/f:filespec :	Identifies the files to be expanded.
/d :	Do not expand; display only a directory of the files in the source. If the source contains more than one file, you must use the **/f:filespec** parameter to identify the specific files to be expanded. You can include wildcard characters.

The destination can be any folder in the system folders of the current Windows installation, in the root of the drive, in the local installation sources, or in the Cmdcons folder. The destination cannot be removable media, and the destination file cannot be read-only. Use the **attrib** command to remove the read-only attribute.

Unless you use the **/y** option, the **expand** command prompts you if the destination file already exists.

FIXBOOT

fixboot *drive name***:**

Use this command to write the new Windows boot sector code on the system partition. In the command syntax, *drive name* is the drive letter where the boot sector will be written. This command fixes damage in the Windows boot sector. This command overrides the default setting, which writes to the system boot partition. The **fixboot** command is supported only on x86-based computers.

FIXMBR

fixmbr ***device name***

Use this command to repair the MBR of the boot partition. In the command syntax, *device name* is an optional device name that specifies the device that requires a new MBR. Use this command if a virus has damaged the MBR and Windows cannot start. This command can damage your partition tables if a virus is present or if a hardware problem exists. If you use this command, you may create inaccessible partitions. We recommend that you run antivirus software before you use this command.

You can obtain the device name from the output of the **map** command. If you do not specify a device name, the MBR of the boot device is repaired, for example:

```
fixmbr \device\harddisk2
```

If the **fixmbr** command detects an invalid or non-standard partition table signature, **fixmbr** command prompts you for permission before rewriting the MBR. The **fixmbr** command is supported only on x86-based computers.

FORMAT

format ***drive*: */Q /FS:file-system***

Use this command to format the specified drive to the specified file system. In the command syntax, */ Q* performs a quick format of the drive, *drive* is the drive letter of the partition to format, and */FS:file-system* specifies the type of file system to use such as FAT, FAT32, or NTFS. If you do not specify a file system, the existing file system format is used if it is available.

LISTSVC

The **listsvc** command lists all available services, drivers, and their start types for the current Windows installation. This command is useful in conjunction with the **disable** and **enable** commands. The list is extracted from the %SystemRoot%\System32\Config\System hive. If the System hive is damaged or missing, the results are unpredictable.

LOGON

logon

The **logon** command lists all detected installations of Windows and then requests the local administrator password for the copy of Windows that you want to log on to. If your first three tries to log on do not succeed, the console quits, and your computer restarts.

MAP

map ***arc***

Use this command to list drive letters, file system types, partition sizes, and mappings to physical devices. In the command syntax, the *arc* parameter tells the **map** command to use ARC paths instead of Windows Device paths.

MD and MKDIR

The **md** and **mkdir** commands create new folders. Wildcard characters are not supported. The **mkdir** command works only in the system folders of the current installation of Windows, in removable media, in the root folder of any hard disk partition, or in the local installation sources.

MORE

more ***filename***

Use this command to display a text file to the screen.

NET

Although the Help file states otherwise, the **net** command is not usable from the Recovery Console. The protocols stack is not loaded for the Recovery Console. Therefore, there is no networking function available.

RD and RMDIR

Use **rd** and **rmdir** commands to delete a folder. These commands work only in the system folders of the current Windows installation, in removable media, in the root folder of any hard disk partition, or in the local installation sources.

REN and RENAME

Use the **ren** and **rename** commands to rename a file.

You cannot specify a new drive or path for the renamed file. These commands work only in the system folders of the current Windows installation, in removable media, in the root folder of any hard disk partition, or in the local installation sources.

SET

You can use the **set** to display or modify four environment options.

SYSTEMROOT

The **systemroot** command sets the current working folder to the %SystemRoot% folder of the Windows installation that you are currently logged on to.

TYPE

type ***filename***

Use the **type** command to display a text file.

Revision

1. Power-on self-test (POST) is the common term for a computer's, router's or printer's pre-boot sequence.
2. The original IBM BIOS reported errors detected during POST by outputting a number to a fixed I/O port address, 80.
3. Debugging Tools for Windows is a set of extensible tools for debugging device drivers for the Microsoft Windows family of operating systems.
4. WinDbg provides source-level debugging through a graphical user interface and a text-based interface.
5. If you have access to the Internet during debugging, you can configure the debugger to download symbols as needed during a debugging session, rather than downloading symbol files separately before a debugging session.
6. The purpose of the debug card is to make the difficult troubleshooting procedure easier and quicker.
7. Attrib command is used to change the attributes.
8. Use BATCH command to run commands that are specified in a text file.
9. Use BOOTCFG command for boot configuration and recovery.
10. Use the cd and chdir commands to change to a different folder.
11. The chkdsk command checks the specified drive and repairs or recovers the drive if the drive requires it.
12. Use CLS command to clear the screen.
13. Use COPY command to copy a file.
14. Use DEL command to delete a file.
15. Use DIR command to display a list of files and subfolders in a folder.
16. Use DISABLE command to disable a Windows system service or driver.
17. Use DISKPART command to manage the partitions on your hard disk volumes.
18. You can use the enable command to enable a Windows system service or driver.
19. Use the exit command to quit the Recovery Console and restart your computer.
20. Use EXPAND command to expand a file.
21. Use FIXBOOT command to write the new Windows boot sector code on the system partition.
22. Use FIXMBR command to repair the MBR of the boot partition.
23. Use FORMAT command to format the specified drive to the specified file system.
24. The listsvc command lists all available services, drivers, and their start types for the current Windows installation.
25. The logon command lists all detected installations of Windows and then requests the local administrator password for the copy of Windows that you want to log on to.
26. Use MAP command to list drive letters, file system types, partition sizes, and mappings to physical devices.
27. The md and mkdir commands create new folders.
28. Use MORE command to display a text file to the screen.
29. Use rd and rmdir commands to delete a folder.

30. Use the ren and rename commands to rename a file.
31. You can use the set to display or modify four environment options.
32. The systemroot command sets the current working folder to the %SystemRoot% folder of the Windows installation that you are currently logged on to.
33. Use the type command to display a text file.

Multiple Choice Questions

1. POST stands for:
   (a) Power-On Self Test
   (b) Power-Off Self Test
   (c) Power-On Save Test
2. MBT stands for:
   (a) Minor Boot Record
   (b) Master Boot Record
   (c) Master Boot Race
3. SAM stand for:
   (a) Security Accounts Mode
   (b) Security Area Manager
   (c) Security Accounts Manager

True/False Questions

1. WinDbg provides source-level debugging through a graphical user interface and a text-based interface.
2. The purpose of the debug card is to make the difficult troubleshooting procedure easier and quicker.
3. Use BATCH command to run commands that are specified in a text file.
4. Use the cd and chdir commands to change to a different folder.
5. Use COPY command to clear the screen.
6. Use CLS command to copy a file.
7. Use DIR command to display a list of files and subfolders in a folder.
8. Use DISKPART command to manage the partitions on your hard disk volumes.
9. Use the exit command to quit the Recovery Console and restart your computer.
10. Use FIXBOOT command to write the new Windows boot sector code on the system partition.
11. Use FORMAT command to format the specified drive to the specified file system.
12. Use MAP command to list drive letters, file system types, partition sizes, and mappings to physical devices.
13. The md and mkdir commands do not create new folders.
14. Use rd and rmdir commands to delete a folder.
15. You can use the set to display or modify four environment options.
16. Use the type command to display a graphic file.

Descriptive Questions

1. What is POST?
2. Describe the various error codes of POST.
3. What are beep error codes?
4. What is Debugging Tools for Windows?
5. What is Debug Card?
6. Describe Windows XP Recovery and Console Debugging.
7. Describe the syntax of the various commands of Recovery Console.
8. How are errors reported?

Answers to Objective Type Questions

Multiple Choice Questions

1. a	2. b	3. c

True False Questions

1. T	2. T	3. T	4. T
5. F	6. F	7. T	8. T
9. T	10. T	11. T	12. T
13. F	14. T	15. T	16. F

18 Data Recovery and BIOS Upgrading

DATA Recovery

Data recovery is the process of salvaging data from damaged, failed, corrupted or inaccessible primary storage media when it cannot be accessed normally. Often the data is being salvaged from storage media formats such as hard disk drive, storage tapes, CDs, DVDs, RAID, and other electronics. This can be due to physical damage to the storage device or logical damage to the file system that prevents it from being mounted by the host operating system. Although there is some confusion as to the term, data recovery can also be the process of retrieving and securing deleted information from a storage media for forensic purposes.

Physical Damage

A wide variety of failures can cause physical damage to storage media. CD-ROMs can have their metallic substrate or dye layer scratched off; hard disks can suffer any of several mechanical failures, such as head crashes and failed motors; tapes can simply break. Physical damage always causes at least some data loss, and in many cases the logical structures of the file system are damaged as well. This causes logical damage that must be dealt with before any files can be salvaged from the failed media.

Most physical damage cannot be repaired by end users. For example, opening a hard disk in a normal environment can allow dust to settle on the surface, causing further damage to the platters and complicating the recovery process. Furthermore, end users generally do not have the hardware or technical expertise required to make these repairs; therefore, costly data recovery companies are consulted to salvage the data. These firms often use Class 100 cleanroom facilities to protect the media while repairs are being made. The extracted raw image can be used to reconstruct usable data after any logical damage has been repaired. Once that is complete, the files may be in usable form although recovery is often incomplete.

According to research by SrA Cyrus Robinson of the Defense Cyber Crime Institute there are also tools available to law enforcement and government agencies only such as ILook IXimager or open source tools such as DCFLdd v1.3.4-1 installed to a FreeBSD operating system that can usually recover all data with exception of the physically damaged sectors. It is important that DCFLdd v1.3.4-1 be installed on a FreeBSD operating system in that studies by the Defense Cyber Crime Institute have shown that the same program installed to a Linux kernel produces extra "bad sectors", resulting in the loss of information that is actually available.

On the other hand, there are many accounts of users getting a bad disk going long enough to pull their data off, often via slightly bizarre tricks. These include making the drive cold (in the freezer) or spinning it manually on the ground, both actions being used to unstick a jammed platter.

Examples of physical recovery procedures are: removing a damaged PCB (printed circuit board) and replacing it with a matching PCB from a healthy drive (this often entails the movement of a microchip from the original board to the replacement), changing the original damaged read/write head assembly with matching parts from a healthy drive, removing the hard disk platters from the original damaged drive and installing them into a healthy drive, and often a combination of all of these procedures.

All of the above described procedures are highly technical in nature and should never be attempted by an untrained individual. All of these procedures will almost certainly void the manufacturer's warranty.

Logical Damage

Far more common than physical damage is logical damage to a file system. Logical damage is primarily caused by power outages that prevent file system structures from being completely written to the storage medium, but problems with hardware (especially RAID controllers) and drivers, as well as system crashes, can have the same effect. The result is that the file system is left in an inconsistent state. This can cause a variety of problems, such as strange behavior (e.g., infinitely recursing directories, drives reporting negative amounts of free space), system crashes, or an actual loss of data.

Various programs exist to correct these inconsistencies, and most operating systems come with at least a rudimentary repair tool for their native file systems. Linux, for instance, comes with the fsck utility, Mac OS X has Disk Utility and Microsoft Windows provides chkdsk. Third-party utilities such as The Coroners Toolkit and The Sleuth Kit are also available, and some can produce superior results by recovering data even when the disk cannot be recognized by the operating system's repair utility. Utilities such as TestDisk can be useful for reconstruction corrupted partition tables.

Two main techniques are used by these repair programs. The first, consistency checking, involves scanning the logical structure of the disk and checking to make sure that it is consistent with its specification. For instance, in most file systems, a directory must have at least two entries: a dot (.) entry that points to itself, and a dot-dot (..) entry that points to its parent. A file system repair program can read each directory and make sure that these entries exist and point to the correct directories. If they do not, an error message can be printed and the problem corrected. Both chkdsk and fsck work in this fashion. This strategy suffers from two major problems.

First, if the file system is sufficiently damaged, the consistency check can fail completely. In this case, the repair program may crash trying to deal with the mangled input, or it may not recognize the drive as having a valid file system at all. The second issue that arises is the disregard for data files. If chkdsk finds a data file to be out of place or unexplainable, it may delete the file without asking. This is done so that the operating system may run smoother, but the files deleted are often important user files which cannot be replaced. Similar issues arise when using system restore disks (often provided with proprietary systems like Dell and Compaq), which restore the operating system by removing the previous installation. This problem can often be avoided by installing the operating system on a separate partition from your user data.

The second technique for file system repair is to assume very little about the state of the file system to be analyzed, and using any hints that any undamaged file system structures might provide, rebuild the file system from scratch. This strategy involves scanning the entire drive and making note of all file system structures and possible file boundaries, then trying to match what was located to the specifications of a working file system.

Some third-party programs use this technique, which is notably slower than consistency checking. It can, however, recover data even when the logical structures are almost completely destroyed. This technique generally does not repair the underlying file system, but merely allows for data to be extracted from it to another storage device.

While most logical damage can be either repaired or worked around using these two techniques, data recovery software can never guarantee that no data loss will occur. For instance, in the FAT file system, when two files claim to share the same allocation unit ("cross-linked"), data loss for one of the files is essentially guaranteed.

The increased use of journaling file systems, such as NTFS 5.0, ext3, and XFS, is likely to reduce the incidence of logical damage. These file systems can always be "rolled back" to a consistent state, which means that the only data likely to be lost is what was in the drive's cache at the time of the system failure. However, regular system maintenance should still include the use of a consistency checker. This can protect both against bugs in the file system software and latent incompatibilities in the design of the storage hardware.

One such incompatibility is the result of the disk controller reporting that file system structures have been saved to the disk when it has not actually occurred. This can often occur if the drive stores data in its write cache, then claims it has been written to the disk. If power is lost, and this data contains file system structures, the file system may be left in an inconsistent state such that the journal itself is damaged or incomplete. One solution to this problem is to use hardware that does not report data as written until it actually is written. Another is using disk controllers equipped with a battery backup so that the waiting data can be written when power is restored.

Finally, the entire system can be equipped with a battery backup that may make it possible to keep the system on in such situations, or at least to give enough time to shut down properly.

Some kinds of logical damage can be mistakenly attributed to physical damage. For instance, when a hard drive's read/write head begins to click, most end-users will associate this with internal physical damage. This is not always the case, however. Often, either the firmware on the platters or the controller card will instead need to be rebuilt. Once the firmware on either of these two devices is restored, the drive will be back in shape and the data accessible.

BIOS Upgrade

You may want to upgrade your existing BIOS, if it does not support the device you want to use in your system. Some old BIOS do not have support for 2.88MB 3.5 inch floppy drives, 20GB HDD, booting them from CD-ROM, etc. In this connection you have two options:

- Either you can buy a new BIOS or
- You can modify your existing BIOS.

Buying a new BIOS and installing it into your system is an easy approach compared to the modification of the exising BIOS. You will need some additional hardware devices and a thorough knowledge of hardware and software to modify your existing BIOS.

BIOS Modification

Other than the BIOS upgrade you can also do the BIOS modification, if you have proper hardware and software knowledge and EPROM programming device. Using these devices you can make any change to the existing BIOS code, you can change the system start up message being displayed, or the error codes displayed, etc.

Copying BIOS

Before making any change in the existing BIOS it is always safe to make a backup copy of your old BIOS code, this will help you if something goes wrong during the modification. The EPROM programmers can read from the EPROM and write to the disk file, this facility can be used to make a disk backup of your BIOS code. You can also copy the disk backup file to an empty EPROM.

Rescue Disks

It is often the case that data recovery and forensics operations cannot be done on a running system; as a result, it is common to use a specialized boot disk, Live CD or Live USB containing a minimal operating system and a set of repair tools.

When floppy drives were still common, the boot disk was typically a very minimal LiveDistro on a floppy disk (such as the Mac OS Classic Disk Tools disk, standard with every system release); however, as operating system complexity has increased, it has become more common for developers to include recovery tools on the same media as the OS installer.

Alternatively, some system administrators use Live CD or Live USB tools such as Knoppix with advanced file management and forensics tools.

Revision

1. Data recovery is the process of salvaging data from damaged, failed, corrupted or inaccessible primary storage media when it cannot be accessed normally.
2. CD-ROMs can have their metallic substrate or dye layer scratched off; hard disks can suffer any of several mechanical failures, such as head crashes and failed motors; tapes can simply break.
3. A file system repair program can read each directory and make sure that these entries exist and point to the correct directories.

4. Some kinds of logical damage can be mistakenly attributed to physical damage.
5. Buying a new BIOS and installing it into your system is an easy approach compared to the modification of the exising BIOS.
6. Other than the BIOS upgrade you can also do the BIOS modification, if you have proper hardware and software knowledge and EPROM programming device.

Multiple Choice Questions

1. BIOS stands for:
   (a) Basic Input/Output System
   (b) Basic Input/Output Software
   (c) Basic Input/Output Solution
2. CMOS stands for:
   (a) Complementary metal–oxygen–semiconductor
   (b) Complementary metal–oxide–semiconductor
   (c) Complementary metal–oxide–semicircle
3. PROM stands for:
   (a) Programmable Read Only Memory
   (b) Program Rcad Only Memory
   (c) Programmable Read Over Memory

True/False Questions

1. Data recovery is the process of salvaging data from damaged, failed, corrupted or inaccessible primary storage media when it cannot be accessed normally.
2. CD-ROMs can have their metallic substrate or dye layer scratched off; hard disks can suffer any of several mechanical failures, such as head crashes and failed motors; tapes can simply break.
3. A file system cannot repair program can read each directory and make sure that these entries exist and point to the correct directories.
4. Some kinds of logical damage can be mistakenly attributed to physical damage.
5. Buying a new BIOS and installing it into your system is a difficult approach compared to the modification of the exising BIOS.
6. Other than the BIOS upgrade you can also do the BIOS modification, if you have proper hardware and software knowledge and EPROM programming device.

Descriptive Questions

1. What is Data Recovery?
2. What causes physical damage?
3. What causes logical damage?
4. How would you modify BIOS?

5. How would you copy BIOS?
6. What are rescue disks?
7. What is logical damage?
8. What sort of toolkits are used?

Answers to Objective Type Questions

Multiple Choice Questions

1. a	2. b	3. b

True False Questions

1. T	2. T	3. F	4. T
5. F	6. T		

19 Laptop Basics

Introduction

A laptop computer, or simply laptop (also notebook computer or notebook), is a small mobile computer, which usually weighs 2.2-18 pounds (1-6 kilograms), depending on size, materials, and other factors.

Laptops usually run on a single main battery or from an external AC/DC adapter which can charge the battery while also supplying power to the computer itself. Many computers also have a 3volt cell to run the clock and other processes in the event of a power failure.

As personal computers, laptops are capable of the same tasks as a desktop computer, although they are typically less powerful for the same price. They contain components that are similar to their desktop counterparts and perform the same functions, but are miniaturized and optimized for mobile use and efficient power consumption. Laptops usually have liquid crystal displays and most of them use different memory modules for their random access memory (RAM), for instance, SO-DIMM in lieu of the larger DIMMs. In addition to a built-in keyboard, they may utilize a touchpad (also known as a trackpad) or a pointing stick for input, though an external keyboard or mouse can usually be attached.

Related Devices

Laptops can be understood as a particular point on the continuum of more or less portable computing devices: the point at which the device is large enough to use substantially the same software as a desktop machine, but small enough to support Mobile computing. Other points on the continuum include:

Transportables, also called portable computers

Computers which can easily be moved from place to place, but cannot be used while in transit, usually because they require AC power. The most famous example is the Osborne 1. A transportable, like a laptop, can run desktop software; but it does not support mobile computing.

Tablets

Computers shaped like slates or (paper) notebooks, with touchscreen interfaces. As of 2007, the most common subcategory is the Tablet PC, which is essentially a laptop with a touchscreen. Some tablets have no keyboard; others, called "convertibles", have a keyboard which can be folded behind the screen. A tablet supports mobile computing, and, commonly, can run some desktop software (possibly with modification), but not all.

Ultra Mobile PCs (UMPCs)

Internet appliances in tablet form. An internet tablet supports mobile computing, but usually does not run any desktop software.

Personal Digital Assistants (PDAs)

Small computers, usually pocket-sized, usually with limited functionality. A PDA supports mobile computing, but almost never runs any desktop software.

Handheld Computers

A high-end PDA or small tablet.

Smartphone

A handheld or PDA with an integrated cellphone.

As will be clear, these categories are blurry at times. For example, the OQO UPC is a PDA-sized Tablet PC; the Apple eMate had the clamshell form factor of a laptop, but ran PDA software. The HP Omnibook line of laptops included some devices small enough to be called handheld computers.

The hardware of the Nokia 770 Internet tablet is essentially the same as that of a PDA such as the Zaurus 6000; the only reason it's not called a PDA is that it doesn't have PIM software. On the other hand, both the 770 and the Zaurus can run some desktop Linux software, usually with modifications.

History

As technology improved during the 1990s, the usefulness and popularity of laptops increased. Correspondingly prices went down. Several developments specific to laptops were quickly implemented, improving usability and performance. Among them were:

- Improved battery technology. The heavy lead-acid batteries were replaced with lighter and more efficient technologies, first nickel cadmium or NiCD, then nickel metal hydride (NiMH) and then lithium ion battery and lithium polymer.
- Power-saving processors. While laptops in 1991 were limited to the 80286 processor because of the energy demands of the more powerful 80386, the introduction of the Intel 386SL processor, designed for the specific power needs of laptops, marked the point at which laptop needs were included in CPU design.

The 386SL integrated a 386SX core with a memory controller and this was paired with an I/O chip to create the SL chipset. It was more integrated than any previous solution although its cost was higher. It was heavily adopted by the major notebook brands of the time. Intel followed this with the 486SL chipset which used the same architecture. However, Intel had to abandon this design approach as it introduced its Pentium series. Early versions of the mobile Pentium required TAB mounting (also used in LCD manufacturing) and this initially limited the number of companies capable of supplying notebooks.

However, Intel did eventually migrate to more standard chip packaging. One limitation of notebooks has always been the difficulty in upgrading the processor which is a common attribute of desktops. Intel did try to solve this problem with the introduction of the MMC for mobile computing. The MMC was a standard module upon which the CPU and external cache memory could sit. It gave the notebook buyer the potential to upgrade his CPU at a later date, eased the manufacturing process some, and was also used in some cases to skirt

U.S. import duties as the CPU could be added to the chassis after it arrived in the U.S. Intel stuck with MMC for a few generations but ultimately could not maintain the appropriate speed and data integrity to the memory subsystem through the MMC connector.

- Improved liquid crystal displays, in particular active-matrix TFT (Thin-Film Transistor) LCD technology. Early laptop screens were black and white, blue and white, or grayscale, STN (Super Twist Nematic) passive-matrix LCDs prone to heavy shadows, ghosting and blurry movement (some portable computer screens were sharper monochrome plasma displays, but these drew too much current to be powered by batteries). Color STN screens were used for some time although their viewing quality was poor. By about 1991 , two new color LCD technologies hit the mainstream market in a big way; Dual STN and TFT. The Dual STN screens solved many of the viewing problems of STN at a very affordable price and the TFT screens offered excellent viewing quality although initially at a steep price. DSTN continued to offer a significant cost advantage over TFT until the mid-90s before the cost delta dropped to the point that DSTN was no longer used in notebooks. Improvements in production technology meant displays became larger, sharper, had higher native resolutions, faster response time and could display color with great accuracy, making them an acceptable substitute for a traditional CRT monitor.
- Improved hard disk technology. Early laptops and portables had only floppy disk drives. As thin, high-capacity hard disk drives with higher reliability and shock resistance and lower power consumption became available, users could store their work on laptop computers and take it with them. The 3.5" HDD was created initially as a response to the needs of notebook designers that needed smaller, lower power consumption products. With continuing pressure to shrink the notebook size even further, the 2.5" HDD was introduced.
- Improved connectivity. Internal modems and standard serial, parallel, and PS/2 ports on IBM PC-compatible laptops made it easier to work away from home; the addition of network adapters and, from 1997, USB, as well as, from 1999, Wi-Fi, made laptops as easy to use with peripherals as a desktop computer.

Upgradeability

Laptops' upgradeability is severely limited, both for technical and economic reasons. As of 2006, there is no industry-wide standard form factor for laptops. Each major laptop vendor pursues its own proprietary design and construction, with the result that laptops are difficult to upgrade and exhibit high repair costs. With few exceptions, laptop components can rarely be swapped between laptops of competing manufacturers, or even between laptops from the different product-lines of the same manufacturer. Standard feature peripherals (such as audio, video, USB, 1394, WiFi, Bluetooth) are generally integrated on the main PCB (motherboard), and thus upgrades often require using external ports, card slots, or wireless peripherals. Other components, such as RAM modules, hard drives, and batteries are typically user-upgradeable.

Many laptops have removable CPUs, although support for other CPUs is restricted to the specific models supported by the laptop motherboard. The socketed CPUs are perhaps for the manufacturer's convenience, rather than the end-user, as few manufacturers try new CPUs in last year's laptop model with an eye toward selling upgrades rather than new laptops. In many other laptops, the CPU is soldered and non-replaceable.

Many laptops also include an internal MiniPCI slot, often occupied by a WiFi or Bluetooth card, but as with the CPU, the internal slot is often restricted in the range of cards that can be installed. The widespread adoption of USB mitigates I/O connectivity to a great degree, although the user must carry the USB peripheral as a separate item.

NVidia and ATI have proposed a standardized interface for laptop GPU upgrades (such as an MXM), but again, choices are limited compared to the desktop PCIe/AGP after-market.

On January 2007, Asus announced XG Station external video card for laptops. XG Station is connected to the laptops using USB-2 and Express card interface.

On February 2007, there is a new standard for external PCI Express cable and connector. Future laptops can be expanded using external PCI Express backplane and chassis.

Performance

For a given price range (and manufacturing base), laptop computational power has traditionally trailed that of desktops. This is partly due to most laptops sharing RAM between the program memory and the graphics adapter. By virtue of their usage goals, laptops prioritize energy efficiency and compactness over absolute performance. Desktop computers and their modular components are built to fit much bigger standard enclosures, along with the expectation of AC line power. As such, energy efficiency and portability for desktops are secondary design goals compared to absolute performance.

For typical home (personal use) applications, where the computer spends the majority of its time sitting idle for the next user input, laptops of the thin-client type or larger are generally fast enough to achieve the required performance. 3D gaming, multimedia (video) encoding and playback, and analysis-packages (database, math, engineering, financial, etc.) are areas where desktops still offer the casual user a compelling advantage.

With the advent of dual-core processors and perpendicular recording, laptops are beginning to close the performance gap with PCs. Intel's Core 2 line of processors is efficient enough to be used in portable computers, and many manufacturers such as Apple and Dell are building Core 2 based laptops. Also, many high end laptop computers feature mobility versions of graphics cards, eliminating the performance losses associated with integrated graphics. So, laptops have improved.

Case Study — Dell Latitude D630

This is just one of the many laptops available in the market. It incorporates a thorough set of features for business—including corporate-level security measures and optional WWAN—for a lower price than its competitors such as the Lenovo ThinkPad T61. It's enough to tempt even longtime ThinkPad users to make the switch; businesses can't go wrong choosing the Dell Latitude D630.

Various features of the laptop are:

Processor	2.0GHz Intel Core 2 Duo T7300
Chipset	Mobile Intel GM965 Express
Memory	2GB of 667MHz
Hard drive	120GB at 5,400rpm
Graphics	Mobile Intel Graphics Media Accelerator X3100 (integrated)
Operating system	Windows XP Professional
Dimensions (LWH)	13.3 x 9.3 (10.3 with extended battery) x 1.3 inches
Screen size (diagonal)	14.1 inches
System weight/weight with AC adapter	5.8 / 6.7 pounds
Category	thin-and-light

The laptop's magnesium alloy case brings an extra sturdiness that you don't see on consumer laptops, and its display hinges are reinforced for the long haul. With its standard battery, the Latitude D630 weighs 5.1 pounds, our unit included an extended battery that brought its weight up to 5.8 pounds. That's near the outer limit for a thin-and-light, though just 0.4 pound heavier than the Lenovo ThinkPad T61. With its AC adapter, the Dell hits the road at 6.7 pounds, which is manageable for travel but not something we'd want to carry with us every day.

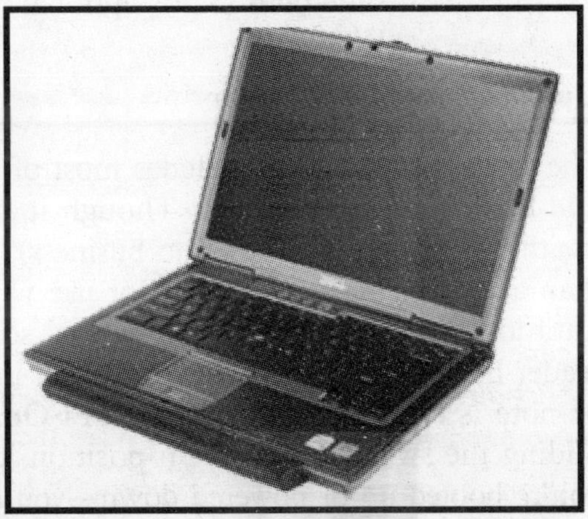

The Latitude D630's 14.1-inch wide-screen display is remarkably bright (223 cd/m^2 in our Labs measurement). Its 1,440x900 native resolution is as sharp as some desktop replacements', which unfortunately can make text and icons appear small. The screen's matte finish makes it a winner for typical office productivity work, though, and its wide aspect ratio lets you comfortably work with two to three windows open side-by-side. Missing above the display are a Webcam and microphone, both of which can be found on competitors' systems, such as the Lenovo ThinkPad R61. It's not a great loss unless you find yourself frequently engaging in Web conferences.

In a world where manufacturers regularly adjust key width and placement to fit the width of their laptops, we appreciate the Dell Latitude D630's standard keyboard, which is quite comfortable for pounding out e-mails and Word documents. If you don't like the nubby, flat-headed pointing stick (not unlike that found on a ThinkPad) with two dedicated mouse buttons below the spacebar, you can use the wide, rectangular touch pad, which has its own activation buttons on the wrist rest. If you opt for biometric security (as we did on our system), Dell squeezes a fingerprint reader between the touch pad's buttons; we appreciate the added security but wish the buttons were a bit larger. Above the keyboard sit all the media controls you'll need on a business laptop: volume up, volume down, and mute. For a business system, the Latitude D630 has some pretty nice speakers; though the sound became muddled at high volumes, sound in the lower three-quarters of the volume range was full and balanced.

	Dell Latitude D630	*Average for thin-and-light category*
Video	VGA-out	VGA-out, S-video
Audio	Stereo speakers, headphone/ microphone jacks	Stereo speakers, headphone/ microphone jacks
Data	4 USB 2.0, mini-FireWire, serial, smart card reader	3 USB 2.0, mini-FireWire, multiformat memory card reader
Expansion	PC Card (ExpressCard with adapter)	PC Card or ExpressCard
Networking	modem, Ethernet, 802.11 a/g/draft-n Wi-Fi,optional Bluetooth ($29), optional WWAN	modem, Ethernet, 802.11 b/g Wi-Fi, optional Bluetooth, optional WWAN
Optical drive	DVD burner	DVD burner

The Dell Latitude D630 includes most of the ports and connections we'd expect on a thin-and-light, plus a few extras. Though it lacks S-video-out and a multiformat card reader (neither of which is essential to business), the Latitude D630 does add one more USB port than average, plus a serial port for use with older, specialized peripherals. In addition, the Latitude D630 piles on corporate-level security measures, including not only a fingerprint reader but also a smart card slot and an internal Trusted Platform Module. Another feature of note is the Latitude D630's Wi-Fi On/Off switch, which incorporates a Wi-Fi finder. Sliding the switch past the On position lets you test for nearby Wi-Fi networks, whether you're booted up or powered down—you don't even have to turn your system on to find a network.

The Dell Latitude D630 was built on Intel's hot-off-the-presses Centrino Duo platform. It also runs Windows XP, the better to help enterprise users who haven't yet made the switch to Vista (though Windows Vista Business is available at no extra cost). Most notably for business users, the Latitude D630 bested its competitors, which measures the computer's ability to multitask with Microsoft Office applications.

Dell's baseline warranty lasts for three years—once the standard among corporate laptops but now somewhat rare; its inclusion of next-business-day, onsite service is further beyond the business norm. Of course, toll-free, 24-7 tech support is also part of the term. In addition, you can attempt to troubleshoot your own issues using various features on the great Dell support Web site, which provides FAQs, troubleshooting tips, real-time chats with a support representative, and a user forum.

Typical Features of a Laptop

General

Windows Vista Certification	Windows Vista Capable

System Type Notebook

Built-in Devices	ThinkLight, Stereo speakers, Wireless LAN antenna
Embedded Security	Trusted Platform Module (TPM 1.2) Security Chip , Fingerprint reader
Width	13.2 in
Depth	9.3 in
Height	1.4 in
Weight	5.5 lbs
Localization	English
Notebook type	Thin-and-light (4-6 lbs.), Vista certified system
Screen type	Wide-screen
Wireless Capabilities	802.11g, 802.11a, 802.11b
Processor	Intel Core 2 Duo T7300 / 2 GHz
Multi-Core processor technology	Dual-Core
64-bit processor	Yes
Data bus speed	800 MHz
Processor features	Intel 64 Technology, Intel Dynamic Acceleration, Enhanced SpeedStep technology, Execute Disable Bit capability
Chipset type	Mobile Intel GM965 Express
Cache Memory Type	L2 cache
Cache size	4 MB
RAM Installed Size	1 GB / 3 GB (max)
Technology	DDR II SDRAM - 667 MHz
Memory specification compliance	PC2-5300
RAM form factor SO	DIMM 200-pin
RAM configuration features	1 x 1 GB
Storage controller type	Serial ATA
Storage Controller / Serial	ATA Interface Serial ATA-300

Storage

Floppy Drive	None

Hard Drive	120 GB - Serial ATA-150 - 5400 rpm
Storage Removable	None
Optical Storage	
Type	DVD±RW (±R DL) / DVD-RAM - Plug-in module
	CD / DVD read speed 24x (CD) / 8x (DVD)
	CD / DVD write speed
	24x (CD) / 8x (DVD±R) / 4x (DVD±R DL)
	CD / DVD rewrite speed 16x (CD) / 6x (DVD-RW) / 8x (DVD+RW) / 5x (DVD-RAM)
Optical Storage (2nd)	
2nd optical storage type	None
Card Reader	
Card reader type	4 in 1 card reader
	Supported flash memory cards MultiMediaCard, SD Memory Card, XD-Picture Card, Memory Stick Pro
Display	
Display Type	14.1 in TFT active matrix
Max Resolution	1280 x 800 (WXGA)
Widescreen Display	Yes
Color Support	24-bit (16.7 million colors)
Features	Anti-glare
Video	
Graphics Processor / Vendor	Intel GMA X3100
	Video Memory Dynamic Video Memory Technology 4.0 - 128 MB
Audio	
Audio output type	Sound card
Audio codec	AD1984HD
Audio output	compliant standards
High Definition Audio	Audio Input Microphone
Input Device(s)	
Input device type	Keyboard, UltraNav, TrackPoint
Telecom	
Modem	Fax / modem

	Max transfer rate 56 Kbps

Protocols & Specifications

ITU V.90	Modem features V.92 upgradable

Networking

Networking	Network adapter
Networking / Wireless LAN Supported	Yes
	Wireless NIC
ThinkPad 11a/b/g	Data link protocol Ethernet, IEEE 802.11a, IEEE 802.11b, IEEE 802.11g, Fast Ethernet, Gigabit Ethernet
Networking standards	IEEE 802.11a, IEEE 802.11b, IEEE 802.11g

Expansion / Connectivity

Expansion Bays	1 x Ultrabay Slim
	Expansion Slots Total (Free) 2 (1) x Memory - SO DIMM 200-pin, 1 (1) x CardBus - Type I/II
Interfaces	3 x Hi-Speed USB - 4 pin USB Type A, 1 x Display / video - VGA - 15 pin HD D-Sub (HD-15), 1 x Modem - Phone line - RJ-11, 1 x Network - Ethernet 10Base-T/100Base-TX/1000Base-T - RJ-45, 1 x Microphone - Input - Mini-phone 3.5 mm, 1 x Headphones - Output - Mini-phone stereo 3.5 mm, 1 x Docking / port replicator - 240 pin docking, 1 x IEEE 1394 (FireWire) - 4 pin FireWire

Miscellaneous

Features	Power-on password, ThinkPad Roll Cage, Hard drive password, Administrator password, ThinkVantage Active Protection System
	Compliant Standards CB, CE, ACA, CCC, CER, CUL, DOC, MIC, NOM, BSMI, GOST, RoHS, SASO, MPR II, MPR III, UL 60950, EPEAT Silver, FCC Part 15 B, EPA Energy Star

Power

Power device from External factor	Voltage Required AC 120/230 V
Battery Technology	6-cell Lithium ion
Installed Qty	1 / 2 (max)
Battery capacity	56.16 Wh
Mfr estimated battery life	5.7 hour(s)

Operating System / Software

OS Provided	Microsoft Windows Vista, Microsoft Windows Vista Business
	Software type PC Doctor, Adobe Reader, Google Picasa, ThinkPad Utilities, Windows Live Search, Fingerprint Software, Windows Live Toolbar, Diskeeper Home Edition, ThinkVantage System Update, Adobe Premiere Elements 3.0, Adobe Photoshop Elements 5.0, ThinkVantage Client Security, Microsoft Office OneNote 2007, ThinkVantage Access Connections, Adobe Instructor Resource Center, ThinkVantage Rescue and Recovery, VitalSource Library College Edition, Multimedia Center for Think Offerings, Lotus Notes Stand-alone Client license, ThinkVantage System Migration Assistant, Norton Internet Security (90 days subscription), ThinkVantage Productivity Center with Away Manager

Manufacturer Warranty

Service & support type	3 years warranty
	Service & Support Details Limited warranty - Parts and labor - 3 years - Pick-up and return, Limited warranty - Battery - 1 year
Environmental Parameters	
Min operating temperature	41 °F
Operating humidity range	8 - 95%
Sound emission	40 dB

Popular Laptops

1. Model: Gateway E-475M

CPU:	2.2-GHz Core 2 Duo T7500
Display Size (inches):	15.4
Wide Screen:	Yes
Total HD Size (GB):	100
Min. Weight (lbs.):	7.2
Price	Around $1300
Bottom Line:	Gateway's E-475M is a blazingly fast, stylish unit that will please everyone.

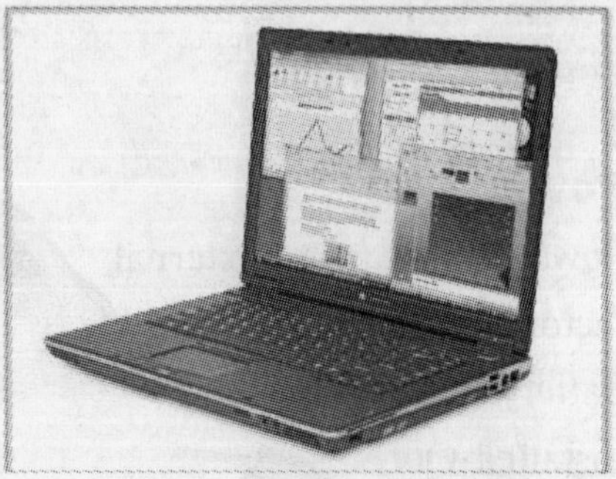

2. Model: HP Pavalion dv6500t

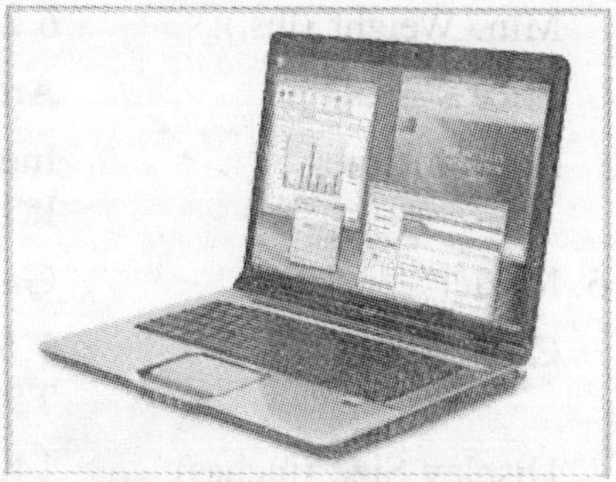

   CPU: 2-GHz Core 2 Duo T7300
   Display Size (inches): 15.4
   Wide Screen: Yes
   Total HD Size (GB): 120
   Min. Weight (lbs.): 6.2
   Price: Around $1079
   Bottom Line: Compact, affordable multimedia notebook has a big screen and a head-turning designer case.

3. Model: Lennova ThinkPad R61

   CPU: 2.2-GHz Core 2 Duo T7500
   Display Size (inches): 14.1
   Wide Screen: Yes
   Total HD Size (GB): 100
   Min. Weight (lbs.): 5.8
   Price: Around $1404
   Bottom Line: The R61's slim size, light weight, and keyboard illumination make it ideal for taking along on the road.

4. Model: HP Pavalion dv2500t

   CPU: 2-GHz Core 2 Duo T7300
   Display Size (inches): 14.1
   Wide Screen: Yes
   Total HD Size (GB): 160
   Min. Weight (lbs.): 5.5
   Price: Around $1344
   Bottom Line: This dv6500t sibling also has a gorgeous imprinted case, but battery life is on the short side.

5. Model: Toshiba Satallite A215-S4757
   CPU: 1.8-GHz Turion 64 X2 TL-56
   Display Size (inches): 15.4
   Wide Screen: Yes
   Total HD Size (GB): 250

Min. Weight (lbs.): 6.2

Price Around $900

Bottom Line: Inexpensive laptop could be a good second PC for the home. It has an ineffective volume wheel, though.

6. Model Gateway T-6815

CPU: 1.5-GHz Core 2 Duo T5250

Display Size (inches): 14.1

Wide Screen: Yes

Total HD Size (GB): 160

Min. Weight (lbs.): 5.5

Price Around $900

Bottom Line: This low-cost portable has a convenient volume swipe; less desirable are the slow performance and dim screen.

7. Model Lennova 3000 N200

CPU: 2.2-GHz Core 2 Duo T7500

Display Size (inches): 14.1

Wide Screen: Yes

Total HD Size (GB): 160

Min. Weight (lbs.): 5.3

Price Around $1299

Bottom Line: The Lenovo 3000 N200 is no multimedia machine, but it has a nice keyboard and is comfortably designed.

8. Model Dell Inspiration 1420

CPU: 2.2-GHz Core 2 Duo T7500

Display Size (inches): 14.1

Wide Screen: Yes

Total HD Size (GB): 160

Min. Weight (lbs.): 6

Price Around $1789

Bottom Line: Midsize consumer notebook has a high-quality design, good performance, and stand-alone media buttons.

9. Model MPC E-295C

CPU: 2.2-GHz Core 2 Duo T7500

Display Size (inches): 14.1

Wide Screen: Yes

Total HD Size (GB): 60

Min. Weight (lbs.): 7

Price Around $1628

Bottom Line: This fast convertible has a huge screen for a tablet—but it's too heavy to hold for long periods.

10. Model Sony VIAO VGN-FZ 180E/B

CPU: 2-GHz Core 2 Duo T7300

Display Size (inches): 15.4

Wide Screen: Yes

Total HD Size (GB): 200

Min. Weight (lbs.): 5.7

Price Around $1999

Bottom Line: Midsize notebook with a nice screen turned in great performance and long battery life.

Revision

1. A laptop computer, or simply laptop (also notebook computer or notebook), is a small mobile computer, which usually weighs 2.2-18 pounds (1-6 kilograms), depending on size, materials, and other factors.
2. Tablet PC, which is essentially a laptop with a touchscreen.
3. Laptops' upgradeability is severely limited, both for technical and economic reasons.
4. Many laptops have removable CPUs, although support for other CPUs is restricted to the specific models supported by the laptop motherboard.
5. For typical home (personal use) applications, where the computer spends the majority of its time sitting idle for the next user input, laptops of the thin-client type or larger are generally fast enough to achieve the required performance.

Multiple Choice Questions

1. PDA stands for:
   (a) Personal Digital Assistants
   (b) People Digital Assistants
   (c) Personal Digital Assignment
2. UMPC stands for:
   (a) Under Mobile PC
   (b) Ultra Mobile PC

   (c) Ultra Motion PC
3. TFT stands for:
   (a) Thick Film Transistor
   (b) Thin Focus Transistor
   (c) Thin Film Transistor
4. STN stands for:
   (a) Super Twist Nematic
   (b) Save Twist Nematic
   (c) Super Two Nematic

True/False Questions

1. A laptop computer, or simply laptop (also notebook computer or notebook), is a small mobile computer, which usually weighs 2.2-18 pounds (1-6 kilograms), depending on size, materials, and other factors.
2. Tablet PC, which is essentially a laptop with a touchscreen.
3. Laptops' upgradeability is not limited, both for technical and economic reasons.
4. Many laptops have removable CPUs, although support for other CPUs is restricted to the specific models supported by the laptop motherboard.
5. For typical home (personal use) applications, where the computer spends the majority of its time sitting idle for the next user input, laptops of the thin-client type or larger are generally fast enough to achieve the required performance.

Descriptive Questions

1. What is Laptop?
2. What are Tablets?
3. What are PDAs?
4. Describe hand held computers.
5. Describe Smartphone

Answers to Objective Type Questions

Multiple Choice Questions

1. a   2. b   3. c   4. a

True False Questions

1. T   2. T   3. F   4. T
5. F

20 Microsoft Windows 2000 Server

Windows 2000 Overview

The Microsoft® Windows® 2000 Server operating system includes integrated Web and application services. These include Internet Internet Information Services (IIS) 5.0, and technologies such as COM+, Message Queuing, and data access. This combination allows developers to use a wide variety of programming languages and tools to build applications that can easily integrate with existing systems, while taking advantage of emerging technologies. By integrating these technologies with enhanced performance, scalability, and reliability, as well as infrastructure features including Microsoft Active Directory™ service and end-to-end security, Windows 2000 provides an application server platform well suited for the next generation of Web-enabled applications.

Introduction to Microsoft Windows

The Microsoft® Windows® operating system platform has become a standard foundation for building and deploying software applications. Its broad programming language support, large third-party developer community, and cost efficiency have helped make Windows the mainstream business operating system and application server platform. With Windows 2000, application developers can use the tools and skills they already have write the new Internet-enabled applications that are increasingly required by businesses.

From Web sites to high-volume transactional applications, Windows 2000 delivers the productivity benefits of component-based development and takes advantage of industry standards for greater interoperability, flexibility, and tools support. These application services are tightly integrated into the operating system to deliver the reliability and manageability that the most demanding traditional and Web-enabled applications require.

This paper provides an overview of the services within the operating system of specific use to application developers. These include:

- Internet Information Services 5.0
- The Microsoft Component Object Model (COM) and COM+
- Microsoft Message Queue Services (MSMQ) message queuing
- Data access technologies
- Common Windows 2000 infrastructure

Because a working knowledge of the component object model used throughout Windows 2000 is particularly helpful to understanding the operating system's application services support, this paper describes the evolution of the component object model and its functionality in Windows 2000. The sections of this paper devoted to distributed applications, the component object model, and transaction services provide the background required to understand how COM+ works.

To fully understand how Windows 2000 helps application developers, it helps to see how the operating system fits into the larger application development picture, Windows DNA 2000. Windows 2000 Server is the foundation for the Microsoft Windows DNA 2000 platform, which includes technologies, tools, and support for application developers. This paper concludes with a brief overview of Windows DNA 2000.

Internet Information Server 5.0

Windows 2000 Server includes the built-in Web service, Internet Information Services (IIS) 5.0, which is accessible from popular browsers. IIS 5.0 is the reliable, scalable HTTP portal through which Web sites and Web applications communicate with the outside world.

IIS 5.0 provides all the standard services users expect from a Web server as well as support for the latest Internet standards, including HTTP 1.1, HTTP Compression, Secure Sockets Layer, and Common Gateway Interface (CGI), and the new Internet collaboration standard, Web Distributed Authoring and Versioning (WebDAV).

In addition, IIS 5.0 goes further than a simple Web server by providing the environment and services application developers need to quickly create sophisticated Web-enabled applications. One of the most significant application development technologies included in IIS 5.0 is Active Server Pages.

Active Server Pages

Active Server Pages (ASP) is a server-side scripting environment that organizations can use to create and run dynamic, interactive Web server applications. With ASP, developers can create a Web-based interface that combines HTML, script commands, and calls to COM+ components.

An ASP page contains a simple program—a script—written in a powerful scripting language, such as VBScript, and executed at the server. ASP pages in IIS 5.0 offer developers many benefits:

- Greatly improved scalability and reliability. With IIS Reliable Restart and other enhancements, IIS in Windows 2000 allows developers to build applications that support more users and stay running.
- Access to COM+ objects. Because an ASP page can create and use COM+ objects, the entire world of component-based applications is accessible to it.
- Integration with COM+-based applications. Because ASP is a COM+ application, all COM+ applications and capabilities are available in ASP.
- Transactional ASP scripts. COM+ integration allows creation of ASP pages that are transactional, meaning that all operations performed by the script can succeed or fail as a unit.
- Process isolation. ASP pages can run in the same process as IIS, offering the best performance, or in a separate process, offering greater isolation in the event of failures. IIS now supports three application protection modes: High Medium and Low,

allowing developers to balance overall Web server reliability with application performance.

- Support for standard, well-known languages. Because VBScript is a subset of Visual Basic, millions of developers are familiar with VBScript today. ASP pages can also be written in JavaScript, another popular and well-supported language.
- Ability to distribute processing load across servers. By using Windows Load Balancing Service (WLBS), included with Windows 2000 Advanced Server, processor-intensive ASP applications can be run on multiple machines to support higher numbers of users.

New ASP features in Windows 2000 Server improve performance and make it easier to write applications that use IIS 5.0 and ASP. These features include:

- Error handling. ASP now has new error handling that lets developers trap errors in a custom error message .asp file. Using the new error method, developers can display useful information, such as an error description or the line number in an .asp file where the error occurred.
- Scriptless ASP. ASP pages that don't contain server-side script are processed as if they were static HTML pages.
- Flow control. Rather than redirecting requests, which requires a performance-impacting roundtrip to the client, Web developers can transfer requests directly to an .asp file without ever leaving the server.
- Performance-enhanced objects. IIS provides updated performance enhanced versions of popular installable components.
- Self-tuning. IIS can determine when executing requests need additional resources and automatically provide more threads when required.

Security Improvements

IIS 5.0 takes advantage of the security features that are fully integrated with Windows 2000. In particular, the Windows 2000 Server Web services are fully integrated with the Kerberos security infrastructure. The Kerberos Version 5 authentication protocol provides fast, single logon to Windows 2000 Server resources within or across Windows 2000 domains. Users can securely authenticate themselves at a Windows 2000 Server Web site and do not have to undergo a separate authentication (logon) to use other resources that may be referenced in the code, such as backend databases. Windows 2000 also includes critical security elements such as enhanced certificate management to allow companies to build a reliable Public Key Infrastructure (PKI).

In addition, Windows 2000 Server now also supports the following standard authentication protocols, which are applicable to Web-based users and ordinary network users alike:

- Digest Authentication: the latest authentication standard of the World Wide Web Consortium (W3C), the organization that sets standards for the Web and HTML.
- Server-Gated Cryptography (SGC): used by financial institutions to transmit private documents via the Internet.

- Fortezza: The U.S. government security standard.

Distributed Applications

When it was introduced, the Microsoft Windows operating system was used primarily to run standalone applications on personal computers. Since then, the capabilities of the Windows operating system have expanded to support distributed applications, which span client and server operations, and the Internet.

The application services in Windows 2000 are designed to support a three-tier (also called n-tier, or distributed) architecture.

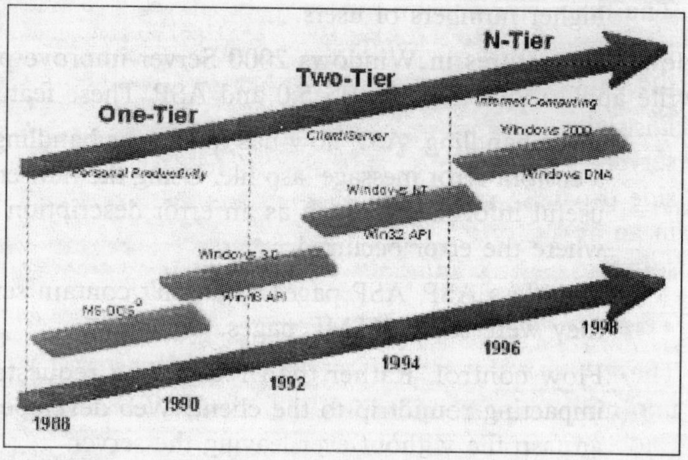

The n-tier architecture separates an application into three distinct components:

- **Presentation**. This is the piece of the application that a user interacts with, such as the order form used in an e-commerce application.
- **Application logic**. This component contains all the business rules and logic associated with the application, such as the credit checking application used to support an e-commerce application.
- **Data**. This is the mechanism that stores and manages the data associated with the application, such as product inventory information for an e-commerce application. Usually this is a relational database, but it can also include other storage containers such as a file system.

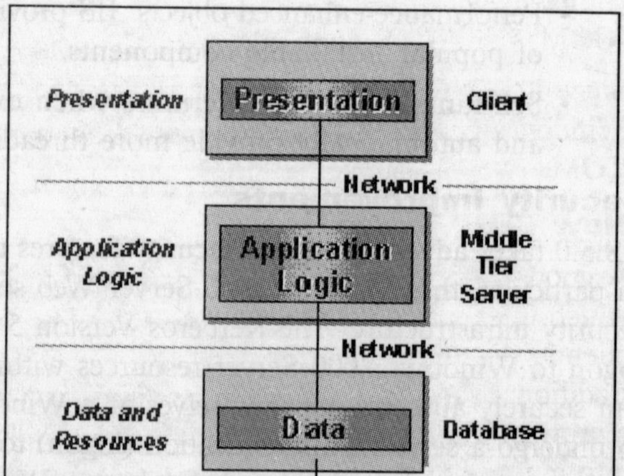

Partitioning applications into presentation, application logic, and data sections results in a simplified programming model that is the standard way to build applications that take advantage of intranet and Internet communications. By adding more hardware where needed, organizations can also expand n-tier applications to handle more users and information.

The n-tier model has proven especially important to developers wanting to integrate Web technologies into business processes. Because the model separates presentation, logic, and database functions, it is much easier to insert a Web server for backend processes and a client browser for presentation processes.

Taking Advantage of Hardware

The move to an n-tier development model is the result of a significant evolution of the personal computer application development model during the past decade. In the late 1980s, applications were generally written to run completely on a single PC. In the early 1990s, the two-tier client-server model emerged. This allowed developers to offload some of the more intensive data-processing work from client machines and move it onto more capable back-end servers. In this two-tier model, presentation software (the user interface) remained on the personal computer, while the bulk of the processing work was moved to the server. The three-tier model adds a further element of separation between the data and the presentation layers, by allowing processing logic to be handled on a separate server from the database and presentation functions.

Distributed applications are written to take advantage of the processing power available on servers—such as those used for database and line-of-business applications—and the client-side capabilities of personal computers and other devices. By dividing the processes used in an application among different computers, organizations can build flexible and scalable software using commodity hardware.

The Component Object Model

The key to building distributed applications is the ability to break software applications into modules, called components, which are the building blocks of distributed applications. Each component is responsible for a specific function. To increase efficiency, these components can be distributed to run on separate computers. The Component Object Model (COM) defines of how Windows-based components work together.

Since it was first introduced in the early 1990s, COM has been an important and evolving Windows technology. In Windows 2000, this model is called COM+. To understand how COM+ works, it helps to understand how the component object model works.

How COM Works

A good example of a distributed application is an electronic-commerce order entry process, which integrates data and processes from a variety of locations, including both servers and clients. In today's development environment, such a process often combines elements of traditional software, such as a database, with those based on Internet technologies, such as a browser. COM allows application developers to break large, complex software applications into a series of pre-built components, which are easy to understand, develop, and change. A component is a software module that is written to handle a particular type of information or a particular process. For example, a customer record can be created using a component that provides for name, address, and other distinguishing information. Components can contain relevant business logic to handle each element of a transaction, for example, specifying the proper length for a telephone number.

Each component is designed so it can be easily modified to address particular requirements. This way, rather than writing the same kind of code over and over, developers can use standard software code, say for an address record, and only adjust the elements that vary for an individual application.

To create a business process, developers connect components together. By reducing the amount of code developers have to write from scratch, this approach reduces the cost of developing software and makes it easier for organizations to modify applications as business conditions change. Because applications built using components can be linked together over networks, component software is also an efficient way to write distributed applications.

Basic COM Features

The following COM features make it a flexible technology for developers to use:

- **Location transparent**. Every COM component can be called within a process, across processes on a single computer, or across multiple computers without being recompiled.
- **Language-neutral**. Because COM is a binary standard, an implementation of COM written in one language is compatible with other COM implementation, making it language-neutral. For example, a Java developer can reuse other COM components written in languages such as Visual Basic or C++. This allows developers to assemble an application from components written in whatever language is appropriate and convenient.
- **Discoverable interfaces**. Discoverable interfaces provide tools and other applications to let developers discover the interfaces and parameters that are supported by the component. This makes it easy for developers to work with the component without the need to understand its inner workings.

COM has evolved to meet the needs of the increasingly sophisticated applications made possible by networked personal computers. In particular, Windows NT® Server 4.0 expanded COM in two major areas. First, Distributed COM (DCOM) extended the COM model to span multiple networked computers. Second, Microsoft Transaction Services (MTS) allowed developers to build component-based applications with transactions that span components and databases.

These technologies have been tightly integrated and refined to create COM+ in Windows 2000. Before going into a deeper description of COM+, the next section provides a general overview of how transaction services work.

Note: You'll sometimes see the entire set of COM-related application service technologies—COM, DCOM, and COM+—referred to generically as COM.

Transaction Services

In the mid-1990s, Microsoft broadened the applicability of COM by introducing transaction processing support as a separate service called Microsoft Transaction Server (MTS). Transaction services help developers write and manage component-based distributed applications by providing much of the software infrastructure needed to execute the business logic that runs in the middle tier of the n-tier architecture. Transaction services include code for connectivity, directory, security, process, and thread management, as well as the database connections required to create a transaction-aware application.

In Windows 2000, COM+ integrates transaction services, as described in the next section of this paper. To make it easier to understand the affect of that integration, this section provides background on how transaction services work.

How Transaction Services Work?

A transaction is a set of events that are committed or rolled back as a unit—either all the events happen, or none of them do. The creation of a complete transaction can require the cooperation of a number of components. In the example illustrated in Figure 4, the order entry application is made of components that, using DCOM, retrieve and process information from several servers. Windows transaction support provides built in programming services that let developers ensure that the entire transaction either succeeds or is completely reversed, without having to write extensive custom code to handle the mechanics of the transaction.

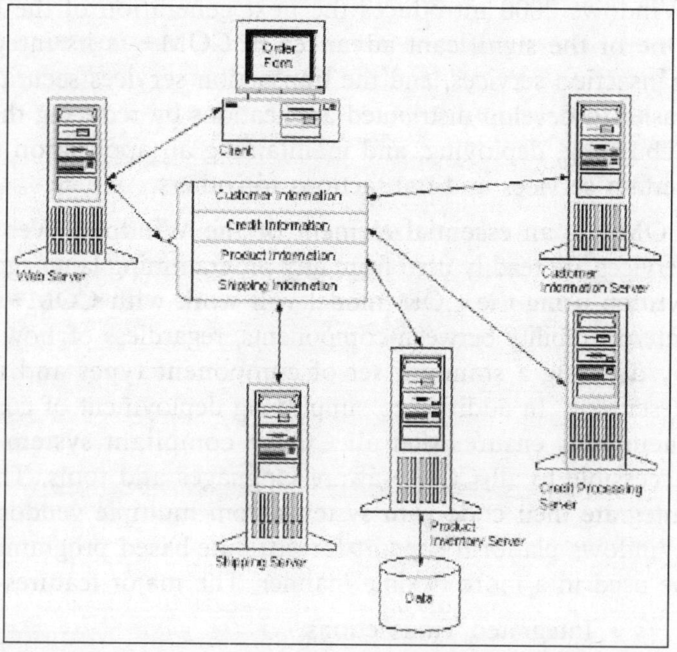

Transaction services and COM work together to increase the capabilities of an application. The easiest way to understand how transactions and COM work together is to look at a typical scenario, illustrated in Figure 4 above. Suppose a customer is ordering products over the Internet. The entire order entry system can be built using COM components containing the business logic required to process orders. The individual elements of the customer's order will likely use several processes and databases, hosted on different servers.

For example, the process would use a customer information database to record the customer's name and address; an inventory database to make sure there is product available to fill the order, a shipping database to track the shipment, and a credit verification process to make sure the customer's credit card is valid.

When the customer places the order, all the processes and database transactions need to be recorded as a whole. The transaction service monitors the entire transaction, and only commits all the changes if the entire transaction is successful. If a communications or hardware failure should interrupt the order processing, the transaction service will either roll back the entire order, or hold it for complete processing when communications are restored. Likewise, should the customer cancel the order, the transaction service can allow the reversal of all the processes and database entries.

Component Services cannot roll back changes to the file system or changes to other, non-transactional resources.

Before transaction support was offered with Windows, developers had to write scripts and components to manually track the requested changes and restore data if any changes failed. With transactions, developers simply have to designate that scripts or components require transactions. This means that developers can put together applications that use components without having to write the specialized code needed to address such issues.

Windows 2000 Components: COM+

Windows 2000 introduces the next generation of the component object model, COM+. One of the significant advances in COM+ is its integration of the previously separate transaction services, and the transaction services security model. This integration makes it easier to develop distributed applications by reducing the work associated with developing, debugging, deploying, and maintaining an application that previously relied on COM for certain services and transactions for others.

COM+ is an essential element of the Windows Web and application services. COM+ services are readily used from any programming language or tool, and components that were written using the COM model will work with COM+. The technology enables extensive interoperability between components, regardless of how they are implemented. It does this by defining a standard set of component types and making all components fully self-describing. In addition to simplifying deployment of components and applications that use them, this ensures that all COM+-compliant system services and components will be accessible to all COM+-aware languages and tools. This makes it easy for developers to integrate their code with systems from multiple vendors. In addition, COM+ extends the Windows platform support for attribute-based programming, which allows components to be used in a more flexible manner. The major features COM+ introduces are:

- Integrated Transactions
- Object Pooling
- Queued Components
- COM+ Events

Integrated Transactions

The major transaction service features within COM+ include:

- Automatic transactions. Automatic transactions allow the transactional requirements of a component to be configured when that component is deployed, thus increasing the potential for component reuse.
- Configurable security. By allowing an administrator to define roles and specify the interfaces and components that can be accessed by clients identified for each role, transactions support greatly simplifies the work required to create secure server applications. For example, an administrator can designate that only those clients identified as managers can change credit history.
- Database connection pooling. Components can reuse existing connections to a database rather than creating new ones, greatly improving application performance and scalability.

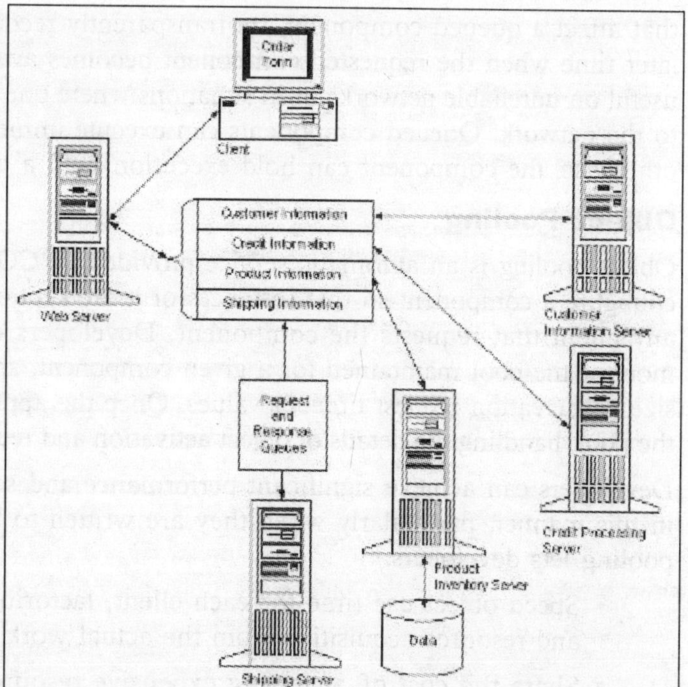

- Support for multiple databases and resource managers. Transactions-based applications can access Microsoft SQL Server™, Oracle and DB2 databases, as well as other resource managers such as the Microsoft Message Queue Service. Transactions-compliant open-database connectivity (ODBC) and object linking and embedding database (OLE DB) drivers are available for many other databases from third-party providers. In addition, COM+ supports two-phase commit transactional access to any XA-compatible database.[2]
- Automatic thread support. Application developers can write single-threaded components, and then let transactions assign threads to those components as needed.
- Process isolation through packages. Individual applications can be grouped into one or more packages, and each package can run in its own process. This allows for greater fault tolerance because the failure of a single component will bring down only the package where that component is located.
- Integration with mainframe transactions. Through the COM Transaction Integrator, available separately, transaction services can initiate and control CICS transactions on IBM mainframes.
- A broad range of development tools. Transaction support allows developers to build applications in any of today's popular languages, including the Visual Basic, Java, C++, and Cobol.

Queued Components

The Queued Components feature takes advantage of Microsoft Message Queuing Services (MSMQ) to let server components logically participate in transactions while unavailable or offline. (MSMQ is described in detail in the next section of this paper.) This allows standard COM components to use MSMQ to deliver asynchronous capabilities. While developers can use MSMQ to write applications that use the capabilities provided by queued components, such development is relatively labor-intensive. Programming with queued components is much faster, and does not require the developer to learn new techniques.

Queued components are typically used for communications between two servers Requests that affect a queued component are transparently recorded, queued, and played back at a later time when the requested component becomes available. Such a model is particularly useful on unreliable networks or in situations where one of the servers isn't always connected to the network. Queued components can execute immediately if the servers are connected; otherwise, the component can hold execution until a connection is made.

Object Pooling

Object pooling is an automatic service provided by COM+ that lets application developers configure a component so that instances of it are kept active in a pool, ready to be used by any client that requests the component. Developers can administratively configure and monitor the pool maintained for a given component, specifying characteristics such as pool size and creation request timeout values. Once the application is running, COM+ manages the pool, handling the details of object activation and reuse according to pre-specified criteria.

Developers can achieve significant performance and scalability benefits by reusing objects in this manner, particularly when they are written to take full advantage of reuse. Object pooling lets developers:

- Speed object use time for each client, factoring out time-consuming initialization and resource acquisition from the actual work that the object performs for clients.
- Share the cost of acquiring expensive resources (such as database connections, sockets, and so on) across all clients.
- Pre-allocate objects at application startup, before any client requests come in.
- Administratively configure pooling to take best advantage of available hardware resources—the pool configuration can change as available hardware resources change.
- Speed reactivation time for objects that use just-in-time (JIT) activation, while deliberately controlling how resources are dedicated to clients.

COM+ Events

Also known as the publish and subscribe events service or Event Notification, COM+ Events is a programming tool that lets application developers write application code (called publishers) that can notify client-side application code (called subscribers) when a particular event happens. For example, COM+ Events can be helpful to developers using queued components to help guarantee delivery of queued tasks.

COM+ Events uses a multicasting publish/subscribe event mechanism that lets multiple clients subscribe to events published by various servers. The COM+ Events system maintains an event database with information about various events, publishers, subscribers, and individual subscriptions.

To see how this works, look again at the order entry application described earlier. Using COM+ Events, the product inventory server can publish a notice when inventory levels on popular items drop below a certain level. Developers writing applications for the purchasing department—or any other areas of the company that are affected by inventory conditions—can readily use this information in their applications by subscribing to the inventory software event notification service.

Message Queuing with MSMQ

MSMQ, a separate technology introduced in the Windows NT 4.0 timeframe, complements the capabilities inherent to COM and transaction services. Because all the steps of an application process may not need to be completed at one time, many distributed applications need the ability to handle delays between a request and a response. MSMQ allows applications to use components that communicate with one another using queued messages, which is a concept similar to e-mail sitting in an inbox.

Being able to write applications that don't require immediate responses from either clients or servers lets developers provide the flexibility required to handle routine pauses within business processes. Using this service also helps developers write applications that are more readily available and more scalable.

How MSMQ Works?

When developers write components that take advantage of MSMQ, their application can send messages to another application without waiting for a response. Those messages are sent into a queue, where they are stored until a receiving application removes them. If a response is expected, the sender can check a response queue when convenient.

Message queuing is a flexible, reliable approach to communication—one that's appropriate for many kinds of applications. Developers don't have to think about the details, and the system architecture takes care of the queuing processes even if the client and server aren't running at the same time.

For example, a developer can use MSMQ to write an application that will let customers submit orders over the Internet, even when the receiving Web server isn't available. Message queuing can also be used to make back-end processing more efficient. For example, when a customer places an order, not all parts of the order need to be processed right away. In the example described earlier, the shipping department does not have to receive the customer order before the rest of the transaction can be completed. Using MSMQ, the order entry application can continue running even if the shipping application isn't available.

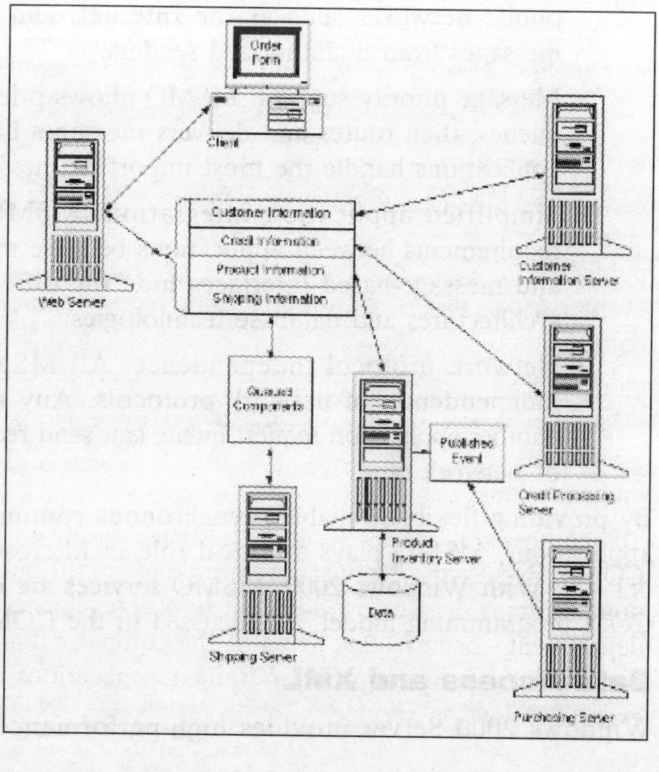

When an order is completed, an order entry component sends a message to a warehouse indicating that the order should be packaged and shipped. Because there's no need for the component to wait for the order to be sent off, this request is made using MSMQ. When convenient, an application in the warehouse then extracts orders from a queue and ensures they are filled. Developers can use transaction services with MSMQ to ensure that the transaction completes properly.

MSMQ Features

MSMQ features that support the capabilities described above include:

- COM-based access. The services of MSMQ can be accessed through a simple interface provided by COM components. This setup makes it straightforward to send and receive messages from within an Internet Information Service Active Server Page script, a transactions-based application or any software that can use COM.
- Integration with transactions. MSMQ operations can automatically enlist in transactions to preserve data integrity.
- Automatic message journaling. If requested, MSMQ will keep copies of messages sent or received by applications. Journals provide audit trails and can also make recovering from some kinds of failure easier.
- Automatic notification. If requested, MSMQ can notify a sending application that messages were (or were not) received and processed correctly. This service lets sending applications know when they can treat messages as delivered or, if failures occur, when they must take corrective action.
- Built-in data integrity, data privacy, and digital signature services. MSMQ can digitally sign and encrypt messages for transfer across the network. This capability protects messages from being viewed or changed during transmission, even when sent over public networks such as the Internet, and ensures that servers do not receive messages from unauthorized senders.
- Message priority support. MSMQ allows priorities to be assigned to messages and queues, then routes and delivers messages based on these priorities. Priorities let applications handle the most important messages first.
- Simplified application integration. MSMQ greatly reduces synchronization requirements between applications because message contents are easy to translate, and message-based interfaces hide the differences between different application architectures and database technologies.
- Network protocol independence. All MSMQ features and functions operate independently of network protocols. Any application that knows the name of another application request queue can send requests and receive responses regardless of network type.

By providing flexible, reliable asynchronous communications between component-based applications, MSMQ plays a critical role in Microsoft component services for Windows NT 4.0. With Windows 2000, MSMQ services are even more tightly integrated with the COM programming model, as discussed in the COM+ section of this paper.

Data Access and XML

Windows 2000 Server provides high-performance access to all types of information (including relational and non-relational data) across an organization from the desktop to the enterprise. The following data access specifications are supported in Windows 2000:

- ODBC. ODBC is the most widely used interface for accessing structured data. ODBC lets applications developers easily access data in over 50 different databases including Microsoft SQL Server, Oracle, Sybase, Informix, DB2, and many others.
- OLE-DB. OLE DB is the Microsoft low-level interface to data across the organization. OLE DB is an open specification designed to build on the success of ODBC by providing an open standard for accessing all kinds of data.
- ActiveX® Data Objects. Active Data Objects are a language-neutral object model, which expose data raised by an underlying OLE DB Provider. The most commonly used OLE DB Provider is the OLE DB Provider for ODBC Drivers, which exposes ODBC Data sources to ActiveX Data Objects.
- RDS. Remote Data Service is used to transport Active Data Object Recordsets from a server to a client computer. The resulting recordset is cached on the client computer and disconnected from the server. RDS uses a subset of the ActiveX Data Objects model, the ADOR.Recordset, to provide a low-overhead, high-performance way to marshal recordset data over a network or web.
- CDO. Collaboration Data Objects are a set of COM objects that provide access to data stored in Exchange.

XML

Windows 2000 Server supports a full range of industry standards to allow you to build applications that integrate with databases, mail servers, XML, and other existing systems. XML is particularly important, because just as HTML lets developers describe the format of a Web document, XML lets them describe complex data structures. Developers can share this information across a variety of applications, clients, and servers. Using the new Microsoft XML Parser, developers can create applications that enable their Web server to exchange XML-formatted data with both Microsoft Internet Explorer and any server capable of parsing XML. Using ActiveX Data Objects 2.5, developers can also access databases and work with ASP pages using XML-enabled code.

Windows 2000 Infrastructure Services

Organizations that build applications on the Windows 2000 platform can take advantage of integrated system services and capabilities. In addition to broad programming language support, Windows 2000 provides the performance, management, reliability, scalability, security, and interoperability required for the increasingly diverse application development requirements faced by today's businesses.

This section provides a brief overview of these Windows 2000 platform infrastructure capabilities. Readers interested in learning more about these aspects of Windows 2000 will find links to helpful resources at the end of this paper.

Performance, Scalability, and Reliability

Windows 2000 Server introduces new levels of performance, scalability, and reliability, which can bring immediate benefits to applications—whether or not those applications were written to take advantage of specific Windows 2000 features. The tight integration between the application services: COM+, MSMQ, and IIS 5.0, and the operating system itself, help to magnify the performance gains throughout applications that use the COM+ technologies.

Programming and Language Support

By integrating COM+, Windows 2000 provides developers with a language neutral approach to building and deploying distributed applications. This lets developers take advantage of the skills and tools they already use, and build distributed, Web-enabled applications in the same way they build stand-alone Windows applications.

Developers can build and reuse components written in Microsoft Visual Basic, C++, Java, and any other language that can generate a COM component. Because Windows 2000 DNA Services relies on a comprehensive and integrated set of services provided by the Windows platform, developers are free of the burden of building or assembling the required infrastructure for distributed applications and can focus on delivering business solutions.

Interoperability

Today's corporate computer environments are often heterogeneous: Many rely on several network operating systems that must interoperate with both newer, intranet client/server environments and legacy computers and applications.

The Microsoft interoperability strategy is based on a four-layer framework that covers network, data, applications and management integration. By supporting key standards, Microsoft is committed to ensuring that the Windows 2000 Server operating system can interoperate with existing platforms and technologies.

Specifically, Windows 2000 Server lets developers create applications that can:

- Communicate with other operating systems using common protocols. Using TCP/IP as a core protocol, a Windows 2000-based server is able to communicate with UNIX and NetWare systems natively over enterprise networks and the Internet.
- Access file shares and printers regardless of environment. Windows 2000 Server provides the services to allow file and print sharing with NetWare, UNIX, Macintosh, and IBM (with SNA Server).
- Reduce the burden of administering multiple systems. With the Active Directory service, organizations can unify and manage the multiple namespaces that now exist in corporate networks—an efficiency that delivers the high level of interoperability required for administering heterogeneous software and hardware environments

Directory Services

The Active Directory service is the integral directory service within the Windows 2000 operating system. It provides a centralized location to store information about people and resources on a distributed network. Developers can use a number of standard interfaces to write applications that use information stored in the Active Directory service about users, other applications, and devices. This can help them write dynamic applications that are simpler to develop and easier to manage.

Because Active Directory is based on standard directory access protocols, such as Lightweight Directory Access Protocol (LDAP), it can interoperate with other directory services employing these protocols. Several application programming interfaces (APIs)—such as Active Directory Service Interfaces (ADSI)—give developers access to these protocols. All Active Directory functions are available through LDAP, ADSI, and MAPI for extending and integrating with other applications, directories, and devices.

ADSI gives developers access to multiple directory service providers through an open set of interfaces. Applications written to ADSI will work with any directory service that offers an ADSI provider. For example, with ADSI, applications can access LDAP, NDS, Active Directory, and other directories with ADSI interfaces as long as the appropriate service providers are available.

Security

Windows 2000 Server includes security services for enterprise-wide network authentication. Developers can build secure intranet, extranet and Internet sites using the latest standards, including 56-bit and 128-bit SSL/TLS, IPSec, Server Gated Cryptography, Digest Authentication, Kerberos v5 authentication, and Fortezza. Because the security infrastructure is integrated into the core of Windows 2000, all Web and Application Services can take advantage of it. From the kernel, through services and applications, all the way to databases on the backend, Windows 2000 provides easy to manage, single-source, high security.

Beyond Windows 2000: Windows DNA 2000

The application services described in this chapter, plus other capabilities such as file and network services, let Windows 2000 provide the foundation for the Windows DNA platform (Windows DNA 2000). The Windows DNA 2000 architecture provides a blueprint that helps developers design and build distributed business applications using technologies that are integral to the Windows 2000 platform.

With Windows DNA, the idea of a platform extends beyond the Windows 2000 Server operating system to include a programming model, tools, database, and application services. Windows DNA 2000 defines a common set of services, including components, Dynamic HTML, Web browser and server, scripting, transactions, message queuing, security, directory, database and data access, systems management, and user interface. These services are exposed in a unified way through COM, enabling applications to take advantage of them easily.

Windows DNA 2000 addresses requirements at all tiers of distributed applications—presentation, business logic, and data, helping developers:

- Create robust, scalable, distributed applications using the Windows 2000 platform.
- Extend existing data and external applications to support the Internet.
- Support a wide range of client devices to maximize the reach of an application.

Windows DNA 2000 enables developers to build tightly integrated applications using familiar tools. Because Windows DNA uses the comprehensive and integrated set of services provided by the Windows platform, developers are free of the burden of building or assembling the required infrastructure for distributed applications. The heart of Windows DNA is the integration of Web and client/server application development models through COM.

Windows DNA 2000 also describes how the family of Microsoft application development products fits together, including Microsoft Windows 2000, Microsoft Visual Studio® development system, Microsoft Exchange Server, Microsoft Commerce Server, and Microsoft SQL Server, as well as new pending products including the next version of Microsoft SNA Server called the Host Integration Server, Microsoft Application Center, and Microsoft BizTalk™ Server (for XML-based business process integration).

Conclusion

The application services in Windows 2000 are the result of years of refinement to meet the requirements of developers who are writing increasingly sophisticated distributed applications. These services have evolved from addressing stand-alone personal computers in the early 1990s to supporting today's diverse distributed networks with multiple servers and large numbers of clients.

IIS 5.0 provides the Web access essential to many new applications. The IIS 5.0 Web server works hand in hand with the component-based application services in Windows 2000.

At the heart of the Windows 2000 application services is the Microsoft Component Object Model (COM). The COM technologies provide a mature foundation for component-based development, and the majority of Windows-based application use COM in some way. With its integrated services and its development tool support from Microsoft and others, COM is a popular foundation for building distributed applications.

Windows 2000 introduces COM+, which fully integrates transaction services to make it easier for developers to write sophisticated, component-based, Internet-enabled distributed applications. COM+ also provides queued components and event services. These features make it easier to write applications that both allow for routine pauses in business processes and can publish information about activities that can be used by other applications.

COM+, IIS 5.0, and the broad base of application development and integrated infrastructure features including directory, security, and data access services in Windows 2000 provide the technology required to let the operating system act as the foundation for the Windows DNA 2000 platform.

Installation of Windows 2000

Minimum Configurations

For a standard server:

- Pentium 133 with ACPI system BIOS available after Jan. 1999.
- 256 MB RAM
- 2 GB HD (1.2 GB free) (Windows will not install if there is less than 850 MB). Winnt32.exe checks for free space before copying

[DiskSpaceRequirements] are in Dosnet.inf

- CDROM or DVD, keyboard, mouse
- Pagefile

Precautionary Steps

Use Microsoft's Readiness Analyzer to identify known software and hardware incompatibilities. (Where x: is the Windows 2000 installation CD-ROM):

```
x:/Winnt32.exe /checkupgradeonly
```

Run on Windows 9x, this generates file %windir%\UPGRADE.TXT. Run on Windows NT, this generates file %systemroot%\WINNT32.LOG. This is not a substitute for application functionality testing.

Upgrade network client computers before upgrading domain controllers.

Have at least one BDC in each domain. This prevents the domain from being orphaned if you lose a PDC during upgrade.

Immediately before performing the upgrade, take clients offline and synchronize the BDC's.

Take one BDC on the domain off-line to preserve the SAM database.

Conduct a full backup, then test restore from backups on a machine to make sure that you can.

Create an Emergency Repair Disk (ERD) before and after upgrades to more quickly recover the system partition.

Start with the forest root, which is automatically the first domain controller installed.

In a dual-boot system, first install the OLDEST OS (Windows 98) in the C:\ drive, then NEWEST OS (Windows 2000).

Preparations (of Ingredients)

What to do before sitting down in front of the server:

Machine Names

How many servers and what are the names of the servers? A medium sized shop would typically have:

- An internal file server inside the DMZ to handle intranet traffic. Conversion from NT4 would involve at least a PDC and BDC's.
- An external web server outside the DMZ to handle customer activity.

Most organizations use a pattern to naming servers consistently. Using real country and city names may cause confusion later. Because Windows creates one pool of alias from both computer names and user names, use different naming schemes for computer and user names. Otherwise, you may get this message from the Service Control Manager on boot-up:

The Messenger service terminated with service-specific error 2270

Static IP Addresses

What is the IP address of your DHCP, Gateway, WINS, Exchange and other servers? Servers must have static IP addresses, not dynamic addresses issued by DHCP.

To list descriptions of TCP/IP /adapters on a machine (and whether each is DHCP Enabled), run this from the Resource Kit:

Cscript "listadapters.vbs"

Domain Names

What is the existing internal and external domain name?

NWLink

Installing a NetWare requires Frame type (default 802.3), Network Number, and Internal Network Number.

Static DNS Root Name and Addresses

The first domain controller is also called the "root" server. This role cannot be dynamically transferred to another machine.

Therefore, a DNS server, gateway server, and/or proxy (accelleration) server must be installed before member servers. Before a server is promoted to be a domain controller, the DNS server must exist or it will install DNS services on the server.

Backup device/media

Rather than installing on top of the existing drive, I prefer completely removing the existing drive and installing a new hard drive. This makes for instant fall-back. The price for a hard drive and the time savings is almost equivalent to a backup media.

International Settings and Localized Versions

All versions of Windows 2000 provide multilingual editing, viewing, and printing capability. To enable the Multilingual Editing and Viewing feature of the English Version to allow users to edit, view, and print information in more than 60 languages, check the "Language Settings For The System" box. To support Greek language system settings, the Greek language group must be installed from the installation CD-ROM. This requires a restart.

For Native Language Support (NLS), install an edition of a Translated Version from separate CD's.

The MultiLanguage Version of Windows 2000 Professional allows the user to dynamically switch among the user interface language. Predefined language schemes define locale information. elect any installed language. However, all 16-bit code, bitmaps, registry keys, values, folders, and filenames are not localized. To install language setting files, use the Windows 2000 MultiLanguage Version Setup utility:

```
MUISETUP.EXE
```

Special Keyboards

Special keyboards are available for some languages (such as French).

Drivers

The three types of drivers are:

- vendor-supplied device drivers.
- generic device drivers for modems and disk drives; and
- standard Plug and Play device drivers for PC Cards, such as Network Driver Interface Specification (NDIS) version 5. x drivers for network adapters and miniport drivers for Small Computer Systems Interface (SCSI) cards; To support Plug and Play capability, Windows 2000 creates a unique device ID called the Card Information Structure (CIS) before installs a driver to support the PC card.

Windows 2000 supports CardBus 32-bit PC Card controllers for high-bandwidth I/O operations such as video image playback. Within the Add/Remove Hardware Wizard, PC Card cards and slots are listed within the PCMCIA Adapters category because that's their legacy.

Automated Installation

Installation of Windows 2000 can be automated at three levels of complexity (A,B,&C below):

A.

If you want to install Windows 2000 from scratch (not upgrading) and have a bootable CDROM :

- change the BIOS to boot first to CDROM, then the C: drive;
- get Setupmgr.exe and use it to create an Unattend.txt file;
- Use a text editor to add calls to create Environemtn strings, shares, etc.
- Copy the Unattend.txt file as WINNT.INF on a diskette. An unattended setup from a bootable CD expects a file named WINNT.SIF on the root of the floppy disk. This file contains information from the unattend.txt file.
- Shortly after booting up the machine, press Enter when you see
- Press Enter to boot from CDROM ...
- Insert the floppy containing the WINNT.INF file
- When you get to the "You have successfully completed Windows 2000 setup" manually install Service Packs and applications.

B.

To totally automate Windows 2000 Server install, including service packs and apps:

- Set the BIOS to boot first to floppy, then C: drive;
- Create a Cmdlines.txt file containing run commands to install service pack and tools;
- Define keystroke scripts for use by Microsoft's ScriptIt tool.
- Create a Windows 98 bootable floppy disk
- Create a Windows Install CD ROOT folder. Under it create an UENGLISH (or

another language) folder. Under that create folders ADV_SRV, PRO, and SERVER, depending on the edition desired.

- Copy the Windows 2000 install CD onto the ROOT folder
- Remove the Read-only attribute from files now on the hard drive
- SlipStream onto the distribution share the latest Windows Service Pack (w2ksp2.exe)
- Create an Unattend.txt file in the I386 folder;
- Optionally ... Bypass the Windows 2000 Serial Check: In folder I386 file setupp.ini, replace the 3 X's at the end of key Pid= with "270".
- Under I386, create the OEM folder and populate it with folders and files containing application installers.
- Make a distribution sharepoint from the modified I386 folder or create a bootable CD
- Insert that CD in the CDROM drive of the machine to be initiated;
- On each machine to be installed, bootup from a floppy or open a Command Console
- Invoke WINNT32.EXE This is automatic if the Unattend.bat file is called from the AUTOEXEC.BAT file on the boot-up floppy disk.
- Use this on Systems Management Server (SMS) to install multiple systems.

Troubleshooting Windows 2000

If it's true, as Mies van der Rohe said, that "God is in the details," then a network is a very holy place indeed. A network administrator's job consists of masses of details, and if you're to cope, you must find ways of handling and tracking them. Microsoft Windows 2000 supplies plenty of tools for this, including ones that allow you to delegate tasks to other users or groups, use scripts to automate tasks, and schedule tasks to run periodically. Nevertheless, administering a network is still largely a process of planning and organization, and in that area there's no substitute for brainpower.

Using the Secondary Logon

Recommended administrative practice dictates that an administrator be logged on to a privileged account (one with administrative rights) only while doing chores that require privileges. For ordinary work, the administrator is supposed to log off from the privileged account and then log on again to an ordinary account. Of course, it's not unusual that ten minutes later a situation arises requiring use of the privileged account. So then it's necessary to log off from the ordinary account and log back on to the administrator account, with the process reversed again a few minutes later.

After a few days of this, even the most security-conscious person begins to toy with the idea of logging on to the administrator account and staying there. And in time, most administrators succumb to the temptation and stay in the privileged account most of the time.

This practice makes Microsoft Windows NT systems highly susceptible to "Trojan horse" attacks. Just running Microsoft Internet Explorer and accessing a nontrusted Web site can be very risky if done from an administrator account. A Web page with Trojan code can be downloaded to the system and executed. The execution, done in the context of administrative privileges, will be able to do considerable mischief, including such things as reformatting a hard disk, deleting all files, or creating a new user with administrative access. When you think about it, it's like handing the keys to your network to a complete (and malicious) stranger.

This problem is finally addressed in Windows 2000 with the RunAs service. This service enables you to work in a normal, nonprivileged account and still access administrative functions without logging off and then logging back on again. To set up the RunAs service, follow these steps:

While logged on with administrative rights, choose RunAs Services from the Administrative Tools menu.

In the list of services, double-click RunAs Service.

Ensure that Startup Type is set to Automatic and that Current Status is set to Started. (If it isn't, click the Start button.) Click OK to close the dialog box.

After performing these steps, create an ordinary user account for your own use (if you don't have one already). Make sure that the user account has the right to log on locally at the machine you want to use.

Note: Windows 2000 views all domain controllers as special cases. On a domain controller, for example, all management of users and groups must be done through the Active Directory Users and Computers snap-in. Also, by default, users can't log on locally to a domain controller. Chapter 9 has more on creating user accounts and granting rights.

Starting a Command-Line Window for Administration

With the RunAs service started, you can log on with your regular user account and then open a command shell for performing administrative tasks, as follows:

After logging on as a regular user, open a command window and enter the command runas /user:< domain\username > cmd. In this case, username is the account with administrative privileges. If you are logged on as a local user, the command is runas /user:< machinename\username > cmd.

A command-line window opens, and you're prompted for the password for the administrative account.

After you enter the password, a second window opens. As shown in the figure here, the title bar of the window clearly indicates that it is running as the account selected.

You can perform any command-line tasks you want from this window. Of course, there are some administrative tasks that can't be done from the command line or that can be done only with great difficulty. Some applications, such as Control Panel and the Printers folder, are launched from the shell at the time of logon, so if you're logged on as an ordinary user, the Control Panel functions stay in that context.

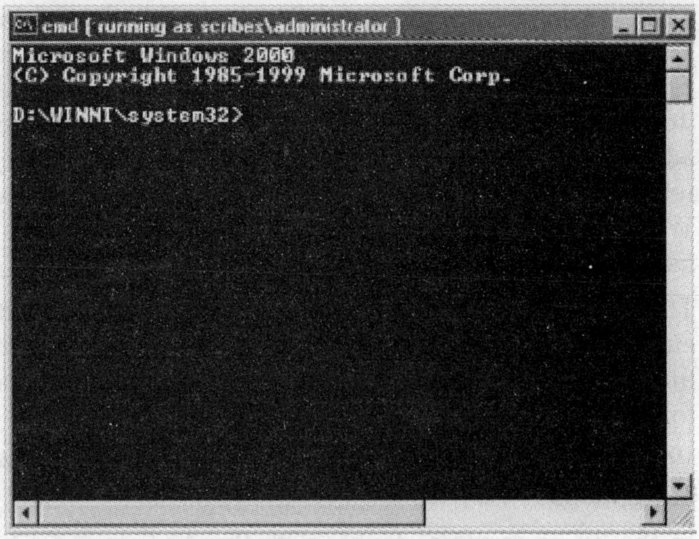

To stop the shell and start it again as an administrator so that you can use functions like Control Panel, follow these steps:

Right-click the taskbar and choose Task Manager from the menu.

Click the Processes tab. Highlight Explorer.exe, and click End Process. A warning message appears. Click Yes. The entire desktop, except for Windows Task Manager and any active applications, disappears.

Select the Applications tab in Windows Task Manager, and then click New Task.

In the Create New Task box, enter runas /user:< domain\username > explorer.exe. As before, username is the account with administrative privileges. If you're logged on locally, use the command runas /user:< machinename\username > explorer.exe.

Enter the password for the user name. The desktop, along with the taskbar, returns. This desktop is in the security context of the user name you specified in the command.

To return to the ordinary user's desktop, use Task Manager to shut down Explorer.exe again. Then start a new instance by typing explorer.exe (without runas, so that Internet Explorer is restarted in the original security context) in the Create New Task dialog box.

Caution: Don't close Task Manager while you're working in the desktop's administrative context—just minimize it to the taskbar. Closing Task Manager can produce unpredictable results and is likely to cost you more time than you can possibly save by using RunAs.

Administration Tools

Most of the tools you'll need for managing a Windows 2000 network come as part of the Windows 2000 Server and Windows 2000 Advanced Server packages, but only a few of them are automatically installed along with the operating system. The following table gives the complete list of Administration Tools.

Administration Tools for Windows 2000

Tool Name	*Description*
Active Directory Domains and Trusts	Administers domain trusts, changes the domain mode, adds and changes user principal name suffixes
Active Directory Sites and Services	Establishes and administers sites, replication, and security services

Active Directory Users and Computers	Manages users, computers, and groups within a domain
Certification Authority	Manages Certificate Services, which issues certificates for public key security
Cluster Administrator (Advanced Server only)	Handles the configuration of clusters and nodes
Component Services	Configures and administers Component Object Model (COM) components and applications
Computer Management	Administers disks, shares, users, groups, and services on the local computer
Configure Your Server	Sets up and configures Windows services
Connection Manager Administration Kit	Manages and customizes local and remote connections
Data Sources	Adds, removes, and configures Open Database Connectivity (ODBC) databases and drivers
DHCP	Manages Dynamic Host Configuration Protocol (DHCP) services
Distributed File System	Manages Distributed file system (Dfs) installation, topology, and replication
DNS	Manages DNS services
Event Viewer	Displays application, security, and system notification logs
Internet Authentication Service	Configures security and authentication for dial-in users
Internet Services Manager	Manages Internet Information Services (IIS)
Licensing	Manages client licenses
Local Security Policy	View and configure user rights, audit policy and other security settings for the local computer.
Network Monitor	Captures frames of network data for detection and analysis of network problems
Performance	Views system performance graphs; configures performance logs and alerts
Admission ControlQoS (Quality of Service)	Assigns network bandwidth by subnet
Remote Storage	Manages the storage of infrequently accessed files

Routing and Remote Access	Administers dial-up, virtual private networking, and internetwork connections
Server Extensions Administrator	Manages Front Page server extensions
Services	Starts, stops, and configures services
Telephony	Manages telephony clients and servers
Telenet Server Administration	Starts, stops, and returns information about Telenet Server.
Terminal Services Client Creator	Makes floppy disks for installing Terminal Service client software.
Terminal Services Configuration	Configures new connections for Terminal Services; modifies and deletes existing connections
Terminal Services Manager	Displays terminal servers in trusted domains
WINS	Administers WINS

Installing Administration Tools Locally

To install the full set of Administration Tools locally, open the i386 folder on the Windows 2000 Server or Windows 2000 Advanced Server CD-ROM, and then double-click the Adminpak.msi file. This starts the Administration Tools Setup Wizard (Figure here), which will install the tools (and later remove them and reinstall them, if you wish). Click Next and the installation proceeds.

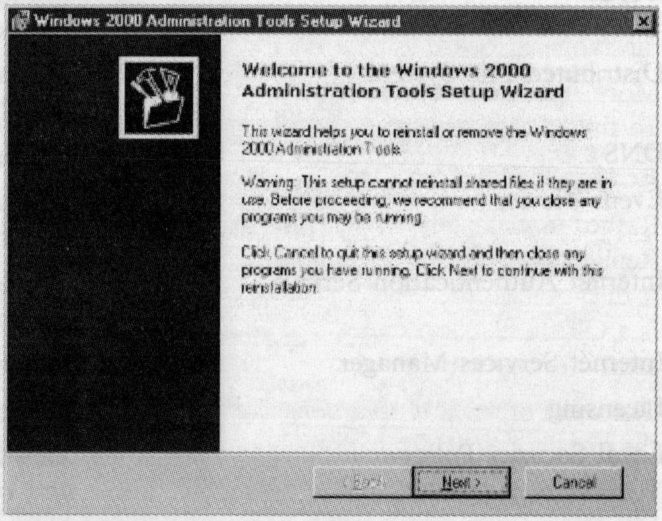

Making Administration Tools Available Remotely

To make the Administration Tools available to others on your network, you can assign the tools to other computers or publish them in Active Directory. Chapter 24 covers the process of assigning and publishing to other users.

Support Tools

The Windows 2000 Support Tools are immensely valuable because they provide functionality not otherwise available in the operating system. You'll probably never use some of the tools, but a few will prove to be worth their weight in Microsoft stock options. This section discusses a few of these utilities. You can see a complete list by choosing Tools Help from the Windows 2000 Support Tools menu.

If you don't see the Support Tools on your Programs menu, you'll need to install them. To install the Windows 2000 Support Tools, insert the Windows 2000 CDROM. Open the Support folder and then the Tools folder. Double-click Setup.

Note: The tools provided on the Windows 2000 CD-ROM are a subset of the tools you can get by purchasing the full Microsoft Windows 2000 Server Resource Kit. The Resource Kit is a separate product with its own companion CD, available from Microsoft Press.

Network Connectivity Tester

Network connections can fail in a spectacular number of ways—at any number of servers and in a variety of client configurations. Determining the source of a problem can be a daunting process. Netdiag.exe can report on an equally spectacular number of functions, running tests on the DNS server, the WINS server, Kerberos, the bindings, the WAN, trust relationships, the IP configuration, the routing table, IPX, NetWare, DHCP, the default gateway, and more. Netdiag.exe can be run on Windows NT and Windows 95/98 as well as Windows 2000, so you can use this excellent troubleshooting tool on servers and clients alike.

Domain Manager

With Netdom.exe, most forms of domain management can be handled from the command line. Machine accounts can be added, removed, renamed, or moved to another domain. Netdom.exe also retrieves information about trusts and lets you establish trusts, synchronize the time, and verify secure channel passwords. The syntax for Netdom.exe is simple, but the range of possible parameters is extensive.

More Info Command syntax and examples are available in the Support Tools Help files. To find the syntax for a specific tool, open a command window and enter tool_name /?.

Active Directory Replication Monitor

Rather than merely monitoring low-level replication among servers, the Active Directory Replication Monitor (Replmon.exe) reports on a wide range of Active Directory functions. It displays the site topology while reporting on the server's properties, indicating whether it is a Global Catalog server, and listing its replication partners, its replication history, and the attributes replicated.

The units of replication among domain controllers are directory partitions that must contain the most current information about objects in the domain. If a server is down or the network is disrupted, the information may not be completely up-to-date. The Replication Monitor can synchronize a monitored server with a specific replication partner to get everything back in order. It also generates status reports for servers throughout a forest for troubleshooting replication errors.

Disk Probe

Disk Probe (Dskprobe.exe) is indispensable when a critical hard disk goes bad. It is a sector editor that you can use to repair damaged partition tables, replace the master boot record, and repair or replace partition boot sectors. Even better, Disk Probe will save master boot records and partition boot sectors as files that can be used to restore the sectors if they become damaged in the future. This can be a great benefit because these data structures aren't part of the file system and are not backed up by any backup program. The following table briefly describes some of the Windows 2000 Support Tools.

Additional Windows 2000 Support Tools

Tool	Filename	Format	Description
ADSI Edit	Adsiedit.msc	GUI	Low-level editor for Active Directory; enables adding, moving, and deleting objects within Active Directory.
Dependency Walker	Depends.exe	GUI	Scans any Win32 module and reports all dependent modules. Used to find the minimum set of files needed to load an application and to find what functions a module uses or exports.
Distributed file system utility	Dfsutil.exe	Cmd	Queries and troubleshoots Dfs.
DNS Troubleshooting Tool	Dnscmd.exe	Cmd	Allows you to view and modify DNS servers, zones, and resources.
Global Flags Editor	Gflags.exe	GUI	Edits global registry settings or flags in use by the kernel.
Memory Profiling Tool	Memsnap.exe	Cmd	Takes a snapshot of all of the memory resources being used by all processes and reports the information to a log file.
Registry Console Tool	Reg.exe	Cmd	Modifies the registry database from the command line. Used to query, add, delete, copy, save, and restore entries.
Remote Command Line	Remote.exe	Cmd	Runs command-line programs on remote computers using named pipes only.
Security Administration Tools	Sidwalk.exeShowaccs.exeSidwalk.msc	Cmd/Cmd/GUI	Manage access control lists.
SNMP Query Utility	Snmputilg.exe	GUI	Graphical version of Snmputil.exe used to troubleshoot Simple Network Management Protocol (SNMP).

Microsoft Management Console Basics

The Microsoft Management Console (MMC) is a powerful addition to the system administrator's arsenal. The MMC works as a packager of system tools, enabling the system administrator to create specialized tools that can then be used to delegate specific administrative tasks to users or groups. Saved as MMC (.MSC) files, these custom tools can be sent by e-mail, shared in a network folder, or posted on the Web. With system policy settings, they can also be assigned to users, groups, or computers. The tools are flexible enough to be modified, scaled up or down, and generally shaped for any use to which you might want to put them.

To build a custom tool, you can either start with an existing console and modify it or start from scratch. In a mature network, you'll most likely use the former method, taking predefined consoles and adding or subtracting snap-ins.

Creating an MMC-Based Console with Snap-ins

Building your own tools with the MMC's standard user interface is a straightforward process. The next few sections walk you through the creation of a new console and describe how to arrange its administrative components into separate windows.

Click the Start button and select Run. In the Open text box, type MMC, and then click OK. An empty MMC window opens, as shown in Figure below, ready for you to add snap-ins.

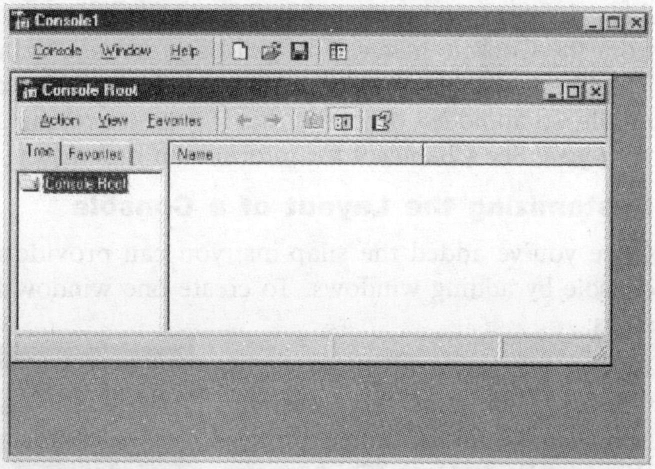

From the Console menu, select Add/Remove Snap-in. (The menu commands on the menu bar at the top of the MMC window apply to the entire console.) The Add/Remove Snap-in dialog box opens. Here you can choose which snap-ins are in the console file as well as enable extensions. In the Snap-ins Added To box, accept the default, Console Root.

Click the Add button. This opens a dialog box listing the snaps-ins installed on your computer (Figure below).

Highlight a snap-in to see a description of its function. Double-click a snap-in to add it to the console. For this example, we'll add Computer Management. The Computer Manager dialog box asks you to select the computer to manage (Figure next).

Select the Local Computer option, and select the check box Allow The Selected Computer To Be Changed When Launching From The Command Line. These options are common to many of the snap-ins. Click Finish.

From the Add Standalone Snap-in dialog box, select Event Viewer, and click Add. As before, select the Local Computer option, and select the check box. Click Finish, then close the

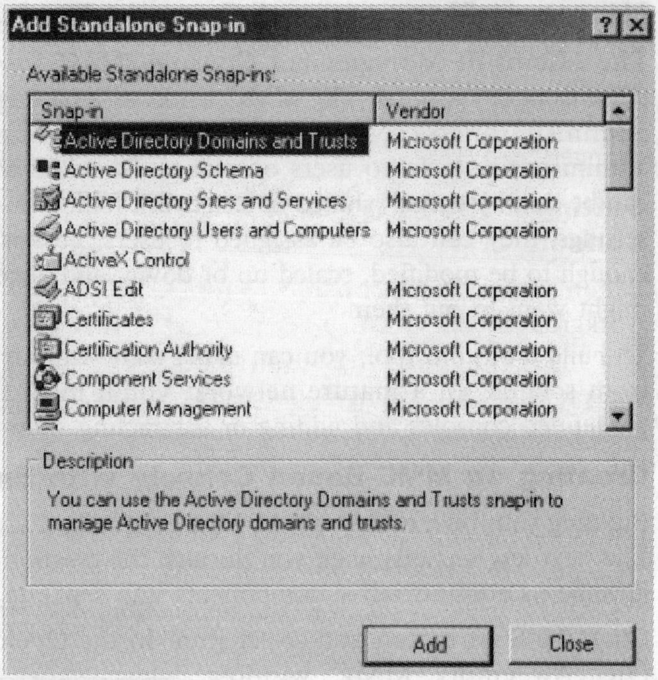

list of available snap-ins. The Add/Remove Snap-in dialog box lists two snap-ins: Computer Management (Local) and Event Viewer (Local).

Click the Extensions tab. By default, the box labeled Add All Extensions is checked, which means that when this console is opened on a particular machine, all extensions that are locally installed on that machine will be used. If this box isn't checked, only extensions that are selected on the list of available extensions will be loaded.

Click OK to close the Add/Remove Snap-in dialog box. The Console Root window now has two snap-ins, rooted at the Console Root folder.

Save the console by choosing Save from the Console menu. You will be prompted for a name—be as descriptive as possible. The file is saved in the Administrative Tools folder by default. This folder is part of your profile, so an added benefit is that if you use roaming profiles, any tools you create will go with you. See Chapter 9 for information on creating roaming profiles.

Customizing the Layout of a Console

Once you've added the snap-ins, you can provide different administrative views in the console by adding windows. To create one window for each of the snap-ins, follow these steps:

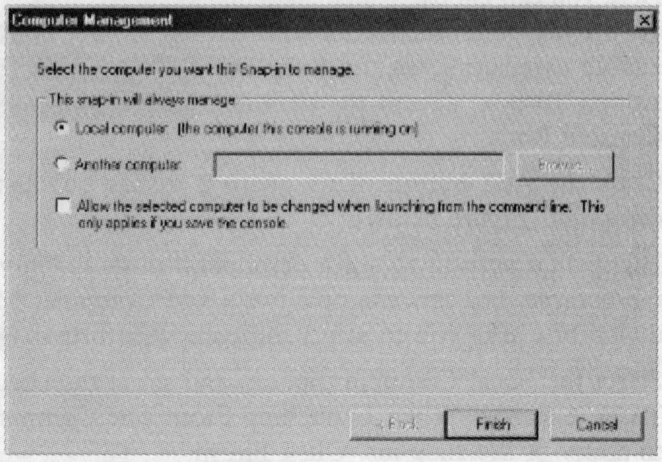

In the left pane of the console window, right-click the Computer Management folder and select New Window From Here. This opens a new Computer Management window rooted at the Computer Management snap-in.

In the Console Root window, right-click the Event Viewer folder and select New Window From Here. Click the Show/Hide Console Tree toolbar button in each window to hide the console tree (Figure next).

Close the original Console Root window. From the Window menu, choose Tile Horizontally. The console window should now look like Figure next.

Note that the buttons and menus in each window apply only to that window. Remember to save your console file after completing the changes.

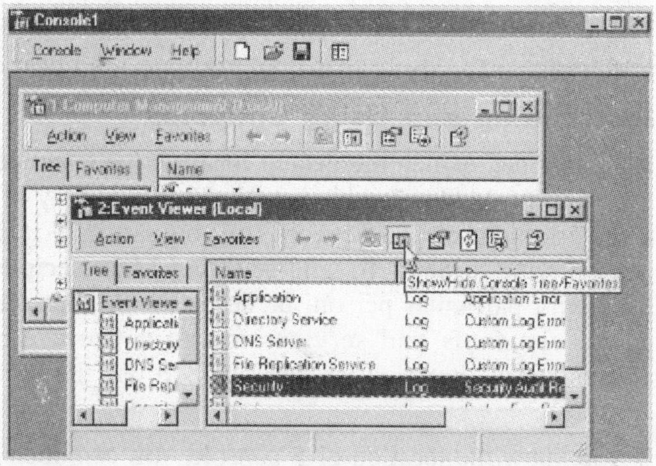

Setting Options for a Console File

When creating consoles for workgroup managers or other users, you may want to restrict how the console is used. Console options can be set so that users can access only the tools that the administrator allows. To set console file options, follow these steps:

With the console file open, click the Console menu and choose Options. This opens the Options dialog box.

Click the Console tab. Choose the console mode:

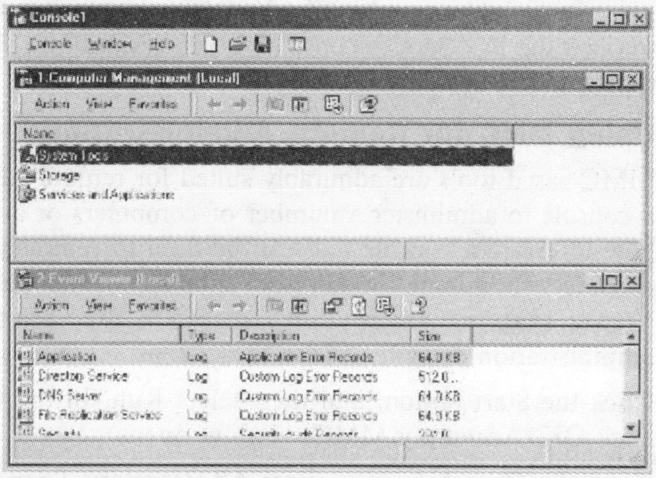

- Author Mode No restrictions. The user can access all parts of the console tree as well as change this console file at will.
- User Mode—Full Access The user can access all parts of the console tree but cannot make changes that affect functionality. Cosmetic changes, such as the arrangement of windows, are saved automatically.
- User Mode—Limited Access, Multiple Window The user can access only the parts of the console that were visible at the time the console file was saved.
- User Mode—Limited Access, Single Window The same as the previous mode, except that only one window is visible.

In all but Author mode, you can also select the Do Not Save Changes To This Console option, so that the console always opens in the same view.

Click OK and save the console file.

Modifying Console Files

After you've saved a console file in any mode other than Author mode, the Console menu is no longer visible, even to administrators. This prevents the user from changing the options. To modify a console file, open a command-prompt window and type mmc /a. The /a switch sets Author mode, overriding any User mode setting, and opens the console window, from which you can open any console file and make changes.

The system administrator can set user profiles to disallow the use of the /a switch, and should do so to ensure that inappropriate modifications can't be made.

Distributing and Using Consoles

As mentioned earlier, the default location for saved console files is the Administrative Tools folder. Console files can be distributed in a variety of ways. You can copy a console file to a shared folder on the network, or you can mail it to another person by right-clicking the file, pointing to Send To, and selecting Mail Recipient. When you assign a console to be used by a particular person, be sure that the person's user profile includes permission to access the tools and services in the console. The user will also have to have any administrative permissions necessary to use the system components administered by the console.

If you know the location of a console, you can open it from Windows Explorer by clicking it as you would any other file. You can also open it from the command line. For example, to open the Fax Service console (which resides in a system folder) from the command line, type mmc % systemroot %\system32\faxserv.msc.

Using MMC for Remote Administration

MMC-based tools are admirably suited for remote administration. You can easily construct a console to administer a number of computers or a single machine. This section describes how to create a console that can be used to remotely administer a domain controller. The console will include the Services snap-in, which manages system services, and the Event Viewer snap-in, which allows access to the various event logs. To make this remote administration console, follow these steps:

Click the Start button, and then select Run. In the Open text box, type MMC, and then click OK. An empty MMC window opens.

From the Console menu, select Add/Remove Snap-in. The Add/Remove Snap-in dialog box opens.

Click Add to open the Add Standalone Snap-in dialog box.

Select Services, and then click Add.

In the This Snap-in Will Always Manage area, select Another Computer, and then click Browse. This will open another Select Computer dialog box.

Highlight the computer you want this snap-in to manage, and then click OK. Click Finish.

Repeat steps 4 through 6, except choose the Event Viewer snap-in. Close the Add Standalone Snap-in dialog box. Click OK in the Add/Remove Snap-in dialog box.

At this point, the console will look like the one in Figure next. Save it under a descriptive name. You can use this console to view events on the remote machine and to start and stop services.

As you can see, consoles can be configured in dozens, if not hundreds, of different ways and then distributed. Snap-ins for every imaginable function will increasingly be available from Microsoft as well as third-party suppliers.

Note: Because consoles are excellent tools for organizing and delegating administrative chores, examples of their use can be found in many other chapters of this book.

Automating Chores with Scripts

Of necessity, most network administrators quickly acquire scripting skills. There aren't enough hours in the day to do everything manually, even if that were desirable. In addition, good scripts are like any program: once the information is entered correctly, there's no need to worry about it until something external changes.

Through ActiveX, Windows 2000 enables scripting options using Visual Basic, Scripting Edition (VBScript); JScript; or Perl. Previously, the only native scripting language supported by Windows was the MS-DOS command language, and many administrators will undoubtedly continue to use MS-DOS scripts because they're very small and very fast. Why use anything else if an MS-DOS script will do the job? The answer is that you shouldn't. However, in a large enterprise or for more complicated scripts, a more sophisticated scripting language is in order.

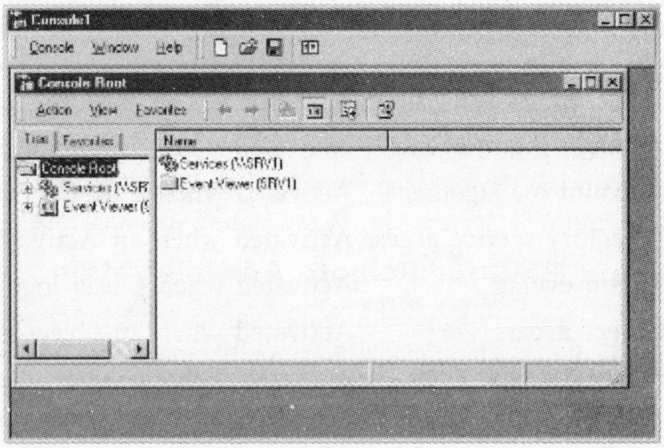

The Windows Script Host (WSH) is built into Windows 2000 and Windows 98. In addition, Windows 95 and Windows NT can run WSH, so scripts are portable across the Windows spectrum. Scripts run under WSH using Wscript.exe and Cscript.exe. Wscript.exe runs in the background, and Cscript.exe runs at the command prompt. To run a script from the command line, the syntax is

Cscript <scriptname.extension> [options] [arguments]

To view the entire list of host options, enter Cscript //? at a command prompt. The most important options are listed below.

- //B Specifies batch mode; script errors and prompts are not displayed
- //D Enables active debugging
- //T: nn Indicates the maximum time in seconds that the script is permitted to run

Real World Uses for WSH WSH is useful for logon and logoff scripts that can be assigned to users—individually or as a group—or to computers. The other important use for WSH is the creation of user accounts, a tedious process at best and, in a large enterprise, quite impossible without scripts. Chapter 9 covers Group Policy objects and the creation of user accounts.

Auditing Events

Auditing certain computers, users, and operating system events is a necessary part of network administration. You choose what's to be audited and then, by reviewing the event logs, track usage patterns, security problems, and network traffic trends. Beware of the impulse to audit everything, however. The more events you audit, the bigger the logs. Reviewing huge event logs is a painful chore, and eventually no one looks at them anymore. Therefore, it's critical to decide on an auditing policy that protects your network without creating a large administrative burden. Also bear in mind that every audited event results in a small increase in performance overhead.

By default, all auditing categories are turned off when Windows 2000 is installed. Table below lists the categories of events that can be audited.

Auditing categories

Event Category	Description
Account logon events	Activated when a domain controller receives a logon request
Account management	Activated when a user account or group is created or changed
Directory service access	Activated when an Active Directory object is accessed
Logon events	Activated when a user logs on or logs off
Object access	Activated when an object is accessed
Policy change	Activated when a policy affecting security, user rights, or auditing is modified
Privilege use	Activated when a user right is used to perform an action
Process tracking	Activated when an application executes an action that is being tracked
System events	Activated when a computer is rebooted or shut down or another event occurs that affects security

Every audited event tells you something, but it's not always something you need to know. For example, auditing successful logons and logoffs may reveal the use of a stolen password, or it may just produce endless pages showing that your duly authorized users are logging on and off as expected. Auditing logon failures, however, will definitely be rewarding if someone is trying a random password hack.

Before you can audit access to Active Directory objects (described in the next section), you must turn on the Audit Policy setting, using Group Policy. To do so, as well as to enable auditing of any of the other categories in Table next, follow these steps:

Choose Active Directory Users and Computers from the Administrative Tools menu.

Right-click the domain name in the console tree, and choose Properties from the shortcut menu.

Click the Group Policy tab and then the Edit button.

In the left pane of the Group Policy console, click your way through Computer Configuration, Windows Settings, Security Settings, and Local Policies to reach Audit Policy.

Right-click the event category you want to audit, and choose Security.

In the dialog box that opens, select the check box to define the setting, and select the option to audit successful and/or failed attempts.

Audit Settings for Objects

Assuming that you've turned on a policy setting for auditing an Active Directory object, you create audit settings by following these steps:

Right-click the object you want to audit, and choose Properties from the shortcut menu. Click the Security tab.

Click the Advanced button, and then click the Auditing tab.

Click Add to set up auditing for a new group or user. Make your selection and click OK.

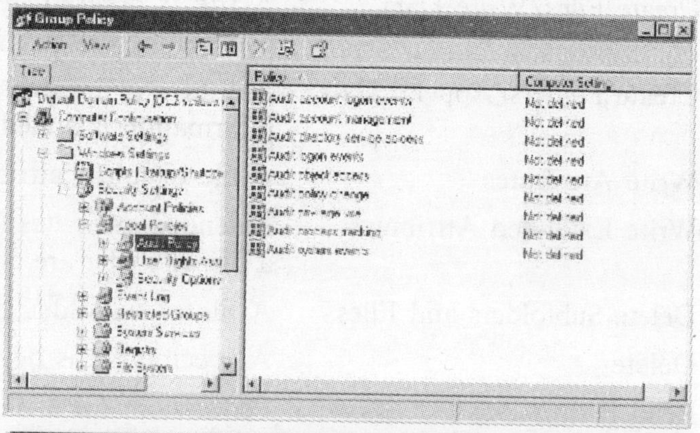

In the Auditing Entry For Collwin dialog box, select the objects you want to audit from the Apply Onto drop-down list. Then, in the Access, select each type of access that you want audited. Click OK when you're finished.

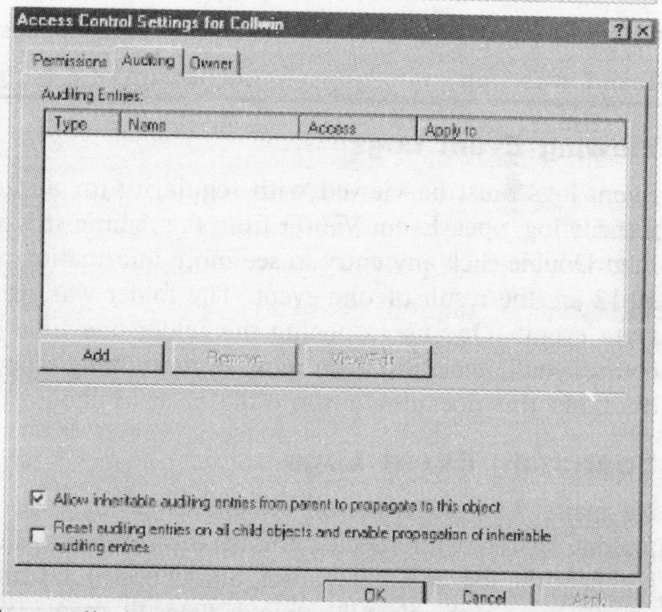

By default, audit settings are inherited by child objects. On the Auditing tab of the Access Control Settings for Collwin box is a check box for allowing inheritable auditing entries. Clear this box and the audit settings for this object will remain constant, even if the parent object's audit settings are changed. In addition, clearing the box will remove any audit settings that have already been inherited. The second check box on this tab resets existing auditing and allows audit entries to be inherited from the parent object once again.

Real World Auditing Cautions Windows 2000 allows such granularity that it's possible—no, easy—to create a real morass when selecting audit settings. So many items can show up in the event log that really important issues may be lost in the crowd. Be very careful when deciding what events need to be audited. Audit as few as is reasonable. You can always add events later as circumstances dictate.

File system events that can be audited

Event	Activated When
Traverse Folder/Execute File	A folder is traversed (that is, someone passes through the folder on the way to a parent folder or a child folder) or an application is run
List Folder/Read Data	A folder is opened or data is viewed in files
Read Attributes	The attributes of a file or folder are viewed
Read Extended Attributes	Extended attributes (defined and created by programs) of a file or folder are viewed
Create Files/Write Data	A file is created inside a folder or a file is changed, overwriting existing information in the file
Create Folders/Append Data	A folder is created inside the folder being audited or information is added to an existing file
Write Attributes	A file or folder attribute is changed
Write Extended Attributes	Extended attributes (defined and created by programs) of a file or folder are changed
Delete Subfolders and Files	A file or subfolder is deleted
Delete	A specific file is deleted
Read Permissions	Permissions for a file or folder are viewed
Change Permissions	Permissions for a file or folder are modified
Take Ownership	Ownership of a file or folder changes

Viewing Event Logs

Event logs must be viewed with regularity for auditing to have any effect. To view the security log, open Event Viewer from the Administrative Tools menu and then click Security Log. Double-click any entry to see more information about it. The security entries in Figure 10-12 are the result of one event. The folder was set to audit successful List Folder/Read Data events. One user opening the folder one time generated all the entries you see. Of course, you'll generally learn more from auditing failed events than from auditing successful ones, but this does demonstrate the need to choose one's auditing battles carefully.

Searching Event Logs

No matter how selective you are, the event logs will mix all sorts of information together, making searches for specific information difficult. To search for a specific type of event, highlight the log in Event Viewer, and choose Find from the View menu. In the Find dialog box (Figure next), select the type or types of events you want returned. Table next describes the other options in the Find dialog box.

Filtering Event Logs

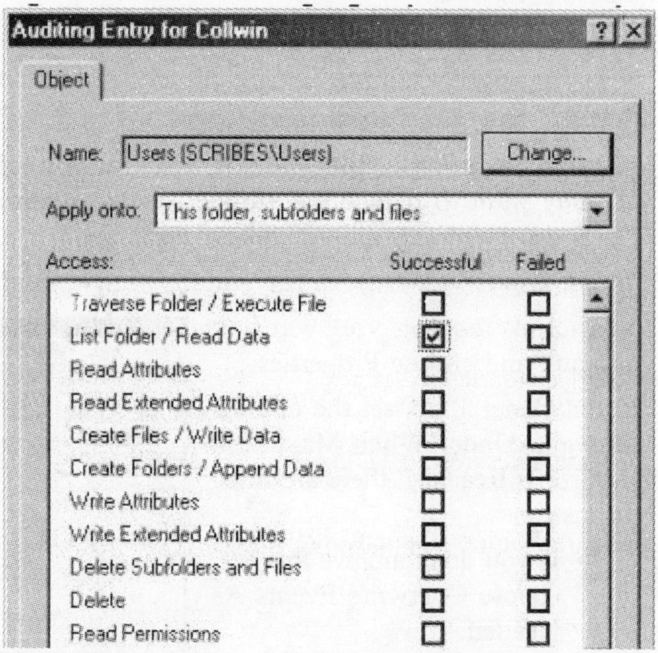

If you don't have enough specific information to locate what you need, you can filter an event log for certain types of information. To use event log filtering, follow these steps:

Choose Event Viewer from the Administrative Tools menu.

Right-click the log you want to search, and choose Properties from the shortcut menu.

Click the Filter tab. Table next describes the fields on this tab. Click OK when you're ready to start the filtering.

The log appears, filtered as you requested. To view the full, unfiltered log again, return to the Filter tab and click Clear.

Options for filtering event logs

Option	Use to Search or Filter For
Information	Notification that some major operation has been performed successfully.
Warning	Notification of some problem or potential problem. Warnings may or may not be significant. For example, replication performed after repeated tries will generate a warning.
Error	Notification of an important event. Errors signify a loss of data or a loss of function. For example, failure of a service to start during boot up will generate an error.
Success Audit	Events audited for success.
Failure Audit	Events audited for failure.
Event Source	A source for an event, such as a system component or a program.
Category	Events by category, such as logon/logoff, policy change, or process tracking.
Event ID	The specific ID number assigned to each logged event.
User	A specific user.
Computer	A specific computer.
From	Events after a specific date. The default is the first date in the log. You can click the drop-down box to select events on a specific date.

To	Events before a specific date. The default is the last date in the file.

Setting the Size of Event Logs

When an event log is full, a dialog box will pop up to notify you. If this happens often, you may want to reduce the number of items being reported or increase the size of the log. To set event log options, follow these steps.

Choose Event Viewer from the Administrative Tools menu.

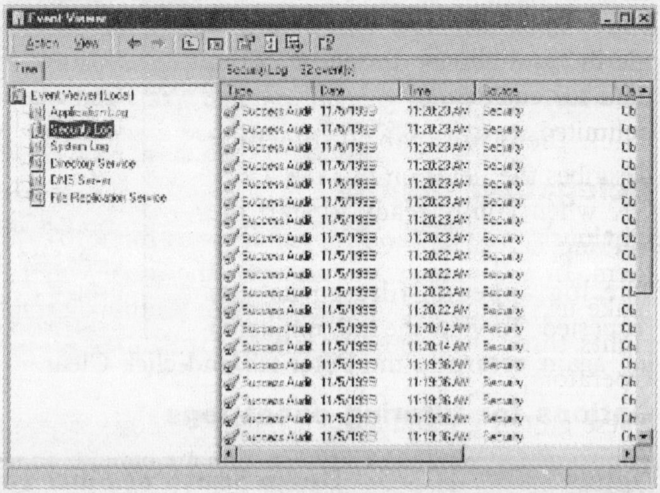

Right-click the log you want to configure and choose Properties.

On the General tab, set the options you want. Under When Maximum Log Size Is Reached, there are three options.

- If you don't archive this log, choose Overwrite Events As Needed.
- If you archive this log at regular intervals, you can select the Overwrite Events Older Than option. Fill in the appropriate number of days.
- Do Not Overwrite Events, the last option, means that the log must be cleared manually. When the maximum log size is reached, new events will simply not be recorded.

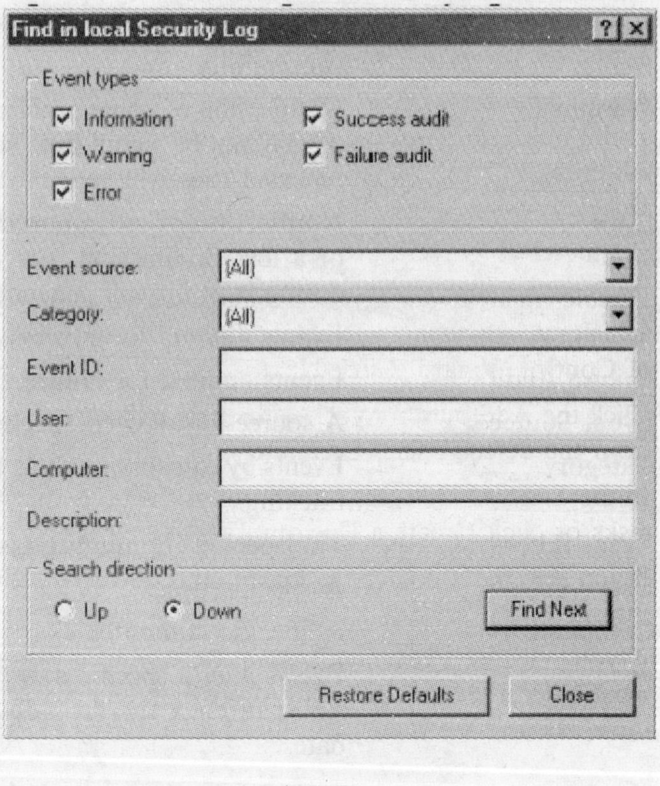

Click OK when you're finished.

Real World Calling a Halt When the Log Is Full Maybe you are so security-conscious that none of the event log options are acceptable. If you absolutely, positively mustn't lose a single security event, you can set the computer to halt when the security log is full. A registry change is necessary to make this happen. First, set Event Log Wrapping to either Do Not Overwrite Events or Overwrite Events Older Than n

Days. Then start RegEdit.exe and proceed to HKEY_LOCAL_MACHINE \SYSTEM \CurentControlSet \Control \Lsa \CrashOnAuditFail, and change the value to 1.

This setting will take effect after a reboot and then, when the log is full, the system will simply stop. After restarting, only administrators will be able to log on until the security log is cleared. This is a drastic measure, but it is necessary in some cases.

Archiving Event Logs

If you will be using event logs to track system usage trends, you must save them. To archive an event log, open Event Viewer from the Administrative Tools menu, and click the log you want to archive. Then, from the Action menu, choose Save Log As. If you save the file in the event log format (.EVT), it can be reopened in Event Viewer, and all the binary data for each event will be retained. You can also save logs as .TXT files or in comma-delimited format (.CSV), but in those cases the binary data isn't saved.

Delegating Control

Obviously, one of the simplest ways to minimize your administrative chores is to delegate them. In a Windows NT network, the usual way to grant broad administrative rights is to make users members of the Domain Admins group. Or you can parcel out administrative rights through some combination of other groups such as Print Operators or Server Operators.

These groups are still available, but Windows 2000 makes delegation even simpler: it allows you to assign responsibility for management of some portion of the namespace to another user or group. The recipient of the delegated authority can have complete administrative control within the area chosen but not the sweeping administrative rights inherent in being a member of the Domain Admins group.

Assign control by organizational unit (OU) whenever possible, because assigning permissions at the object level quickly becomes too complicated to be worthwhile. Records of security assignments are critical, so keep track of all delegations. To delegate control, use the Delegation of Control Wizard, which always assigns permissions at the OU level.

Open Active Directory Users and Computers from the Administrative Tools menu.

Double-click the domain node, and then right-click the container whose control you want to delegate and choose Delegate Control from the shortcut menu. This starts the Delegation of Control Wizard. Click Next.

Click the Add button to select the user or group to be granted control. Make your selection from the Select Users, Computers, or Groups screen (Figure next).

In the Tasks to Delegate screen, select the tasks that you want to delegate. Select predefined tasks or click Create a Custom Task. Click Next.

If you selected a predefined task, you're essentially finished. Review the summary and click Finished.

If you selected Create a Custom Task, you're presented with more specific choices as to what objects you're delegating control on and the specific permissions to be granted. When those choices are made, you'll see a summary of the delegation. Click Finished.

Using Task Scheduler

While it's true that you could—and still can—schedule tasks using the AT command, as described later in this chapter, Task Scheduler provides a graphical interface and is much easier to use. Tasks can be scheduled during off-hours and to run repeatedly. The Task Scheduler service is started at boot up and runs in the background. To use Task Scheduler, open Control Panel, double-click the Scheduled Tasks folder, and then follow these steps:

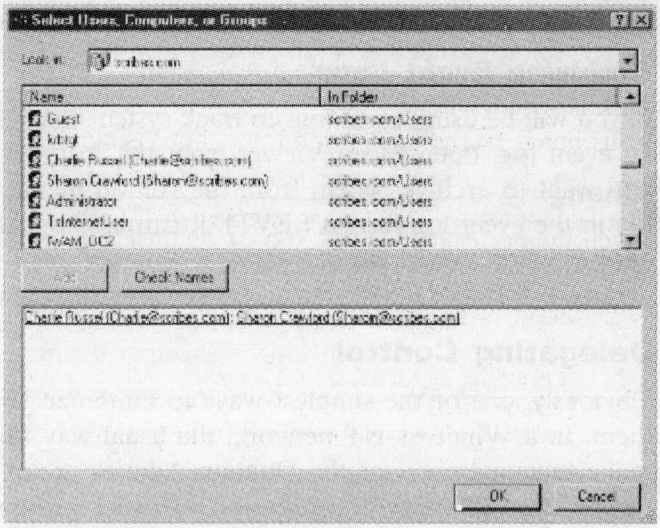

In the Scheduled Tasks window, double-click the Add Scheduled Task entry. This starts the Scheduled Task Wizard. Click Next.

Select a program from the screen (Figure next), or click the Browse button to locate another program. Click Next.

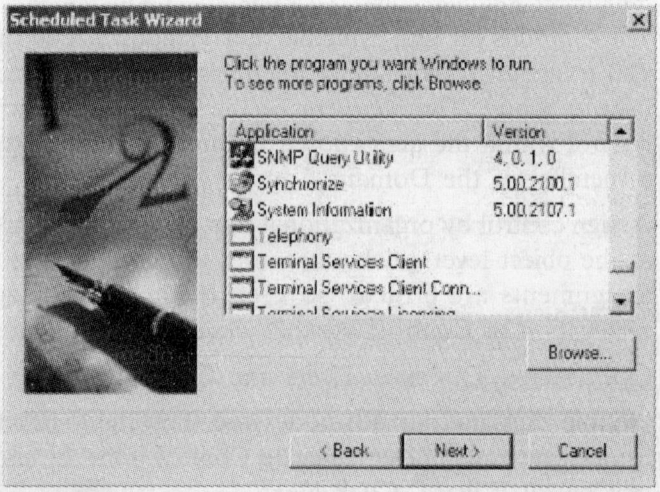

Supply a name for the task, and then indicate how often you want it performed. Click Next.

Select the time of day you want the task performed. Depending on the timing you've selected, you'll also need to specify one of the following:

- Daily Task Every day, every n days, or weekdays only.
- Weekly Task Every n weeks; supply the day of the week.
- Monthly Task Select the day of the month, and select which months.

Supply the user name and password for the user who will be scheduling tasks. Click Next. Note that the account you specify must have the privileges necessary to run the task. For example, if you're scheduling a backup program, the user must have backup rights.

If you need to specify parameters for the task being scheduled, select the check box next to Open Advanced Properties, and then click Next.

Make the necessary changes, and click OK.

For tasks to run as expected, it's important that the computer's date and time be set correctly. Many programs will start to run in Task Scheduler and then pause, waiting for input that never comes—or that comes much later, when someone looks at the machine to see what's going on. To make sure you have all of the parameters for a task to be able to run successfully, open a command prompt and type program_name /?. Then right-click the task in the Scheduled Tasks window and choose Properties. Enter the necessary parameters in the Run text box and click OK.

You might want to schedule a task to run right away so you can test its performance. If a task is scheduled by a user and that user isn't logged on at the scheduled time, the task still runs but is in the background and not visible.

Changing a Schedule

Even the best schedule can run up against reality now and again, so you need to be able to adjust your planned events.

- To run a task immediately, right-click the task's icon in the Scheduled Tasks window and choose Run from the shortcut menu.
- To stop a task that's running, right-click the task's icon in the Scheduled Tasks window and choose End Task. If the scheduled task has been set up to start another task, the End Task command will halt only the original scheduled task.
- To temporarily halt all Task Scheduler actions, open the Advanced menu in the Scheduled Tasks window and choose Pause Task Scheduler. Any tasks that do not start because Task Scheduler is paused will run again only at their next scheduled time. To start Task Scheduler up again, click the same menu and choose Continue Task Scheduler.
- To stop using Task Scheduler, open the Advanced menu in the Scheduled Tasks window and choose Stop Using Task Scheduler. No scheduled tasks will run, and the Task Scheduler service will no longer start automatically when the system is rebooted.

Tracking Task Scheduler

The system maintains a detailed log of Task Scheduler's activities. To view the log, double-click Scheduled Tasks in Control Panel. From the Advanced menu, choose View Log. This opens a log like the one shown in Figure next, with the most recent entry at the bottom of the window. The Details view in the Scheduled Tasks window displays information about each task (Figure next).

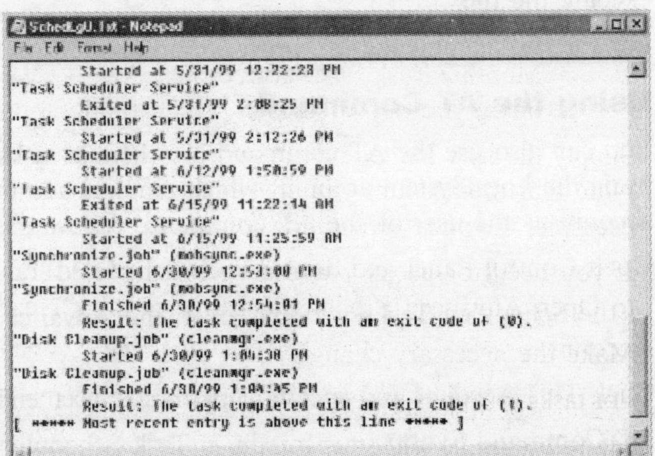

The Task Scheduler log.

The Details view for scheduled tasks.

If a scheduled task doesn't execute as expected, right-click the task in the

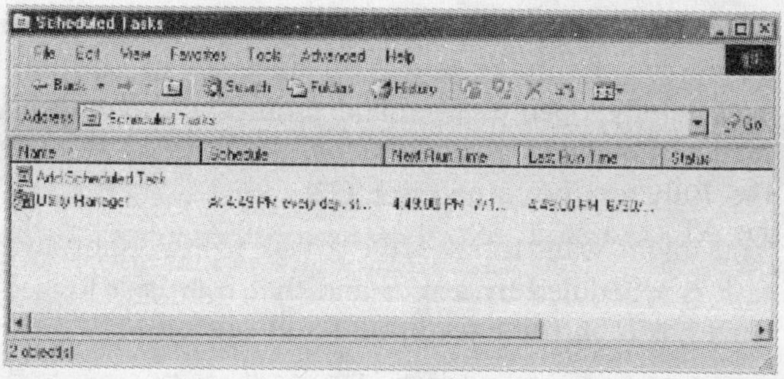

Task Scheduler window and choose Properties from the shortcut menu. Verify that the task is in fact enabled. (The Enabled check box in the Task Properties window should be selected.)

Viewing Tasks on a Remote Computer

If you are an administrator of a remote computer running Windows NT or Windows 2000, you can view and edit the Task Scheduler settings on that computer. Find the computer in the My Network Places window (in Windows 2000) or in the Network Neighborhood window (in Windows NT), and then double-click the Scheduled Tasks folder.

To view and edit scheduled tasks on computers running Windows 95 or later, the remote computer must

- Have remote administration enabled
- Specify your user account as having remote administrative access
- Share the hard disk on which the Scheduled Tasks folder resides

Real World Autocompletion on the Command Line The command line may be moribund, but it's far from dead. Windows 2000 includes actual improvements in command-line functions, such as file and folder autocompletion. To turn this feature on, open a command-line window and type cmd /f:on. Now you can avoid typing long file or folder names at the command line. For example, to navigate into the Program Files folder from the root of the system drive (typically C:\), you'd type c:\cd p and then press Ctrl+D. The command will expand immediately to c:\cd "Program Files". Press Enter to invoke that path.

The feature will also work with files. Let's say you're in C:\Program Files\Windows Media Player and you would like to execute Mplayer.exe. At the command line, type mp and then press Ctrl+F. The path will expand to include Mplayer.exe. Press Enter to actually execute the file.

For the full documentation, open a command window and type help cmd.

Using the AT Command

You can also use the AT command to schedule tasks. By default, the AT command is run using the LocalSystem account, which requires administrative privileges. To specify another account as the user of the AT command, follow these steps:

Open Control Panel and double-click Scheduled Tasks.

In the Scheduled Tasks window, open the Advanced menu and then choose AT Service Account.

Click This Account and specify a particular user and password. Click OK.

AT Command Syntax

The command structure for the AT command is as follows:

AT [\\computername] [id] [[/delete]|/delete [/yes]]

AT [\\computername] time [/interactive] [/every:date[,...] |
/next:date[,...]] command

The following parameters can be used with the AT command. Used without parameters, the AT command returns a list of scheduled commands.

- \\computername Specifies a remote computer. Without this parameter, the local computer is assumed.
- id Indicates the identification number, if one is assigned.
- /delete Cancels a scheduled command. If no identification number is specified, all scheduled commands on the computer will be canceled.
- /yes Forces a yes answer to all system queries when canceling all commands.
- time Specifies when the command is to run, expressed as hours:minutes in 24-hour notation.
- /interactive Allows the task to interact with the desktop of the user logged on at the time the job is run.
- /every: date [,...] Runs the command on the date specified. The date can be specified as one or more days of the week (M, T, W, Th, F, S, Su) or as one or more days of the month (numbers 1 through 31). Separate multiple dates with commas. If this parameter is omitted, the current day of the month is assumed.
- /next: date [,...] Runs the command on the next occurrence of the specified day. If this parameter is omitted, the current day of the month is assumed.
- command Indicates the program, batch file, or command to be run. If a path is required, use the Uniform Naming Convention (UNC) path.

Here are some important facts to keep in mind about the AT command:

- The AT command doesn't automatically load Cmd, the command interpreter, so if the command parameter docsn't point to an executable file, you must explicitly specify Cmd, followed by the /c switch, at the beginning of the command.
- Commands scheduled using AT run as background processes, so there is no displayed output. To redirect output to a file, use the redirection symbol (>). The redirection symbol must be preceded by the escape symbol (^), so a sample command would be at retrieve.bat ^>c:\daylog.txt.
- If you have to use a drive letter to connect to a shared directory, include an AT command to disconnect the drive when the task is completed. Otherwise, the assigned drive letter will be neither available nor seen at the command prompt.

You can switch back and forth between the AT command and Task Scheduler, although there are some limitations. For example, if you schedule a task using AT and later modify that same task using Task Scheduler, the task is then "owned" by Task Scheduler and you can no longer access it using AT.

Repairing Windows 2000

Here are some of the new commands available in the Recovery Console DOS window: • chkdsk—Works pretty much the same way it does in any Windows NT environment. You can enter the chkdsk command to diagnose hard disk problems, or use chkdsk /f to fix problems. This version of chkdsk works with FAT 16, FAT 32, and NTFS partitions. • disable—Disables a malfunctioning service. For example, suppose that the Alerter service is malfunctioning and causing a blue screen of death on boot-up. In such a situation, you can enter the command disable alerter to correct the problem.• diskpart—Works similarly to fdisk, in that it allows you to create, delete, and manage hard-disk partitions. Of course, fdisk still exists and functions properly within the Recovery Console.• enable—Works like the disable command. It is used to enable services that have been disabled.• exit—Exits the Recovery Console and reboots the computer into Windows 2000. If you don't want to do an immediate reboot, it is safe to power off the system while running the Recovery Console.• extract—Extracts files from the Windows 2000 CD. As you probably know, the Windows 2000 system files are compressed on the CD to save space. Should you need to replace a damaged file, you can use the extract command to extract the needed file from its CAB file on the Windows 2000 CD.• fixboot—Writes a new boot sector to the hard disk. You'll use this command if your boot sector has been damaged by a virus or other catastrophe.• fixmbr—Writes a new master boot record to the hard disk.• helpLists more commands than space permits me to cover. It also covers the syntax of each command and some common uses of the various commands.• listsvc—Displays the names of and some basic information about all the services on the system. Obviously, the enable and disable commands are useless to you if you can't remember the exact name of the service in question.• logon—Lets you log in to the Recovery Console using a different user account.• systemroot—Automatically takes you to the system root folder (usually \WINNT\SYSTEM32). This command is basically a shortcut. It's especially useful if you're unsure which folder is acting as the system root.

As you can see, repairing a failed copy of Windows NT 4.0 can be difficult and time consuming, at best. However, Windows 2000 has a much better solution directly built into the operating system. The Recovery Console utility lets you access the hard disk of a failed system directly from the command prompt.

Once you access the command prompt, you can perform a variety of hard-disk repair functions by using built-in utilities. You can also perform any necessary file manipulations regardless of the file system or the type of hard disk the files reside on.

About the only edge ERD Commander Professional (discussed in the sidebar "Repairing Windows NT with ERD Commander Professional") has over the Recovery Console is the ability to reset passwords. This ability is very handy, should someone "accidentally" change the Administrator password, because you can't access the Recovery Console without providing the Administrator password. Fortunately, according to the Winternals Web site, ERD Commander Professional will work with Windows 2000 as well as with Windows NT 4.0. Therefore, I recommend keeping a copy of ERD Commander Professional around for resetting changed or damaged passwords. I recommend using the Recovery Console for all other critical Windows 2000 repairs.

Revision

1. The Microsoft Windows 2000 Server operating system includes integrated Web and application services.
2. Windows 2000 Server includes the built-in Web service, Internet Information Services (IIS) 5.0, which is accessible from popular browsers.
3. The key to building distributed applications is the ability to break software applications into modules, called components, which are the building blocks of distributed applications.
4. Microsoft broadened the applicability of COM by introducing transaction processing support as a separate service called Microsoft Transaction Server (MTS).
5. Windows 2000 introduces the next generation of the component object model, COM+.
6. MSMQ, a separate technology introduced in the Windows NT 4.0 timeframe, complements the capabilities inherent to COM and transaction services.
7. Windows 2000 Server provides high-performance access to all types of information (including relational and non-relational data) across an organization from the desktop to the enterprise.
8. Organizations that build applications on the Windows 2000 platform can take advantage of integrated system services and capabilities.
9. The Windows DNA 2000 architecture provides a blueprint that helps developers design and build distributed business applications using technologies that are integral to the Windows 2000 platform.
10. Microsoft Windows 2000 supplies plenty of tools, including ones that allow you to delegate tasks to other users or groups, use scripts to automate tasks, and schedule tasks to run periodically.
11. Recommended administrative practice dictates that an administrator be logged on to a privileged account (one with administrative rights) only while doing chores that require privileges.

Multiple Choice Questions

1. MTS stands for:
   (a) Microsoft Transaction Server
   (b) Microsoft Transit Server
   (c) Microsoft Table Server
2. COM stands for:
   (a) Common Oriented Model
   (b) Component Object Model
   (c) Common Object Model

True/False Questions

1. Windows 2000 Server includes the built-in Web service, Internet Information Services (IIS) 5.0, which is accessible from popular browsers.
2. Microsoft broadened the applicability of COM by introducing transaction processing support as a separate service called Microsoft Transaction Server (MTS).
3. Windows 2000 introduces the next generation of the component object model, COM–.
4. Windows 2000 Server provides high-performance access to all types of information (including relational and non-relational data) across an organization from the desktop to the enterprise.
5. The Windows DNA 2000 architecture provides a blueprint that helps developers design and build distributed business applications using technologies that are integral to the Windows 2000 platform.
6. Recommended administrative practice dictates that an administrator be logged on to a privileged account (one with administrative rights) only while doing chores that require privileges.

Descriptive Questions

1. What is Windows 2000?
2. What Distributed Applications?
3. Describe The Component Object Model.
4. How Windows 2000 handles Data Access and XML?
5. What is Windows DNA 2000?
6. Describe the various options of installing Windows 2000.
7. How would you repair Windows 2000?
8. Which tools are used in repairing Windows 2000?

Answers to Objective Type Questions

Multiple Choice Questions

1. a 2. b

True False Questions

1. T 2. T 3. F 4. T
5. T 6. T

T Model Test Papers

Max. Marks 100

Time: 2.30 Hrs

Model Test Paper 1

Computer Applications and Hardware Section

Q.1 Fill in the blanks **(1 marks x 10)**

1. SIMM stands for _____________.
2. EPROM stands for _____________.
3. MBT stands for ________________.
4. UMPC stands for ____________
5. The three main units of computer are: Keyboard, Central Processing Unit and ____________.
6. PC XT ran on Intel ____ processor.
7. The mouse which is now commonly used is ______________
8. USB keyboards are compatible with ______________
9. POST stands for _______________
10. TFT stands for ______________

(Monitor, Erasable Programmable Read Only Memory , Thin Film Transistor, Windows, Ultra Mobile PC, Single In-line Memory Module, Power-On Self Test, Optical, 8088, Master Boot Record)

Q.2 T/F write correct answer in Bracket [] **(1 marks x 10)**

1. RAM is Random Access Memory . [ ]
2. Intel released the first version of AGP; appropriately titled "AGP specification 1.0," in 1977. It included both the 1x and 2x speeds. Specification 2.0 documented AGP 4X and 3.0 documented 8X. [ ]
3. Depending on their use, bus is divided into three major types: Data bus, Address bus and Control bus [ ]
4. An EPROM has a quartz window on the face of the chip that exposes the chip's interior circuits. [ ]
5. New floppy disk need not be formatted. [ ]
6. Keyboard need 7 W of power supply. [ ]
7. DMP printers can print multiple copies of print output at a time. [ ]
8. Keyboard is the main ouput device of the computer. [ ]

9. A web camera is basically a low-end digital video camera with low resolution and fixed focus lens. [ ]
10. An extended partition is secondary to the primary partition(s). [ ]

Q.3 Multiple Choice Questions (1 marks x 10)

1. RAM stands for:
   (a) Random Allowed Memory (b) Ready Access Memory
   (c) Random Access Memory
2. Maximum memory in PC AT could be ___ MB:
   (a) 8 (b) 16
   (c) 32
3. CISC stands for :
   (a) Complex Instruction Save Computer
   (b) Complex Instruction Set Computer
   (c) Complex Instruction Small Computer
4. PPI stands for .
   (a) Program Peripheral Interface
   (b) Programmable Peripheral Interleave
   (c) Programmable Peripheral Interface
5. A Zip drive is used to:
   (a) Storage backup (b) Compress data
   (c) Hide data (d) None of these.
6. Every new floppy disk has to be _______.
   (a) stored (b) formatted
   (c) labelled
7. CD-ROM stand for:
   (a) Current Disk Read Only Memory
   (b) Compact Disk Read Only Memory
   (c) Close Disk Read Only Memory
8. WORM stands for:
   (a) Write Once, Read Many (b) Write Once, Read Maybe
   (c) Write Over, Read Many
9. Web camera is
   (a) a camera (b) an input device
   (c) both.
10. Processor is attached to:
    (a) Motherboard (b) Monitor
    (c) Keyboard.

Q.4 Short answer type questions (2 marks x 10)

1. What is BIOS?
2. Give difference between ROM and RAM.

3. What is the command to display a directory pagewise?
4. What does the symbol \(backslash) stand for?
5. What is prompt command used for?
6. What do you understand by Cache Memory?
7. Describe Motherboard.
8. What is Super I/O Chip?
9. What do you understand by Access Time?
10. What is WORM?

Do any five of the following

Q.5 Answer the following: (5 x 2 Marks)

(a) Describe hand held computers.

(b) What are rescue disks?

Q.6 Answer the following: (5 x 2 Marks)

(a) What is Data Recovery?

(b) What is POST?

Q.7 Answer the following: (5 x 2 Marks)

(a) How would you install Windows 98?

(b) What is SMPS used for?

Q.8 Answer the following: (5 x 2 Marks)

(a) Explain the working principal of LASER printer?

(b) What is an Erasable disk?

Q.9 Answer the following: (5 x 2 Marks)

(a) Why are CDs more common?

(b) What is Controller Chip?

Q.10 Answer the following: (5 x 2 Marks)

(a) Describe the Rename command.

(b) What is Central Processing Unit?

Q.11 Answer the following: (5 x 2 Marks)

(a) Describe the various types of operating systems.

(b) Describe the various bus slots.

Q.12 Answer the following: (5 x 2 Marks)

(a) What all was there on PC AT motherboard?

(b) What is SCSI hard disk?

Answers to Objective Type Questions

Fill in the blanks

1. Single In-line Memory Module
2. Erasable Programmable Read Only Memory
3. Master Boot Record
4. Ultra Mobile PC
5. Monitor
6. 8088
7. Optical
8. Windows
9. Power-On Self Test
10. Thin Film Transistor

True False Questions

1. T	2. F	3. T	4. T
5. F	6. T	7. T	8. F
9. T	10. T		

Multiple Choice Questions

1. a	2. b	3. b	4. c
5. a	6. b	7. b	8. a
9. c	10. a		

Max. Marks 100

Time: 2.30 Hrs

Model Test Paper 2

Computer Applications and Hardware Section

Q.1 Fill in the blanks (1 marks x 10)

1. The main directory of the hard disk is ______________
2. Display card generates ______________
3. UART stand for ______________
4. DDR SDRAM stands for ______________
5. SAM stand for ______________
6. Time shows the time in hh:mm and ___ format:
7. FDC stands for ______________
8. PROM stands for ______________
9. Pen drive is based upon ______________
10. STN stands for ______________

(Universal Asynchronous Receiver Transmitter, Floppy Drive Controller, Double Data Rate Synchronous Dynamic Random Access Memory, ss, Super Twist Nematic, Program Read Only Memory, Security Accounts Manager, Optical technology, Root directory, Graphics)

Q.2 T/F write correct answer in Bracket [] (1 marks x 10)

1. DVD stand stands for digital video disc or digital versatile disc, is the next generation of optical disc storage technology. [ ]
2. Most time-sharing systems use time-sliced, non pre-emptive scheduling. [ ]
3. Use BATCH command to run commands that are specified in a text file. [ ]
4. Use CLS command to copy a file. [ ]
5. Some kinds of logical damage can be mistakenly attributed to physical damage. [ ]
6. Laptops' upgradeability is not limited, both for technical and economic reasons. [ ]
7. RD command is used to create a directory. [ ]
8. DDR2 SDRAM is very similar to DDR SDRAM, but doubles the minimum read or write unit again, to 4 consecutive words. [ ]
9. ROM is Read Over Memory. [ ]
10. The SATA power and data cables are the most noticeable change from Parallel ATA. [ ]

Q.3 Multiple Choice Questions (1 marks x 10)

1. A copy of the current instruction is stored in:
   (a) Instruction Register (b) Working Register
   (c) General Register

2. LPX stands for:
   (a) Low Profile Extended (b) Low Period Extended
   (c) Low Profile Extra
3. DIMM stands for :
   (a) Dual In-line Memory Mode (b) Dual In-line Memory Module
   (c) Duet In-line Memory Module
4. RTC stand for :
   (a) Real Time Clock (b) Real Time Clear
   (c) Road Time Clock
5. DDR3 SDRAM stands for .
   (a) Double Data Rate Two Synchronous Dynamic Random Access Memory
   (b) Double Data Rate To Synchronous Dynamic Random Access Memory
   (c) Double Data Rate Three Synchronous Dynamic Random Access Memory
6. Which one is optical storage media:
   (a) HDD (b) Floppy disk
   (c) Pen drive (d) DVD.
7. DVD stands for:
   (a) Direct Video Disc (b) Data Video Disc
   (c) Digital Video Disc
8. Average power needed by motherboard is :
   (a) 30 W (b) 35 W
   (c) 25 W
9. To rename a file, you give the command as:
   (a) name (b) REN
   (c) re
10. Hard disk is a ______ device.
   (a) Storage (b) Display
   (c) Removable

Q.4 Short answer type questions (2 marks x 10)

1. What are the different options of the DIR command?
2. How is it possible to see the system date?
3. What is the root directory?
4. How is memory used in personal computer?
5. Where is battery placed in the motherboard?
6. What are the types of storage devices?

7. Describe the cables and connectors of eSATA
8. What is floppy disk? Explain contraction and its working?
9. What are Optical Disks?
10. What is multimedia keyboard?

Do any five of the following

Q.5 Answer the following: **(5 x 2 Marks)**

(a) Describe the various error codes of POST.

(b) Describe the working of DVD.

Q.6 Answer the following: **(5 x 2 Marks)**

(a) What is access time of hard disk?

(b) What is Debug Card?

Q.7 Answer the following: **(5 x 2 Marks)**

(a) What is DOS used for?

(b) Explain the working of Mouse.

Q.8 Answer the following: **(5 x 2 Marks)**

(a) How would you copy BIOS?

(b) How would you install the hard disk?

Q.9 Answer the following: **(5 x 2 Marks)**

(a) Which are the different type of scanners?

(b) How would you install floppy disk drive?

Q.10 Answer the following: **(5 x 2 Marks)**

(a) What is a Combo drive?

(b) Describe zip drive.

Q.11 Answer the following: **(5 x 2 Marks)**

(a) What is Laptop?

(b) Compare SMPS with the main supply.

Q.12 Answer the following: **(5 x 2 Marks)**

(a) How would you install the CD Drive?

(b) What is an operating system?

Answers to Objective Type Questions

Fill in the blanks

1. Root directory
2. Graphics
3. Universal Asynchronous Receiver Transmitter
4. Double Data Rate Synchronous Dynamic Random Access Memory
5. Security Accounts Manager
6. ss
7. Floppy Drive Controller
8. Program Read Only Memory
9. Optical technology
10. Super Twist Nematic

True False Questions

1. T	2. T	3. T	4. F
5. T	6. F	7. T	8. T
9. F	10. T		

Multiple Choice Questions

1. a	2. a	3. b	4. a
5. c	6. d	7. c	8. b
9. b	10. a		

Max. Marks 100

Time: 2.30 Hrs

Model Test Paper 3

Computer Applications and Hardware Section

Q.1 Fill in the blanks (1 marks x 10)

1. PDA stands for ________________
2. CMOS stands for ______________
3. BIOS stands for ______________
4. IDE stands for ___________________
5. Line printers print a _____ at a time.
6. CD ROM storage is ____________ MB.
7. RPM stands for ______________________
8. RISC stands for ________________
9. SRAM stands for _________________
10. DRAM stands for ____________

(Basic Input/Output System, line, Revolutions Per Minute, Integrated Device Electronics, Personal Digital Assistants, Static Random Access Memory, Line, Dynamic Random Access Memory, 750, Reduced Instruction Set Computers, Complementary metal–oxide–semiconductor)

Q.2 T/F write correct answer in Bracket [] (1 marks x 10)

1. The main CD subassembly called a drive engine, which uses to hold eject, spin, and read the disk. [ ]
2. Dot-matrix printers are also called serial printers. [ ]
3. In the Serial Interface Technique, the data is transmitted as 0-bit at a time through a single wire. [ ]
4. A firewall is a system that prevents unauthorized use and access to your computer. [ ]
5. Tablet PC, which is essentially a laptop with a touchscreen. [ ]
6. A password is a form of secret authentication data that is used to control access to a resource. [ ]
7. There are seven generation of computers. [ ]
8. A Sound card can input and output sound under control of computer programs. [ ]
9. The operating system does not form a platform for other system software and for application software. [ ]
10. The Athlon 64 X2 is the first dual-core desktop CPU manufactured by AMD. [ ]

Q.3 Multiple Choice Questions (1 marks x 10)

1. RAM consists of binary numbers 1s and :

   (a) 0s (b) 2s

   (c) 3s

2. For listing the files widthwise, we give the command as?
   (a) DIR/P (b) DIR/W
   (c) DIR
3. PC-ATs full form of:
   (a) Personal Computer Area Technology
   (b) Personal Computer Advanced Technology
   (c) Personal Computer Advanced Techniques
4. Spinning speed of each platter of IDE Hard disk is
   (a) 10,000 rpm. (b) 5,000 rpm.
   (c) 7,200 rpm. (d) 6,000 rpm.
5. There are two types of floppies 5¼ and ____:
   (a) 3½ (b) 3¼
   (c) 5½
6. A male connector for the serial interface can have 9 or __ pin:
   (a) 30 (b) 20
   (c) 25
7. Mouse can be used by clicking, double-clicking and :
   (a) biting (b) eating
   (c) dragging
8. Full form of LASER is:
   (a) Light Amplification by Stimulate Emission of Radiation
   (b) Low Amplification by Stimulate Emission of Radiation
   (c) Light Around by Stimulate Emission of Radiation
9. Computer Virus is a:
   (a) Hardware (b) Computer Device
   (c) Software program
10. Operating system is:
   (a) Hardware (b) Computer Device
   (c) Software program

Q.4 Short answer type questions (2 marks x 10)

1. What are PDAs?
2. What is Disk Utility?
3. What is BIOS?
4. What is DVD?
5. What is flash drive?

6. What is a serial port?
7. What is Itanium Processor?
8. What display does your monitor show when you type CD?
9. Describe the personal computer.
10. Draw back panel of CD ROM drive.

Do any five of the following

Q.5 Answer the following: (5 x 2 Marks)

(a) Describe the various connectors of motherboard.

(b) Describe Smartphone

Q.6 Answer the following: (5 x 2 Marks)

(a) List out the various popular operating systems.

(b) What is a 3D mice?

Q.7 Answer the following: (5 x 2 Marks)

(a) Describe the working of PC AT.

(b) How the hard drive works? Explain its internal working.

Q.8 Answer the following: (5 x 2 Marks)

(a) Describe the various classifications of computers.

(b) Describe the syntax of the various commands of Recovery Console.

Q.9 Answer the following: (5 x 2 Marks)

(a) Describe Windows XP Recovery and Console Debugging.

(b) What are CISC and RISC?

Q.10 Answer the following: (5 x 2 Marks)

(a) How would you remove virus?

(b) Which are Electrostatic Printers?

Q.11 Answer the following: (5 x 2 Marks)

(a) What parameters you have to set in Advanced CMOS Setup.

(b) What is a modem?

Q.12 Answer the following: (5 x 2 Marks)

(a) Describe the various formats of DVD.

(b) What is a USB device?

Answers to Objective Type Questions

Fill in the blanks

1. Personal Digital Assistants
2. Complementary metal–oxide–semiconductor
3. Basic Input/Output System
4. Integrated Device Electronics
5. Line
6. 750
7. Revolutions Per Minute
8. Reduced Instruction Set Computers
9. Static Random Access Memory
10. Dynamic Random Access Memory

True False Questions

1. T	2. T	3. F	4. T
5. T	6. T	7. T	8. T
9. F	10. T		

Multiple Choice Questions

1. a	2. b	3. b	4. c
5. a	6. b	7. c	8. a
9. c	10. c		

Max. Marks 100
Time: 2.30 Hrs

Model Test Paper 4

Computer Applications and Hardware Section

Q.1 Fill in the blanks (1 marks x 10)

1. The command which will transfer to the root directory is ______________
2. You can change the status of the file using the command ___________
3. Backup files can be restored using the command called ___________
4. The command which is used to shift the command from one directory to another is __________
5. DMA stands for ________________
6. The command would you use to create a new directory ________________
7. BIOS stands for ___________________
8. SRAM stands for ___________________
9. PROM stands for ___________________
10. UART stand for ________________

(CD, Restore, Static Random Access Memory, MD, CD\, Basic Input/Output System, Program Read Only Memory, Universal Asynchronous Receiver Transmitter, Direct Memory Access, Atrib)

Q.2 T/F write correct answer in Bracket [] (1 marks x 10)

1. A digital camera cannot store many more pictures than an ordinary camera. [ ]
2. CD-ROMs can have their metallic substrate or dye layer scratched off; hard disks can suffer any of several mechanical failures, such as head crashes and failed motors; tapes can simply break. [ ]
3. DMP printers have a good photo quality. [ ]
4. A primary (or logical) partition contains two file system. [ ]
5. A hybrid disk, called magneto-optical (MO), combines the best features of magnetic and optical disk technologies. [ ]
6. NLX. known as New Low Profile Extended, motherboard has been a form factor in use with desktops for quite some time. [ ]
7. ROM can be of three type: PROM, EPROM, and EEPROM. [ ]
8. FDD cable consists of 43 pin connector, which is connected between Floppy Drive Controller (FDC) and floppy drive. [ ]
9. A USB cable has four wires: power, ground, D+ and D–. [ ]
10. Mouse is an input device. [ ]

Q.3 Multiple Choice Questions (1 marks x 10)

1. CPU contains Primary Storage, Arithmetic Logic Unit and
   (a) Control Unit
   (b) Data Unit
   (c) Alpha Unit

2. Which of the following does not belong to the Intel's Processor's series:
   (a) 8086 (b) 80186
   (c) 80486 (d) 8051
3. The files in DOS are named in which format ?
   (a) 9 + 2 (b) 10 + 1
   (c) 8 + 3
4. Three types of bus are, Data bus, Address bus and :
   (a) Control Bus (b) Cover bus
   (c) Clear bus
5. Floppy drive connector is of .... Pins.
   (a) 34 (b) 50
   (c) 72
6. The main keys of the Keyboard are Alphabetic, Arrows, Numeric and :
   (a) Function (b) Future
   (c) Faulty
7. SMPS stands for :
   (a) Switched Main Power Supply (b) Switching Main Power Supply
   (c) Save Main Power Supply
8. Printer is a _______ device.
   (a) Input (b) Pointing
   (c) Output
9. USB is a _______ device.
   (a) Input (b) Output
   (c) Both
10. Prompt command is used to change the command prompt from:
   (a) c:\ (b) c:
   (c) c

Q.4 Short answer type questions (2 marks x 10)

1. What are Tablets?
2. What is a boot disk?
3. How mouse works? Explain.
4. Why are CD-ROM preferred over the floppy disks?
5. Type the command to remove a directory. Where must the cursor be to remove a directory or subdirectory?
6. How does USB handle software?

7. Describe Intel 915 Motherboard.
8. Is it possible to see the system time, how?
9. Describe Double Core processor.
10. What is the purpose of Disk Partitioning?

Do any five of the following

Q.5 Answer the following: **(5 x 2 Marks)**

(a) Describe web camera.

(b) Describe troubleshooting of floppy disk drive.

Q.6 Answer the following: **(5 x 2 Marks)**

(a) What are Chain, Band and Drum printers?

(b) Describe what is there in the mechanical and electronic section of floppy disk drive.

Q.7 Answer the following: **(5 x 2 Marks)**

(a) What causes logical damage?

(b) How would you take care of the CD Drive?

Q.8 Answer the following: **(5 x 2 Marks)**

(a) Explain the types of HDD availlable in the market along with the difference.

(b) What is a parallel port?

Q.9 Answer the following: **(5 x 2 Marks)**

(a) What are the features of Intel 910GL Motherboard?

(b) Describe the various functions of the operating system.

Q.10 Answer the following: **(5 x 2 Marks)**

(a) What causes physical damage to the devices?

(b) Describe the various processors in the Xeon family.

Q.11 Answer the following: **(5 x 2 Marks)**

(a) How would you install a keyboard??

(b) How would you modify BIOS?

Q.12 Answer the following: **(5 x 2 Marks)**

(a) Describe the working of Flat-bed scanner.

(b) What are Zip disks?

Answers to Objective Type Questions

Fill in the blanks

1. CD\
2. Atrib
3. Restore
4. CD
5. Direct Memory Access
6. MD
7. Basic Input/Output System
8. Static Random Access Memory
9. Program Read Only Memory
10. Universal Asynchronous Receiver Transmitter

True False Questions

1. F	2. T	3. T	4. F
5. T	6. T	7. T	8. F
9. T	10. F		

Multiple Choice Questions

1. a	2. d	3. c	4. a
5. a	6. a	7. a	8. a
9. c	10. a		

Max. Marks 100

Time: 2.30 Hrs

Model Test Paper 5

Computer Applications and Hardware Section

Q.1 Fill in the blanks **(1 marks x 10)**

1. UMPC stands for ___________
2. POST stands for _______________
3. SIMM stands for ____________.
4. STN stands for ______________________
5. Pen drive is based upon _______________
6. Time shows the time in hh:mm and ___ format:
7. SRAM stands for ________________
8. MBT stands for _______________.
9. You can change the status of the file using the command ___________
10. Backup files can be restored using the command called ______________

(Ultra Mobile PC, Atrib, Static Random Access Memory, Restore, Master Boot Record,Optical technology, ss, Super Twist Nematic, Single In-line Memory Module, Power-On Self Test)

Q.2 T/F write correct answer in Bracket [] **(1 marks x 10)**

1. A file system cannot repair program can read each directory and make sure that these entries exist and point to the correct directories. [ ]
2. Use FORMAT command to format the specified drive to the specified file system. [ ]
3. WinDbg provides source-level debugging through a graphical user interface and a text-based interface. [ ]
4. There are two main types of printers: Impact and Non impact printers. [ ]
5. There are three basic types of Mouse: Mechanical Mouse, Optomechanical Mouse and Optical Mouse. [ ]
6. BIOS, in computing, stands for Basic Input/Output System also correctly known as Basic Integrated Operating System and occasionally Built In Operating System. [ ]
7. REN is used to rename a file. [ ]
8. It's logical then that data stored on read-only memory (ROM) cannot be changed, as its name implies. [ ]
9. The main parts of the computer are: Mouse, Central Processing Unit and Keyboard. [ ]
10. CD-ROM (Compact disk-read only memory) are created at a mastering facility. [ ]

Q.3 Multiple Choice Questions **(1 marks x 10)**

1. Computers are classified into _______ generations:

   (a) 7 (b) 3

   (c) 5

2. A directory whithin a directory is called:
   (a) Sub directory (b) Part directory
   (c) Junior directory
3. What is the new name of IA-64?
   (a) Itanium (b) Pentium
   (c) Athlon
4. Numbers of heads/platter are ....
   (a) 1 (b) 2
   (c) 3
5. Formatting is the process of arranging:
   (a) Tracks (b) Sectors
   (c) Both (a) and (b) (d) None of these.
6. .... is used to write protect a floppy.
   (a) Write Protect Notch (b) Write Paper Notch
   (c) With Protect Notch
7. Mouse is a _______ device.
   (a) Input (b) Pointing
   (c) Output
8. Dot matrix printers are so called because they print characters in terms of :
   (a) Squares (b) Dots
   (c) Circles
9. A modem performs
   (a) Modulation
   (b) Demodulation
   (c) Analog to digital and digital to analog conversion
   (d) All of these.
10. USB cable has __ wires:
   (a) 3 (b) 4
   (c) 5

Q.4 Short answer type questions (2 marks x 10)

1. Describe the various generations of computers.
2. Describe PC chipset.
3. What does the command Backup do?
4. Define the various capacities of DVD.
5. What are AT and ATX power supply?
6. What are the advantages and disadvantages of Dot Matrix Printers?

7. What all you need for installation of the computer?
8. What is Window 98?
9. What is a Computer Virus?
10. What are the technical specifications of USB 2.0?

Do any five of the following

Q.5 Answer the following: (5 x 2 Marks)

(a) What are the characteristics of Chipsets?
(b) What is microprocosser? Explain its working?

Q.6 Answer the following: (5 x 2 Marks)

(a) Describe the process of troubleshooting the mouse.
(b) Describe the various uses of the motherboard.

Q.7 Answer the following: (5 x 2 Marks)

(a) Describe what is available in CMOS.
(b) What is an operating system?

Q.8 Answer the following: (5 x 2 Marks)

(a) Describe the various components of the Motherboard.
(b) How would you troubleshoot the hard disk?

Q.9 Answer the following: (5 x 2 Marks)

(a) What is Debugging Tools for Windows?
(b) Which type of memories are used by personal computers?

Q.10 Answer the following: (5 x 2 Marks)

(a) Is it possible to remove the root directory of your hard disk by using the RD command? If yes, how?
(b) What are the features of USB?

Q.11 Answer the following: (5 x 2 Marks)

(a) Describe the various Sockets and Slots.
(b) Describe Intel 865G Motherboard

Q.12 Answer the following: (5 x 2 Marks)

(a) Describe the various type of printers.
(b) What is Random Access Memory? Explain its construction.

Answers to Objective Type Questions

Fill in the blanks

1. Ultra Mobile PC
2. Power-On Self Test
3. Single In-line Memory Module
4. Super Twist Nematic
5. Optical technology
6. ss
7. Static Random Access Memory
8. Master Boot Record
9. Atrib
10. Restore

True False Questions

1. F	2. T	3. T	4. T
5. T	6. F	7. T	8. T
9. F	10. T		

Multiple Choice Questions

1. c	2. a	3. a	4. b
5. c	6. a	7. b	8. b
9. d	10. b		